ON MONEY AND MARKETS

A Wall Street Memoir

HENRY KAUFMAN

McGraw-Hill
New York   San Francisco   Washington, D.C.   Auckland   Bogotá
Caracas   Lisbon   London   Madrid   Mexico City   Milan
Montreal   New Delhi   San Juan   Singapore
Sydney   Tokyo   Toronto

Library of Congress Cataloging-in-Publication Data

Kaufman, Henry.
  On money and markets : a Wall Street memoir / by Henry Kaufman.
    p. cm.
  Includes bibliographical references and index.
  ISBN 0-07-136049-2
  1. Kaufman, Henry.   2. Capitalists and financiers—United States—Biography.
  3. Finance—United States—History—20th century.   I. Title.

HG172.K38 A3 2000
332'.092—dc21
  [B]   99-086024

McGraw-Hill

A Division of The **McGraw·Hill** *Companies*

FIRST EDITION

ISBN 0-07-136049-2

Printed and bound by R. R. Donnelley & Sons Company.

1 2 3 4 5 6 7 8 9 0 DOC/DOC 9 0 9 8 7 6 5 4 3 2 1 0 9

McGraw-Hill books are available at special quantity discounts to use as premiums and sales promotions, or for use in corporate training programs. For more information, please write to the Director of Special Sales, Professional Publishing, McGraw-Hill, 2 Penn Plaza New York, NY 10121-2298. Or contact your local bookstore.

This publication is designed to provide accurate and authoritative information in regard to the subject matter covered. It is sold with the understanding that neither the author nor the publisher is engaged in rendering legal, accounting, or other professional service. If legal advice or other expert assistance is required, the services of a competent professional person should be sought.
—*From a Declaration of Principles jointly adopted by a Committee of the American Bar Association and a Committee of Publishers.*

 This book is printed on recycled, acid-free paper containing a minimum of 50% recycled, de-inked fiber.

To my parents and grandparents,
who were always there for me in my formative years.

And to my wife, Elaine,
and my sons, Glenn, Craig, and Daniel,
who have enriched my life since.

FOREWORD

By Paul A. Volcker

Ordinarily on a long plane trip my priority is sleeping. Not on my last flight to Tokyo. I took along a draft of Henry Kaufman's memoir. It kept me not only awake but fascinated.

I cannot claim scholarly detachment and lack of bias. I have counted Henry as a close friend and trusted professional colleague for forty years. We are close in age. We were both apprenticed in the same institution—the Federal Reserve Bank of New York, which for many years has educated budding financial economists for a role on Wall Street. Our subsequent careers followed different but parallel tracks. In many respects our thinking has overlapped.

For all of that, I will not be alone in finding *On Money and Markets* both an important book and a lively read. It provides fresh and striking insights into Wall Street and some of the people and institutions that populate it. It compels attention to its analysis of the implications—both highly promising and potentially dangerous—of global finance. And it reveals a warm and affecting human story of a man who has found so much in America and has returned so much to his adopted land.

Henry Kaufman, born in a bucolic German village, was one of many children who found their normal life turned upside down by Nazi terror. Without significant resources his family suddenly had to adjust to the very different and difficult environment of life in New York City. Like many of his refugee contemporaries, Henry seldom spoke of those troubled times, at least not to friends who hadn't shared that experience— those of whom he writes, with a tinge of longing, as having lives flowing, "with a peaceful and predictable rhythm. Born into well situated families (with) . . . know(n) career paths at an early age."

That is maybe a rather simplistic generalization of the life of middle-class Americans, but there can't be any doubt that an escape from the Holocaust provided a trial by fire beyond the comprehension of most Americans. One cannot help but wonder whether the unique challenges faced by Henry Kaufman, and by those with similar experiences, have brought a special quality to their lives. They have developed a strong bond of attachment to a country that respects both the rule of law and personal liberty, one that has succeeded better than most in combining tolerance with a sense of moral conviction.

One recurrent theme in this memoir is the inherent tension for those trading securities and managing money between the need to compete, to prosper, to grow, and the need to treat clients fairly, to maintain high fiduciary standards, and to respect the broad public interest reflected in regulation and supervision. No one can read this book without sensing Henry Kaufman's pride in pioneering financial market analysis and building a strong and independent research staff in a leading investment bank, his exultation in becoming a partner and an integral part of that great trading house, and his strong sense of responsibility as he became part of the senior management of the firm. His writing makes equally plain his increasing uneasiness about the difficulties of maintaining that sense of personal and professional responsibility as the competitive pressures intensified, as his firm like others became fixated on the need to maintain earnings in the short run, and as impersonal new technology became pervasive. In the end, Henry became more comfortable spending the last years of his professional life in a small firm he could call his own, with the collateral advantage of freeing himself to comment as he saw fit on pressing issues of public policy—and not so incidentally, as it has turned out, to write a memoir.

Much of the book is devoted to restating and elaborating long-standing concerns about the potential excesses and fragility of global financial markets, and the consequent need for more effective international approaches toward regulation and supervision. He, rightly in my judgment, calls attention to the weaknesses and uncertainties in so-called modern risk management and trading techniques rooted more in mathematical constructs than in clear understanding of the characteristics of financial markets and of human nature, now as always prone to excesses of exuberance and despair. One can question the efficiency or practicality of some of his specific proposals of institutional reform, but governments and market participants alike should, in their own

interest, be aware of elements of fragility that Henry has so convincingly identified.

These past two decades or so have brought unprecedented prosperity to Wall Street and to those with the wit and means to invest in
financial instruments. Innovation, globalization, and the removal of
many regulatory restraints have dramatically changed the financial
landscape. Theories of a new era and expectations of a serene investment outlook abound—matters particularly convincing to a generation that has come of age in the midst of the greatest equity market
boom in all of American—and for all I know—world history.

But there have also been plenty of alarm bells for those who are listening. The recurrent Latin American debt crises, the recent conta-
gious financial breakdown among the fabled Asian economic "Tigers,"
the persistence of the Japanese economic doldrums following their
stock market "bubble," the struggles only a decade ago of our thrift and
banking institutions to step back from crisis—all that gives point and
pertinence to Henry's analysis and concerns. For that reason alone, *On
Money and Markets* should be prescribed reading for all those whose
future and fortunes are tied to the performance of our financial system. But more than that, the book is an absorbing story, a saga of how
one man, starting as a butcher's son in a German village and thrust as
a refugee into the citadel of capitalism, could make an important contribution to the world of finance and to the educational and cultural
life of the city at the center of that world.

Henry touches all too lightly in the book on the role he has played
in providing support for his alma mater, the New York University Stern
School of Business, the main building of which now bears his name.
Reflecting his concern that economic education was straying too far
from the lessons of practical experience, he has taken particular care to
endow professorships specifically dedicated both to teaching economic history and to exposing students to the thinking of men and
women with careers in business or public life.[1] That interest in education has extended internationally, to important support for exchange

---

[1] I felt especially honored to be the first Henry Kaufman Visiting Professor at the
Stern School.

students and for Israeli professorships. Moreover, there is a broad range of artistic and humanitarian institutions in New York City that have benefited from the conviction of Henry—and of his wife, Elaine—that there are greater values in life than the strictly economic. It is the breadth of those interests and the depth of his thinking that will be the enduring hallmarks of Henry Kaufman's life.

Paul A. Volcker
Former Chairman of the Federal Reserve

ACKNOWLEDGMENTS

To begin with, I owe special thanks to David Sicilia of the University of Maryland. A specialist in business and economic history, David offered sage advice about the substance and style of the manuscript, especially the historical and biographical segments. His keen editorial eye made this a much better book.

Several members of my firm, Henry Kaufman & Company, graciously pitched in to help with this project. At the center of the whirlwind was my secretary, Helen Katcher, who dug up obscure documents, proofread and printed, phoned and collated. In many ways Helen knows my career better than I, and her knowledge has been invaluable not only for contributing to this project, but also for sustaining my professional life since coming to work for me more than 32 years ago. Peter Rup, assisted by NYU intern Esther Chwei, meticulously researched much of the data that appear in the book's text and graphs.

I also managed to recruit several dear friends and associates to the cause. I consulted on a number of key issues with the ever-judicious Charles Brophy, who also read and commented on several chapters. Roger Kubarych, a long-time colleague and a first-rate economist, helped me think through quite a few issues in finance and banking through stimulating discussions and insightful critiques. I am grateful to Robert DiClemente for providing some of the financial information in these pages.

For their efforts and good judgment in bringing this book to market, I wish to thank Philip Ruppel and Jeffrey Krames of McGraw Hill, and my literary agent, Reid Boates.

And then there is my wife, Elaine, who never complained as this book consumed scores of my evenings and weekends. She has been the center of my world for more than four decades, and has shared all of the strains and triumphs of my life and career. How could I ever acknowledge her enough?

CONTENTS

Permission of Doris Ettlinger, Doris Ettlinger Studio.

1

From Nazi Germany to the New World

We knew what we had to do. As my father had warned, Germany no longer was a place for Jews.

For some, life flows with a peaceful and predictable rhythm. Born into well-situated families, they know their career paths at an early age. Some follow the footsteps of their parents to become doctors or lawyers or enter the family business. They live for the rest of their lives in the same community. A few even marry childhood sweethearts. Enduring bonds are formed with neighbors, friends, and others that contribute to the stability of everyday life.

That was not to be my lot. Although I was born in a small German village, called Wenings, where everyone knew each other, the stability of living that often accompanies such a setting was to be short-lived. Born in 1927, I enjoyed a quiet boyhood for a time, until my family and I were swept up in the greatest human tragedy of the twentieth century: the Holocaust. Fortunately, we managed to escape with our lives by fleeing Wenings when I was 9, and continued on to the United States 11 months later. It was a jarring transition, not merely from one nation to the next, but also from a tiny farming hamlet to the world's greatest metropolis, New York City. When we arrived, Wall Street meant nothing to me, and, of course, I meant nothing to Wall Street.

My Childhood in Rural Germany

Wenings was a remote farming village of some 1,200 people in the upper Hessen district of Germany. The farmers lived in town, tending their fields on the outskirts and moving their harvests by horse and buggy back into town. The nearest railroad was a town away, and only a few local people owned automobiles. Even travel by bicycle was arduous, for the countryside was hilly and most roads were in poor condition.

We lived in an extended family, with my mother's parents and one of my grandfather's brothers. My father and grandfather were butchers and cattle traders, who often traveled into the region to buy and sell livestock. On occasion, they brought cattle home for slaughter, a messy event that I sometimes witnessed but never welcomed. Since my family ran a kosher butcher business, the cow had to be slaughtered by ritual, with one swift stroke of a large knife. The torrent of draining blood and the carving up of the carcass was a startling sight for a young boy, and I never grew accustomed to the ritual.

Ours was a modest house. On one side was the butcher shop and slaughterhouse; on the other, a living room and my grandparent's bedroom and kitchen. Upstairs were several bedrooms, including that of my parents, as well as a second living room, which for some reason sat unused. Heating and cooking were by potbellied stove, and our house—like most in the town—had no indoor toilet. But we did have two modern conveniences: electric lighting and a telephone. The conditions of my boyhood home stand in stark contrast with those of my New Jersey residence today—with its six bathrooms, central air conditioning, four televisions, and telephones in nearly every room. But in the 1920s, we were reasonably prosperous and knew no other lifestyle.

My grandparents' roots in this little town went back a century or more. My grandfather, Daniel Rosenthal, was an extremely hard-working man with a straight, tall bearing and an aura of dignity. Opa, as I always called him, normally was a quiet man, but could erupt like a volcano when he lost his temper. Unfortunately, the hyperinflation of the early 1920s devastated him financially and emotionally. Prior to the great inflation, he was worth about 200,000 marks, which gave him a good measure of comfort and security, or so he thought. The problem was that most of his money was in deposits and loans to farmers that were secured by mortgages or land. After the great inflation hit, borrowers came with bushel baskets of worthless money to pay off their debts. These episodes, which my grandfather told again and again, were my first lessons in economics and finance.

My grandmother was very protective of my grandfather. She hovered over him, regulating his diet to reduce his high blood pressure; some days were meatless, others were restricted to fruits, and garlic was a staple. Judging by modern nutritional standards, this diet most likely prolonged his life. He died in 1945 at the age of 79. Whereas Opa had 2 brothers, my Oma—grandmother in German—was the oldest of 11 brothers and sisters. She became the matriarch of her large family. Although I was an only child, I was never alone, in part because my Oma also hovered over me. Whatever the vicissitudes of everyday life, even in our extended household, I could do no wrong in her eyes. She prepared special dishes for me. She presented me with my first bicycle. Even in the last few years of her life in New York, when I was going to college and sleeping late on weekends, she served me breakfast in bed.

My father came from a larger town, Niederrodenbach, near Hanau, which today is virtually a suburb of Frankfurt. He was one of four brothers. I saw my paternal grandparents only infrequently. Several members of my family—including my paternal grandmother, an aunt, an uncle, and two cousins—were victims of the Holocaust. My father was an engaging man, a keen observer of human behavior, and generous in his dealings with others. I could never find fault with him or my mother as parents, or with their warm marital relationship. My mother had been born in Wenings in 1901, the only child in her family. A beautiful woman, she had an outgoing personality that allowed her to make friends easily. She was always there when I needed her, and was very devoted and close to her parents.

My mother's devotion to me came to the fore when I was struck with polio at the age of 4 in 1931. I still recall coming home on a summer day, dragging my deadened left foot along and complaining of a severe headache. My mother quickly took me to Frankfurt, where I underwent my first operation. To my great disappointment, the surgery overcorrected the bend in my left foot, so a second operation was required 2 years later. During the painful weeks I was hospitalized each time, my mother remained at my bedside from in the morning until in the afternoon, often reading popular German children's stories aloud. Some of my favorites—including *Max and Moritz* and *Der Strupfelpeter*—I could recite from memory.

When I left the hospital, I remained immobilized for weeks, forced to wear a cast on my leg and largely confined at home. This prevented me from socializing with children my own age or attending school regularly. For years, I was required to wear a leg brace, and to this day I wear a specially made arch and tend to drag my left foot when I'm tired. It is difficult to judge what role this early disability may have played in shaping my character. I am certain it made me more dependent on my family, especially my parents, than I would have been without the need for such care and nurturing. Although I believe I later overcame whatever negative effect the illness had on me, there is no way of knowing this for certain.

Apart from the hardships of polio, my early childhood in Wenings lives on today in pleasant memories. Often, I accompanied my grandfather to synagogue on Friday evening or Saturday morning. There were about 60 to 70 Jews in town, and all were Orthodox. I recall the delicious assortment of fresh foods that inevitably accompanied the major religious holidays such as Rosh Hashanah (the Jewish New Year)—the apple, plum, and crumb cakes, piled high and even served at breakfast time. When apples were in season, Oma made a tasty apple shalit (similar to deep-dish apple pie) especially for me to eat with the Sabbath meal. The pace of life was leisurely. Trips to nearby towns with my father or grandfather were by horse-drawn buggy or sled. And there were neighborhood children to play with and, presumably, grow up with in our tranquil village.

Gathering Clouds

That vision of a tranquil village began to cloud over with the rise of the Nazis after 1933. Despite the quiet of my very early years in Wenings, the Germany of my youth was quite unstable. The Treaty of Versailles, imposed on a defeated Germany by the Allied Powers, contained a "war guilt clause" that blamed Germany for starting the war. It also required Germany to pay huge reparations—132 billion gold marks—to the Allies, whose high tariffs in turn made it virtually impossible for Germany to garner sufficient funds with exports to meet its reparations payments. The result was enormous resentment and economic chaos. In 1914, the ratio of the mark to the dollar had been 4.2 to 1; by early 1921, the mark traded at the rate of 64 to the dollar. Soon thereafter, as the German government ran the printing presses, the mark spiraled into near worthlessness. When Germany failed to meet a reparations payment in 1923, France seized the Ruhr. Meanwhile, Germany was plagued with assassinations and attempted assassinations, as well as attempts to overthrow the new Weimar government.

In 1924, under the terms of the Dawes Plan, the reparations amounts were lowered and the French occupation ended. Reforms followed, and the German economy stabilized and resumed growth. Germany was readmitted into the European community. But the resentments remained, not far from the surface, and could be seen in the growth of both the Communist and National Socialist (Nazi) movements; the latter group was headed by Adolf Hitler, who blamed the Jews for the defeat in World War I and whose anti-Semitism would become more obvious over time. In this period, however, the historic sites for anti-Semitism were Russia and France. The great wave of Jewish migration to America before World War I originated in Eastern Europe, where Jews were made the objects of pogroms, not in Germany.

A number of German Jews did go to America, but rarely because of religious intolerance. Rather, they tended to be businesspeople. Some of them went to Wall Street, where they organized what became some of the Street's most powerful investment banks. During the post-Civil War period J. & W. Seligman funneled German money to American railroads, much like the blue-blooded Drexel, Morgan had done for English investors. The firm had offices in New York, San Francisco, New Orleans, London, Paris, and Frankfurt, presided over by the eight

Seligman brothers. Kuhn, Loeb, Lehman Brothers, and Goldman Sachs had all become major Wall Street investment houses by the time I arrived on American shores, though I knew nothing of this at the time.

This is not to say that Jews were accepted fully in German society. There was anti-Semitism there, too. Nevertheless, quite a few German Jews achieved great prominence in science, the arts, business, and even government. German Jews had joined the German armies in the war, my father among them. In fact, Jews were integrated more thoroughly into German society than into most other European nations.

During the late 1920s, Germany was struck by the Depression, which in time would affect the entire world. In March 1930, 2.3 million Germans were unemployed, and the figure rose to more than 6 million just 2 years later. Although the Nazis had captured only 12 seats in the Reichstag (and the Communists 54) in the 1928 election, 2 years later the Nazis won 107 seats, the Communists 77. Of the two totalitarian movements, the Nazis clearly were surging ahead. They attracted many of the unemployed, who joined the party's paramilitary organizations. By 1932, more than 1 million Nazi storm troopers marched in the streets, stiffly uniformed and menacing.

In July 1932, when the Nazis received 37 percent of the popular vote and won 230 seats in the Reichstag, Hitler demanded to be named chancellor, but President Paul von Hindenburg refused. Another election was called in November, and in this one the Nazi vote declined to 33 percent and the number of seats the party received was 196. For a brief period it appeared the democratic forces in Germany might stage a comeback, but this was not to be. The difficulties in ruling Germany obliged von Hindenburg to ask Hitler to form a government, which he did, becoming chancellor on January 30, 1933. There was yet another election in March, and in this one the Nazis received nearly 44 percent of the vote. Hitler's power was now secure. It seems providential, in retrospect, that Franklin D. Roosevelt was sworn into office in Washington that same month (March 1933). The two great antagonists in the greatest war of the twentieth century appeared on the historical stage at almost the same time.

I was just 5 years old when Hitler became chancellor, still in the midst of my trials and tribulations with polio. Even at that young age I sensed something was amiss. My father and grandfather started to have difficulties in buying cattle from farmers. Slaughtering cows according to the Jewish tradition became illegal. These were foreboding signs, but none of us anticipated the horrors that were to come.

Hitler's power and popularity grew as Germany recovered from the Depression, largely due to his militarization efforts. As time went on, the virus of Nazism seeped into the minds of almost all Germans, even the children. By 1935, few of my classmates would play with me. Fortunately, my teacher was a very righteous man, who prohibited anti-Semitic outbursts in class. He also was very helpful to me during my absence from school because of my second polio operation.

But the anti-Semitic disruptions continued to grow in size and scope as time went on. More and more local men donned the Nazi uniform. Some of the young boys in town wore the uniform of the Hitler Youth organization. Members of the small Jewish community began to stay indoors at night. Farmers who were indebted to us delayed payments. The words "dirty Jew" were heard more frequently.

My father was arrested and held for a short time by the Nazis. They somehow heard that he had a small pistol, which he had brought back with him from World War I. Ironically, in 1934 he had been awarded the "Ehrenkreuz Für Frontkämpfer" (an honor cross for being in the advanced forces during the war). He actually was among those who, with his cavalry battalion, had crossed the Marne River. It took a bribe of 10,000 deutsche marks to free my father. On another occasion, my father was nearly arrested by the Nazis during army maneuvers, but an army officer interceded in my father's behalf. The World War I papers that my father always carried impressed this officer sufficiently to force the Nazis to back off.

It was my father who urged my grandparents and mother to leave Wenings early on. He would raise the topic during dinner conversation, more frequently and urgently after Hitler took power. My grandparents, however, would not budge, so deeply were their roots planted in the little town. Then in their sixties, they couldn't imagine what life would be like elsewhere. But my father was much closer to the grim realities of the situation through his travels and association with others of his age, and continued to advocate that we leave.

The climactic end to our life in Wenings occurred during the evening of Saturday, January 30, 1937. Snow and ice covered the ground on that bitterly cold night—the anniversary date of Hitler's coming to power. A few people in town told my father of plans for a torchlight parade, and warned him to expect some trouble. Late that evening, sometime perhaps between 10 and midnight, we heard marching. Even though it was bedtime, we were all fully dressed. Knowing that the Nazis were targeting young Jewish men, my father told us he was going to hide in the woods and return later, and then jumped from the first-floor back window and disappeared into the night. Huddled upstairs in my parents' bedroom were my grandparents, my mother, my grandfather's older brother, and I. The parade stopped in front of our house. (I never learned the size of the mob.) Our shutters were tightly closed. Within moments, we heard the crash of the door being smashed in, the sound of breaking glass and smashing furniture, followed by the sickening thud of footsteps on the stairs. This was followed by another crash, as someone in the second-floor hallway threw my mother's sewing machine down the stairs.

As I cowered in the darkened room with my family, who now seemed pitifully powerless in the face of the menacing horde, I counted the seconds before the inevitable. The door would burst open . . . and then what? It was difficult for my childish mind to imagine the details, but the terror that gripped me was almost overwhelming. Then, the most unexpected happened. No one entered my parents' bedroom. We were not forced to confront the racist intruders. Instead, the rabble faded away, leaving behind quite a bit of destruction—and an unmistakable message. That night, no one lifted a finger in our defense—not the presumably friendly neighbors, not the mayor, not a single member of the small community where my family had lived for generations.

Sometime past midnight we heard voices from the backyard calling my mother and grandparents. It was an elderly Jewish couple, standing in their night clothing, each bleeding from wounds to the head and wanting to come into our house. They stayed until morning, when my father returned from his hiding place in the forest.

We knew what we had to do. As my father had warned, Germany

no longer was a place for Jews. Somehow that night—for reasons that perplex me to this day—we had been given a reprieve. My family was not about to bet on a second chance. Like the thousands of German Jews fortunate enough to outrun the concentration camps (as they would later learn), we sold our house and other properties under duress for a fraction of their real value. The day after the attack, we left Wenings and headed for Frankfurt, home to several of my grandmother's brothers and not far from my father's family.

An Aside—Returning to Wenings in the Future

I returned to Wenings three times later in my life. The first was in 1959, just 22 years after we fled the town. My wife, Elaine, and I took a 4-week holiday through Western Europe. The town seemed smaller than I remembered, as did the house in which I had lived as a child. One of our neighbors, who had been friendly with my family, welcomed us as if nothing had happened. She marched my wife and me through a good part of the village, introducing us to people whom my grandparents and parents probably knew, but who were nearly all strangers to me. The synagogue was still standing. It had been converted to a Catholic church, with a plaque stating its former status. We also visited the Jewish cemetery to pay homage to my great grandfather whom I vaguely remembered from my early childhood. I felt out of place and strange in Wenings. While I could still speak conversational German, I wanted to speak only English.

The second time I returned was in 1978, when, following a family trip to Israel, our three teenage sons wanted to see my birthplace. When we drove into the town, I stopped at the school that I attended for a few years, and suggested that we walk through the schoolyard and perhaps visit the school itself. Suddenly, there was a roar of fighter planes overhead. Tanks and half-track vehicles rumbled along the road. It was the American army on maneuvers. I experienced a flashback that glued me to the spot for a minute or so. It took me back to the time in 1935 when the German army was on maneuvers. The schoolchildren, myself among them, lined the street to watch Hitler pass through the town. He passed no more than 6 or 7 feet from me, his right arm outstretched in

the Nazi salute as he stood in the open Mercedes that was so often pic-
tured in the newspapers. The people were jubilant.

I have visited Germany often since then. In 1990, I returned to
Wenings, following an invitation from the mayor, who had read about
me in the German press. I had been visiting Frankfurt frequently, giving speeches at conferences and meeting with some of the German
business and financial leaders. The mayor hoped I would go to Wenings to accept an invitation to become an honorary citizen. After some
hesitation, I accepted. But there was a slight misunderstanding. I
thought the ceremony would take place on that visit, but the mayor
wanted to discuss the event with me first. It turned out that he also
wanted to apprise me of some recent developments in the town.
Apparently, a Jewish doctor from Israel settled in the neighboring
town of Gedern, married a gentile woman, and started to practice
medicine. Thereafter, swastikas appeared on his house, and one day the
doctor's house burned down. Shocked by the story, I never returned to
accept the mayor's invitation. Sadly, part of the community's dark
experiment with the Nazis seemed to have lived on.

More recently, while I was on a speaking engagement in Europe in
October 1999, my wife and I stopped over in Frankfurt for the specific
purpose of trying to locate the grave of my paternal grandfather. I had
a death certificate dated July 1940, well after the start of World War II
and the Holocaust. Perhaps my grandfather was still buried in Frankfurt's Jewish cemetery. Fortunately, the cemetery's ledger contained the
information I sought. I found my grandfather's grave in a far corner of
the deserted cemetery, and as I brushed aside the fallen leaves that partially covered his very modest, weathered headstone, childhood memories of my father's parents came rushing back. As I stood there I
realized that I was the first person in 59 years to visit this forgotten
grave. Neither my father nor his brothers had a chance to fulfill the
Jewish tradition of visiting the grave of their parents each year—Hitler
had seen to that. While most of us are lost in history after a few generations, I was there that day in Frankfurt to say, "That time had not yet
come for my grandfather."

Even so, my childhood malice toward Germany has mostly faded
away. Germany staged an extraordinary recovery in the aftermath of

World War II, with considerable support from the U.S. It has become the dominant country in Europe, and seems to have put in place a democratic political system with strong footings. In my career, I have met with many very talented German business and financial leaders. A new generation of Germans is taking hold, a generation of the post-World War II era. The question that used to pop into my mind when I met Germans—"Where were you and what were you doing during the Hitler years?"—no longer seems relevant.

From Frankfurt to the United States

To go back to our plans to emigrate to the United States, we planned to stay with our relatives in Frankfurt until our visas were approved, and then continue on to the United States. We spent the first night en route to Frankfurt in the nearby town of Buedingen. After struggling to fall asleep, I was later awakened by my mother, who was shaking me to bring me out of a nightmare in which I relived the frightening events of the night before.

Soon we moved into a rental apartment in Frankfurt, and I began attending a well-known Jewish school called Philanthropin. Anti-Semitism was on the rise, although at that time it was not as noticeable in Frankfurt as it was in the smaller communities and in some other cities. My father became even more insistent on leaving Germany. There was no work for him there and my grandfather's business life ended the day we left Wenings.

Fortunately, we were relatively well positioned to make the voyage. Two of my grandfather's sisters lived in the United States, having emigrated there at the turn of the century. I suspect they had made the move in order to increase their chances of marriage. Although both were attractive and intelligent women, tradition held that daughters should bring dowries to their mates. Since my grandfather's parents were not wealthy, their daughters' possibilities for marriage in a small German town were much more limited than in the sprawling and "modern" United States.

The plan apparently worked. One sister married a butcher who came to own a large meat processing plant and became very prosperous. When the couple returned to Germany for a visit in the 1920s, they brought along their large chauffeur-driven automobile, which of course made quite a splash in Wenings. The other sister married a man who owned a sizable delicatessen. So they had more than sufficient financial capacity to sponsor us. Their affidavit to the American authorities even included a letter of support from New York Senator Robert Wagner.

My father left Germany before us, because by the latter part of 1937 younger Jewish men were being arrested frequently. He first went to Amsterdam, where he stayed with his brother for several months before sailing to New York. It was then up to my mother to shepherd her parents, my grandmother, an aging uncle, and me to the United States. We could take very little with us. The most portable assets were Leica cameras and Zeiss field glasses, which were quite marketable in the United States.

New American Ways

On December 10, 1937, we departed Germany from Hamburg aboard the German passenger ship *Deutschland* (sunk in World War II by the Allies). After 7 stormy days at sea, we arrived at the port of New York. It was a murky, blustery afternoon, and to a 10-year-old boy from the German countryside, Manhattan looked overpowering. But family was there to cushion the shock and take us in—not only my grandfather's two sisters, but also their families, my grandfather's brother and his family (who had left Wenings for New York several years before us), and several of my mother's cousins.

Within a few weeks, we moved into a two-bedroom apartment on Forrest Avenue in the East Bronx, a habitat dictated by our meager financial situation and by the close proximity of several relatives. Now that we had an official residence, my mother accompanied me to P.S. 23 just a few blocks away. I was 10, but when the principal of the school realized that I knew very little English, he assigned me to the first grade. That demotion meant that a lot of what I was being taught was redundant—the alphabet, math, even reading, except for the English language. It took about a year or so before I entered my rightful grade.

After a while we moved into an apartment on nearby Jackson Avenue. We settled into our new home, and I was becoming adjusted to school in America.

Making a living was another matter. It was, after all, 1938. The beginning of mobilization for World War II was helping to lift the economy out of the Depression, but the recovery was erratic. The unemployment rate was 19 percent, and fears of another economic set-back still ran deep. But while these uncertainties were acute, my family and other recent German immigrants were hardly discouraged; the news from those who remained behind was bleak and getting worse by the day. German Jews on both sides of the Atlantic spent much of their time finding sponsors willing to write affidavits for those left behind.

My father and mother found jobs, even though they were not doing what they preferred. For a while, my father delivered milk for 25 cents an hour, but he was forced to give up that job after falling off the milk truck one day. He then went to work at the meat processing plant owned by my grandfather's brother-in-law, the same man who had provided the affidavit that allowed us to come here. Workers at the plant put in 6 long days per week. A 60-hour workweek for my father was not unusual.

My mother began doing housework for a number of families, and eventually took a job in a brassiere factory in the garment district in Manhattan. Although my grandmother did the cooking and some of the housework in our family, my mother still had plenty to do when she came home from work at night. Rising at 6, she often finished her day around midnight. She finally quit her wage job around 1945.

How we all managed, adjusted, and got along together in the extended household is still difficult for me to fathom. By the time we moved to the larger apartment on Jackson Avenue, our family had grown to 8, thanks to the addition of two of my mother's cousins in their early twenties whom we had helped bring to the U.S. just before World War II broke out. We all shared a single bathroom. But no one really complained. We had escaped the clutches of Hitler, and saw assimilating into American life as a challenge.

The members of our extended family met that challenge with varying degrees of enthusiasm and success. For my grandparents, language was the greatest of several challenges. Then in their late sixties, they found it difficult to adjust to some of the new ways, although they took enormous comfort in the fact that they escaped the Holocaust and were with their family and some of their friends.

My parents had little time for themselves in those early days in this country. Besides having to work long hours, they often played host to an apartment full of visitors. Friends and relatives frequently showed up unannounced, as was common in the German-Jewish community. Many stayed for afternoon coffee and cake and some even for dinner. It was a kind of intimacy and spontaneity in family living that has largely disappeared in modern life.

Unlike my grandparents, for me the language barrier came down rather quickly. Like many a New Yorker, I learned to play stoopball, stickball, and softball. Unfortunately, the vestiges of polio had left me with a weakened left foot, which slowed down my running. That handicap demolished my childhood ambition of becoming a great major league baseball player, although the fantasy comes back to me occasionally when I watch a baseball game. Still, I became an avid New York Giants baseball fan. When my friends and I couldn't get into the Polo Grounds (the stadium in Manhattan where the Giants played their home games) on free Police Athletic League passes, we would go up to Coogan's Bluff, a vantage point from which most of the outfield and a good part of the infield were visible. I also discovered the public library and became an avid reader, especially of American and English literature.

Shortly after my bar mitzvah at the age of 13, we moved to Washington Heights, a section in upper Manhattan that had become a major enclave of middle-class German-Jewish families. I attended George Washington High School, having been preceded there by Henry Kissinger and Alan Greenspan, among others. I did quite well academically and made the honor society. As I approached graduation, the big question in my family was: Where would I go to college? I had no real inkling about a career path. But my mother and grandmother did; they wanted me to become a doctor, a typical hope at that time for a Jewish boy.

I enrolled at New York University's campus at University Heights in the Bronx, where nearly every student either was pre-med or pre-law or was enrolled in the engineering school. Unlike NYU's Washington Square campus, which was coed, the University Heights campus consisted of all males, many of whom were former servicemen just returned from World War II. They tended to be more serious and goal-oriented than the young recent high school graduates. I required no additional prodding to work hard and perform well. It was never said to me directly, but my family expected me to be an achiever and to persevere in my studies. I sensed their ambition for me, and understood their sacrifice on my behalf.

Actually, there were many things unsaid in my family, but I believe that they were understood. My family, as I suspect was true of other German Jews, was rather stoic, so that expressions of personal endearment were rarely heard. I wasn't taught to say to my parents or grandparents "You're the greatest," "I love you," and the like. No matter how much I believe that these unspoken words were not necessary in our intimate family life, I still wish that I had spoken them to my parents.

The unspoken words of my family concerning my future path prodded me to enroll in summer classes, taking the maximum of 12 credits, including 8 credits of a chemistry class in quantitative analysis. I struggled through that summer, realizing that a career in medicine might not be in my future. In contrast, I enjoyed history and literature. After an introductory course in economics, which I liked immensely, I took a course in money and banking. Among other assignments, we were asked to read Frederick Hayek's 1944 book, *The Road to Serfdom*, a defense of free markets. Hayek saw economic planning as a major step on the way to totalitarianism. The book resonated with a generation that had just endured Hitler, Stalin, and Mussolini, but was not very popular among stalwart New Dealers. An abridged version was published in *Reader's Digest,* and it was in vogue for a while, which was rather interesting in view of the popularity of the ideas of John Maynard Keynes and Alvin Hanson, who had very different opinions about the proper role of the state.

By my junior year, I continued to enjoy and do well in history and literature, but knew that I would follow a career path in some aspect of economics or finance. Those subjects appealed to me because they brought me into the realities of life as I had experienced them, while the sciences seemed to me much more abstract.

In looking back at my formative years, I have no doubt that the experiences of my youth left a deep imprint on both my personal behavior and my economic and financial thinking later in my professional career. After all, I was a child who was brought up in the aftermath of the German hyperinflation, in the period and in the country where Hitler came to power, and also in the pluralistic and democratic United States. My strong anti-inflationary views, which in later years I expressed in writings and press interviews, were rooted in the stories told over and over again by my grandfather about the devastation that the hyperinflation inflicted upon him and his homeland. In those desperate times, barter more and more became the medium of exchange, and debts were paid off by worthless currency. The financial system could not carry out its fundamental function, the efficient allocation of resources.

These stories also suggested to me that it is dangerous to disenfranchise the middle class, which inflation certainly does. The very poor lose very little from virulent inflation in the short term. Over the longer term, inflation forces them to remain destitute. Debtors actually do very well during an inflationary period. The very rich can escape some of inflation's hardships, except in circumstances like Germany's, where it was the incubation of political and social upheaval. My professional training confirmed what I observed directly during my early years: that financial institutions and markets play a unique and special role in our society. They are essential if the economy is to allocate savings efficiently; and for that to happen, as I will explain in more detail later, there needs to be a balance between entrepreneurial drive and fiduciary responsibility.

Having found refuge in this country at an early age, yet still old enough to understand the perilous place from which I escaped, I am perhaps more sensitized than many native-born Americans to economic developments that might endanger this country. Such a background probably heightened my concern as an economist about the destabilizing influence of the inflationary spiral in the 1970s, the rapid growth of debt in the 1970s and 1980s, the fiscal policy excesses of the 1980s, and the lack of fiduciary responsibility displayed by many financial institutions in recent decades. I take great pride in being an American. Consequently, when financial excess threatens our economic moorings, and thus our extraordinarily dynamic and pluralistic nation, I have often spoken out for saner behavior and more effective policies.

Nevertheless, I've never declared any strong political preferences for one or the other party or its candidates, until this past year, when I have actively supported Senator Bill Bradley for the Presidency. In my discussions with him, I have continually been impressed by his integrity, his probing questions, and his understanding of the complex issues facing our increasingly interrelated economic and financial world. Bill Bradley achieves a rare balance in his commitment to both fiscal and social responsibilities.

In my early years in the U.S., my idol was President Franklin Delano Roosevelt. Many Jewish refugees identified with him. He understood early the Hitler menace, and tried to rally the country to oppose him. I also idolized FDR because he did not let polio stand in the way of his ambitions. Indeed, he suffered far more from polio than I did. That suffering was, of course, well hidden from the public. All I ever saw from newspapers or newsreels was this tall and broad-shouldered man with an infectious smile, his extraordinary voice exuding confidence over the airwaves. What an inspiration and a great leader he seemed to us, having just escaped the evilness of Hitler!

Since that time, historical research has revealed that FDR—and many others, including some Jewish leaders—could have done more to help the Jews in Europe. In later years, I also realized some of the legislation passed in the Roosevelt era to prevent the occurrence of another depression was overzealous. The National Recovery Administration was a mistaken attempt to substitute central planning for market economics. The Glass-Steagall Act that separated commercial and investment banking was an overreaching effort to punish the bankers that figuratively closed the barn door after the horses had escaped.

Many other laws forged in the New Deal era were misguided as well. That should not be surprising, however. Many times in the past when the economic and financial pendulum swings to one extreme, the swing away is to the other.

All this helps explain how the historical context of my youth influenced me to become an economist. Economics brought me in touch with some of the concerns my father and grandfather had expressed to me about their experiences in Germany after World War I. It also helped me to understand the Great Depression that plagued the world as I was growing up. Economics seemed like a promising career, a means to attain upward mobility. And if I were successful, I might contribute in my own small way to solving some of the nation's economic problems. As I embarked on my career, however, I did not have a clear idea of how I might accomplish any of this.

In choosing that career path as an undergraduate at NYU, I should add, I was not inspired by any individual teacher. Rather, the subject itself captivated me. Influential mentors appeared later, in graduate school and in my employment. But I did have some inspirational teachers in other subjects. There was Theodore Jones, who taught history; Professor Robert Fowkes, a German teacher; and Professor John Knedler in English literature, who introduced me to Geoffrey Chaucer in a stimulating way.

In the ongoing debate in higher education about whether teaching or research is more important in the making of faculty members, I weigh in for teaching. The great teachers I had stirred my thoughts by their presence in the classroom, not through what they wrote. I will be writing about giants I met in graduate school such as Marcus Nadler and Peter Drucker, who wrote some very influential books and articles that have remained influential for decades. But their teaching was if anything more influential. In saying this I do not mean to minimize the importance of research. In the process of their research for publication, Drucker and Nadler obtained the information and developed the ideas they brought to the classroom. This is certainly important. But as teachers they had a talent for making very complex subjects comprehensible and interesting. There are hundreds, perhaps thousands, of men and women, ranging in age from their thirties or forties to their seventies (like me), who were affected by Nadler, and even younger students by Drucker; we, in turn, influenced others, and so it went, down the line.

My junior and senior years came and went quickly because I continued to take the maximum number of classes allowable during the summer, permitting me to graduate in 2½ years, in January 1948.

At that time, working experience was not essential for entering a graduate business school. I was accepted at Harvard, Columbia, and the University of Michigan. Harvard did not accept new students for entry at midterm, and I did not want to wait nearly 8 months to begin my graduate work. I registered at Columbia for a 1-year master of science degree, hoping to eventually begin a career in banking or in the securities market. I did well in most courses, especially banking and economics.

But I struggled in security analysis, taught by Professor David Dodd. A legendary figure, Dodd, as is well known, was the coauthor with Benjamin Graham of *Security Analysis*, a standard in its field for many years. I now realize my problem was due to inadequate preparatory course work in accounting and finance—a realization that became clear only in retrospect. However, at the time I simply stumbled along, hoping that I was doing the right thing to prepare myself for a career with a Wall Street firm or with a bank.

2

The Road to Wall Street

*"At Salomon you can hear the cash registers ring
every minute of the day," Nadler said.*

━━━━━━━━━━

I completed the master of science program at Columbia University in
January 1949. This gave me a great sense of accomplishment—and
yet my dream of a career on Wall Street seemed a dim possibility. For
one thing, I had no personal contacts on the Street who could help me
land a job. More than that, business schools in those days, including
Columbia, were not geared up to place their graduates. (This is in
sharp contrast to today, when graduate programs bring recruiters to
the campus before students graduate, and many provide summer
internships to graduate candidates.) But the biggest problem was simply that there were few jobs in banking at the time. The economy had
entered a recession, as the initial wave of pent-up wartime demand
passed and as millions of soldiers returned to civilian life. Many veterans had gone to college in 1945 and were now entering the labor force,
contributing to a rise in unemployment.

In the financial community of that day—a very different world
structurally and behaviorally from what we see now—activity was far
from booming. The 272 million shares traded for the entire year of
1949 would today not even make for a busy morning. Compared with
present-day levels, the over-the-counter market of a half century ago
was tiny and lethargic. Banks and insurance companies were highly
liquid. The former, for example, had loan-to-deposit ratios of less than
60 percent, whereas today the ratio is over 100 percent. (This is possible because many banks now rely not only on deposits but also on
other borrowings as a source of funds.) There were also many savings

and loan associations and savings banks, a large number having since disappeared as a result of hard times or mergers. Mutual funds were in their infancy, and the flow of savings into private pension funds was modest.

One of the most distinguishing features of American finance at that time was the segmentation of responsibilities among institutional groups. In the aftermath of the financial debacle of the 1930s, legislation circumscribed the activities of the major financial institutions such as banks and securities firms. There were, for instance, interest rate ceilings on savings deposits and residential mortgages. In corporate finance, the net issuance of bonds totaled $2.9 billion, which today roughly equals a single day's worth of underwriting.

In the government bond market, the ⅜ percent peg on Treasury bills was just being lifted, and a heated debate was raging about whether the 2½ percent peg on bonds also should be lifted. (This didn't happen until the Federal Reserve–Treasury accord in 1951.) Few financial institutions had meaningful economic research staffs, and a kind of gentlemen's agreement among major institutions that they would not raid each other for financial management talent kept job hopping to a minimum.

Learning the Ropes in Industrial Banking

Following a 6-week search, I began my banking career in March 1949 as a credit analyst at Peoples Industrial Bank. Peoples recently had moved to a new building on the Avenue of the Americas and 30th Street, the heart of the fur district, on the fringe of the garment district, and not far from the flower wholesalers. The locale was quite a distance from the Wall Street area where all of the major securities firms and banking institutions were headquartered. My salary was $45 a week. It was a start, and I actually learned a lot that later proved helpful to me on Wall Street.

I doubt that any industrial banks still exist today. In 1949, the major difference between a commercial bank and an industrial bank was that the latter financed mainly small and medium-sized businesses through a variety of financing techniques that were not yet acceptable to most commercial banks. These included accounts receivable financing, chattel mortgage loans, field warehousing loans, the rediscounting of notes receivable, and even a variety of consumer loans. Peoples also financed many small and medium-sized finance companies.

The credit department was small: a manager and about four others. I received informal, on-the-job training, which wasn't optimal but was offset by many advantages. I was thrown into a variety of credit work, which gave me close contact with the senior management, including the president and senior loan officers. These were people who did not have much of a theoretical base to their knowledge, but had considerable "street smarts," obtained from rubbing shoulders on a daily basis with their clients. Their business required a level of intimacy with borrowers not demanded in the field of investment banking, but which might well prove useful in that segment of the business.

The credit approval process began with the analysis of balance sheets and profit and loss statements. For those who know how to unlock their secrets, these documents can contain hidden traps, as I soon discovered—and was later reminded by some of the more spectacular credit problems of recent decades. Balance sheets tend to overstate assets and understate liabilities. Inventories commonly are assigned a large cash value after they have become obsolete, while receivables that are ostensibly current are quite often in arrears. Inadequate reserves constitute yet another common weakness that is poorly reflected in these statements. A receivable is a current asset, but it could be a slow asset.

It is important to keep in mind that a balance sheet is a snapshot of one moment in time, and thus presents a very limited view of a business. To a good banker, therefore, a business is much more than its balance sheet. Likewise, a profit and loss statement is not simply a collection of figures, but rather—for the perceptive banker—a window into the nuts and bolts of the business, from its method of operation to its management philosophy. In short, good bankers understand the shortcomings of accounting and know how to correct for them.

By this definition, the people I worked with at Peoples were good bankers. Their knowledge and instincts were well suited for the tasks they had to perform. But I suspected that they were not equipped to range beyond their normal business domain. I also had ambitions to use my academic training in other financial venues, but for the time being the work at Peoples Industrial suited me well.

In one of my early assignments, I was asked to review the quality of receivables of a medium-sized finance company to which the bank had made a number of unsecured loans. To my surprise, I found that more than half of the loans that the finance company had made to its customers had been renewed by the borrowers many times, even though quite a few of the borrowers had made no payments within a year. Nevertheless, the receivables all were listed as current assets, with only a small fraction recorded below the current asset line. On another occasion, in reviewing the credit merits of a large retail appliance store, I discovered that the borrower was taking into income all the finance charges on outstanding receivables, thus inflating the profits of the firm. Such accounting gimmickry unfortunately has made a comeback in recent years.

Most of all, I learned quickly how vital it is to know the quality and integrity of the borrower's management methods. Secured loans, for instance, are an indication of weaknesses on the part of the borrowers. And single-purpose assets often are assigned inflated net worths, considering what they could fetch in the marketplace. This was true in a case where I had to determine the collateral value of a very specialized mammoth printing press. As it turned out, because the usefulness of the machinery to others was quite limited, the collateral value was substantially *below* the purchase price.

Then there was the time I checked on a loan made to a manufacturer of corrugated containers. The borrower held a large loan that was collateralized by a field warehousing agreement; that is, the loan was secured by inventory kept on the borrower's premises—in this case, a portion of the firm's inventory of giant rolls of kraft paper used to make corrugated boxes. One of the firm's employees had been designated as a trustee over the collateralized inventory. When I visited the plant, however, I discovered that inventory designated as collateral was stored in an outside yard, where it had become damaged by weather.

Inside were many undamaged rolls—a much more valuable inventory that could be used to secure the loan. My written analysis of the situation somehow reached the vice chairman of the bank, who promptly reprimanded the loan officer and made sure the loan was properly collateralized.

The challenge of deciphering a firm's management, however, is a complex matter. Four years after joining Peoples Industrial Bank, I was promoted to Credit Manager. Soon thereafter, the bank's attorney came to see me, and he was obviously disturbed about something. He had been in the Latin Quarter, a well-known nightclub at the time, where he saw one of our large borrowers. The client—a man of about 60—was accompanied by a very young lady. It was clear to the attorney that the two, by the way they were behaving, hardly were relatives or platonic friends. "What do we do now?" the bank's lawyer asked me intently. I replied that we are not responsible for his personal conduct, and that the real question was whether the client's personal life was putting at risk the financial well-being of his business.

Fortunately, it was just the end of the month. I asked the bookkeeping department to bring us the canceled checks for both his business and personal account. Quite a few business and personal checks, some for large amounts, were for jewelry, furs, nightclubs, flowers, and rental payments for an apartment, which definitely was not his residence in New York City. We naturally didn't confront the client about this matter, but we reduced his credit line sharply. He transferred his account to another bank, and 2 years later, declared bankruptcy. High integrity and morality are not reported in financial statements. Nor are they verified by the accompanying statements of certified public accountants.

During my first 5 years at Peoples, the bank changed hands twice: first when it was sold to Household Finance Company in 1951, and then when it was resold to Manufacturers Trust Company in 1953. I became a junior loan officer in 1954, but I continued to yearn for an occupation that would allow me to apply my academic training more fully. In fact, for the last several years (since 1950) I had been advancing my graduate education by working toward a doctorate degree.

From Commercial Banking to Central Banking

Columbia University did not offer night courses at the Ph.D. level, so I enrolled at New York University's Graduate School of Business Administration, then located at 90 Trinity Place, next door to the American Stock Exchange. From 1950 to about 1956, I worked full time at the bank during the day and attended classes four evenings a week. I took summer classes as well. I devoted part of each weekend to catching up with homework. But I thoroughly enjoyed the courses, especially those in the money markets, international capital markets, and financial history, and a smattering of specialized courses in finance.

I even took several courses in business management, mainly because I wanted to see what Peter Drucker was all about. When I sat in his class in the mid-1950s, Drucker already commanded a national reputation. His book, *The Practice of Management,* was widely acclaimed. What fascinated me then about Drucker, and still does, is how he infuses his broad perspective on business issues with philosophical and historical considerations.

At the same time, there is a wonderful human side to Peter Drucker. I experienced that side of the man firsthand during my Ph.D. oral examination. For three hours, six professors questioned me about three major subject areas. The first hour focused on financial markets. One of the professors (not Drucker) queried me about war finance through the use of federal budget deficits, and asked me to illustrate on the blackboard the accounting impact of such wartime finance using a debit and credit approach. It was abundantly clear to everyone, including myself, that my diagram and explanation left much to be desired. My stomach sank at the puzzled looks on the faces of the six professors.

Mercifully, we took a short break halfway through the examination. Peter Drucker followed me on my way to the bathroom and stopped me in the hall. "Henry, you started off terribly," I can still hear him say, "but if you maintain the pace of the last hour, you will have no trouble." It was a kind and decent gesture to someone he hardly knew. Encouraged, I did keep my stride and passed the exam.

The professor who had the most influence on my career was Marcus Nadler, who was also my favorite teacher. Nadler became my mentor, and later on we became friends. He had an exceptional persona. At 5 feet 7 inches or so, with dark hair and glasses, Nadler was not physically imposing. His demeanor was always serious, and he invariably held a cigarette in his hand, the likely cause of his death from lung cancer. Nadler was a lecturer who appeared before very large classes, especially one on contemporary economic problems, which was so popular at NYU that former students would return to audit the class.

Nadler had a steady way of speaking and a wonderfully logical mind. As a teacher he had a rare ability to break down complex subjects into more palatable and understandable points. In other words, he had a great capacity to simplify, to turn abstract ideas into practical applications. A consultant to several businesses, including the Hanover Bank, Nadler often brought real-life problems into the classroom, thereby giving his students a sense of reality to their textbook learning. Nadler also presented his material in a balanced and judicious manner, with no perceptible bias; he tried hard to examine problems from all sides. And like all great teachers, Nadler exhibited an almost religious fervor about his field, an enthusiasm that easily infected his students.

Not surprisingly, Nadler had a large student following. Many returned after graduation to reenroll in his classic course, "Current Money Market Problems." He gave his students lots of personal attention, and I prized the many hours we spent together. His lectures helped shape my belief that financial institutions and markets must balance entrepreneurial drive with fiduciary responsibility. And his fairness and openness to opposing points of view influenced me to conclude that no one school of economic thought has a monopoly on wisdom.

Nadler's advice had a profound influence on my professional career as well. One incident remains vivid in my memory. As the date of my daunting, three-hour Ph.D. oral examination approached, Professor Nadler offered me three pieces of sage advice. To begin with, he said, read everything ever written by the six professors on the exam committee who would be sitting across from me. Second, pay a visit to each of those professors to introduce myself and offer to answer any questions they might have. Finally, Nadler suggested that during the exam itself I take a moment after each question to organize my thoughts, and then speak slowly and deliberately when giving answers. Quick responses, he explained very practically, would allow time for more questions!

Fortunately, the exam went well. Months later, when I was well along toward completing my Ph.D., Nadler again offered helpful career guidance. Confirming what I had been restless about for some months, he acknowledged that my work at the bank seemed limiting. The Manufacturers Trust branch seemed to offer me few opportunities to utilize what I had learned in my classes or to develop my ideas. Nadler suggested that I request a transfer to the main office, or perhaps seek a position at a large international firm where I could bring my academic knowledge to bear.

Following Nadler's advice, I obtained an interview at Manufacturers' main office with Raymond Deering, an Executive Vice President and Treasurer. It was a cordial interview, and Deering called me a few weeks later. After complimenting me on my academic achievements and the excellent credit work I was doing at the branch, he recommended that I put off transferring to the main office and instead become a loan officer at one of the bank's large branches, such as the one at the Empire State Building.

Meanwhile, another opportunity came my way. I had applied at the Federal Reserve Bank of New York, not for any particular job, but rather to be considered for any suitable post. I was surprised, therefore, when a representative from the New York Fed called me. It was about to launch a major study of the problem of providing funds to small business, and was looking for someone with banking experience. I had some working experience in this area, but more importantly, was nearly finished writing my Ph.D. dissertation—which was propitiously entitled "Financing Small Business."

As I usually did when confronted with a major professional decision, I sought the advice of Nadler. When I laid out the options—a large branch of the bank or the New York Fed—his response was immediate. "Don't even think about it. Go to the Fed and a new world will open up to you." Perhaps the Fed had called him about me. Robert Roosa, the head of research at the Federal Reserve Bank, knew Nadler, and Madeline McWhinney, my first boss at the Fed, was one of his very gifted former students. (I always felt that if her career had started 10 years later, she would easily have become a Governor of the Federal Reserve Board.) In any case, I'm as certain as I can be (without the luxury of being able to replay history) that Nadler had once again given me sound advice.

My starting salary at the New York Federal Reserve Bank in 1957 was $7,000. It was more than I was earning at Manufacturers Trust, and when Ray Deering called to ask when I would like to transfer to the Empire State branch, I had considerable satisfaction in telling him that I was leaving. An interesting follow-up to this encounter came a year or so after I joined the Federal Reserve Bank. I received a call from one of the officers in the Personnel Department of Manufacturers Trust. It seemed that Manufacturers' new Chairman, Gabriel Hauge, wanted an assistant with a broad academic background as well as some banking experience. Would I consider coming back? Again, the answer was no.

As Nadler had predicted, I encountered a whole new environment at the New York Fed. At Manufacturers, credit work had required a lot of contact with a diverse group of clients. In contrast, in research I worked with other researchers, and met only occasionally with individuals from private institutions or with personnel from elsewhere in the Fed system. It was quite a change for me. Not only had I moved from a single bank to the central bank, but I had also moved completely away from dealings with small businesses to money and capital markets—the domain of big institutions and big markets.

The research activities at the New York Fed involved studies on credit quality, commercial bank lending and investing, developments in the foreign exchange market, the role of mutual savings banks and life insurance companies in the capital markets, consumer credit, and borrowing from the Fed. In addition to this institutional research, there was an ongoing effort to track and evaluate business and money market conditions as well as international economic and financial developments.

The Federal Reserve Bank of New York has a unique role among the 12 Federal Reserve Banks. It is the most important because it is located at the heart of the money and capital markets. It carries out the open market operations agreed upon by the Federal Open Market

Committee, of which the President of the New York Fed is Vice Chairman and a permanent voting member. Thus, the research effort at New York tended to rival that of the Federal Reserve Board in Washington.

The new job also demanded that my writing become more succinct and disciplined. The first article I wrote for the Bank's *Monthly Review* certainly brought this home to me. It dealt with the earnings of commercial banks, a subject about which I thought I had some knowledge, having worked in a bank and conducted a great deal of credit work. To my dismay, Alfred Hayes, the Bank's President, returned the draft to me and the other economists with scores of penetrating criticisms—enough to bring down my self-assuredness several notches. By the time we handed over the article to the printer, I recognized only small fragments of my original draft.

The most exciting dimension of my new job was the fact that, at long last, I was seeing classroom concepts applied to important worldly matters. The *Monthly Review* article became the first of many that I would publish in my career for an economically literate audience (a complete bibliography of my writings and speeches is included at the end of this book). At the same time—initially by happenstance—I began what would become a long career as a public speaker on financial and economic subjects. Bruce MacLaury (who would go on to become President of the Federal Reserve Bank of Minneapolis and head of the Brookings Institution) had been temporarily assigned to public information, with the task of giving some talks on money markets and the Fed. When MacLaury fell ill, I stepped in.

I recall the experience vividly. I was to give a talk on the money market at the Graduate School of Savings Banking, a 2-week-long seminar at Brown University. Accompanied by Tom Waage, I went to Providence well prepared—and not merely because I was a novice at public speaking. I had been given specific instructions to limit my talk strictly to the allotted 50 minutes. If I went over, even by a minute, I was informed, someone in the back of the room—in keeping with a tradition at the Brown seminar—would begin to play marching music on the phonograph, at which time the audience would stand up and march out of the room.

I managed to avoid that embarrassment, but not a different one a short time later in my public speaking career. On that occasion, I was addressing an audience at the Trust Investment School in Binghamton, New York. Again, the subject was the money markets. It was a topic that fascinated me, but I was nevertheless pleasantly surprised when the audience began to punctuate my lecture with applause and cheers. The accolades didn't seem to correspond well with my pithiest lines, but no matter—I had the audience in the palm of my hand. Soon, though, I discovered that the applause was directed elsewhere—toward the man who appeared on stage every few minutes with a makeshift sign showing the scores of the World Series game then in progress. As well as I may have been doing, the favored team was faring even better.

As my months on the job at the Fed turned into years, my understanding of financial markets deepened considerably, and the books I had read on the subject took on greater meaning. I became involved in forecasting the factors that affect bank reserves, and I put in a stint as an observer at the trading desk where open market operations were conducted.

The year 1957 was a banner year in my life. Not only did I take the job at the Fed, but I also married, beginning a partnership now in its fifth decade. I had met Elaine Reinheimer of Newark, New Jersey, on Labor Day the previous year. It was a blind date, arranged by my uncle. One does not forget first encounters with people who become so important in one's life. We went to Asbury and saw the movie *High Society*. Elaine had attended Russell Sage Institute and Fairleigh Dickinson University, and was working as an assistant buyer for a company that purchased dresses for retailers throughout the country.

It didn't take long for our mutual affection to deepen into love. We became engaged in February 1957, shortly before I moved to the Fed, and were married on September 15, soon after I began my new job. We found an apartment in upper Manhattan. Our first child, Glenn, was born on November 5, 1961, and this prompted a move into a larger apartment in the same complex. Our second son, Craig, was born on August 12, 1964. Then, when Glenn was ready for school, we moved to a house in Glen Rock, New Jersey, primarily for its well-regarded school system. Our third son, Daniel, was born on November 3, 1969, and later we moved into a larger house in another community. Elaine stayed at home to raise the children. After they grew up and left home, Elaine devoted much of her energies to the multifaceted arts institution in Manhattan that I endowed in her name. The Elaine Kaufman Cultural Center houses the Merkin Concert Hall, the Music School of America, for gifted children, and the Lucy Moses School, which offers classes in music, dance, and theater.

During my time at the Fed (from mid-1957 to the end of 1961), the central bank had to deal with several cyclical swings in the economy and in the financial markets. Interest rate fluctuations were actually quite pronounced, although the absolute levels were very low by current standards. The yield for the 3-month bill fell from 3 percent in 1957 to ⅝ of 1 percent early in the second quarter of 1958 in response to monetary easing undertaken to reverse a business recession. Surprisingly, a lot of bond speculation occurred in the market, especially in one U.S. government issue—the 2⅝ percent due in the early 1960s. Interest rates then rose sharply, forcing many investors to take significant losses. In short, it was a fascinating time to work at the Fed.

One of the highlights of my years at the Fed was my association with a very professional and talented peer group. This included Ernest Bloch, Lawrence Ritter, Jack Guttentag, and Robert Lindsay. All four went on to long and successful academic careers. Andrew Brimmer and Emmett Rice eventually became Governors of the Federal Reserve Board. Tilford Gaines took charge of investments at the First National Bank of Chicago, and then became Chief Economist at Manufacturers Hanover. Francis Schott left the Fed to become Chief Economist for the Equitable Life Assurance Company. As noted earlier, Bruce MacLaury, after becoming President of the Minneapolis Fed, went on to head the Brookings Institution. Peter Sternlight moved out of research to head the open market desk at the Bank. Paul Volcker, of course, became Chairman of the Federal Reserve Board. Albert Wojnilower moved to Citicorp, and then spent many years as Chief Economist for the First Boston Corporation.

While many distinguished economists and financial experts remained at the Fed for their entire careers, this roster suggests that the

Federal Reserve served as a training ground for many of the nation's most talented analysts. The same is true today. It was and is a wonderful place to gain an understanding and experience about the actual workings of monetary policy as well as an overview of the financial markets and their linkages to the economy, and also to get involved in some of the very narrow aspects of the economy and financial markets. Thus, while newcomers moved into the Research Department of the bank, others moved out, some to other areas within the Federal Reserve System, some into the financial world or to universities.

Joining Salomon Brothers

Although I was thriving at the Fed, in my third year there several new job opportunities prompted me to reexamine my career path. The first offer came from Bob Roosa, who invited me to take on a 2-year assignment in Turkey as an adviser on money market and banking matters to the Turkish central bank. At first blush, this sounded quite appealing. I had been married only a few years, and the opportunity to travel to the Middle East seemed exciting, perhaps even romantic. But my mentor and adviser, Doc Nadler, thought otherwise. "Why do you really want to go there, and what will you accomplish?" was his first remark to me when I told him about the offer. Then he added quickly: "There are two reasons why you shouldn't take on this assignment. First, when you come back in two years, who will really need an expert on Turkish banking? Second, when you return to the New York Fed, you will have lost ground in experience and knowledge. You will be out of the loop." He was right. I declined the offer.

The second opportunity came to me through a friend who had given my name to a headhunter friend of his. The Franklin National Bank was looking for a loan officer and an adviser to the bank's President, Arthur Roth. Long Island–based Franklin National was then planning to open its main office in Manhattan's financial district, with aspirations of becoming a money market institution. I met with Roth, but came away from the meeting unenthusiastic. I realized why when Doc Nadler said to me, "Why do you want to work for a regional bank

at this stage of your career?" This offer, too, I declined. As a footnote to
the story, Franklin National Bank failed in 1974, after guessing wrong
on currency movements shortly after the United States went off the
gold bullion standard, which caused currencies to fluctuate. There was
then virtually no expertise in the area of currency fluctuations, as
Franklin National learned the hard way.

My third offer that year was from Smith, Barney, already a well-
established securities firm in 1961. Smith, Barney wanted a European
representative with a broad academic background and some banking
or institutional experience. I was excited about the offer; for one thing,
the pay was more than twice my salary at the Fed. More importantly, I
had long desired to join a well-known Wall Street firm. And the European travel appealed to me a great deal—certainly more so than
Turkey.

For his part, Doc Nadler was ambivalent about the offer. He wasn't
sure how Europe would fare. In 1961, Europe lacked the vitality it
would later exhibit. What ultimately induced me to turn down the job
was his statement, "Henry, you should also understand that with your
religious affiliation you probably will never become a senior partner in
that firm." I had to admit, painful as it was, that he was probably right.

Fortunately, much has changed on that score since Doc Nadler
made that insightful statement to me in 1961. Today, Smith, Barney is
owned by CitiGroup, whose Co-CEO is Sandy Weill, a Jew. Moreover,
the religious barrier to advancement in Wall Street has nearly disappeared. Merrill Lynch has a Jewish CEO and an African-American
senior manager. Morgan Stanley—until a few decades ago, a thoroughly white-shoe, Ivy League institution—is no longer so. By the
same token, many of the so-called Jewish-dominated securities firms
are so only in name: Lehman, Goldman Sachs, and Salomon began as
Jewish firms, but today are comanaged by non-Jews at the senior level.

Still, even today, some doors remain closed to minorities at some
leading financial institutions. But the situation has improved, especially since World War II. Women are making gains as well, though
they are not yet as visible on Wall Street as they should be. Some no
doubt have been stymied by the fact that males still dominate the top

management of most nonfinancial businesses. And while some women find securities trading unappealing—because of its high stress level, confrontational nature, and often abusive language—many women are making their mark in research. I have no doubt that, within a decade, a growing number of women will move into the senior management of financial institutions.

For all that Marcus Nadler did for me—as an exemplary teacher, mentor, confidant, and friend—it is hardly surprising that he was instrumental in my decision to join Salomon Brothers, one of my life's most important choices.

The genesis of my move to Salomon began at a dinner of the Money Marketeers, an association created by and composed solely of former students of Marcus Nadler. Members ranged from aspiring newcomers to highly successful senior managers. Three or four times a year, we had dinner meetings at which Nadler would speak about one or another critical economic or financial issue, always placing the matter in historical perspective. One of the dinner get-togethers each year would feature a comedy skit that somehow involved the Doc. (I recall writing some satirical lyrics to be sung to a tune from *My Fair Lady*.) These occasions were a wonderful way to honor Professor Nadler, and to bring together the ambitious young with the more experienced and accomplished.

In 1961, I became secretary of the Money Marketeers, and found myself sitting next to the organization's treasurer, Charles Simon, at one of the dinners. Charlie (as he was known to friends and associates) was a senior partner at Salomon Brothers & Hutzler. He was, quite simply, an extraordinary individual. He had gone to work at Salomon right out of high school, as an office boy. Intelligent, hard working, and ambitious, Charlie soon was offered a position in sales.

Physically, Charlie was an imposing figure—stocky, with broad shoulders, a large round head, very piercing eyes, and weight that fluctuated widely. So did his attire, which ranged from very conservative to outlandish, often highlighted by double-breasted suits with wide lapels. Charlie pursued knowledge relentlessly, even though he was not formally educated. Nor did he disdain academia. To the contrary: Year in and year out, he sat in on Nadler's classes, listening to lectures on contemporary and financial issues. And he devoured books on a broad range of subjects, from art, economics and finance, literature, and American history, to psychology, biographies, and military history.

On many occasions after I joined Salomon, my phone would ring at 10 or 11 in the evening, sometimes later. It would be Charlie, eager to recite the latest insight he had gained from a book he had recently finished reading. The following morning, Charlie would hand out copies of the stimulating book to all whom he had called the night before. (I suspect some Salomon folks have a section of their study devoted to Charlie.) He reveled in newfound knowledge, locked it away in the many crevices of that huge head of his, from whence he could retrieve it days or years later. As a tribute to Charlie's warm friendship, acuity, and inexhaustible curiosity, I endowed the Charles Simon Chair in Finance at NYU's Stern School of Business.

When Charlie and I met, I was an unknown economist from the New York Fed, he a well-known senior partner at Salomon—hardly an unusual arrangement at a Money Marketeers dinner. By the end of the evening, Charlie had learned quite a bit about my background, while I heard just a smattering of things about Salomon.

Salomon was not yet the powerhouse it later became. I knew little of its history and present position on Wall Street, but enjoyed the evening's conversation at the Money Marketeers party with an interesting and prominent man.

The next day, Charlie called to invite me to lunch the following week. When I asked what time, he replied in typical Charlie style, "I'll be here waiting for you anytime it's convenient for you." When I arrived at Salomon's headquarters at 60 Wall Street, Charlie, again in his typical fashion, didn't take me to the guest dining room but rather to the partner's dining room, an intimate and rather elegant parlor with a large rectangular table that seated 12. Charlie seated me at the head of the table, which I later learned was usually occupied by Ben Levy, then a senior partner. For the next hour, Charlie regaled me with his rendition of the firm's history. I felt somewhat awkward, not knowing the purpose of the luncheon, nor why Charles Simon was directing so much attention my way.

When the lunch was nearly over, Charlie explained to me that a year earlier Salomon had recruited Sidney Homer from Scudder, Stevens and Clark, where he had developed a number of analytical techniques for measuring bond values and served as a bond portfolio manager. Charlie had brought Sidney to the attention of the firm, with the hope that Sidney would establish a fixed-income research operation at Salomon. Charlie hoped that I would agree to meet with Sidney Homer to discuss the possibility of serving as his assistant in the new research effort.

No research unit of that kind, at least of any significance, existed on Wall Street at the time. More generally, research had become more important since the 1950s. Billy Salomon—the firm's acting managing partner and son of one of the firm's founders—along with Charles Simon and Sidney Homer predicted (correctly, as it turned out) that research would become a crucial function for the firm. Initially, Salomon's customers had not called for an ambitious research effort, but over time they began to rely upon it more and more each year.

Sidney was given a free hand in creating a bond market research operation. Years later he wrote a short, privately printed memoir with the engaging title *Fun with Bonds*. As he recalled this turning point in the firm's history:

> In a flash I knew exactly what he [Bill Salomon] meant and saw how valuable would be a combination of their unbeatable bond trading and bond underwriting skills and my valuable studies. . . . The firm backed me up with unlimited resources. Never in the ten years I spent there was any limit ever suggested to the costly program of research and publication that I developed.

Sidney was taken into the firm as a general partner when he was nearly 60 years old. Unusual at the time, such a step would be impossible today, when partnerships are rare on the Street, and most top executives either retire or leave the securities market before they reach 60.

I agreed to meet with Sidney Homer the following week. As I soon discovered, Sidney was completely different from any of the other partners. He was a Harvard graduate. He had an extraordinary family background. His mother, Louise Homer, sang with Enrico Caruso at the Metropolitan Opera, and his father, also named Sidney, was a composer and conductor. Sidney was related to Samuel Barber, the composer, and Winslow Homer, the artist. He liked to tell the story of his mother's reaction upon learning that her son intended to become what he called, "a bond man." "Where did we go wrong?" she wailed.

Sidney had great historical perspective, not merely in financial matters, but also when it came to social and political developments. In contrast, his partners were very near-term-oriented. Whereas the typical Wall Streeters of that time often spent evenings with clients, overeating and overdrinking, Sidney led a very disciplined and organized life. His workday began promptly at 8:30 a.m. and ended at 5:15 p.m., followed by cocktails with his wife, perhaps a little piano or chess, and then to bed.

Sidney wrote with great clarity. He could close the door to his office and emerge a few hours later with a 10-page memo to portfolio managers that demanded little editing. I later came to appreciate his great historical sensibilities when he asked me to review and edit a draft of a book he had just completed entitled *A History of Interest Rates*, which he described as covering 40 centuries and 40 nations. Following his instructions, I read that draft aloud—all 594 pages, including 73 statistical tables. Like many good writers, Sidney knew that I would spot more grammatical errors and other problems by reading the book aloud. Years later, when I decided to fund a directorship at the Salomon Center at NYU's Stern School of Business, I was eager and gratified to endow it in Sidney's name.

When Sidney and I met, he explained to me that he was looking for an assistant to help him build a research department devoted solely to money and bond markets. At the start, the assistant (working with an analyst, a research assistant, and a secretary) would be expected to carefully analyze Federal Reserve and U.S. Treasury borrowings, and to build on Sidney's work on the supply and demand for credit and on interest rates. All of this would provide the foundation for the firm's bond market research effort. Few were working in this area, and still fewer were doing it well.

In a follow-up meeting, Sidney also indicated that he would not expect me to write speeches or memos for him, but hoped that I would write under my own name. A few days later, he called me with a job offer, and asked that I meet with Bill Salomon to discuss compensation.

Should I accept? Salomon did not have the standing or the prestige of Lehman Brothers, Goldman Sachs, Morgan Stanley, or, for that matter, Smith, Barney, whose earlier offer I had declined. But Salomon had established itself as a strong trading firm in very high-quality securities. More than that, it was clear to me that Sidney Homer would be pioneering; research of the kind he described was not being done with any degree of professionalism.

Needless to say, I consulted with Doc Nadler. When I walked into his office, he greeted me with, "I know why you're here. You have an offer from Salomon Brothers."

"What do you think about it?" I asked.

"Now, you have a critical decision to make," he said. He then opined, "You can stay at the Fed and probably carve out a very nice career. There is nothing wrong in that. Or you can try your hand at investment banking."

"But why Salomon Brothers?" I interrupted.

"At Salomon," he responded, "you will soon find out whether you will sink or swim. And at Salomon you can hear the cash registers ring every minute of the day." Nadler was never in better form.

I met with Bill Salomon a few days later. He offered me a starting salary of $13,000, well below what Smith, Barney had offered. I told him that I thought I should receive another $1,000, to which he quickly replied: "Take it or leave it." I took it. While an additional $1,000 seemed a lot to me at the time, in hindsight it was entirely irrelevant.

To put this offer in perspective, start by considering that I would be arriving as an assistant to a partner, a man in an unusual position not only at Salomon, but also throughout Wall Street. In that period, partners were assessed by how much business they generated. But Sidney was not bringing in clients or customers directly; rather, he was engaged in generating information that was relevant for the operation of the business. The firm's salespeople utilized such information to help educate clients, which in turn encouraged them to make certain kinds of transactions with Salomon. So Sidney was performing an extremely valuable function for the firm. And I was to be his assistant.

Even for nonresearch partners, Salomon's compensation structure did not promise lavish riches. In 1958 the Administrative Committee, led by Billy Salomon, initiated new rules on compensation. A partner was to receive a salary decided upon by the Committee. As one partner summarized the situation, "Even if you did well, you would be living on $100,000 or less," which was, he accurately concluded, "quite modest by the standards of the time." I was to receive a small fraction of that amount. Down the road—far down the road, given my status and age—there might be a partnership; but at least I had something to shoot for. After all, Sidney Homer was starting a new department with considerable potential. He impressed me enormously with his insights. And the open working environment was quite a contrast from the more bureaucratic setting at the Fed.

I accepted the offer. I had traversed from Wenings to Wall Street along a circuitous path. In my early years in Wenings, I never could have imagined this destination. Nor did I envision when I began college that my career would lead me to Wall Street.

When I walked into Salomon Brothers & Hutzler on January 13, 1962—my first day on the job—I was filled with anticipation, not knowing exactly what to expect. To be sure, Sidney Homer and Charlie Simon had already given me a rather good briefing. And I already knew a great deal about the money and capital markets, the influence the Federal Reserve had on operations like Salomon, and the importance of information flows to money market firms. I also knew that securities firms were involved with a wide range of financial market participants including banks, savings institutions, insurance companies, pension funds, mutual funds, and foreign governments and institutions. In contrast, the Federal Reserve Bank of New York conducted open market operations on behalf of the Federal Reserve mainly in short-dated U.S. Government securities ("U.S. Governments"), and then only when the Fed had to offset seasonal factors influencing bank reserves or when it wanted to change its credit posture. The Fed therefore enjoys periods of relative inactivity.

Not so in investment banking. What impressed me most when I started at Salomon was the third-floor trading room. The epicenter of the firm, it was where a wide range of securities changed hands, from short-dated to long-dated fixed-income issues, from railroad obligations to U.S. Governments, from Treasury bills to bankers' acceptances and commercial paper. To this mix were added in later years mortgage securities, junk bonds, foreign bonds, stocks, and financial derivatives. The trading room was crowded with people—traders, salespeople, and some support staff. The largest number hovered around the U.S. government and money market desks, followed by the station where corporate and municipal bonds were traded, the railroad desk, and lastly the preferred stock desk. (Only a few salesmen and traders were involved in equities when I arrived.) They sat cheek to jowl, usually in shirtsleeves, calling one another by first name. All, that is, except Ben Levy, who invariably wore a dark suit and answered only to "Mr. Levy" or "B.J."

The topography of the firm was revealing. Most partners sat on the trading floor, including Billy Salomon, the managing partner. (Billy had a small office in the back that he rarely used.) Everyone's actions were open to the scrutiny of everyone else. Salomon's open trading venue—first at 60 Wall Street, and later on a much larger scale at One New York Plaza—was unique for many years until other firms began to emulate it. Such openness had much to commend it. The general noise level was a sure indicator of whether markets were active or listless. The lack of physical barriers facilitated the rapid flow of market information from one desk to another, and thus decision making.

The room also encouraged meritocracy. Amid the din of shouted bids and jangling telephones, an atmosphere of informality prevailed, even between partners and rank-and-file employees. It was easy to look over a trader's shoulder at his desk blotter and learn his trading positions, and easier still to note changes in facial expressions or intonation. Accomplishments were quietly noted, as were failures. Competition was encouraged, but at the same time cooperation was needed for the firm to thrive. Marcus Nadler was right when he said to me, "At Salomon you will soon know whether you will sink or swim."

In stark contrast to the trading room, Sidney Homer's office—the best in the firm—featured two large windows that overlooked Wall

Street. Even so, the path to Sidney's office traversed the trading room, past the men's bathroom. My office, to use the term loosely, was partially partitioned, no larger than 7 by 8 feet. Behind stood a radiator that clanked according to its whim, and a window that looked out on the building's dark interior well. Our secretaries and two research assistants occupied an open space nearby. Sidney graciously offered to share his office with me when I became a partner several years later, but I declined. Modern offices would come later, when the firm moved to a new building at One New York Plaza.

It didn't take long—only about 2 weeks—for the informality and directness at Salomon to hit me, and drive home the fact that I was no longer at the Federal Reserve Bank. I was in the bathroom when Billy Salomon rushed in looking for me. "Henry, the books will close soon on a major U.S. Government refunding. What do you think we should do?" he asked. The question unnerved me a bit. At the Federal Reserve, the President never would have sought me out like that. He would have called Robert Roosa, the head of research, who might have called me, after which I would have written a memo. Here, communication was direct, and the need for information—however imperfect—immediate.

I arrived at Salomon at the right place and the right time. Salomon was not one of Wall Street's largest or most influential investment houses. Far from it. But its potential was enormous, for Salomon then possessed the key ingredients—trading expertise, a willingness to take risks, and a large reservoir of securities—that it would need to expand and prosper from the dramatic changes beginning to unfold in American finance.

It was during Wall Street's great postwar expansion that Salomon Brothers entered the ranks of the leaders—Merrill, Lynch; Morgan, Stanley; Goldman, Sachs; and their peers. It did so by dramatically expanding in investment banking and by focusing on institutional trading, especially bonds, mortgage-backed securities, and derivatives. Building on its existing strengths and connections in that area—especially its roster of top-notch institutional clients—Salomon astutely took advantage of the institutionalization of savings that would become one of the hallmarks of postwar finance. Connected intimately with the market through its knowledgeable cadre of partners, traders, and salespeople, Salomon catapulted into leadership by pioneering new financial instruments, by dominating the derivatives market for many years, and by moving aggressively into securities underwriting.

Salomon's growth over the next generation would astound even its most optimistic partners. As the 1960s began, the firm's net worth stood at $10 million; by the end of the 1970s, it would reach $230 million, only to expand another 10-fold by the middle of the 1980s. By that time, Salomon—with tax-exempt offerings, corporate offerings, and Eurobond offerings each in the neighborhood of $35 billion to $45 billion—had become the largest investment firm on Wall Street.

And as we would all come to see to our amazement, Salomon's rise was reflected in broader and equally dramatic transformations in the financial markets—as credit burgeoned, financial crises occasionally rocked the markets, prices and interest rates moved with new volatility, institutions underwent massive shifts, and monetary policy emerged as the dominant force in sustaining economic growth.

3

The Growth and
Transformation of Markets

Today's financial markets are a tribute to the triumph of capitalism, to the progress of technology, and to the gains made by those favoring economic democracy over political control.

<hr>

I began to catch glimpses of Salomon's auspicious future as I plunged into flow-of-funds analysis, at the suggestion of Sidney Homer, during my early months at the firm in 1962. The more I examined the data, the more astonished I was by what they suggested about the likely shape of the financial markets several years hence.

In 1965, I was given an opportunity to share my findings about the rapid expansion of financial markets with the partners and other senior executives at Salomon by giving an address on the subject of what the markets might look like 10 years out. My basic methodology was to project nominal GNP for the next decade, and thereby estimate the size of the credit market in 1975, based on the assumption that the two would continue to grow in roughly the same relation to each other as they had historically. Even though I based my calculations on rather conservative assumptions, my projection still indicated that the credit market would more than *double* in size over the next decade.

Most members of the audience at Salomon were stunned. Some fired off questions pertaining to their own market specialty. Others wanted to know more about the institutional structure 10 years hence. Still others asked where all the money would come from to finance the credit demands that I had projected.

Ironically, the passage of the decade would prove my estimates that day in 1965 to have been too conservative. And had I been asked to project the nature and size of the credit market to the end of the century, I would have missed the mark even more. As few experts, if any, anticipated in those days, the already robust growth of the 1950s and 1960s would be dwarfed by the expansion of the last three decades of the twentieth century.

The Dramatic Growth of Postwar Financial Markets

That dramatic expansion is an essential starting point for understanding the various transformations in domestic and international financial markets that are the subject of this book. The geometric growth of America's postwar financial markets was both a cause and a consequence of the nation's broader economic expansion. The boom was unprecedented in its scale, scope, and duration. Simply put, America's postwar generation experienced the greatest economic expansion in the history of the world. Never before did so many people partake of material prosperity.

The United States emerged from the war an economic powerhouse, producing half the world's output with a mere 6 percent of its population. Only part of this had to do with the fact that combat never reached American shores. Going into the war, the United States had led the world in most major industries—iron and steel, automobiles, agriculture, banking and finance, among many others—and it continued to dominate throughout the postwar period.

Between 1948 and 1973, the U.S. economy grew at an average annual rate of 3.7 percent, while real weekly wages—a key indicator of economic well-being—rose an average 2.9 percent per year. Unemployment hovered between 3 and 6 percent (apart from a couple of years, when it approached 7 percent). And the inflation rate (aside from a couple of temporary spikes) remained below 3 percent until the late 1960s. Little wonder many began to believe that poverty in America might soon be eliminated.

America's postwar economic strength flowed from a potent combination of forces. Government spending expanded dramatically: to contain communism throughout the world, to house and educate a generation of veterans, to build interstate highways, to expand social programs for millions of Americans. At the same time, federal officials rarely changed tax codes, enacted regulations, or pursued antitrust actions. Big business enjoyed generous profits, paid high wages, and pumped out goods and services for the world's largest middle class. For their part, American consumers were ready and willing to buy. Through 15 years of depression and war (1930–1945), they had been unable to spend liberally on goods and services—in particular, expensive durables such as homes, automobiles, radios, and washing machines. The war brought full employment, as women poured into the factories to join the men who had not been sent to fight overseas. Earning two or more incomes and working overtime, yet with few opportunities to spend, American families saved a hefty portion of their income. In 1945, they held an astounding $140 billion in government bonds and bank accounts. And they were eager to buy houses, cars, appliances, and other goods so long denied them by the hardships of depression and war.

For a time after the end of the war, millions feared the return of economic hard times. (After all, the war, rather than Roosevelt's New Deal, had ended the Great Depression, and now the war was over.) But that didn't happen. Instead, businesses invested and built, and consumers spent. The boom was on.

This was the economic context when I began work at Salomon Brothers in 1962. The postwar boom was well under way. Still, few on Wall Street had an inkling of the geometric growth of financial markets that was beginning to unfold, and fewer still were analyzing the major developments in financial markets in any kind of systematic way. The dimensions of this expansion, and the inner dynamics that were driving it, soon began to become apparent to me as I undertook flow-of-funds analysis at Salomon under the direction of Sidney Homer.

One of the most profound transformations in postwar finance was the explosion of domestic nonfinancial debt. This index—the combined borrowings of business, households, and federal, state, and local governments—ballooned from $724 billion in 1960 to $16.1 trillion in 1998, for a 22-fold increase. By comparison, nominal gross domestic product (GDP) expanded 16.5-fold over the same period, rising from $527 billion to $8.7 trillion (see Exhibit 3-1).

The American bond market has grown from outstandings of $485 billion in 1970 to an estimated $13 trillion at the end of 1998 (see Exhibit 3-2). This annual rate of growth of 19.5 percent also far outstripped the growth of GDP. Bonds remain the largest fixed-income market in the world, with a 43 percent share (although they were proportionally a larger 62 percent in the 1970s, when other markets were more docile). Not surprisingly, the surge in the value of outstanding bonds has been accompanied by a pronounced rise in the volume of bond trading. For example, the daily average volume of trading in U.S. Governments totaled $189 billion in 1998, compared with $129 billion and $72 billion 5 and 10 years ago, respectively.

Outside the United States, the combined fixed-income markets for the industrialized nations have grown from $291 billion in 1970 to $13 trillion in 1997, an average annual rate of 15 percent (see Exhibit 3-3). There, too, debt has grown much more quickly than GDP. This is a pattern specific to the advanced economies of the world. While the fixed-

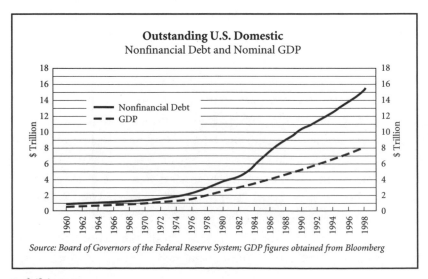

Outstanding U.S. Domestic
Nonfinancial Debt and Nominal GDP

Source: Board of Governors of the Federal Reserve System; GDP figures obtained from Bloomberg

Exhibit 3-1

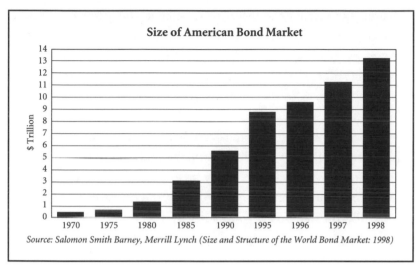

Exhibit 3-2

income markets of the largest emerging nations have shown irregular but spectacular growth over time, their size remains small relative to the markets of the industrial nations.

The stock markets have enjoyed their own boom. Among the 10 leading industrialized nations, the total market value of equities topped

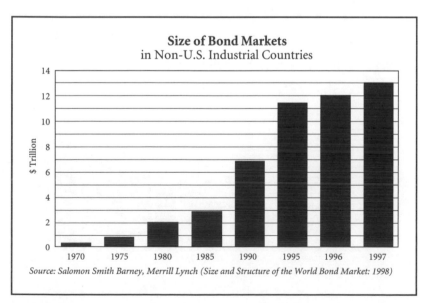

Exhibit 3-3

an estimated $25 trillion in 1998, up 121 percent from just 5 years before, 184 percent from 10 years before, and an astounding 1,004 percent since 1980 (see Exhibit 3-4). At the beginning of the 1990s, U.S. gross domestic product still exceeded the market value of stocks by 55 percent; but by the end of 1998, stock values exceeded GDP by 71.6 percent (see Exhibit 3-5).

Even more astonishing is the overwhelming increase in stock trading activity (see Exhibit 3-6). In 1960, 767 million shares were traded on the New York Stock Exchange. Today, an even greater number of shares change hands on the NYSE *each day*. Now, the turnover rate (the volume traded on the Exchange divided by the volume of shares outstanding) is 76 percent, compared with an average of 51 percent for the 1980s, 22 percent for the 1970s, and 17 percent for the 1960s.

Financial derivatives (the subject of Chapter 4) played a modest role in finance for decades, but began a precipitous climb in the 1980s. One key measure of this—the notional principal value of outstanding interest rate swaps—amounted to only $683 billion in 1987, and then rose to $2.3 trillion in 1990 and to $36.3 trillion at the end of 1998 (see Exhibit 3-7).

Yet another market that exploded in the postwar period was currency trading. Once the domain of a few specialists, the currency market has broadened sharply. According to estimates made by the Bank for

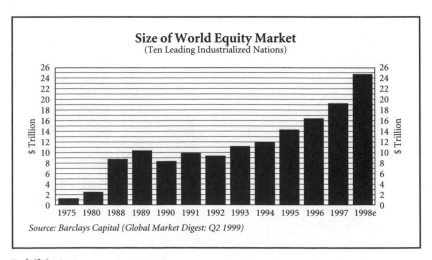

Exhibit 3-4

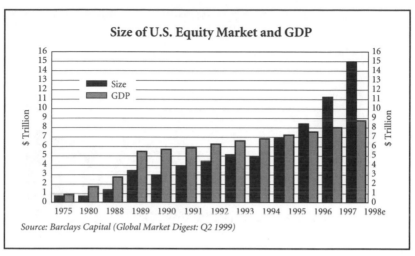

Exhibit 3-5

International Settlements, foreign currency turnover totaled $206 billion in March 1986, $1 trillion in April 1992, and $2 trillion in April 1998.

What were the forces behind these extraordinary developments in the financial markets?

In the case of the debt explosion, the historically high inflation that began in the mid-1960s (with the irresponsible financing of the

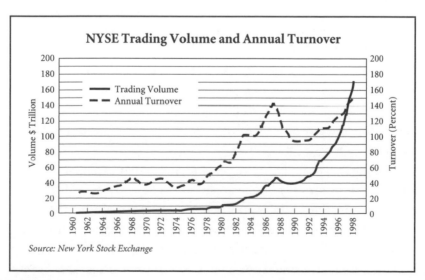

Exhibit 3-6

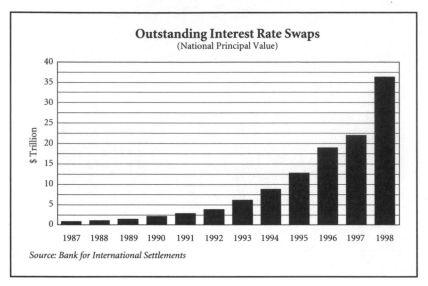

Outstanding Interest Rate Swaps
(National Principal Value)

Source: Bank for International Settlements

Exhibit 3-7

Vietnam War), and erupted into double-digit inflation in the late 1970s, certainly was a factor—but not the only one. In fact, the growing divergence between inflation rates and debt has become a distinguishing feature of our times, and the reason has much to do with federal government borrowing.

As we have seen, domestic nonfinancial debt grew moderately in the immediate post-World War II period, and advanced in close alignment with the increase in nominal GDP. Even with the onset of the "great inflation" in the mid-1960s, the two indices (the growth of debt and of GDP) moved in tandem, hovering around 7 percent in the 1960s and 11 percent in the 1970s. But the 1980s brought a dramatic surge in debt, while the growth rate of nominal GDP ebbed, as did inflation, though in a more erratic pattern.

On the face of it, this decoupling seems to defy explanation. After all, inflation historically has been one of the key drivers of debt. But a closer examination of the economy of the 1980s reveals that the standout generator of debt was the United States government, which accumulated huge budget deficits as a result of tax cuts and increased spending for defense and the major entitlement programs. Federal debt rose by a staggering 206 percent in the 1980s, compared with 22 percent in the 1960s and 120 percent in the 1970s. This is not to say that households and corporations were parsimonious. Both stepped up their borrowings in the 1980s.

The result of the U.S. government's borrowing binge in the 1980s was a debt burden that contributed to a severe business recession and a financial crisis. (I discuss the latter in Chapter 14). The hard-won financial rehabilitation that followed in the 1990s brought debt growth once again into closer alignment with the growth of GDP. By that time, several divergent patterns had become visible. In the early 1990s, federal government borrowings remained extremely large, while private-sector borrowings subsided sharply. By the middle of the decade, U.S. debt growth slowed, and then contracted, as the government began at long last to generate budget surpluses, while the growth of private-sector debt once again began to accelerate.

The massive expansion of public and private debt reflected a crucial and widespread shift in attitudes about borrowing in the postwar period. The initial hesitancy to borrow in the late 1940s and 1950s—a legacy of the generation that had endured the hardships of the Great Depression—was eclipsed by a much more expansionist view of debt. Later, the deregulation movement of the 1970s and 1980s reinforced the trend toward heavier and heavier corporate borrowing by spurring competition. In earlier times, when markets were more compartmentalized and institutions more restricted in their activities, the pressure to compete through leveraging and other means was not as acute, even though this may have caused some economic and financial inefficiencies.

The Securitization of Credit

Another powerful force driving the postwar transformation of financial markets has been securitization (that is, the conversion of non-marketable assets into marketable ones). Very likely the most far-reaching development in modern finance, securitization has changed the very nature of financial assets, as well as the character of market behavior. One major consequence of widespread securitization has been the creation of a vast and sometimes bewildering assortment of securitized assets. Securitization has permitted the packaging, resale, and trading of a large array of obligations that one time were locked up in the portfolios of original lenders and investors. Now, virtually every major variety of financial asset is packaged and ready for sale and resale, with consequences that many Wall Streeters have not considered fully.

Securitization started slowly, gaining its first boost with the rise of that large commercial paper market in the 1950s and 1960s. It then picked up considerable momentum in the late 1970s with the creation of home mortgage pass-through securities, followed by the invention of collateralized mortgage obligations (CMOs) and real estate mortgage investment conduits (REMICs). The packaging of outstanding bank loans to less developed nations in the form of instruments such as Brady bonds marked another giant step in the spread of securitization. We now have massive securitization of credit card receivables, auto loans, commercial mortgages, home equity loans, and even some commercial and industrial loans.

As these new marketable instruments have proliferated, joining the many other kinds of obligations now available, they have replaced assets that once were lodged on the balance sheets of conventional financial institutions, and that rarely if ever were marked to market. Thanks to securitization, those same assets can be traded, priced, and marked to market daily—as Eurodollar bonds, interest rate and currency swaps, junk bonds, zero coupon bonds, equity derivatives, options in Eurodollar and U.S. Treasury futures, and in many, many other forms.

For many Americans, the most vivid illustration of securitization is the way home mortgages are secured today as compared with years ago. In the early 1960s, banking was a local affair. Those who sought a mortgage typically visited a local savings and loan, where they met with a loan officer who drew up a profile of the family's financial situation. The loan application was forwarded to a committee for review, and within a couple of weeks or so the applicant would have an answer. If the loan was approved, the money came from the passbook savings of residents in the community. And because the federal government tightly regulated the interest rate that savings and loans could pay, there was little variation in the loan rates offered from one bank to the next, and thus little reason to shop around. In short, the home mortgage market was local, personal, and predictable.

Today, the mortgage market is national, intensely competitive, and dazzlingly complicated. The days of interest rate ceilings have long passed, so banks have much greater latitude in what rates they can offer. Even more striking, the players in the game have changed. The local savings and loan has greatly diminished in importance, following the colossal collapse of that industry in the 1980s. In its place, a wide range of financial institutions began to offer mortgages, from commercial banks to insurance companies to mortgage brokers.

Then there is the question of what happens to the mortgage debt once it is issued. No longer is it domiciled in the originating institution. Instead, it is likely to be transformed into discrete packages of debt (that is, securitized) which are then marketed and remarketed like shares of stocks or bonds. The mortgage customer might visit the local banker, but more likely he will consult a number of newsletters, magazines, or Web sites for up-to-the-minute information on rates and other features. An increasing number of facilitators even approve or decline loans based on statistical profiles of applicants rather than a thorough review of the documentation. And there are scores of new mortgage "products" to choose from, making the traditional 30-year fixed mortgage seem clunky and unsophisticated by comparison. Thus, the volume and velocity of information available to the mortgage shopper, the array of financing options, and the kinds of financial players participating in the business—all have multiplied many times over since the early postwar years.

In addition to mortgage borrowers, many other demanders of credit—who in earlier times depended heavily on bank loans—now have access to the open credit market. This graduation to the realm of open markets has involved not only companies, but also sovereigns. It spans both investment-grade and below-investment-grade credits. Bonds of poorer quality have become part of the growing wave of securitized assets that are traded and priced on a continual basis, rather than remaining passively lodged on the balance sheets of commercial banks or other traditional institutions.

What have been some of the major consequences of securitization? First, the large-scale shift from nonmarketable to marketable assets has had the significant side effect of dispelling the illusion that nonmarketable assets by nature have stable prices. In doing so, however, some of the new securitized instruments have magnified the volatility of financial asset prices. Second, securitization has opened up literally trillions of dollars worth of financial assets to the harsh glare of the marketplace. For a long time, traditional institutions such as banks and insurance companies carried their nonmarketable financial assets (such as loans and mortgages) at par, regardless of interest rate movements. But now that many of these assets are in marketable form, their values are accordingly determined by the marketplace. Third, securitization has given market access to borrowers who previously had depended heavily on bank loans. These new participants in the open markets range from ordinary households to business corporations and sovereigns.

Fourth, the shift to marketability makes accurate pricing of securities essential. It is now the key ingredient in measuring and controlling risk, in calculating profit and loss, and in evaluating performance. But even under normal conditions, this is hardly a cut-and-dried procedure, except in the case of some liquid sectors, such as U.S. Governments. Rather, for most corporate debt obligations, for virtually all securities issued by borrowers in emerging markets, and for many segments of the mortgage securities market, attaining valid pricing is an imprecise science. In the case of financial derivatives, this is most apparent in the pricing of over-the-counter options and of securitized derivatives, notably structured notes.

That highly securitized markets are, on the whole, more volatile than less securitized markets has important implications. In volatile markets—as in recent times, and surely during periods in the future—liquidity may disappear suddenly, accurate pricing becomes exceptionally difficult to obtain, and marking to market may be practically impossible.

Why is this so? And what are the consequences? To begin with, the price of the last trade may be completely invalid in rapidly moving markets, particularly for illiquid securities and certainly for most options. Moreover, the price that a dealer is prepared to quote may be little more than an *indication* of what the security is worth, not the price at which the dealer is actually willing to trade. Another dealer may quote—on that same "indications-only" basis—a wildly different price. For the institution trying to mark that position to market, there is simply no reliable arbiter of "true" price.

More than that, the price quoted may be valid for trading only a very small amount, not the full amount that the investor has in his portfolio. And in the case of already existing options, dealers may be calculating prices on the basis of highly questionable assumptions. Of course, marking such positions to market is problematic because other dealers may be relying on radically different assumptions, which in any event cannot be verified.

These difficulties have been around to some degree for a long time. But they have intensified in recent years with the growing volatility of many asset prices. With more and more debt in marketable form, financial institutions are finding it necessary to reprice those assets on a continuing basis. At the same time, debt securities themselves have become more complex, and thus harder to evaluate. It is particularly difficult to price instruments that possess a high degree of what is known technically as "optionality." The consequences of not being able to mark to market accurately are often far from trivial. At best, dealers face embarrassment when clients call attention to inaccurate estimates of portfolio returns. At worst, they face the calamity of enormous losses and the impairment of capital.

Perhaps the most important of all, widespread securitization has had the broad effect of loosening the credit process. Credit standards have been lowered, and the credit market has grown enormously. This should not be surprising, given the role of the investment banker in the securitization process. It is his job to facilitate the securitization process—after all, his fee depends on the successful distribution of the issue—and in doing so, the investment banker's due diligence is limited by his analytical focus on the borrower's current financial situation. This, in effect, leaves much of the judgment in the hands of the investor. A securitized investment also encourages the investor to believe that he can quickly sell the obligation when a credit problem brews, thereby passing off the problem to someone else. Again—in this instance at the time when the investment is undertaken—we see the making of the liquidity illusion.

By transforming trading practices, by fostering the creation of a dazzling array of new instruments, and by facilitating the explosive growth of modern financial markets, securitization has emerged as arguably the most potent and influential development in the financial history of our times.

The Globalization of Financial Markets

Today there is general agreement among financial experts that we live and work in an economic environment that is much more "globalized" than at any other time in history. Without the rapid strides in the securitization of financial assets and vast improvements in technology, the globalization of markets could not have taken place, at least not at the rapid clip we have seen in recent decades.

To be sure, international lending and investing hardly were inventions of the postwar period. They were born with the emergence of the first capitalist city-states (most notably fourteenth-century Venice), whose leading merchants invested across national and continental borders, albeit at a snail's pace compared with today. In the nineteenth century, British bond investors funded America's sprawling railroad networks, and by the turn of the century, several giant U.S. manufacturing firms had become truly multinational.

Meanwhile, international finance among sovereigns oiled the wheels of war, beginning with the American Revolution, in which the colonial revolutionaries borrowed heavily from France, Spain, and Holland. During World War I, the United States went from being a debtor nation that owed foreigners $3.7 billion to a creditor nation to whom foreigners owed $12.6 billion. And America's role in international finance expanded enormously during and after the Second World War, as U.S. multinational corporations entered a boom period, and the federal government invested $13 billion of Marshall Plan money in Western Europe between 1948 and 1951, while dominating the Bretton Woods/IMF international monetary regime of the postwar era.

Still, international finance in the last few decades has been defined by an important transformation—part of the new dominance of free-market capitalism around the world. This is the shift from capital markets that were rigorously controlled by central governments, segmented, and frequently inefficient to those that are far more open, broadly interconnected, and inventive. We have seen a transition from fixed exchange rates and highly regulated interest rates to an environment of market-determined exchange rates and interest rates, with all of the characteristic volatility—at times of breathtaking magnitude—of unencumbered capital markets.

It is important to recognize that this transformation was not premeditated; that is, it did not come through careful, deliberate planning by government officials, academics, or market participants themselves. Instead, it came in fits and starts. It was spawned by repeated bursts of financial opportunism, as borrowers, lenders, and intermediaries sought ways to avoid regulations, sidestep taxes, gain access to cheaper sources of funds, trade currencies or securities at lower cost and without onerous restrictions, or find new avenues for speculative activity. In the process, institutions at the forefront of innovation made a considerable amount of money, and their achievements in turn attracted numerous imitators, not all of whom were successful.

As a general rule, the financial authorities of the main industrial countries were of two minds about the eclipse of the postwar status quo, with its ostensibly strong and effective regulatory oversight. (See Chapter 12 for a detailed discussion of financial supervision and regulation.)

It is often forgotten that when the International Monetary Fund was established, its Articles of Agreement specifically sanctioned restrictions on movements of capital across national boundaries. Nor did the IMF's founders intend the organization to criticize member nations for applying controls on domestic credit creation, which was accepted practice at the time. Liberalization of current account transactions was deemed to be far more important than liberalization of capital account transactions. Even when some began to seriously contemplate the merits of international capital mobility and open credit markets in the 1960s and early 1970s, most major industrial nations were reluctant to abandon entirely the exchange controls, capital controls, or other devices that allowed them to directly influence the flow of credit and the movement of capital.

But government officials and politicians also appreciated the value of competitive markets, and thus hesitated to apply regulatory muscle so stringently that their national banking institutions were kept from pursuing what seemed to be profitable new financial activities. For one thing, they didn't want their leading corporations to be shut off completely from less costly foreign sources of credit. So they turned a blind eye to many ruptures in the barriers to international flows of funds, while in effect accrediting the most effective means of breaking down obstacles to international capital mobility: the Euro-currency markets.

Just the same, the bias in favor of direct intrusion into capital markets persisted in several key nations, even as financial flows were opening up elsewhere. Only quite recently did the last of the major European Community (EC) members with meaningful capital controls (France and Italy) agree to scrap them as part of the EC's Single Market Initiative.

The present-day architecture of global financial markets includes many large institutions, myriad tradable obligations, and instantaneous transmission of information through computer networks. It is now commonplace to issue stocks and bonds globally. With markets operating in one hemisphere or another at any given time, transactions can be consummated around the clock. Indeed, traders often neutralize the risk in a position at the end of a day by consummating trades in markets operating in different time zones. Shortly after New York markets close, Tokyo markets open. Trading desks worldwide are covered longer, and the NYSE is now planning to extend its trading hours. The contrast with earlier years is striking. In the 1960s, I would typically arrive at Salomon Brothers around 7:30 a.m. to find the trading floor mostly deserted. Two decades later, the floor already was buzzing with activity when I arrived early in the morning, as closing information poured in from Asia, and the European markets already had stirred to life.

Both the blinding speed of information flow and the nimbleness of market responses were brought home to me in the early 1980s, while

I was attending a meeting at the Bank of England. It was a Friday, a day when the U.S. was scheduled to release unemployment figures. At 2:30 p.m. London time (8:30 a.m. in New York) I briefly stepped out of a meeting to call my office in New York. After exchanging a comment or two with a member of my staff on the telephone, I headed back to the meeting. Passing me in the hallway, a member of the Bank of England remarked to me: "Henry, your employment data was very strong. The dollar is rallying in the Forex market and European bonds are down sharply."

Institutions and Portfolio Management

As markets and assets have changed dramatically with the emergence of a new global financial system, so has the composition of financial institutions themselves. The power and influence of traditional commercial banks, savings and loans, and insurance companies have diminished, while a new breed of institutional participants has come to the fore. These institutions are distinguished by their emphasis on short-term investment performance, their heavy use of leverage, and their willingness to move in and out of markets—whether equities, bonds, currencies, or commodities—in a relentless quest to maximize returns. The new breed includes the often-reviled hedge funds, although they are neither the sole nor the leading contestants. In fact, most prominent banks, securities firms, and even a few insurance companies possess departments that emulate the trading and investment approach of the hedge funds. Even the corporate treasuries of a number of nonfinancial corporations are engaged in this activity. Once arcane and exotic, the hedge fund approach to investment has been mainstreamed.

Mutual funds have been central to this realignment. Within a few short years, they emerged as a dominant market force. As shown in Exhibit 3-8, mutual funds were barely noticeable in the 1970s, when they accounted for only 1 percent of the funds supplied to the credit market. In 1997, 1998, and the first half of 1999, they supplied 11.4 per-

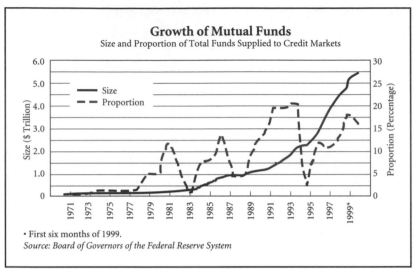

Exhibit 3-8

cent, 17.9 percent, and 15.7 percent, respectively. Their role has been especially pivotal in the stock market, which was long dominated by private and public pension funds. But as private pension funds increasingly have shifted from defined benefits to defined contributions—thereby encouraging beneficiaries to select their own portfolio risk profiles—mutual funds have attracted billions of dollars of pension fund assets.

The mutual fund revolution has been a major component of a larger trend toward greater discretionary investment—including risk-bearing investment—on the part of the household sector. Compared with earlier periods, the last 25 years or so have seen a dramatic increase in household financial wealth in the stock market, partly through new investment in individual company stocks and stock mutual funds, but also through the sharp rise in stock values, especially in the last 5 years. As shown in Exhibit 3-9, corporate equity investments by households now account for 36.6 percent of household wealth (in 1998), compared with 21.8 percent a decade ago (1989). Indeed, the lure of the stock market has encouraged quite a few individuals to become day traders to use leverage in order to achieve

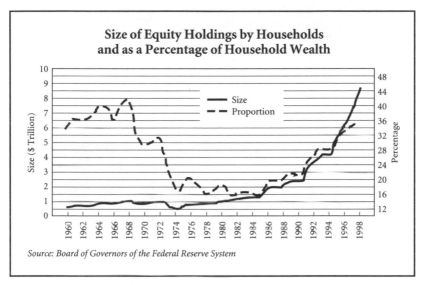

Source: Board of Governors of the Federal Reserve System

Exhibit 3-9

higher rewards, and thus to focus on near-term financial objectives rather than longer-term goals.

As household financial wealth has grown, personal savings has diminished as a key component of household investment strategy. In fact, some data suggest that middle-class households in the aggregate are "saving" at a negative rate, probably because they are emboldened by the generous returns from their stock portfolios. The pattern of rising household financial wealth and declining personal savings, shown in Exhibit 3-10, surely is one of the extraordinary features of the last decade, a development I noted in a number of speeches in the early 1990s.

These key trends—securitization, improvements in technology, globalization, and greater household participation in financial risk taking—have transformed financial markets in fundamental ways since my early days on Wall Street. Yet, behind the high-tech wizardry, the staggering array of new financial instruments, the democratization of risk, and the ongoing reconfiguration of financial institutions, financial markets still operate based on a core set of fundamentals. They still involve borrowers and lenders, investors and creditors,

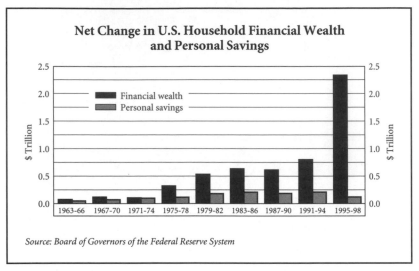

Exhibit 3-10

stock investors and corporations. And in the case of debt creation, these parties still enter into lending arrangements in which the borrower agrees to repay at a stipulated time and at a predetermined interest rate as compensation to the lender. In ancient times, as now, this arrangement has been the underpinning of financial transactions. To be sure, today many transactions are very complicated; some require complicated contracts and time to consummate, while others are done in a matter of seconds by telephone or computers. But they still depend on the fundamental precepts of honest exchange and timely repayment.

In the vast majority of cases, the parties involved honor their commitments. If they didn't, markets would function poorly, or not at all, financial and economic resources would be allocated inefficiently, and economic progress itself would be slow or would stall altogether. Viewed in this way, effective financial markets are a wonder to behold. They reflect the exercise of objectivity, trust, and a blend of entrepreneurship and fiduciary responsibility—though not always, of course. At times, these basic tenets are ignored or forgotten, leading to overcontrol or overindulgence, neither of which is healthy for the economy.

Today's financial markets are a tribute to the triumph of capitalism, to the progress of technology, and to the gains made by those favoring economic democracy over political control. Nevertheless, the task of preserving the efficient operation of today's markets is extraordinarily demanding. Markets are far more complex than years ago, and this complexity poses new challenges for investors, senior managers at financial institutions, regulators, central bankers, and other key financial players.

4

The Derivatives Revolution

How will derivatives perform under a less favorable set of conditions? That question haunts the future of the derivatives revolution.

———————

In the last two decades or so, Wall Street has become enamored with a seemingly new category of financial instruments known as derivatives. As we saw in Chapter 3, financial derivatives are probably the fastest-growing segment of the financial scene today. Given the speed and scale with which it swept through the international investment scene in recent years, the derivatives revolution deserves careful re-examination.

Salomon Brothers was in the forefront of the derivatives revolution—and understandably so. We had a long history of market making, as well as detailed knowledge of the financial instruments that go into the derivatives mix. Salomon was a leader in trading U.S. Governments, money market obligations, and a wide range of corporate bonds, and its research capabilities were well suited to support the new derivatives business.

For these reasons, I was not surprised when John Meriwether and a few others from Salomon's Government desk came to the Executive Committee to ask for authority to broker interest rate swaps in the early 1980s. Nor was I surprised a few months later when the Committee was asked for permission to position these derivatives, that is, to become a dealer with an inventory. It didn't take very long for these positions to mushroom.

I always thought this was a good business for Salomon, especially because we had a firm grasp of the characteristics of underlying markets. But I did have some reservations. What was going to be the magnitude of our participation in the overall derivatives market? As our positioning grew rapidly, the magnitude of risk taking started to stretch out in maturity and even in credit quality. For some reason the Executive Committee found it difficult to establish analytical tools that would set the parameters for this activity. Indeed, there were instances when other activities were curtailed because the capital was needed to hold these securities to maturity in order to gain the profit benefit. However, Salomon did well in the derivatives business even though we continued to enlarge our total exposure.

Drivers of Growth

Ironically, much about this quintessentially "modern" development is not new at all; several of the most common varieties of financial derivatives have been around for many decades. Still, new derivatives instruments have appeared on the financial scene in recent years, and these tend to be the most complex—and least understood—of the breed. It is therefore important to identify which kinds of derivatives are new, why they gained popularity so quickly, and what particular economic and financial conditions have nurtured them. Understanding those conditions helps explain derivatives as a historical phenomenon, but also raises the crucial question of whether derivatives markets will continue to expand and work smoothly in future years, when different conditions are likely to prevail.

More than that, the proliferation of financial derivatives has—perhaps more than any other single development of the last two decades—placed new strains on our already obsolete system of financial supervision and regulation. As the derivatives revolution has gained considerable force and momentum, our laws and regulatory institutions are struggling to remain relevant and effective. The transformation of financial markets—including but not limited to derivatives markets—has been so sweeping and fundamental that patchwork fixes will not do.

The economic and financial market that nurtured the derivatives revolution is defined by six key elements. First, inflation has been waning worldwide. This has encouraged investment in financial assets—stocks and bonds alike. As professionally managed portfolios have increased in size and scope internationally, many investment managers have sought to limit exposure to market risks by making use of derivatives. That, in turn, has been a steady source of business for financial institutions that specialize in providing financial derivatives as instruments for risk management.

A second macroeconomic trend hospitable to derivatives has been the positively sloped yield curve that has prevailed most of the time in recent years in the United States and in a handful of other developed nations. This curve has had the indirect yet significant effect of enabling a wide range of market participants to boost profitability, and thus overall financial strength, without having to take on greater credit risk. And that market condition, in turn, has encouraged greater participation in derivatives markets on the part of a growing number of financial institutions.

The disintermediation of the credit-creation process that has been taking place on a large scale in many advanced economies is yet another underpinning of the derivatives revolution. These shifting competitive conditions in the financial sector have encouraged many well-established financial institutions to plow additional resources into a widening range of capital market activities—including derivatives. Once developed, those organizational capabilities are not easily dismantled, even if economic expansion causes loan demand to pick up again.

A fourth condition favorable to financial derivatives has been the emergence of large pools of risk capital under the direction of managers who aggressively seek high rates of return, and who are able to amass large open positions in currencies, bonds, or stocks. The fact is, for every cautious portfolio manager hoping to use financial derivatives to limit risk, there must be a willing risk taker on the other side. Without the active participation of prominent speculators, the market would be lopsided, which would make the cost of derivatives prohibitive for risk-averse businesses as well as for investors who are trying to hedge open exposures.

Still another trend fostering the proliferation of derivatives has been the unusual volatility in a number of underlying markets in recent times. Consider, for example, the eruptions in the European exchange rate mechanism in the early 1990s. Those erratic conditions enabled risk-averse businesses and investors to acquire the hedges they desired, and speculators to take open market positions that (they believed) would rise in value because few expected that European financial authorities would be willing or able to sustain prescribed exchange rate relationships.

That assumption proved to be correct in the end, but some market participants got caught leaning the wrong way. Moreover, segments of the derivatives markets (notably, certain kinds of over-the-counter options) performed poorly under stress. By and large, however, the private sector reaped large profits, while the central banks of Europe sustained heavy losses. The question then emerges: What would have happened to many private market interests if the central banks had made profits?!

Finally, technological advancement also has helped set the stage for the derivatives revolution. The development of powerful mathematical tools for quantifying many of the underlying risks involved in exotic financial instruments has helped popularize derivatives, as has the plummeting price of computer power, which is needed to carry out the intricate calculations involved in managing complex exposures in swaps and options. It was precisely the application of such state-of-the-art analytical tools to the practical side of the new business that initially gave the pioneers in financial derivatives their competitive advantage.

Falling inflation, a rising yield curve, large-scale disintermediation, the search for historically high rates of return, price volatility in key financial markets, and new computational techniques—this powerful combination of underlying conditions has ushered in an unprecedented level of activity in financial derivatives. But it is important to recognize the uniqueness of this convergence. How will derivatives perform under a less favorable set of conditions? That question haunts the future of the derivatives revolution.

Points of Consensus

It is striking that on some issues related to derivatives—which were debated fiercely as recently as a year or two ago—there is now a consensus of views, while other aspects of the derivatives revolution continue to generate debate and controversy, perhaps more so than ever.

Consensus has emerged in at least four aspects of financial derivatives. To begin with, we now have a much better understanding than we did just a few years ago of how financial derivatives fit into the overall picture of financial markets. Nearly every serious observer has come to recognize that financial derivatives—whether in the form of futures, forwards, swaps, options, or securities that embody derivatives—cannot be understood in isolation. They are merely one part of the far-reaching structural changes in our financial markets that have emerged and evolved over the past three decades.

This new financial world is defined by widespread securitization of credit; by the internationalization of borrowing, lending, and investing; by unprecedented volatility in the prices of assets; by the declining relative position of traditional institutional lenders and investors who tended to buy and hold; by the emergence of "hi-octane" portfolio managers with very near-term investment horizons, who are willing to use greater leverage to achieve higher returns; by the dramatic expansion of mutual funds, many of which employ derivatives or hold securities that embody derivatives; and by a persistent blurring of the lines between distinct kinds of financial institutions. One might even say that the lines between the real and the financial aspects of business life have become blurry as well.

Many experts now see financial derivatives as an outgrowth of these broader historical processes of financial transformation. The *interaction* of the financial system's component elements tends to nurture financial risks, which in turn motivates investors, companies, and financial institutions to look for new ways to profit and new hedges against risk. Increasingly, derivatives seem to be an attractive option. But they are not merely an answer to increasing risk. Derivatives have themselves become an agent of change in the broader financial picture. It is now axiomatic that they must be considered within this broader context.

A second point on which opinion has converged is that the term "financial derivatives" is too broad to be very useful; and that we need to take care to distinguish among the varieties of derivatives in order to understand their financial and economic implications. Market professionals appreciate that the term covers a wide range of financial instruments and techniques, each with unique origins, purposes, and risks. The practical consequence of this diversity is that the discussion of financial derivatives has shifted from its earlier focus mainly on interest rate swaps (as in the case of the path-breaking study published by the Group of 30 in mid-1993) toward the very different—and considerably more complex—markets for over-the-counter options and securitized derivatives.

Consider, for example, the case of forward foreign exchange swaps. These often are classified as a new variety of financial derivative. But currency forwards have been in use for generations, sometimes as hedging vehicles, at other times for speculation. To be sure, there are a few fresh wrinkles. Two decades ago, hardly anyone wrote 5- or 10-year forward contracts, whereas today it is easy to find a bank or securities firm that will take them on. More than this, the rate of turnover in forward markets has mushroomed, thanks to the advent of flexible exchange rates, which in turn have been spurred on by the heightened volatility of currency values and by the latest information revolution, with its lightning-fast telecommunications and real-time price quotations. Apart from this greater velocity and volume, however, the whole foreign exchange market operates essentially the same as it has for decades—including the large risks inherent in currency trading. Modern computers allow dealers and their customers to keep better track of the exposed positions they are taking, but they certainly don't provide surefire predictions about whether to go long or go short!

Third, opinion has begun to converge on the basic risk character-istics of derivatives. Not long ago, advocates of these instruments argued that they were primarily "risk management" products. This view carried the typically unspoken assumption that derivatives had the overall effect of *reducing* risk in the financial positions of end users—in other words, that derivatives were tools to help hedge against already present risk. However, a string of large and highly publicized losses incurred by a number of institutions that were heavily invested in derivatives (including nonfinancial corporations and commercial banks) has made this view untenable. Rather, many market partici-pants now acknowledge (some reluctantly) that financial derivatives facilitate not only hedging but also speculation. More to the point, everyone seems to agree that it is dangerous when users of derivatives are exposed to risks that they either do not understand or cannot quantify accurately. Even those who ordinarily are considered to be quite sophisticated as participants in traditional financial markets can find themselves over their heads when contending with the bewilder-ing complexity of some of the novel products created by derivatives specialists.

An important consequence of these developments is that dealers and end users alike have come together in calling for better evaluation of the kinds of credit risks—also known as counterparty risks—that arise in trading financial derivatives. The credit judgments that matter most are those that relate to the exposures from transactions with new types of organizations. These include leveraged funds, to which con-ventional credit ratings simply do not apply, and subsidiaries of nonfi-nancial corporations, which may have a complex—and somewhat ambiguous—relationship with the parent.

This raises several difficult questions. How often are credit reviews done in these cases? How good are the data that are fed into the review process? Who makes sure the data are correct, or updated frequently? Prior to the now notorious misadventures in the markets of several large end users that surfaced in the mid-1990s, these questions were roundly dismissed as hypothetical. No longer. To be sure, it will take a long time to actually implement a robust credit review system; but no one seriously disagrees any more with the need to do so.

Finally, we now have a much better understanding of the great range of financial institutions that are actively involved in originating, packaging, marketing, and trading the various types of financial derivatives. The scope of this activity is dazzling and continually expanding. It includes puts and calls on shares of individual companies, equity indexes, government bonds, bond and stock futures, currencies, commodities, interest rate caps, and floors and collars; and it extends to a whole class of hybrid instruments that combine futures, swaps, and options, and even to an emerging category of contingent options, where payoffs are a function of multiple conditions taking hold. The institutions involved in trading these instruments include commercial banks, securities firms, insurance companies, finance companies, and even some units of nonfinancial corporations. Their basic businesses differ in important ways. But when they deal in financial derivatives, these traditional distinctions evaporate. When institutions market derivatives, all are essentially in the same business.

The business of writing over-the-counter options, particularly the more complicated ones, is very different from the traditional activities of a bank or securities firm. Conceptually, it is akin to the risks taken by casualty insurance companies when there is no true actuarial basis for setting a premium. Over-the-counter options writings face the additional challenge of properly valuing complex options during their effective life. This is especially difficult in today's environment, when the value of financial assets is so volatile. Such conditions raise questions about the credibility of pricing models for standard options, for which an estimate of future volatility is a crucial variable.

Moreover, because financial options create risks that cannot be hedged perfectly without, in effect, undoing the transactions altogether, investors often turn to dynamic hedging to manage the new risks. But dynamic hedging is an inexact science, one that relies on extraordinarily complex computerized models, which themselves are far from infallible (because they are built on historical data). More than one major financial institution is now jeopardizing its viability by depending on the power and reliability of models for critical functions—from the pricing of complex options, or securities and swaps with embedded options, to identification of exposures, to evaluation of positions under changing circumstances—now known to the trade as "stress testing"—to portfolio risk management. The problem is that no one knows how robust these models will be in the face of unusual market developments.

Disagreements and Blind Spots

It is reassuring that these points of consensus about derivatives have emerged within the financial community in a relatively short time. They mark great improvements in our collective understanding of the way the market functions and the risks that are at stake. Regrettably, however, there are still many blind spots in our understanding of the nature and consequences of these financial instruments.

To begin with, derivatives are a transinstitutional phenomenon, which raises important policy implications for our current regulatory system. After all, that system is organized according to industry categories that have been made obsolete by derivatives (and other recent financial innovations). Since many kinds of financial institutions have been caught up in the derivatives revolution, effective supervision and regulation of these complicated financial instruments will be impossible without an extraordinary level of cooperation among many regulatory bodies.

This degree of cooperation historically has been very difficult to achieve in the international arena, given the great variation in official supervisory and regulatory structures from one nation to the next. In the United States, the task is particularly challenging. In order to have effective supervision and regulation of financial derivatives domestically, we would need to move beyond the standard list of federal authorities to embrace regulatory bodies at the state level (for instance, state insurance commissioners). The greater challenge is coming to grips with the fact that totally unregulated financial institutions are operating in the marketplace alongside regulated ones. Thus, even those who are most comfortable with the present regulatory structure must concede that the system does not produce a level playing field for all market participants who are active in financial derivatives.

There is also little agreement about how the markets for derivatives are likely to fare in the future, when conditions are likely to differ a great deal from those in which derivatives first thrived. The extraordinary volatility in the third quarter of 1998 demonstrated clearly the vulnerability in the use of financial derivatives. In the Russian economic debacle, for example, derivatives were employed where the counterparty was the Russian banks. This turned out to be a great mistake because the creditworthiness of the Russian banks was not assessed correctly.

Not surprisingly, there is a wide range of opinion about whether the markets for financial derivatives can function well in a bear market for stocks and bonds. Still, it is worth noting the trading results of some prominent participants in the market, which suggest that it is much harder to carve out attractive rates of return from derivatives when interest rates rise than when they are falling.

What may be even more significant is that demand for financial derivatives seems to vary considerably among certain classes of end users. Some have been burned badly in their early encounters with some of the more exotic instruments, and are now gun-shy. Others—including several mutual funds and a few corporate treasury departments—have stretched internal guidelines in order to acquire securities with embodied derivatives, and now are restricted by more explicit investment rules. I would be surprised if the overseers of marginal participants—the financial units in state and local governments, in universities, or in health care facilities, for instance—will continue to be receptive to the use of derivatives. This is not to say that genuinely sophisticated participants in the market—who understand the risk-reward trade-offs of derivatives, and who accept the higher risks inherent in the quest for higher returns—will drop out. Still, the prospects are good that at least some kinds of derivatives likely will be hampered as potential end users come to better understand what they are getting into when, for instance, they acquire a complex and highly leveraged structured note.

Related to this is the question of computer modeling. The major players in the derivatives market rely heavily on computer modeling to calculate risk. Those institutions with the most sophisticated models are justifiably proud of them, and believe they provide a competitive advantage in the marketplace. But there is reason for caution. How well will these models work in the face of unusual market developments? We can't be certain. Modeling that is liberal will tend to project greater profit, just as conservative modeling will yield smaller perceived profit. And if the models break down, the consequences of such a breakdown are difficult to predict. Indeed, since most financial derivatives, especially over-the-counter options and related instruments, are scarcely a decade old, the market has yet to be tested under any number of difficult scenarios—most notably, by a period of extreme stringency in monetary policy.

A second key point of contention about derivatives continues to be whether a highly developed market for derivatives increases or decreases the volatility of underlying financial assets. This issue has inspired diametrically opposed views among experts. Those who believe that derivatives may decrease the volatility of interest rates, exchange rates, and equity prices generally rely on the concept of "stabilizing speculation." They argue that if derivatives make it easier for investors to take speculative positions in markets, and if speculation is generally stabilizing, then volatility should gradually diminish with the proliferation of financial derivatives.

I belong to the opposing camp. Some varieties of derivatives have irreversibly changed the behavior of the underlying financial markets on which they are based. Into this category I put the various futures markets (and their associated options markets) on equity indexes and on government bonds. These derivatives have introduced greater symmetry in position taking. In other words, they make it just as easy for the investor to go short on stocks or bonds as to go long, just as currency forwards always have done in the foreign exchange markets. And because bond and equity futures make it cheaper to switch positions, they can divert transactions that ordinarily would have been in the associated cash markets.

In doing so, they also introduce phenomenal *leverage* into the system. It is this insertion of greater leverage that can make for greater volatility in the system, whether or not the speculators' actions can, at the end of the day, be judged as "stabilizing" in some abstract sense. Of course, we can see clear examples of this kind of volatility in the stock

market crash of October 1987 as well as in the swings in the summer of
1998. More generally, research has shown that price and rate volatility
for most financial instruments varies a great deal over time.

In my judgment, that variation over time comes from the ability to
apply leverage. In more placid times, when volatility was less than it is
today, that ability was constrained. Well before the development of
financial derivatives—that is, in the 1960s, 1970s, and early 1980s—a
variety of financial innovations made leveraging more commonplace.
At the same time, values in financial markets became more volatile.
Recently, the derivatives revolution has ratcheted up the ability to
leverage by several more notches. With this has come even greater
volatility in markets. And the trend is likely to continue.

One very popular derivative, interest rate swaps, also has become
immensely important with respect to the functioning of underlying
credit markets. In their simplest and most easily described form, interest rate swaps are a form of arbitrage. For example, two companies
with differing credit quality and market acceptance may find that they
can borrow more cheaply by arbitraging the difference in their *relative*
credit quality. The higher-rated company will be able to borrow at a
relatively narrower spread to U.S. Treasury bonds at the long end of the
maturity spectrum, while the lower-rated company can borrow at a
relatively narrower yield spread (although, of course, wider in *absolute*
terms) at the short end. The interest rate swap makes both firms better
off—enough so to pay the fees of the banker who structures the deal.

This kind of arrangement, although straightforward in concept,
was unknown two decades ago. In recent years, it has blossomed to the
point where an astonishing $36.3 trillion worth of interest rate swaps
are now outstanding. Financial institutions and companies in virtually
every developed country—and in quite a few emerging markets as
well—are now engaged in the interest swap business. Not surprisingly,
this has squeezed profit margins accordingly. Pricing has become so
tight that originating banks probably are not being compensated fully
for the residual credit risks they have assumed even in the simpler varieties of swaps.

Still another critical issue that has generated vastly differing views
is the deceptively simple question of how financial institutions actually

make profits in their derivatives activities. Is it from making markets for customers? Or is it from proprietary trading? No outsider really knows. According to the principal market makers in financial derivatives, they are in the business of helping their clients meet their perceived needs for risk management products. While admitting that much of their profitability stems from that function, they also concede that their traders take sizable positions for the institution's own account—whether the institution is a bank, securities firm, insurance company, or finance company. Few dealers have revealed precisely how much of their profits come from market-making activities and how much from proprietary trading. And fewer still have indicated the magnitude of the open exposures they are carrying on average, nor the maximum exposures taken, nor the scale of risk associated with these exposures.

I suspect that more sunshine will be cast on this hazy corner of the derivatives business. Regulators are likely to demand more complete and timely information. Litigation also may generate some light, as a welcome by-product. But the financial institutions themselves are likely to play the leading role, as they come to see the advantages of greater transparency to their own interests. Accordingly, they will supply more complete—and comparable—information on where derivatives-based revenues come from and on the risks incurred in the business. Otherwise, investors may think the institutions have something to hide. And they may be right.

Still another key issue that remains unresolved is the importance of accurate marking to market, which remains woefully unappreciated in the derivatives business. Such marking is the key ingredient for measuring and controlling risk, for calculating profit and loss, and for evaluating performance. Even under normal conditions, this is not a simple and straightforward process, except in certain highly active sectors (such as listed equities and on-the-run U.S. government securities). Rather, for corporate debt obligations, for securities issued by borrowers in emerging markets, and in many segments of the mortgage securities markets, valid pricing is an inexact science. This is most apparent in the pricing of over-the-counter options and of many securitized derivatives, most notably structured notes. In volatile markets, liquidity may disappear suddenly, making the process of marking to market virtually impossible for many of these instruments.

Why is this so, and what are the consequences? To begin with, in rapidly moving markets the price of the last trade may be completely invalid, particularly for illiquid securities, and certainly for most options. Second, the price that a dealer is prepared to quote may be little more than an indication of what the security or option is worth, not the price at which the dealer is prepared to trade. On that same indications-only basis, another dealer may quote a wildly different price. For the institution trying to mark that position to market, there is no reliable arbiter of the "true" price. Third, the price quoted may be valid for trading only a very small amount, not the full amount in the investor's portfolio. Fourth, the dealer's assumptions, as he provides a price for an existing option, may be highly questionable, and marking that option position to market cannot be verified with other dealers.

This unsatisfactory state of affairs is hardly new. But the situation has worsened as the volatility of asset prices has surged, as more and more credit obligations have been securitized, and as the securities themselves have become more complex. This is especially true in cases where there is a high degree of what is known technically as "optionality."

The consequences of inaccurate marking to market can be calamitous, as in the 1994 failure of a highly leveraged mortgage portfolio manager and during the turmoil in the financial markets in the summer of 1998. More generally, an inability to mark to market is a continuing source of uncertainty in risk management and can potentially distort performance returns. It also raises pressing questions about the credibility of assertions by leading market participants, who claim to be capable of monitoring all their outstanding risk exposures and to be able to use dynamic hedging to control such exposures effectively—all on a real-time basis. How can that be true when absolute control requires flawless marking to market? After all, that degree of precision cannot be attained when underlying markets become illiquid and when the availability of accurate pricing evaporates. Under such conditions, dynamic hedging cannot be depended on to protect an institution from adverse market developments.

At the very least, the difficulties associated with the accurate pricing of derivatives argue strongly for the additional stress testing of risk management systems. And this should be done under conditions in which market liquidity has been radically reduced, and even assuming that no transactions are possible for extended periods of time.

Finally, there is little agreement in the financial community about what, if any, impact derivatives have on broader economic and financial performance. How do derivatives affect the business cycle, and thus the course of monetary policy? Some experts see only a benign connection between derivatives markets and the larger economic and financial system. According to this view, derivatives exist to redistribute risk from those less prepared to deal with risk to those more equipped to do so. In this way, the argument continues, economic and financial activity can proceed with fewer fits and starts, since there will be fewer negative surprises and unforeseen losses that undercut business decisions.

But this line of reasoning, although valid up to a point, is flawed because it misses the true significance of financial derivatives. What the proponents of the benign impact view miss is the potential for derivatives to amplify the business cycle by introducing more leverage into the system and thus expand credit availability, especially for marginal borrowers. During an upswing in the business cycle, this additional borrowing capacity allows the private sector to withstand monetary restraint for a longer time. As a result, the central bank eventually will need to engineer considerably higher interest rates—with correspondingly lower asset values—than are normally expected in order to cool down the economy to achieve noninflationary growth. And, conversely, after a business recession, interest rates will have to drop more than is generally anticipated in order to revive economic activity.

Policy Implications

These characteristics and consequences of derivatives markets hold important policy implications. To its credit, Congress has been trying to reshape the legislation presently regulating and supervising derivatives markets. But I have yet to see an approach that gets at the heart of the new regulatory challenges posed by the recent explosion of derivatives.

We can begin by acknowledging that the current federal regulatory apparatus already possesses the resources and power to accomplish much that is needed in the derivatives arena. What is needed is closer cooperation among existing agencies. They can do many useful things under present legislation, without the need for Congress to pass new laws that may have negative unintended consequences for the financial markets. New legislation is unpredictable, and unpredictability in financial markets is inherently destabilizing.

More than this, it would be a mistake to pass new laws targeted specifically at derivatives. Such an approach would ignore a much broader reality: that sweeping changes in the structure of financial institutions and markets have rendered obsolete our overall system of financial supervision and regulation. To be beneficial, therefore, regulatory reform must extend beyond the domain of financial derivatives; it must deal comprehensively with all of the dynamically changing elements of financial institutions and markets that now make up the global financial system. The legislation proposed in Congress in recent years, in spite of its attributes, falls far short of the broad scope of reforms needed.

This is not to say that the market should be left to regulate itself. Such a laissez-faire approach would not work, nor serve the public interest. For one thing, newcomers to the market may seek to wrest market share away from market participants by relaxing credit standards or pricing aggressively, which would increase the risk-return trade-offs for everyone. Rather, any properly refashioned system of financial supervision and regulation must encompass specific rules and guidelines governing financial derivatives and other financial instruments as part of a broader effort to improve supervision of our dramatically changed financial institutions and markets.

The rapid proliferation of financial derivatives is outpacing the ability of investors and regulators alike to assess risks in timely and responsible ways. Some of the more exotic products are frequently too complex to be understood and managed by those who trade them. Unfortunately, self-regulation by the financial community has not worked in the past, and probably won't work in the future. The Group of 30's recommendations for effective management and supervision of derivatives were there for all to adopt. Nevertheless, Long Term Capital Management had a derivatives exposure so huge—an estimated $1.4 trillion—that its crisis threatened the viability of our financial markets in 1998. A few years back, a Japanese trading company suffered huge trading losses in copper through trading activity involving derivatives by a trader whose activities were poorly managed. And Nicholas Leeson incurred derivatives-based losses large enough to force the sale of the venerable Baring Brothers to a Dutch insurance company.

In spite of such travails, the growth of financial derivatives will continue. Indeed, the over-the-counter derivatives market, probably the most robust growth section in the larger derivatives picture, grew by more than 500 percent—to $51 trillion—from the beginning of 1994 to the end of 1998. While most of this business involves the routine trading of interest rate exposures by financial institutions, a sizable number of OTC derivatives deals are designed for much more dubious ends. Some investment bankers sell derivatives as a tool for regulatory arbitrage. Others are selling structured note derivatives (which look much like bonds) to institutions that are otherwise excluded from engaging in foreign exchange. Still others— including many of the investment bankers who were active in Mexico prior to its 1994–1995 financial crisis—use derivatives to foil banking margin requirements and exchange controls.

Derivatives offer a very tempting brew, one with difficult-to-resist ingredients: high leveraging, varying maturities, and, at first blush, large profits for market makers. Because they are essentially bilateral contracts between individual banks, it is next to impossible to know how many derivatives have been created. There are, as I have suggested, some steps that regulators can take to rein in the abuses in these rapidly changing markets. But the more pressing question is: How will financial derivatives fare when financial markets are under severe constraints in the future? To avoid a calamity, official supervisors need more detailed and timely information and a more intimate involvement in the market process.

5

The Corporatizing
of Wall Street

*Salomon Brothers was entering the age of the giant
corporation.*

In the last half century, Wall Street has undergone dramatic transformation. Most of the financial instruments and investment banking
functions of today would be unrecognizable to Wall Streeters of the
early 1960s, when I began my career at Salomon Brothers.

One of the most profound changes has been the shift from the partnership to the corporation as the predominant form of organization in
American investment banking. This shift came about largely in response
to the larger forces that have revolutionized Wall Street since the 1960s,
most notably the geometric expansion in the volume and variety of
investment banking activities and instruments (see Chapter 3).

These changes brought new opportunities, but also placed new
strains on the traditional partnership structure of Wall Street's leading
investment houses. Two of the most pronounced strains were the burgeoning need for more permanent capital—as securities firms moved
into the business of extending credit—and the shift of market knowledge and earning power away from partners and toward mid-level
managers and traders. I was fortunate to participate in the drama of
Wall Street's transformation, for my career at Salomon Brothers corre-
sponded with that firm's rise from a minor player in an off-Broadway
play to a major star on the Street. How Salomon Brothers struggled to
manage the rapidly broadening scale and scope of financial activities
reveals a great deal about the larger patterns of change that swept
across investment banking.

The story of this evolution over time is essential groundwork for understanding the challenges that now face investment bankers. Today's modern, globalized, securitized, homogenized high-tech financial world is extraordinarily flexible and innovative. But it is getting harder and harder to manage.

Partnerships on Wall Street

When I joined Salomon Brothers & Hutzler in 1962, the investment banks of Wall Street were partnerships. They were mainly involved in two activities. They floated new securities—corporate, government, and municipal obligations—for cash. Or, more ambitiously, they also made secondary markets in outstanding issues by buying and selling securities. For this, the firms acted either as a broker (that is, intermediary between buyer and seller) or as a dealer, in which case they carried out the market-making function, placing their own capital at risk in the process in order to finance the inventories of stocks that they bought but did not want to sell immediately.

The scope of investment banking and commercial banking alike was largely defined by legislation that had been fashioned in response to the collapse of financial markets during the Great Depression. The centerpiece of this legislation—the Glass-Steagall Act of 1932—sharply curtailed the permissible activities of the commercial banks. No longer could commercial banks underwrite new issues of corporate stocks or bonds, nor act as brokers or dealers in these obligations (although they could still underwrite and trade U.S. government and municipal bonds). That function now became the sole domain of the investment banker. By separating investment and commercial banking, Glass-Steagall began a regulatory regime that would endure for nearly a half century.

The two kinds of financial institutions were distinct in other ways as well. Whereas commercial banks were owned by stockholders, investment banks were for the most part organized as partnerships. Savings banks and savings and loans, in contrast, were mutual entities, owned by their depositors. Some leading insurance companies were mutuals, too. As we will see, this pattern has changed dramatically in recent decades, as more and more financial institutions have moved to stock ownership—including Wall Street investment houses.

The intensely personal nature of partnership-based investment banking was reflected in the names of the leading firms. As with law partnerships, the Wall Street firms proclaimed the names of founding members in their titles. Kuhn, Loeb & Co., Goldman Sachs & Co., Hornblower and Weeks, Lazard Freres & Co., Lehman Brothers, Blyth & Co., and Kidder, Peabody & Co. were among the better-known investment houses of the day. Today's Merrill Lynch carried the fuller name Merrill Lynch, Pierce, Fenner & Smith in the 1960s.

Many of Wall Street's great investment houses dated back to the late nineteenth century, and quite a few were the creations of German Jews who emigrated to the United States in the 1830s and 1840s. (Abraham Kuhn and Solomon Loeb, Marcus Goldman, Joseph Seligman, and the Lehman brothers were among the more notable in this group.) By the time I came to Wall Street, few firms (most of them recent upstarts) were still run by their founders and namesakes. Still, most leading investment houses featured one or two prominent partners who played key leadership roles within their firms, while also occupying highly visible positions in the broader financial community. These included John Schiff at Kuhn, Loeb; Sidney J. Weinberg and Gustave Levy of Goldman Sachs; Cy Lewis of Bear, Stearns; Robert Lehman of Lehman Brothers; and Albert H. Gordon of Kidder, Peabody. Still alive and well in New York finance, partnerships not only gave these firms a personal identity, but also reflected the nature of a business built largely on personal connections and reputation.

Salomon Brothers: From Partnership to Corporation

Salomon fit the mold well. Organized in 1910 by the three Salomon Brothers—Arthur, Herbert, and Percy—and Baltimore department store tycoon Mortimer Hutzler, Salomon Brothers & Hutzler began life as a money market and bond house. The brothers built up the business by canvassing banks to find out their money market and bond requirements and then trying to fill them. Meanwhile, Benjamin Levy, their first hire, would remain back in the office, taking orders on the phone and keeping order. By 1961 all were gone but Ben Levy, who had risen to a major post at the firm.

By then Salomon Brothers & Hutzler was a relatively small but highly respected firm, still strongly identified with the bond market. With considerable strength in the secondary markets, Salomon did well in the competitive bidding for new issues of corporate bonds, particularly utility and railroad obligations. It also had become a leading dealer in U.S. Government securities, but was at best a minor underwriter of negotiated offerings and did very little business in equities. All in all, the firm had an excellent reputation among its customers and clients, but was not a leader on the Street.

Unlike their blue-blooded counterparts, the partners at Salomon were not the products of Ivy League schools. In fact, few if any held college degrees. But the lack of formal education was not a liability then, as it is now. According to a Salomon Brothers history, one of the brilliant senior men at Salomon once boasted that he was not a high school dropout, but rather an *elementary school* dropout. Percy's son William Salomon—the inheritor of the family name and the firm's leader—had not gone beyond preparatory school. When Bill decided to marry, his father urged him to work to support his family rather than continuing in school. Given this environment, it was quite unusual for Salomon to hire me—or anyone, for that matter, with my qualifications. As the first person at Salomon—and possibly on Wall Street—to hold a doctoral degree, I represented the first glimmering of a trend in the financial community toward greater analytical sophistication that would broaden and deepen in later decades.

Along with its modest educational credentials, Salomon Brothers was, in the early 1960s, an intimate place to work. With a total net worth of merely $12 million and with fewer than 20 partners, the firm was small enough to sustain close working relations from top to bottom. This was reinforced by the physical layout at the headquarters at 60 Wall Street. There, fewer than a handful of partners had private offices. Most worked in sales or trading, their desks situated right on the large, open trading floor, a bustling center of activity described in company advertisements as a "financial supermarket." Many of the firm's top executives had begun their careers in the "back office" and worked their way up to partner.

To make partner, of course, was to reach the top of the profession. It was a singular distinction. My own recollection of making partner at Salomon in September 1967 remains a vivid memory more than three decades after the fact. When Sidney Homer called me at home with the good news, I felt that I had "arrived." It was a feeling not only of accomplishment, but also of belonging. This sense of belonging—one of the great attributes of the partnership structure—fosters a strong sense of loyalty to the firm, for partnership status also brings the promise of lifetime employment. Very few partners jettisoned the esteemed position to join another firm; and in the 1960s it was also uncommon for nonpartners to change firms.

The predominance of partnerships at Salomon and elsewhere on Wall Street had other important and interesting consequences as well. Whereas directors and managers share power within corporations, partners exercise utter control in a partnership arrangement. Unfortunately, for some partners in investment banking, the firm merely was a vehicle for enhancing one's personal fortune. At the end of each year, the partners in such firms set aside sufficient capital to keep the business viable, and then divvied up the rest according to their partnership participation. But not all partnerships operated that way. At some investment houses, the controlling partners preferred to reinvest retained earnings in order to expand the business, rather than maximizing partner earnings in the short term. Under the brothers' leadership, Salomon Brothers & Hutzler pursued such a strategy. As Bill Salomon's star rose, Salomon increasingly retained capital for expansion. He was determined to make the firm a major force on the Street.

Partnerships remained the prevalent form of organizational structure for securities firms for most of the twentieth century. A few converted early, such as the old Boston house of Lee, Higginson, whose partners were forced by a financial crisis in 1932 to liquidate and sell their securities business to a corporation that operated under the same name. Mostly, the conversion to the corporate form was a postwar phenomenon. Kidder, Peabody made the change in 1964; Morgan, Stanley in 1970. Merrill Lynch, which diversified into U.S. government securities through the 1964 acquisition of C. J. Devine, went public in 1971.

Salomon Brothers & Hutzler was a latecomer to the trend. The business expanded rapidly in the 1960s, culminating in a move from the 60 Wall Street offices (occupied by Salomon since 1922) to a giant headquarters building at One New York Plaza in 1970, when the firm was renamed Salomon Brothers. But the partnership did not give way to corporate governance for another decade, on October 1, 1981.

Salomon's incorporation was a logical response to a larger set of forces that were transforming the financial community more broadly. Chief among these was the dramatic growth of the securitized portion of the financial markets in the 1960s and 1970s. Salomon deftly positioned itself to exploit key sectors of this market. It did so by cultivating skills in the pricing of corporate and government obligations; by making markets on difficult trading days, taking securities into inventory to do so; and by bidding successfully for corporate underwritings in the face of stiff competition. In these and other ways, Salomon demonstrated a willingness to compete fiercely in the then burgeoning market for government debt and corporate commercial paper and debt.

One of the clearest illustrations of Salomon's competitive zeal is the story of how it won a giant IBM bond issue away from Morgan Stanley in the fall of 1979. Like many blue-chip firms, Big Blue had been an exclusive client of Morgan Stanley for years. But Salomon was determined to break that exclusivity. A good opportunity presented itself when IBM came to the financial markets with the first large new bond issues in its history: $500 million of 5-year notes and another $500 million due in 15 years. This came at a time of great turbulence in the financial markets: Inflation was soaring in the double digits, and interest rates were volatile and on the rise. Given the size of IBM's offering and the state of financial markets, it was hardly a propitious time for the giant computer maker to consider jumping to a new underwriter.

After many conversations and meetings between IBM and Salomon, negotiations came to a head during a critical meeting in September. The Salomon contingent included John Gutfreund (then Salomon's managing partner), Jon Rotenstreich (the partner assigned to the account), and myself (as a senior partner and head of research). At one point in the conversation, an IBM executive asked me when I thought the issue should come to market. For me, the answer was clear: as soon as possible! This was because I was convinced that interest rates would continue to climb, that the Federal Reserve was going to tighten credit even further, and that foreign confidence in the dollar would continue to erode in the near future. IBM subsequently invited in Salomon as a lead comanager on the deal. When Morgan Stanley refused to give Salomon equal billing, the computer giant approached Merrill Lynch to serve as a comanager, and that firm accepted.

In bringing the offering to market, Salomon really showed its competitive strength. We priced the two issues very tight to the yield on U.S. bonds that had the same maturities. The 5-year IBM issue yielded just a few basis points above U.S. government bonds, while the long 15-year issue produced a mere 18-basis-point premium. Enthusiasm for the new offering ran high, and the issues would have sold out except for an unexpected turn by the Fed. We had priced the issues late in the week. That weekend, Federal Reserve Chairman Paul Volcker announced the Board's intention to engineer a modest growth in the money supply, while letting interest rates seek their own levels. With the reopening of markets on Monday, interest rates rose sharply. Of course, this was bad news for Salomon's thinly structured IBM deal; and in spite of some shorting of government issues to offset the underwriting risk, we lost money on the IBM offering. Still, fighting that battle helped us win the larger war. Salomon continued to get business from IBM. More important, by acting as lead manager of a large offering by one of the great American corporations, we had boosted the firm's profile in the financial community. More and more, Salomon Brothers was gaining a reputation as a key player on Wall Street.

Salomon moved from large bond placements to the trading of large blocks of stock relatively easily. As this kind of business became increasingly common on Wall Street in the 1960s, it seemed like a natural addition to the firm's range of activities. After all, assessing the risks in large-block stock trading was roughly analogous to evaluating and pricing bonds; and our clients in this business were for the most part the same institutional investors. Once again, Salomon found itself breaking into a market dominated by larger, well-established firms. In this case, however, Salomon's entrée was eased by deregulation. On May 1, 1975—which became known as the famous "May Day" on Wall Street—the Securities and Exchange Commission decreed that commissions on stock transactions of all sizes could be negotiated. (The SEC hitherto had lifted set commission rates on the largest transactions.) By opening up stock trading more completely to market forces, this move favored the likes of Salomon, which was willing to compete for business fiercely on price.

Salomon's scope of activities further expanded in the 1970s, when the firm formally entered the international arena. Although for decades the firm had done business internationally, it now opened its own offices in Hong Kong, Tokyo, and London. The latter two offices developed into very large trading operations, while the Hong Kong office enjoyed only modest growth.

Still another new business direction for Salomon—one in which we spearheaded a new direction in Wall Street—was the securitization of mortgages. This initiative, led at Salomon by Robert Dall and then Lewis Ranieri, transformed mortgage obligations from local credit instruments into securitized obligations that were bought and sold in a national market—yet another manifestation of the broad trend toward financial securitization in the postwar decades. Now, mortgages were packaged in bundles and sold in the form of discrete obligations, much like bonds. The business involved some intricate challenges, particularly because mortgages can be prepaid, and because they possess varying maturities and credit quality characteristics. Such complexities forced Salomon to staff up, but also moved the firm into a profitable new domain with relatively few competitors at the start.

The Business of Lending

Along with the expansion of Salomon Brothers and its Wall Street peers and traders and market makers—thanks to the geometric growth of trading and the proliferation of new credit instruments—came a more fundamental change. Increasingly, the Street's investment houses played the additional role of creditors in a variety of transactions. In the simplest form, they lent securities with large repurchase agreements. Such arrangements included not only high-grade bonds and highly tradable stocks, but also securities of lesser quality. Eventually, this activity extended to myriad financial derivatives, some of which were exchange-traded, but many others—such as interest and currency swaps—were custom-tailored with much longer maturities. This drew the securities firms into counterparty risks, wherein they served as either debtor or creditor, depending upon their transaction role at a given time. In this way, securities firms began to emulate commercial banks, which long had been in the business of making credit judgments and extending credit. Now, with the proliferation of derivatives, the tables were turned: Commercial banks followed the securities firms as lenders in the new business.

Consider two illustrations of the new, more complex realities that Salomon faced in the 1960s and 1970s. When Salomon Brothers took the lead in securitized mortgages, it discovered new opportunities in mortgage securities by involving investors through repurchase agreements. In the early 1980s, Salomon made such an arrangement with American Savings and Loan of California (a charter company of Financial Corporation of America of Delaware), led by Charles Knapp. After buying a large block of securities through Salomon, American became financially strained. It then entered into an agreement with Salomon to borrow funds temporarily from Salomon to meet its obligations, using the newly acquired securities as collateral. The advance allowed a few points of margin, and Salomon earned as compensation 50 basis points more than the typical rate charged for such a repo transaction. Since the loan approached $2 billion, Salomon earned a tidy profit.

But beneath the sheen of this seemingly straightforward deal lurked some complex and thorny issues. To begin with, a repurchase agreement normally is a short-term accommodation. But in this instance, American—unable to regain its financial footing as soon as expected—renewed the repurchase agreement loan again and again. In effect, Salomon unwittingly became banker to the West Coast firm. The ostensibly short-term credit relationship was evolving into a long-term one. What if interest rates continued to climb? This would put greater strain on the thrift institution, as well as force down the collateral value of its securities, forcing Salomon to raise its collateral requirement from the borrower. Or suppose Salomon compelled the liquidation of the loan through the sale of the collateral securities? That kind of forced sale would very likely depress the value of the securities to the point where they may not garner enough capital to pay off the loan. Worse still, the savings and loan might fail, in which case the legality and enforceability of the repurchase agreement might be called into question.

In the end, Knapp was entangled in legal troubles. Fortunately, Salomon's loan was repaid. But the episode further convinced me that this kind of very sizable arrangement (at the time) with securities clients was inappropriate for the firm because—as in the case of American Savings and Loan—Salomon could find itself acting as an ongoing creditor to a firm that was betting that interest rates would fall.

In the same period, Salomon for the first time began to confront another, related challenge: strains on its capital base. This magnifying problem grew out of the same set of internal and external forces that were driving the corporatization of Wall Street—from the expansion of trading and underwriting in traditional securities, to the proliferation of new credit instruments, to the enlargement of the investment firm's lending activities. To be sure, Salomon's capital resources were growing at a fast clip. In the two decades between 1961, when I joined the firm, to 1981, when Salomon incorporated, its capital expanded from some $12 million to roughly $240 million.

This 20-fold growth was due in large measure to the strict capital retention policies that Bill Salomon sustained during his tenure as managing partner. Consider the rules in place in 1967, when I became a partner. I was permitted to draw an annual salary of $25,000, plus advances up to 5 percent of my share of the firm's capital, plus about $6,000 for each dependent and advances for tax payments and charitable gifts. There were occasional exceptions, but these needed the personal approval of Bill Salomon, who frowned on excessive cash drawings, especially if the money was intended to support an ostentatious lifestyle. The contrast with the culture of Wall Street today is, of course, striking. Beginning with the excessive 1980s and continuing through the 1990s, junior-level "yuppie" brokers and traders, some in their early twenties, bought mansions and exotic sports cars and hosted lavish parties, while their firms made little effort to curb such free-spending conspicuous consumption.

The partnership structure had important implications for how Bill Salomon and the partners ran the business strategically. Unlike the publicly traded corporation, which must be accountable to shareholders, we had the independence to take large markdowns on securities without having to worry about their impact on quarterly or yearly earnings. Bill Salomon ran the firm conservatively in an accounting sense, but very aggressively as a competitor. And with our capital bound up together and dependent upon the firm's success, the partners felt a sense of drive and commitment that is difficult to overemphasize.

For all these benefits, however, the partnership structure had a great offsetting weakness: its failure to meet the capital needs of the rapidly expanding firm. True, the firm's capital rose sharply in the 1960s and 1970s. But consider again the pace at which the economy and financial markets grew in the same period. From 1961 to 1981, U.S. government debt rose from $259 billion to $1.1 trillion; local and state government debt from $76 billion to $444 billion; corporate bonds from $92 billion to $544 billion; commercial paper from outstandings of $7 billion to $215 billion; and the market volume of equities from $387 billion to $1.1 trillion. At the same time, the mortgage market—which reached outstanding obligations of $1.6 trillion in 1981—was being securitized at a rapid clip, a dazzling array of financial derivatives were coming into vogue, and financial markets were being jostled by the forces of globalization.

The depth and breadth of the broadening range of business opportunities demanded proportionately larger capital requirements than did Salomon's traditional businesses, such as U.S. government securities, with its thin financing margins. More and more, Salomon was handling new kinds of marketable credit instruments and confronting an enlarged volume of credit demands, which were exacerbated by inflation and increasingly being packaged in the form of securitized instruments.

With this kind of growth, raising new capital became increasingly problematic and cumbersome under the old partnership structure. The best candidates for general partner possessed a rare combination of proven ability and personal wealth. But such individuals were very hard to find. So were new limited partners who were willing to invest large sums in the business, but without a continuing voice in its operation and without the liability exposure of a general partner. Too often, limited partners were well past retirement age and did not contribute enough to the firm to make a meaningful difference. This problem was hardly unique to Salomon; in recent years, Goldman Sachs—one of the few remaining successful surviving partnerships—has turned to institutional investors to meet its long-term capital needs, and recently converted to the corporate form through a public stock offering.

Closely related to this problem was the somewhat more subtle issue of *permanence* of capital. When older partners retired at Salomon, they became limited partners, which allowed them to continue earning as much as 20 percent on their invested capital. Limited partners also could withdraw their capital piecemeal over a period of years, and those who followed this path further taxed the firm's limited asset base. Incorporation eased the strain by allowing thousands of new investors to buy into the firm by buying its stock. (Ironically, it also may have accelerated the withdrawal of partner assets. I suspect that some partners used the occasion to diversify their risks and to cash out some of their Salomon capital, although I never heard this view expressed at the senior level.)

The rapid growth of the business placed new strains on the old management structure as well, yet another reason behind the shift to the corporate form. Salomon's management structure was quite straightforward in the 1960s and most of the 1970s. Major decisions were handled by the Administrative Committee—later the Executive Committee—composed of managing partner Bill Salomon and six or seven other partners, including myself. (I became a senior partner at Salomon in 1972.) The system worked well in large measure thanks to Bill Salomon's almost uncanny ability to recruit and nurture talented professionals. His style was to give us all considerable leeway, which cultivated a sense of shared responsibility. The roster of today's

Salomon alumni is chock full of prominent individuals—too numerous to mention here—whose skills and potential were initially recognized and cultivated by Bill Salomon.

Yet another of Bill Salomon's stellar attributes was his insistence that employees at every level of the firm maintain high ethical standards. For Salomon, the firm's success depended heavily on the trust of clients and creditors, a point that he continually drove home at every opportunity. One particular occasion that I recall exemplifies this aspect of Bill's leadership. It happened during an Executive Committee meeting sometime in the early 1970s. One of the firm's bond traders interrupted the meeting to report gleefully that we had just consummated a $100 million bond trade—a huge transaction for the time—with one of our institutional clients. When Bill asked how much we made on the trade, the trader beamed "1 point." But for Bill Salomon, the profit was too generous, given the size of the trade and the importance of the large institutional client. He immediately ordered the partner in charge of the trade to return part of the profit. In addition, Bill reduced the partner's fiscal year profit participation. Today such an action would be out of place on the Street. The trust and intimacy that once typified relations between investment banks and their clients has been supplanted by a transaction-driven ethic that favors profit maximization at every turn.

Nor would Bill Salomon's managerial style work well in today's complex competitive environment. Up until the time he stepped down as managing partner in 1978, Salomon met with the Executive Committee infrequently, on an as-needed basis, and with no formal preparation. There were no regular budget reviews or planning sessions. Indeed, for many years after I took charge of the entire research effort, I never had to present a research budget. Bill was consulted individually on large underwritings and trades, while the firm's overall administration remained intensely personal and informal. In short, the senior partners were not properly groomed to manage the complexities of a much-expanded business.

The rapid expansion of trading at Salomon was inevitably accompanied by a rapid staffing-up. In order to build management capabilities quickly—more quickly than could be achieved through the traditional partnership system—the firm had to define new, nonpartner titles for those who were not yet ready for partnership, nor perhaps ever would be. The early morning breakfasts in the partner's dining room—a Salomon tradition for decades—seemed to lose their color and intimacy. And as the firm's payroll climbed from the hundreds into the thousands, even knowing the names of the firm's employees became an impossible task.

In these and other ways, Salomon Brothers was entering the age of the giant corporation.

6

Salomon's Growing Pains

We could not be Tiffany's and K-Mart at the same time.

―――――――

The burgeoning volume of trade, the voracious new demand for investment capital, the management challenges associated with rapid expansion—these were key forces behind the corporatizing of Wall Street in the 1960s and 1970s. Even so, each firm that traveled from partnership to corporate form followed a unique route. At Salomon Brothers, the particular events leading to incorporation seemed to unfold almost by happenstance, though surely the time was ripe for the change. Such is the nature of historical change: The larger context provides the ingredients that are catalyzed by the actions of individuals.

The Phibro-Salomon Merger

Salomon Brothers incorporated by joining forces with Phibro Corporation, a giant commodities trading company. The genesis of the merger was a 1980 visit to my office by Phibro Chairman and CEO David Tendler, and the firm's President, Hal Beretz. Under its earlier name Philipp Brothers, the company had joined forces with Engelhard Minerals & Chemicals, but the merger failed. The separation that followed produced a new, publicly traded corporation called Phibro.

Yet—as Beretz and Tendler explained to me in confidence that day—Phibro was still looking to diversify its business. The firm had been generating large profits from commodity trading, particularly in petroleum. Thanks to the shrewd foresight of Ludwig Jesselson, one of the firm's high-ranking executives, Phibro had moved aggressively into the petroleum sector just before the OPEC oil embargo of 1973 drove up worldwide crude prices dramatically. Now Phibro, flush with cash, was looking to diversify its base of operations.

Up to this point, the histories of Salomon and Phibro, as well as the lives of Jesselson, Tendler, Beretz, and myself, had intersected from time to time. I had been acquainted with several men from Phibro, in some cases through ties going back to Germany. Phibro's founders were German Jews, and the parents of Hal Beretz had lived in my old hometown of Wenings until fleeing the rise of Hitler, like my own family. Our parents had stayed in touch after immigrating to the United States, and though I had never come to know Hal personally, I had learned from my parents that the Beretzes were very forthright and honorable people. Salomon Brothers had earlier ties with Phibro as well. We had marketed its commercial paper, and even served as an adviser to Philipp Brothers when it split with Engelhard.

At one point in the long discussion of Phibro's investment alternatives that day, I suggested to Tendler and Beretz that they consider buying an insurance company. They seemed interested, so I arranged a meeting with Mike Frinquelli, a well-regarded insurance company analyst working for me in the Stock Research Department. With the help of our investment bankers and Frinquelli, Phibro made an offer to N.N. Corp (Northwestern National Insurance Company). All looked promising, but the deal fell through at the last minute: N.N. Corp reneged because Armco Steel topped Phibro's acquisition bid by a mere 50 cents per share. The N.N. Corp gambit would be the closest Phibro would come to making an acquisition in more than a year of hard searching.

Through this working relationship, however, Phibro's search for a partner came to the attention of more and more senior partners at Salomon, while at the same time Phibro's executives became more familiar with our firm as their search became more difficult and protracted. It was therefore not totally unexpected that Beretz and Tendler one day suggested a Phibro-Salomon Brothers merger.

The proposal struck a chord at Salomon for a variety of reasons. As I described earlier, resources pressures were mounting on Wall Street that made incorporation look more appealing by the day. Salomon had watched many of its key competitors go public in recent years, and was now one of the few remaining major partnerships on the Street.

More than that, Salomon had been struggling through an especially difficult year when Tendler and Beretz proposed a merger. By the close of 1980, skyrocketing interest rates had driven the yield on 3-month Treasury bills to 15.2 percent and the yield on long Governments to 12.3 percent. The prime loan rate was rising, rapidly exceeding the 20 percent mark. And the yield curve—the difference between long- and short-term yields—was inverted sharply, with short-term yields being much higher than yields on long bonds. All this made the burden of carrying positions extremely costly.

Compounding this problem was the fact that operating activities—trading securities and investment banking—were not generating the kind of consistent profits needed to expand the partnership's capital fund, which in turn was needed to underpin heavy borrowings for Salomon's larger and more diverse financing activities. As noted earlier, the withdrawal (or potential withdrawal) of capital by recently retired partners under the terms of their limited partnership made it difficult to sustain a permanent and predictable capital base. And Salomon Brothers faced still another constraint on the financial side: Much of its new partnership capital had been generated from proprietary investments. The gains from these holdings (in oil and gas wells and other stocks), and from occasional stock and bond trades, were set aside for long-term capital gains.

Highly secret negotiations to merge were in full swing by the early summer of 1981. On Salomon's side, Ira Harris and Richard Rosenthal (both of whom were partners and members of the Executive Committee) took primary responsibility for the negotiations. Within the Committee itself, discussions were intense, sometimes emotional, often around questions for which there were no tidy answers. Not surprisingly, the question of whether to convert a 71-year-old partnership into a corporation elicited a range of responses among the partners. Retired limited partners, many who had mentored current partners, had no vote on the matter and presumably would oppose or even resent the idea of merger if consulted. Indeed, Bill Salomon—son of one of the founders of a firm that still carried the family name—was terribly upset when informed after the fact of the decision.

Even among the current staff, the proposed merger posed wrenching questions. Should incorporation be an occasion for encouraging the retirement of some of the general partners? In many instances, the answer was yes, and the unpleasant task of informing those individuals fell to John Gutfreund and me. The meetings were among the most difficult in my career, for many of the departing partners had been associates of long-standing.

Incorporation also raised questions about how the firm could retain talented junior members. Would the best of the breed stay with Salomon if the possibility of making partner were no longer available? Fortunately, Ira Harris supplied an answer: an attractive new compensation package for key employees and some of the more junior partners. The package contained a "phantom pool" of 1.2 million shares of Phibro common stock at $30 per share. Holders of these shares would receive the cash equivalent (per share) of the highest price attained by the Phibro shares in the next 5 years. Ira's plan seemed to work: The number of defections following incorporation was lower than anticipated. Soon, not surprisingly, other firms on the Street were emulating Ira's innovation.

Mergers inevitably raise the questions about fit and power. The former has to do with how well the corporate styles or cultures of the formerly distinct firms will not merely coexist, but rather achieve some kind of synergy that makes them more than the sum of their parts. The question of power is more obvious: Will one of the two firms command more control than the other?

The merger plan called for the creation of a publicly traded holding company named Phibro Salomon Inc., which would own and control two subsidiaries—Salomon Brothers and Phibro. Salomon's Executive Committee and Phibro's senior management would serve as board members of the corporation. John Gutfreund and David Tendler became co-chairmen. But the presidency went to Hal Beretz, and the board was dominated by Phibro people and outside directors chosen by them.

Divergent Paths

It was soon abundantly clear that the merger was not going to fulfill the hopes of its architects. As one of those architects, I had naïvely expected that the joining of the two giant trading firms would produce a dominant global firm. But fundamental differences in culture, function, and markets scuttled those hopes. To begin with, securities trading and commodities trading were different creatures. Whereas Salomon did business with prominent institutions in the industrial world, Phibro dealt with developing nations and their indigenous firms, where standards of business behavior varied greatly from the lawful and ethical to the utterly corrupt. Whereas the clearing of securities transactions was an evolved and seamless process, the clearing of commodities often was a complicated and bumpy process. And whereas Salomon was a highly innovative firm, Phibro was not.

Most importantly, the success rate of the two entities in the new holding company diverged sharply. It soon became clear that Phibro's business had peaked around the time of the merger, for soon thereafter its revenues and profits began to fall precipitously. The prices of several key commodities—including oil, in which Phibro was invested heavily—were now declining irregularly, belying the conventional wisdom at the time that petroleum prices would continue to rise. In the 3 years following the merger, Phibro's contribution to the holding company's profits had plummeted from $364 million to $165 million.

In sharp contrast, Salomon's business blossomed. We maintained a dominant position in U.S. Governments. We solidified a strong position in investment banking, which in turn reinforced our key role as a secondary market trader in corporate bonds. We held the lead in the securitizing of mortgages, an activity that burgeoned in the 1980s when a variety of new home financing instruments were invented to boost the stagnant real estate market. Our Tokyo office achieved profits beyond expectations, thanks largely to the trading acumen of

Shigeru Myojin. And we continued to innovate, pioneering a host of new credit instruments and techniques ranging from original issue discount (OID) bonds to certificates of accrual on Treasury securities (better known as CATS). With all this, Salomon's revenues increased from $2.3 billion in 1982 to $3.4 billion in 1984, while profits rose at an even faster pace in the same period, from $421 million to $557 million.

Not surprisingly, the divergent fates of the two entities created frictions, which soon escalated into a struggle for control of the firm. The acrimony soon gravitated to the outside directors who were not strongly allied with either Phibro or Salomon interests. To lobby on Salomon's behalf, Richard Schmeelk and I visited two outside directors: Maurice (Hank) Greenberg, of the AIG Insurance Company, and William May, former head of American Can. I also traveled with John Gutfreund to South Africa to meet with Phibro-Salomon's largest shareholder, the legendary Harry Oppenheimer. Even so, neither the outside directors nor the firm's large stockholders wished to become embroiled in a management struggle, and only agreed to a plan reluctantly and after long discussions.

In the end, Salomon's interests prevailed. John Gutfreund was appointed sole CEO of Phibro-Salomon, no longer awkwardly sharing the position with Phibro's Tendler. Phibro was radically downsized, and its key management people departed in short order. Symbolizing the power shift, the Phibro name was removed from the holding company's name in 1986. Henceforth, the corporate name of the newly refocused firm would be, simply, Salomon Inc.

For all the distress between Salomon and Phibro, the merger proved to be enormously beneficial for Salomon. Above all, it gave us access to capital on a large scale, which Salomon craved in order to continue to grow. In September 1981, just before the merger, Salomon had capital of $300 million. One year later, the combined net worth of the two entities was $1.8 billion. And as Phibro was downsized, its capital resources served as a cash cow for Salomon's rapid expansion. More than that, incorporation allowed Salomon to tap both the money markets and the capital markets by issuing short-term and longer-dated obligations.

Aggressive Leveraging for Growth

Even with this much broader capital base, Salomon's thirst for capital seemed insatiable. As markets continued to securitize and globalize at a rapid clip, Salomon's need for capital continued to grow. It was how the firm quenched this thirst—by greater and greater reliance on leveraging—that began to trouble me, and eventually contributed to my departure from the firm after 26 years.

Salomon always had been leveraged to some degree, of course. But incorporation, and the new management regime, had ushered in a new era. In earlier days, the partners had been careful to scrutinize the firm's leveraging. Certainly, doing so then was a much simpler matter; the universe of obligations was much smaller, and it was made up of a higher proportion of securities with shorter maturities and high-quality ratings compared with what would follow in the late 1970s and 1980s. For these reasons, I was comfortable with the firm's leveraging practices.

Two stories bring home the point. The day I became a partner in 1967, Sidney Homer used the occasion to quip: "You can tell your wife that you are now personally liable for $1 billion." I did tell Elaine, my wife, who immediately asked, "Why did you do that?" I explained that there were offsetting assets of rather high quality and liquidity. The same matter came up again in early 1972 when André Meyer, the then illustrious head of Lazard Freres, invited me to lunch. I was surprised to learn that Meyer wanted to recruit me to his firm. Within minutes of sitting down at lunch, he asked me, speaking in his distinctively formal manner, "Dr. Kaufman, how do you sleep at night?" He then went on to say, "Your firm carries huge positions and has huge liabilities. You're a general partner, so if anything goes wrong, you are personally liable. Here at Lazard, we don't do that. When I walk in every morning, I know my overhead costs, which at a minimum are covered by known income." In response, I explained to him that our inventory was turning over once every two days, and that most of it was short-dated and high-quality. But I suspect that Meyer, who was schooled in the restrained ways of European investment banking, found little of this convincing.

I stayed at Salomon, but in the late 1980s I began to question that decision. The leveraging was growing endemic, and I tracked the size of our borrowings from week to week with growing concern. To calculate what I considered to be a more revealing measure of the firm's leveraged risk, I added total borrowings to our outstanding contingent liabilities in derivatives and in repurchase agreements, and to obligations in subsidiary entities. In other words, I grossed up rather than netting out. The figures were disturbing, and I began to warn of the trend at meetings of the Executive Committee. A few members shared my concern, such as Dick Schmeelk and Ira Harris, and also raised the issue before the Committee. But most did not.

Largely in response to my repeated expressions of concern, John Gutfreund asked the three members of the Executive Committee responsible for the firm's major trading areas in fixed-income obligations—Tom Strauss (Governments), Bill Vouté (corporates), and Lew Ranieri (mortgages)—to prepare a detailed report on Salomon's leveraging and risk taking. But they never produced it, at least not before I left the firm in the spring of 1988. It struck me as more than a little ironic that a firm that specialized in the creation and management of debt would not have a clear and systematic picture of its own leveraging and financial risk taking.

In retrospect, the reasons why the Executive Committee as a whole did not confront the issue of overleveraging head-on seem clear enough. Under the governance structure of the business at that time, the Committee did not manage the firm in its entirety. We certainly met frequently enough; unlike the intermittent gatherings that characterized Bill Salomon's regime, John Gutfreund presided over a formal meeting each Tuesday morning and Thursday afternoon. But the division of responsibilities among the senior partners tended to encourage factions, infighting, and inefficiency. Most members of the Committee, except John Gutfreund, were responsible for a specific area—one for corporate finance, another for equity markets, another for mortgages, one for municipals, myself for research, and so on. Each member commanded great influence over his particular area. But the broader view of the firm often was not well represented. Adding to this fragmentation were the ongoing tensions—roiling beneath the surface, and sometimes boiling over—between the firm's traders and its investment bankers. With distinct methods, aspirations, and cultures, these two groups possessed interests that were chronically difficult to reconcile.

There had been conflicts as long as there had been partners, and the switch to the corporate form did little to dispel the hothouse atmosphere. Keen competition among the units and factions within the firm made it difficult for members of the Executive Committee to forge personal friendships. It was an intense group, whose members were animated by a potent brew of high ambition, extraordinary talent, competitive drive, and shrewdness. Thus, meetings of the Executive Committee were seldom dull. There were dramas within dramas, and one had to keep hidden agendas in mind, and read subtle signals in order to anticipate likely outcomes.

My Departure: A Painful Decision

This mix of strong personalities and fragmented structures of authority allowed the firm to largely ignore the leveraging issue. Unfortunately, John Gutfreund practiced a permissive style of leadership that allowed too many abuses to go unchecked. He could not bring himself to discipline those who erred but contributed heavily to profits, or those who strayed in their personal behavior. All this, it seemed to me, was undermining the strength of the firm. Too often, John Gutfreund's long-term vision was blurred by near-term considerations. Rather than putting in place a formal procedure for allocating capital, or conducting rigorous risk-profit analysis—ironically, just the kind of analysis we routinely conducted for our clients—we lurched ahead, paying only intermittent attention to the growth of leverage that supported our operations.

Heavy leveraging was not the only issue for which I was out of step with some of the other senior partners. Another was junk bonds—the low-rated, high-yielding bonds that would come to epitomize the rough-and-tumble excesses of Wall Street in the 1980s. In 1985, when the junk bond market was running at a fevered pitch, several of

Salomon's senior executives advocated that we challenge Drexel Burn-ham—the pioneer and leader in the market, thanks to Michael Milken and his minions—by moving into junk bonds in a big way. I opposed the move on broad philosophical grounds.

Certainly, there were handsome profits to be made from junk bonds. But a major move in this direction would cause Salomon to lose its vision and focus, I argued in the Executive Committee. Simply put, we could not be Tiffany's and K-Mart at the same time. Salomon had plenty to do, domestically and internationally, in the investment-grade business. A strong move into low-quality bonds might bewilder the firm's traditional customers, and perhaps even pose conflicts of interest. Added to this, diversification into the junk market would mean further leveraging of our capital position. At some point our own credit rating would be at risk. A modest involvement seemed rea-sonable to me, but a major shift in our priorities did not.

In 1986, John Gutfreund announced the establishment of a new senior management group at Salomon. This move reinforced the firm's transition from partnership to corporation by concentrating managerial control into a small group of five men. But the reorganiza-tion had a deeper significance. Those who were invited to serve in the new Office of the Chairman—and it was a revealed fact that I was not—favored a higher level of risk taking, especially when it came to leveraging the firm.

Before this event but several years after the merger, I had been appointed Vice Chairman of Salomon at the recommendation of David Tendler to counterbalance the elevation of Phibro's Tom O'Mal-ley to Vice Chairman. So when John Gutfreund told me of his plans for the new, very senior management group, which was to exclude me, I replied that I intended to resign both as Vice Chairman and as a mem-ber of the board. Given my long-standing opposition to the heavy leveraging of the firm, this latest John Gutfreund move seemed to me to be a step in the wrong direction. More than that, it seemed clear to me, my exclusion from the group would diminish my influence on the policies of the firm, would undermine the objectivity of Salomon's research, and probably would place me in the awkward position of having to contradict key positions held by senior management in front of the corporation's public board—an entity that was not thoroughly familiar with the intimacies and intricacies of the business. It was a messy and politically perilous position to be in—hardly appropriate for a Vice Chairman.

John seemed taken aback at my stance. But neither he nor I changed our positions. I resigned the two positions, and—more importantly—began to resign myself to the realization that I might not finish out my career at Salomon.

The end came somewhat sooner than I expected, when Salomon took yet another major strategic step in what I considered to be in the wrong direction. In 1987, I served on a task force of senior managers that conducted a series of long and arduous meetings with area operating heads to review profitability, management strengths and weaknesses, and action plans. Then came a series of astounding decisions. The firm would accelerate its efforts to develop the high profit margin business (a.k.a. junk bonds), while closing down its commercial paper and municipal departments.

On the face of it, our commercial paper business was not a moneymaker. But it nevertheless served a crucial function for the firm, and therefore deserved to remain. Salomon's trade in commercial paper linked us to both the Treasury and to chief financial officers of leading corporations—relationships that were enormously helpful in garnering other business for the firm. As for the Municipal Department, secondary market trading was bringing in dismal returns, but the underwriting of new issues was generally profitable. Unfortunately, both areas were not strongly represented in the strategic discussions.

Soon thereafter, I told John Gutfreund that I wanted to resign effective March 31, 1988. I suggested that the announcement come at the end of the calendar year, when I would finish out my term on the Compensation Committee. John and other members of the Chairman's office tried to persuade me to stay. But I knew that the firm was now headed in a direction I fundamentally opposed and that nothing I would say would change that course.

During my final days at Salomon Brothers, a dramatic episode unfolded that carried an important lesson about the interests of managers in a corporatized Wall Street—namely, that senior managers are no more compelled to act in the best long-term interests of the firm than they had been under the old partnership system.

It began in November of 1987, when famed financier Ronald Perlman attempted to take over Salomon Brothers. Looking for a "white knight," John Gutfreund turned to Warren Buffett, who agreed to pump $750 million into Salomon in return for convertible preferred stock paying a 9 percent dividend. At first blush, the rescue seemed perfect; Perlman failed, and an independence of the firm was preserved. Given the options available, Salomon's senior managers seemed to have succeeded in preserving their own position first and foremost.

In fact, there probably had been an alternative. Maurice "Hank" Greenberg of American Insurance Group (AIG), who sat on Salomon's board, was, I believe, prepared to have his firm take a large position in Salomon to deflect the Perlman threat. He was not given that opportunity. Had a merger of the two firms followed—a likely scenario—the result would have been a powerful international financial institution. AIG's involvement and influence, to carry the inference further, most likely would have kept Salomon out of the scandals that would soon envelop the firm. But Greenberg's hands-on management style was well known on the Salomon board, and probably was a key factor preventing John Gutfreund and the remaining Salomon board members from turning to Greenberg.

My decision to leave Salomon Brothers was, for me, extraordinarily painful. I had been part of a phenomenal success story—the rise of Salomon Brothers from anonymity to the highest level of investment banking. Fortunate to join a unique group of talented people at the right time, I had built my career hand-in-hand with the company's emergence to leadership. Indeed, the financial independence that now enabled me to leave the firm had come from our mutual success over the last three decades.

Salomon Brothers' journey—from partnership to corporation, from trading securities to involvement with high-credit-risk transactions, and from guarding client relationships to much more impersonalized transactions—has been a microcosm of the broad transformation of Wall Street in the postwar period. When viewed in the context of larger forces at work in the global financial marketplace, Salomon's story carries important lessons about the challenges that now face investment banking's leaders.

The corporatizing of Wall Street firms was inevitable. It facilitated the merger and consolidation of Wall Street institutions. Today, we have very large and diversified securities firms. We have some firms that have become subsidiaries of other financial institutions such as banks. We also have banks and insurance companies that have branched out into the domain of securities firms. With all this, it is not surprising that the tasks of the senior management of these large institutions have become daunting, a subject I will return to in a later chapter.

7

The Americanization of Global Business and Finance

*The United States just may be the fullest expression
of economic democracy in the world today.*

———

During my frequent business trips abroad, especially to Europe and Japan, I came to see more and more clearly what is distinctive about the American approach to business and finance. Perhaps I had been sensitized to cross-cultural differences by my German upbringing. What struck me was not merely the relative informality of American business meetings, or the tendency of Americans to reach decisions more quickly than their European and Japanese counterparts. It was also their willingness to adapt to change and to innovate that impressed me. These differences had been apparent for some time, but they did not come into clear focus until the closing decade of the twentieth century, when America displayed its remarkable flexibility and capacity to adjust. Those traits proved to be invaluable to the United States for meeting new competitive challenges, and enabled the American economy to experience a sustained era of economic expansion.

Business expanded at a robust pace for the last 8 years of the 1990s, marking the century's longest period of uninterrupted growth. The boom featured a spectacular rise in business profits and in the value of financial assets, as well as a sharp increase in employment. The financial net worth of American households rose an astonishing $12 trillion, an advance of more than 50 percent. In recent years, U.S. per capita wealth has led the world. This economic success—buttressed by the political stability and unrivaled military power of the United States—has been exerting a powerful *Americanizing* influence on business and economic practices throughout the world.

Given America's unrivaled economic supremacy, it is not surprising that the United States is admired and emulated by business and political leaders in virtually every corner of the globe. American business practices are widely seen as second to none. Our economic values are respected, if not always embraced. Our financial market innovations are imitated, although sometimes grudgingly. All of this reflects American power, which appears to be unassailable. To be sure, there are weaknesses in our economic system, problems that seem intractable. But even some of these are giving way in the face of sustained economic growth and prosperity. Each month, for example, segments of the U.S. population that had endured chronic unemployment are being drawn into the workforce. In this way and others, Americans of all backgrounds and income levels are benefiting from the strong economy.

It was not always so. You would have to go back to the decade of the 1950s to find a comparable period of American dominance and self-confidence. Like the 1990s, the 1950s were a period of political and military dominance, and an era of good economic growth (punctuated by short and mild recessions) with low inflation, relatively modest unemployment, a nearly balanced federal budget, and a firm dollar. The 1950s and early 1960s were a heyday in American economic and political history.

That golden era unraveled over the course of three decades, however. The Vietnam War proved to be not only a military and strategic nightmare, but also an occasion for poor economic policymaking that sparked a long wave of high inflation. Then came the collapse in the value of the dollar, outsized government deficits, two major oil shocks, lost industrial prowess, and a nearly debilitating spate of financial excesses. Only recently—following the fall of the Berlin Wall and the subsequent breakup of the Soviet Union, which together marked the end of the Cold War—has America regained much of its economic and political standing on the world stage.

Consider, for a moment, an alternative—and hardly implausible—scenario. If the Cold War had continued, the world probably would be a very different place than it is today. Germany would not be unified, and thus not well positioned to dominate the continent economically; but at the same time West Germany would not be encumbered by the vast financial burdens of integration. Western Europe as a whole would be cooler toward the United States than it is, and less willing to tamper with its centuries-old corporatist economic and financial structure. Eastern Europe would not be privatizing. Ideological divisions would continue to block economic progress in much of Latin America and Africa and in individual emerging nations such as Vietnam. As a consequence, the Americanization of global financial markets and business would not have advanced nearly as far as it has in recent years.

But it has: The forces of history have created a powerful dynamic that compels all to consider, and many to embrace, the tenets of Americanization. This, in turn, has raised some fundamental questions about the contours of America's imperfect economic democracy: What is the nature of Americanization? How is it achieving such great success? Is it a legitimate model for other countries to emulate? What are the prerequisites for American-style methods and institutions to be imitated by or transplanted into another political body, without causing unpleasant symptoms or outright rejection? And—keeping in mind a certain epic about an "unsinkable" ship built and commanded by supremely confident men—what are some of the vulnerabilities of the American juggernaut? There is, as I will discuss, a dark side to Americanization.

The Concept of Economic Democracy

What do I mean by the Americanization of business and finance? The phenomenon has many key elements, some of which are intertwined and difficult to define separately. It is perhaps best to begin with the closely related notion of *economic democracy*. Democracy itself is a complex concept. The dictionary equates democracy with *egalitarianism*, but that hardly simplifies matters because the word "egalitarianism" itself contains two powerful, and seemingly contradictory, strands of thought.

One strand of egalitarianism has to do with the leveling of economic differences. It is the guiding principle of what has come to be known as *social democracy*. Social democracy has been the prevailing organizing principle of government and politics in Europe and Japan throughout much of the last half century. That is now being challenged. The outcome of that contest is not clear. Social democrats seek to promote equality of rewards, rather than merely equality of opportunity. They are notoriously uncomfortable with markets, especially with the sometimes cruel logic that markets impose. And they oppose the often vastly unequal rewards and punishments that markets mete out. Thus, social democracies often employ mechanisms to ameliorate inequalities, such as steeply progressive income tax rates that redistribute income from the successful to the less fortunate. In contrast to free-market advocates, social democrats are comfortable with intimacy between government, business, and finance because they see corporatism as a natural adjunct to the welfare state.

But there is another breed of economic democracy—of which the United States is an example—that has grown out of a very different egalitarian tradition. In this tradition, *impartiality* rather than social democracy is the dominant guiding principle. Equality of opportunity, not equality of outcomes, takes precedence. Whereas social democrats look to legislatures, elected officials, and elite bureaucrats to determine economic and financial outcomes, free-market democrats (for lack of a better term) look to market forces to determine such outcomes. They accept the fact that great economic disparities between winners and losers are a normal and inescapable consequence of the free-market system. At the core of undiluted free-market democracy is the belief that this process of winnowing out the successful from the unsuccessful is fair, efficient, and necessary for maximizing overall economic growth.

On closer examination, however, a great many Americans seem to be ambivalent about their competitive economic democracy, and downright troubled by some of its more extreme manifestations. This ambivalence can be seen in the wide range of checks and balances on the behavior of business and financial enterprises that we have incorporated into our market system over time. Even after a generation of deregulation, our system remains honeycombed with regulations. U.S. tax codes intrude on the game of winning and losing in scores of ways, from moderately progressive income tax rates to hefty inheritance taxes. At the local, state, and federal levels, government plays an active role in economic affairs. And the American social safety net—while hardly as extensive as those in Europe—extends broadly enough to support the full citizenry as well as a host of industries (most notably agriculture) deemed to have special needs.

Nor does our system tolerate well the harshest of competitive outcomes—business failure—especially when it comes to the largest corporations, banks, and other enterprises. In America's imperfect economic democracy, these entities are, in effect, "too big to fail." Historically, when they have gotten into serious trouble, the government—weighing the immediate social and economic costs—has shown a propensity to step in to shore up the faltering giants with loan guarantees, tax breaks, and other subsidies. Under the strict rules of market capitalism, such firms would be left on their own to endure the rigors of market discipline; indeed, market purists would argue that faltering firms are, by definition, weaker firms, and that their failure is good for the economy.

Because of these and other forms of government activism, the United States is in fact an *imperfect* economic democracy. Ours is not a "pure" form of market capitalism, nor does it purport to be. Still, America's economic democracy is closest to that ideal than virtually any other major political economy in the world today. What, then, are the defining characteristics of America's economic democracy?

America's Unique Economic Democracy

According to the idealized view of America's economic democracy, business is disciplined by the marketplace. Governed by an active market for corporate control, corporations are run primarily to serve the interests of shareholders, not for the benefit of insiders or so-called "stakeholders" (workers, communities, the government, and the like). This does not mean that successful companies are necessarily antisocial or exploitative. To the contrary, say the proponents of unfettered market capitalism, the corporations that survive the rigors of competition and earn profits are the firms that supply healthy tax revenues, generate investment, and create and sustain jobs. They are, in short, the economy's engines of growth.

But this is not always the case. Capital and human resources are churned continually by changing technologies and production processes, and by the frequent abandonment by corporations of no-longer-profitable activities. While this process may optimize shareholder value along the way, it is hardly painless or risk-free.

An active market in corporate control normally involves a considerable number of mergers, acquisitions, divestitures, and other forms of restructuring. Hostile takeovers, although they are rarer than is commonly perceived, are accepted practice. In fact, many investors not only tolerate regular corporate restructuring as a natural feature of a fluid market economy, but *applaud* this feature of America's economic democracy. According to this philosophy of business, new combinations, new activities, new business lines, new organizational structures, new products, and new managers encourage ongoing innovation. Because the business environment is ever-changing, the leaders of today cannot be assured that they will dominate in tomorrow's marketplace.

This view, too, goes a bit too far. For one thing, stability is not always the enemy of innovation. Firms that know more or less what to expect in their regulatory and competitive environments are more likely to invest than those that face a far less certain set of challenges. As Harvard Business School Professor Howard Stevenson has shown, predictability is an essential component of business success. More than that, many mergers are simply poorly conceived and wasteful; they fail to create enterprises that are more efficient and competitive than were their component parts.

America's economic democracy also is distinguished by its high degrees of transparency and accountability. Investor-oriented businesses must disclose useful information based on common accounting standards so that investors can know what is happening and can make comparisons among companies. Honest accounting and timely reporting are critical. It is difficult to escape such disclosure, and the few firms that bypass the rules often pay a heavy price.

In the United States it is the mandate of the Securities and Exchange Commission, a highly respected independent regulatory authority, to ensure that business corporations disclose enough about their operations to permit adequate oversight. The SEC has gained a formidable reputation as a guardian of the interests of shareholders. America's economic democracy also has evolved ways of softening the harsh consequences of business failure by trying to *anticipate* failure and make it as painless as possible for all concerned. We have, for example, developed a fairly elaborate and tested framework of corporate bankruptcy proceedings, overseen by a specialized court system, a system that typically provides an orderly way out of unhappy situations.

When it comes to relations between business and government, America's economic democracy also possesses some unique features. We strive for an arm's-length relationship in order to ensure a high degree of independence on the part of both private enterprise and the state. But at times government-business relations in America have been more than arm's length: They have been downright adversarial. Mistrust has been rampant on both sides, as demonstrated by thousands of business conduct cases that have filled American courts in the twentieth century. This contrasts sharply with the intimate and cooperative relationships common in other major industrialized nations. Here, in America, antitrust actions, environmental protection mandates, equal employment opportunity complaints, and the like are daily fare; the civil court system plays an active role in arbitrating disputes; and product liability lawsuits are used to promote consumer interests more aggressively than elsewhere in the developed world.

In this uneasy relationship, the government often appears to act very inconsistently, both within a given regulatory body and between one part and another. Why, for example, do some parts of the federal government encourage automobile companies to reduce exhaust emissions and improve mph performance, while others keep gasoline taxes the lowest in the industrialized world, thereby encouraging a dependency on the automobile that leads to greater pollution?

Still, it is important to recognize that, for the most part, government regulators take a very pragmatic approach in dealing with corporate America—an approach that often gives the *impression* of inconsistency. The federal government often finds it expedient to support particular industries when the political stars are in alignment. It has, for example, provided subsidies for ethanol production at a time when energy markets were glutted. And, of course, the federal government has a long tradition of supporting exporters, not only with protective tariffs, but also (in recent years) through the Eximbank and controversial trade missions.

There are other occasions as well when the adversarial posturing of business and government in America takes an about-face. In the eyes of the government, some companies are simply too important—whether for domestic political reasons or national security considerations—to fail. When such enterprises have gotten into trouble in recent decades, government officials have not been shy about getting directly involved. The threatened collapses of Chrysler and Lockheed in the late 1970s are prime examples. It is also true that powerful Washington lobbies have enjoyed some success in bending the federal government to their wishes, to the detriment of the majority. Even so, these are exceptional cases that prove the rule: The United States just may be the fullest expression of economic democracy in the world today.

For the American system to work, however, government must play a pivotal role as referee. This does *not* mean government should assume control of business decision making. But for transparency and disclosure to work, the SEC and other independent regulatory authorities must continue to ensure that corporations act on behalf of their shareholders. There is, after all, no federal incorporation in the United States, a mechanism that could enforce certain minimal yet vitally important strictures on businesses that operate (as so many do these days) in many states or regions. Because the U.S. Constitution confines business incorporation to the state level—with obvious limitations—there is a persistent need for the kind of national-level oversight provided by the SEC.

Nowhere is the ambivalence in the American system of business-government relations more apparent than when it comes to the question of corporate consolidation and concentration in business and finance. Since the passage of the Sherman Anti-Trust Act of 1890, federal officials have tried to enforce antitrust as a way of minimizing "restraint of trade." And antitrust actions have indeed been an integral part of our business and financial history. But the U.S. government's position on consolidation runs hot and cold. Many major industries in America—such as banking and insurance—are *for regulatory reasons* much less concentrated than in other major industrial countries. And as the recent decision in the Lockheed-Northrop merger suggests, the government can quickly change from supporting consolidation in an industry to actively opposing it. But in many circumstances, leading industries are permitted to consolidate to high degrees, though never (except in the case of regulated public utilities) to the level of monopoly. In the United States, the typical pattern in core industries is oligopoly, a kind of halfway house that tries to preserve a degree of competition in core industries while allowing high levels of concentration.

When it comes to the matter of the foreign ownership and control of domestic enterprises, American thinking runs hot and cold as well. Most of the time, foreign investors are greeted by a large welcome mat. This is especially true for companies (such as Honda and Toyota in automobiles) that are expected to keep American firms on their competitive toes. States have been aggressive in trying to attract foreign firms; many set up elaborate investment offices abroad, and woo foreign companies with sweet, even delectable, tax concessions. More than one U.S. state governor owes his reelection to success in this domain.

Still, with some regularity, the foreign purchase of U.S. assets, whether in industry or in real estate, has garnered strong criticism from some quarters. The foreign purchase of prominent American properties (which can hold great symbolic value) seems to draw the most fire, as when Japanese investors bought Rockefeller Center and the Pebble Beach golf courses in California several years ago. At the same time, some industries (notably in defense and in telecommunications) have been excluded from foreign ownership and control. Here, as in so many realms, open markets prevail in most but not every instance. Pragmatism and national interests have a veto on occasion.

Yet another defining characteristic of American-style economic democracy is broad access to credit, a tradition with deep roots in the American past. In contrast to the "lead bank" approach that prevails in Germany and Japan, American companies have long sought access to open credit markets as soon as they have demonstrated sufficient creditworthiness. Today, there are very few American corporations of any size that cannot access the open market, and they do so more or less regardless of credit rating. This is a unique feature of the American system of the financial markets, one that is unrivaled by any other major country. European and Japanese companies have begun to gain access to the open markets, and more will do so over the coming years. Banks continue to be more important sources of credit to the corporate sector abroad than in the U.S. They will resist losing their privileged position, but in the long term securitization will prevail.

The Americanization of Global Financial Markets

These key features of America's unique form of economic democracy—primacy of shareholder value, transparency and accountability, adversarial relations between business and government, and general openness to foreign investment and credit markets—are also the hallmarks of America's financial system. It is perhaps inevitable that a highly decentralized economic system would tend to promote a financial system that is itself quite entrepreneurial and resistant to government interference. Like the larger economy, the U.S. financial system is based on the Darwinian philosophy of the survival of the fittest. At its best, it is relatively pristine. For example, it suppresses collusive behavior, and disdains mechanisms that tend to smooth out differences between winners and losers, such as the Japanese-style "convoy approach."

While these long-standing tenets of the American economic democracy are gaining popularity around the world, it is principally the *newer* features of American finance that are spreading the most quickly. We can observe, in fact, the Americanization of global financial markets in no less than six major areas of finance.

First is securitization, the powerful trend that I discussed in Chapter 3. No other nation has demonstrated America's proficiency at assembling, packaging, and reselling traditional loans, turning them into instruments that can be priced and traded continually in an open credit market. Securitization—which first burgeoned with the commercial paper market of the 1960s and later matured with the explosive growth of the U.S. mortgage securities market—has become a truly global phenomenon in recent years. Today, global markets are pulsing with a dizzying range of collateralized loan obligations, including packages of auto loans, credit card receivables, and (more recently) the commercial loans of U.S. subsidiaries of Japanese banks.

Second, performance-driven asset management has become increasingly important in country after country. New types of institutional investors have dramatically changed the nature of modern capital markets. A generation ago, insurance companies, banks, and the personal trusts of wealthy families dominated the financial scene. These kinds of investors generally followed buy-and-hold investment strategies with long time horizons. The practice of marking portfolios to market based on *current* asset prices was rare to nonexistent. Since the 1980s, however, much of this has changed, and the changes have originated for the most part in the United States.

Initially, waves of new corporate pension funds and state and local retirement funds spawned a new breed of professional portfolio manager. Competition was fierce, and the pressures increased on the portfolio managers to outperform certain performance benchmarks. That, in turn, led to new techniques for the precise measurement of portfolio performance in many market sectors. As methods such as "credit scoring" became common, lenders were set free of local constraints, bankers became less closely tied to their clients, and the lender-borrower relationships generally became much more impersonal.

On the positive side, the American financial system is more open and responsive than its counterparts in other nations, even capitalist ones, and it is becoming more so with each passing year. Supported by open credit markets, portfolio managers have become less and less willing to hold on to unprofitable enterprises. This has the positive effect of opening up investment opportunities for new businesses. But it also encourages lenders and portfolio managers to become more and more focused on near-term performance, to push hard to outperform their benchmarks and their competitors. Over time, they are expected to beat their bogies over shorter and shorter time horizons. Accordingly, their investment strategies have become more trading-oriented and less strategic.

Another defining feature of modern American finance that has spread to leading foreign financial centers is the *indexation* of portfolio performance. This practice was largely invented and developed in the United States with the encouragement of a small cadre of prominent academic economists. At many leading financial centers, especially in the pension funds areas, a growing number of large institutional investors became disenchanted with the performance of their outside managers and concluded that they could do well enough—at least during an extended bull market—by simply replicating the behavior of an equity or fixed-income index. A new industry emerged to provide these services, one offering sizable economies of scale and relatively modest fees.

Like the other leading American financial innovations of the last two decades, indexation offers both benefits and risks. Indexation works generally as expected during periods of rising asset values. But during bear markets, it can pose problems that extend beyond the obvious loss of asset value. The Asian crisis of 1997 demonstrated the dark underside of indexation. When credit ratings agencies downgraded the bonds of many Asian issuers from investment-grade to junk bond status, indexers were suddenly compelled to sell their bonds in very disorderly markets. Unlike traditional bonds, indexed bonds could not be subject to independent credit evaluation. In those unstable conditions, many clients suffered severe losses.

High leveraging, through hedge funds and other strategies, is a fourth global financial trend that grew largely out of the American scene in recent decades. Investors who take this approach sit at the far opposite end of the risk-return spectrum from buy-and-hold investors and indexers. They seek extremely high rates of return for their investors by participating in investment pools that take large risk positions in the financial, currency, and commodity markets. High leveraging is one of the main ways that such investors seek to enhance returns.

Hedge funds are hardly the only institutions that leverage in this way. Several kinds of traditional institutions do as well, from banks and insurance companies to securities firms and the finance departments of nonfinancial corporations. Some of the latter have set up units that function much like independent hedge funds. The most successful of these outfits have become modern legends, famed for outwitting slower-moving institutions and even central banks in their quest for maximum return. They are not particularly faithful investors and do not hesitate to close out a position that does not immediately pay off. Their activities often lead to increased volatility in the financial markets. But they represent a potent force in the marketplace, and their numbers continue to climb at a rapid pace.

As I described in Chapter 4, derivatives emerged as a major force in financial markets since the 1980s. Here, too, America led the way. The U.S. firms that were the driving force behind the derivatives revolution are now major players in the business of originating, selling, and trading a fantastic range of swaps, futures, forwards, options, and complex instruments that blend combinations of them (which collectively are known as derivatives). These kinds of instruments permit participants to shift risks on to other investors who are willing to take on those risks. They also permit greater leverage to be deployed in the management of portfolios. As such, they have the potential to magnify rewards for winners and to explode losses for losers. Because many derivatives are highly complex financial instruments—beyond the comprehension of even moderately sophisticated market participants—and because the legal status of contracts in financial derivatives is not well defined, losers have been known to sue their counterparties. For these reasons, derivatives combine several aspects of American-style economic democracy: innovation, high performance, and litigation.

Mutual funds make up a sixth major component of the financial world to have emerged in the last generation. Invented in England, mutual funds have become a distinctively American phenomenon in size and scope, and one that is being felt in all corners of the financial world. They are also a major means by which risk taking has become democratized, and therefore a kind of investment that resonates well with the optimistic American belief that everyone—no matter what their wealth or knowledge about financial markets—has the God-given right to make a profit in stocks and bonds. But profiting in the financial markets is seldom easy, and therefore mutual funds, too, have proved to be a mixed blessing.

Spearheaded by more than a dozen giant organizations, the mutual funds industry has grown to massive proportions in the last decade. After emerging as a major force in the United States, mutual funds are becoming somewhat more important in Europe. They have not yet taken hold in Japan, but the potential market for mutual funds there is enormous. Consider this comparison: Japanese households keep roughly 60 percent of their financial assets in deposits of one sort or another—that is, in financial assets with fixed capital value and no exposure to market risk. In the United States, by contrast, households hold barely 15 percent of their total financial assets in the form of deposits or money market funds. Instead, they own more than $2 trillion of mutual funds, alongside nearly $6 trillion of common stocks and another $2 trillion of credit market instruments. And none of this factors in their indirect ownership of stocks and bonds held on their behalf in pension funds and other financial institutions. Americanization means risk taking.

To summarize the key strengths of American-style economic democracy: It creates a strong dynamic for change and for efficiency. It tends to promote a better allocation of resources at all levels—the company level, the national level, and the global level. It promotes entrepreneurial spirit, which fosters innovation and competitiveness. It respects the interests of investors, demanding full information and punishing companies that try to subvert transparency. It encourages a vibrant venture capital industry that helps to spawn exciting new companies, especially in the high-technology area. It broadens risk taking across society and breeds a healthy awareness of the benefits of profit. To the extent that it enfranchises all elements of society as potential investors, it tends to break up powerful elites and to promote a classless society.

Despite these considerable benefits, however, the American system is not perfect. To the contrary, it poses a number of complex challenges that must be weighed against its attributes.

To begin with, American-style economic democracy has a built-in tendency toward excesses. This was quite apparent in the 1980s, with the excessive development of commercial real estate and the emergence of highly leveraged companies that became highly vulnerable to subsequent developments. And the phenomenon seems to be reemerging in recent years. For example, a number of deals have been done on the basis of inflated value of equities. The question is: What will happen if and when the stock market is challenged? That might happen if interest rates rise because the economy starts to overheat and inflation rises or because a revenue slowdown puts a squeeze on corporate profits.

Second, Americanization does not put an end to the business cycle. To the contrary, it threatens to introduce an asymmetrical response to changes in asset prices that will over time complicate the task of formulating an appropriate monetary policy. The chief reason is the broader participation of the household sector in the financial markets. As more and more household assets are held in securities or in mutual funds which will always fluctuate in value, there will tend to be a greater response to a fall in stock and bond prices than to a rise in prices. That will tend to increase the cyclicality of consumption because of the so-called "wealth effect."

Third, Americanization may improve economic efficiency, but it poses considerable problems for the central bank. The greatest challenge is how to take account of changes in the value of financial assets in the formulation of monetary policy. This puts the central bank in an uncomfortable position. There is virtually no political support for the central bank tightening credit conditions to interfere with a rise in stock prices. With the broadened participation in the stock market through mutual funds, stock price advances are now welcomed by practically everybody. The fear of perpetuating a speculative bubble in the markets is virtually nonexistent. However, there will be pressure on the central bank to ease monetary conditions in the event of a significant fall in the value of equities, regardless of economic circumstances at the time.

Finally, it is important that would-be emulators of America's economic democracy acknowledge that a freewheeling financial system driven by entrepreneurial behavior requires a rigorous, astute supervisory system. It may seem paradoxical that the less commercial banks are central to the credit-creation system, the more important it is for the official supervisory authorities, especially the central bank, to maintain strong oversight. That is because banks are the lenders of last resort to their customers, and when access to the open credit markets is closed off, the demand for bank credit can quickly increase. The recent Asian financial debacle reaffirms the point. The buildup of short-term loans to Korean, Indonesian, and Thai borrowers was inadequately supervised by the authorities of the United States and the other major industrial countries.

As America's political economy is emulated throughout the world—especially by developing nations—our policymakers, as well as those of the other leading developed nations, have a responsibility to minimize the abuses and disruptions that can easily erupt along the way. One of the best ways for policy leaders to act responsibly is to work hard to ensure that international lending is governed by due diligence. There is no better example of how such diligence can break down, with dire consequences, than the flood of U.S. lending to Latin America and Asia in the last few decades. Simply put, no one forced U.S. lenders to make such large loans to those Asian and Latin American buyers. Such debt flows have become much easier in recent decades, thanks to the increasing opening of international credit markets. Unfortunately, those markets have no built-in mechanisms to ensure responsible behavior.

Lenders and investors in America and other free-market nations alike see the trend toward the Americanization of global business and finance as a positive step toward freedom and openness. But as the foreign loan debacle of the 1980s and 1990s aptly illustrates, irresponsible lending can easily turn into, in effect, a form of economic and financial *imperialism*. When the borrower nations in such circumstances find themselves unable to service their debts, the result can be a tragic series of currency devaluations, hyperinflation, and general impoverishment. This, in turn, offers investors in the developed nations an enticing opportunity to step in and buy assets in the debt-burdened nations at bargain prices. This kind of scenario, while profitable for individual investors and institutions, is hardly a way to promote economic democracy among the world's developing nations. Moreover, a major economic setback in the United States also would run the risk of derailing the trend toward the democratization of business and finance in the industrial countries.

The Depersonalization of Financial Relationships

One of the most salient features of American-style economic democracy, but one that has not received the attention it deserves, is its tendency to depersonalize relations among lenders, borrowers, portfolio managers, and investors. It is an ironic fact that the considerable economic success of the United States since the Second World War—including the current economic boom that began in the early 1990s—has not produced a corresponding sense of comfort and security among many investors. Rather, in spite of the great achievements in the U.S., there is an uneasiness in the land that cannot be traced to the objective analysis of economic statistics or the Dow Jones Industrial Average. It has to do with deep feelings of uncertainty and anxiety, and with a growing number of disconnects in our business and our personal relationships. These feelings of discontent and restlessness are driven to an important extent by the rapidity of change and by a kind of depersonalization that envelops aspects of our lives.

What is there about the rapidity of change that is so unsettling? Above all, while change is the very essence of life, most of us are creatures of habit; we prefer repetition and constancy in our relationships. But in economics and finance, predictability and reliability are growing increasingly harder to attain because the underlying structure is shifting dramatically.

Consider, for example, the realm of technology. Within the space of less than two decades, American offices have gone from treasuring their speedy electric typewriters to acquiring the extraordinary machines called word processors, to switching to something called a personal computer, to upgrading to the most up-to-date information technologies, including Internet access, fax capabilities, and software supporting professional-quality desktop publishing. Nowadays, PCs are so widespread and inexpensive that 7-year-olds use them to learn their spelling and to play games with graphics capabilities that surpass anything outside the Disney studios of just a few years back.

The consequences are far-reaching for an array of workers. Life will never again be the same for secretaries, for draftsmen, for printers, for librarians struggling to conform to an electronic world, for accountants who must become spreadsheet specialists, even for the U.S. Postal Service, which must compete not only with Federal Express but also with e-mail. Lawyers who once drafted ordinary wills now let their clients do that through cheap off-the-shelf software while concentrating instead on more challenging activities such as creating complex trusts. Doctors will lose their Olympian stature as patients arrive already having digested up-to-the-minute information from the Web about their particular illness.

In these and other ways, inexpensive technology is being fused with an irregular improvement in the knowledge of how to use it effectively. The result is a profound change in the nature of work and the set of skills needed to do that work. It represents a kind of change that disturbs the common rhythms of life, as when experienced middle-aged managers and professionals discover that their youngest subordinates often have superior skills. For many, learning the new skills is hard. And this is a worldwide phenomenon.

The rapidity of change in financial life has been equally sensational. Radical changes in the structure of finance have led to a revolution in the way credit is created, in the volume of sales, distribution, and trading of marketable securities, and in the volatility of financial asset values. Just think back to what it used to be like to get a mortgage compared with what it's like today. Whereas a mere two decades ago, this process involved a personal visit to a local bank or savings and loan, today dozens of banks, thrifts, and mortgage specialists advertise their 800 numbers. You call in or fill out a form and get an approval within days or even hours. Your loan ends up being packaged with hundreds of others in securitized form, is sold off in the open market, and becomes part of the ebb and flow of the daily swirl of transactions.

The story is the same in other sectors of the financial markets. There has been the rapid growth of credit cards and the instant access to credit provided by them. Corporate America has shifted financing in the space of a generation from close reliance on the banking system, to floating-rate financing, to commercial paper, to leasing of all kinds, then to a burgeoning open market for corporate bonds, and most recently to the use of financial derivatives that inject even more leveraging into the system. There has been a shift to securitization, to the greater use of the open credit markets, and to the institutionalization of investing, all of which have required the ability to continuously mark investment portfolios to market. In turn, the practice of marking to market has changed the mentality of decision making, almost ordaining short-term investment horizons and aggravating volatility in the marketplace. There has also been the globalization of finance, which has introduced these rapid changes into all the major financial markets.

Whether in industrial fields or in the financial realm, rapid change almost inevitably produces big winners as new products or services go from concept to prototype, curiosity, and then broad usage with remarkable speed. Yet, overall growth in the economy may be moderate. As a result, people employed in many segments of the economy do not feel the surge of elation that is mainly felt by the few industries and relative handful of firms that are at the leading edge of innovation. Change comes unevenly, in fits and starts, and it creates losers as well as winners.

The other aspect of the current sense of national unease stems from a growing depersonalization of many aspects of life. Consider, for example, the transformation of our medical care system. As Milton Friedman has noted (borrowing a theme of the great novelist Solzhenitsyn), we have traversed from a system based on the rather low-tech family doctor, informal counselor, and family confidante to the high-tech world of specialists, masters of their craft but essentially anonymous to their patients, and then to HMOs, where you're treated by teams and seldom see the same physician twice.

The transformation of the workplace is equally dramatic. The process of mergers and consolidations often leads to depersonalization as smaller firms are absorbed by medium-sized firms that are in turn absorbed by giant corporations. Moreover, outsourcing is a manifestation of depersonalization. In both cases, there is a sense of randomness at work in the economy. In the financial community, as I described in Chapter 5, the partnerships that once dominated Wall Street have been supplanted by publicly traded corporations where the interpersonal decision making is more formalized and loyalty and devotion to the firm are difficult to inculcate.

The combination of rapid change and depersonalization gives a sense that the pressures are never-ending, that there is no relief, that no dependable new steady state can be created. To be sure, competition from companies within the standard group of major industrial countries is a permanent condition of our global economy. In addition, the emerging nations are getting better and better at making world-class products, and we accept the fact that they will continue to get even better in the future.

Why is there a tendency to overlook the upside? Much of the answer lies with the unevenness of who gets the benefits in our economy. Our corporations making high-value-added products of all types—which is where our powerful comparative advantage lies—will do well. Who would doubt that? But a number of industries that employ a lot of workers will not be direct beneficiaries—although they may be indirect beneficiaries to the extent they can respond to change, find niches, and trade off quality for cost. Ever since Adam Smith and David Ricardo we have been taught that specialization in production creates efficiencies; but what if you're employed today in a sector in which the United States does not appear to have a long-term comparative advantage? You have to either move to another industry or another line of work or stay and accept the likelihood of continuing pressures for restructuring, compressed pay, and so on.

What can be done to respond to the mood of economic insecurity and anxiety? To begin with, it is important not to deny its existence—but also not to pander to the realities of economic uncertainty and depersonalization. When leaders focus exclusively on positive overall economic statistics or sermonize that the stock market is way up and thus things must be getting better, this only irritates the public and reinforces the notion that those in authority are callous. But by the same token, careless criticism of economic conditions that are generally quite good leaves the misimpression that some person or persons in a position of authority—whether the government or the central bank or business leaders—are maliciously keeping the country from enjoying more prosperity. Economic progress does not come easily. It requires not only hard work, but also strong organizational abilities, a high degree of inventiveness, and a compliant Mother Nature—and it is mischievous to assert otherwise.

Second, we must end the practice of subsidizing the losers indefinitely. It's expensive, it destroys government budgets, and it imposes tremendous economic costs, because it retards the shift in resources to more productive sectors. It is false compassion. Countries that try to do this have found themselves with lower growth and much higher unemployment rates than countries, such as the United States, that are more tolerant of change.

Third, continuing education for adults and explicit retraining programs have a role to play. But we must not *overstate* their potential. After all, some of the most anxious and disgruntled in our society are those who have been casualties of rapid economic change and corporate downsizing: managerial and professional staff. By any standard, they are highly educated people, with experience and good skills.

Fourth, where education has most promise is in broadening the number of people who can qualify for jobs, but helping young people become employable is more than a matter of schooling. It is a matter of being honest about the underlying obstacles to educational attainment, particularly in deprived urban areas. The local culture has to change, and government alone or government primarily can't make that happen. The absence of time-tested family structures is fundamental to the problem.

What we need are efforts that break the cycle of dysfunctional families, inadequate education, stilted job prospects, and despair. This will require that we make education a 12-month-a-year proposition *and* create opportunities for youth to get out of their neighborhoods.

In the final analysis, a world of rapid changes and depersonalization is a world of greater individual freedom. My upbringing in the very structured economy and society of prewar Germany has given me an acute appreciation for the value of freedom and openness in all aspects of life, from the social and political to the financial and economic. America's meritocracy, however imperfect, offers individuals who are not born with great social standing or family wealth (myself included) opportunities to rise to positions of prominence and influence.

But if we are to live in an improving world, freedom has an accompanying requirement—namely, responsibility. In the prayer book called the *Haggadah,* from which I read on Passover evening, there is the following passage:

> The struggle for freedom is a continuous struggle
> In every age some new freedom is won and established
> Yet each age uncovers a formerly unrecognized servitude
> Requiring new liberation to set man's soul free.

As capitalism spreads to more and more regions of the world, its strengths and weaknesses will be multiplied and amplified. It can only benefit economic policymakers and investors in Europe and Japan—and in other developed and developing regions—to be clear about the promise and problems of American-style economic democracy. It is true that the homegrown American way cannot be transplanted whole cloth from U.S. shores to foreign lands and foreign cultures. At the same time, however, the American experience has much to teach those who would emulate our imperfect economic democracy.

One of the most effective ways to encourage such transnational understanding is through student exchange. For this reason, for the last eleven years I have served as chairman of the Institute of International Education, the largest nonprofit organization in the United States administering student exchange programs. Each year, IIE brings thousands of foreign students to American shores and sends thousands of American students to study abroad. This benefits foreign students by introducing them to our system of government, our business institutions and methods, and our broader culture. When they return to their country of origin, and as they continue to grow professionally, some will look to their experience in the U.S. as a source of inspiration. Similarly, American students gain a much richer sense of cultural diversity through direct experience in a foreign land. In the end, the integration of the world's economic systems will not make headway in the 21st century unless tomorrow's financial leaders develop a deep appreciation for institutions and cultures outside of their own.

8

The Rise of Financial
Forecasting

*There is, simply put, no constancy in the financial
markets, but rather continual ebbs and flows, with
occasional major structural changes.*

Yet another way in which Wall Street has been transformed in the
postwar period is in the art and science of economic and financial
forecasting. When I began my career, this kind of research was confined almost completely to the academic world. Over time, business
school researchers continued to work in the area of forecasting. Eventually, they were joined by economists at financial institutions, who
gradually took the lead in the field. Today, forecasting is an essential
component of modern business and finance. I was fortunate to have
been at the center of this transformation. Indeed, my reputation on
Wall Street grew mainly from my work as a forecaster of interest rates
and of many other financial market dynamics.

This is not to say that the academic underpinnings were unimportant. In fact, decades before forecasting became commonplace on Wall
Street and in corporate America, a number of economists and economic historians did important work in the field, from F. R. Macauley
and Leslie Mitchell to Simon Kuznets, Raymond Goldsmith, and Brad
Hickman. Not surprisingly, much of the curiosity about financial
crises and panics was driven by a desire to understand that greatest of
all modern economic calamities, the Great Depression. Nor was business and financial forecasting invented entirely in the postwar period.
In one form or another, its roots extend back to ancient times, for it has

always been in the interest of individuals and societies to anticipate the contours of material life over the next horizon.

In the 1950s and 1960s, forecasting was beginning to make its way into Wall Street as well. But the few techniques practiced were crude by today's standards. At the time I joined Salomon Brothers & Hutzler in 1962, forecasting in the financial industry was neither specialized nor particularly sophisticated. There were no asset allocation models, for example, and forecasters tended to focus on domestic equity markets rather than taking a more global perspective. The few researchers who knew how to perform technical analysis were beginning to find an audience, but their techniques had yet to gain the attention and respect of mainstream portfolio managers.

Watching the Fed and Flows of Funds

When Sidney Homer joined Salomon in 1960, bond research on Wall Street was a rarity. Rarer still were any attempts to apply systematic analysis to the economy and financial markets as integrated systems. Only a handful of firms published quotation sheets that featured daily or weekly prices and yields on outstanding U.S. government bonds or on publicly traded corporate or municipal bonds. Here and there in the business press one could find brief commentaries on the bond market. And, of course, such information flowed intermittently via telephone and the mails. But the systems that today move mountains of bond market information at lightning speed—computer networks, Bloomberg, Telerate, and the like—were still years in the future.

Sidney Homer liked to describe himself as a "bond man." This reflected his self-deprecating desire to downplay his rigorous understanding of interest rate theory. But his grasp of interest rate theory was as strong as that of most economists, and he had few peers as a historian of the subject. Sidney's chief interests in the field were interest rate history, debt structure, real-world linkages, and a variety of special subjects—from short and long maturities, to low-coupon and high-coupon bonds, to the relationships among obligations at various levels of credit quality.

Most importantly, Sidney was the first Wall Streeter to take a comprehensive approach to fixed-income research. His book, *A History of Interest Rates*—published the year I arrived at Salomon—demonstrated his mastery of the subject. I became aware of this during my first few months at Salomon, when he walked over to my desk with galleys of his book and asked me to read them—with one important proviso: I was to read the text *aloud* to my secretary, who would follow along in her duplicate copy. Naturally, I asked why. He explained that the technique would help me spot errors and poor sentence structures. And he was right. I read out loud every one of the 594 pages, including the 73 statistical tables on interest rates, some of the data stretching back centuries.

Sidney knew at the time that we would need to do more than analyze the entire interest rate spectrum. In order to ferret out important new trends in financial markets—in particular, new values in bonds—we would also need to monitor the operations of the Federal Reserve and the U.S. Treasury, as well as the flow of credit through the financial system. These tasks—my first assignments at Salomon—became my entrée into forecasting. Our work in this area buttressed Salomon's emerging strengths in U.S. government securities, while also helping our institutional clients to better understand some of the key forces influencing financial values.

These early assignments were not difficult for me, given my Fed experience; but I'll admit they were tedious at times. I had a secretary, but little other help. Salomon's entire research operation then consisted of Sidney and myself, our two secretaries, Richard Johannesen (an excellent bond analyst), and a junior assistant. There were mountains of data to plow through, little of the data compiled into readily available databases as they are today. And since personal computers had not yet come to Wall Street, we were forced to sort and compile all of the data by hand.

To be sure, some data about the Fed and Treasury were available in the early 1960s. Bob Roosa, a former head of research at the New York Fed, had written an excellent booklet on Federal Reserve open market operations. Hobart Carr, a researcher at the New York Fed (and later an NYU professor), published an excellent interpretation of Federal

Reserve statistics. And the Federal Reserve itself had published articles
on several of the factors affecting bank reserves.

Even so, there were no readily available data on many of these subjects, including the *seasonal* behavior of the Treasury and Federal
Reserve. To track that behavior, I compiled weekly data going back
many years on factors affecting bank reserves, such as currency in circulation float and Treasury balances. Those statistics, in turn, enabled
us to figure out the Fed's involvement in the market 1 week hence.
Would the Fed (for seasonal reasons) try to absorb reserves by selling
securities? Or would it be supplying reserves by buying securities?* In
effect, I attempted to replicate the Fed's own analysis, albeit with a
thinner stream of information.

Even more challenging than seasonal forecasting was the task of predicting changes in the Federal Reserve's fundamental monetary posture.
Was the Fed going to ease or tighten the money supply? Shift direction?
To answer these questions, I began to analyze the reports of the Federal
Open Market Committee (FOMC) for the previous 5 years. (Unlike
today, when those reports are issued every 45 days, in the early 1960s they
appeared only once a year.) From the FOMC reports I identified a list of
factors that influenced the Committee's decisions. My analysis showed
that the most common factors were changes in the money supply,
employment levels, interest rates, inflation, industrial production, bank
credit, bank reserves, time and savings deposits, retail sales, U.S. Treasury
financing, balance of payments, and capital outflow. How much emphasis the FOMC placed on each of these variables was (and is) a difficult
puzzle to solve because the relative importance of these variables varies
considerably over time. Even so, we took a great step forward by identifying the list of variables on which the Fed focused its attention—a list
that has changed remarkably little since the 1960s.

Then, as now, monetary policy shifted glacially. The slow pace of
change could encourage a kind of risky complacency. Since the FOMC
changed the Fed's discount rate an average of only once or twice a year

---

*The Fed can expand or absorb reserves either outright or temporarily through
repurchase or reverse repurchase agreements, respectively.

between 1957 and 1965, it would have been easy enough for me to achieve a remarkable 96 percent accuracy rate simply by predicting *no change* in monetary policy week after week! But the real challenge was to forecast correctly the remaining 4 percent of the time, when Fed policy shifted, and with important consequences.

Nor was the discount rate the only meaningful indicator. Indeed, throughout the 1960s and 1970s both the Fed and Wall Street shifted priorities and attention from one indicator to another. In the early 1960s, the Federal Reserve targeted net free or net borrowed reserves, which actually fluctuated widely because of seasonal changes and other unanticipated factors. For many years, market participants riveted their attention on this target, in spite of its shortcoming as a gauge of policy. In the late 1970s, when Fed Chairman Paul Volcker announced a strict adherence to monetarism, Wall Street began to focus on the money supply.

Even at the Fed, change was a constant. Rather than defining the money supply narrowly, the Fed introduced new categories such as M1a and M1b; and after that, the central bank shifted its attention to M2, supplementing it with the bank credit proxy. By the 1980s, the Federal Reserve was moving away from this strict adherence to monetarism, at which time the Federal funds rate became a money condition target.

Today, most Wall Streeters consider the money supply to be relatively less important than before. Rather, they look to the Federal funds rate and to the monthly releases of economic data such as consumer and wholesale prices, unemployment, and other measures of economic performance that may influence FOMC decisions on the near horizon. Given the Fed's current reliance on judgment rather than on definitive benchmarks, new and more complicated targets are sure to emerge in the next few years. And this is as it should be, for the complexities of economic and financial life cannot be unlocked by following the trends in just a few variables.

In retrospect, my early assignment as Salomon's Fed watcher was exquisitely well timed. As noted, only a handful of Wall Streeters were doing the same thing, and they had very little visibility. Today, an army of financial analysts tracks every nuance of Federal Reserve and U.S. Treasury activity and policy. Present-day investors are privy to a seemingly endless stream of analysis of Fed open market operations, of official pronouncements, and of economic developments that will affect Fed and U.S. Treasury decisions. Much of this information is supplied by news retrieval services, and by the Fed itself, which feeds the investment community a steady diet of press releases, testimony, and speeches. So commonplace is information about the Fed and Treasury that it is packaged and distributed much like ordinary commodities. The situation was much different in the 1960s, when such information possessed special value because it was so rare. Accordingly, there was enormous pent-up demand for this kind of analysis. It is therefore not surprising that my findings and forecasts quickly gained a large audience of investors, fund managers, economists, and policymakers.

Along with my early interest rate work, Sidney Homer gave me a second early assignment that also proved to be pivotal in my career. He charged me with the task of tracking what we called "the supply and demand for credit," or what the Fed referred to as "flow-of-funds analysis." In this domain—as with our research on interest rates and Fed and Treasury activity—we were not the first to conduct such research, but we were certainly among the earliest on Wall Street. Bankers Trust, Scudder, Stevens & Clark, and the Life Insurance Association already had begun to work in the flow-of-funds area, and the Fed periodically published flow-of-funds data. Sidney Homer himself had brought a simple model of selected credit flows with him when he joined Salomon.

For his part, Sidney focused on selected net demands for long-term investment funds. These included the demand for credit for real estate mortgages, corporate bonds, state and municipal bonds, and foreign and international bank bonds. After picking the brains of experts in each of these fields, Sidney would forecast demand for credit in each category 1 year into the future. Then he would estimate how these demands would be financed, that is, how much long-term financing would be supplied by each of the key nonbank institutions (insurance companies, savings banks, savings and loan institutions, corporate and state pension funds, and so on). Whatever credit was not supplied by these institutions, of course, would have to come from commercial banks and individuals. It became clear to us that whenever commercial banks and individuals were called upon to finance a large portion of credit demands, this would put upward pressure on interest rates.

Within a few years I developed a far more comprehensive model of credit flows, one that was oriented toward a financial market perspective. My model incorporated demand for short- and long-term credit by each major sector of borrowers. I also disaggregated credit flows by type of institutional and noninstitutional lender. In this way, I showed how a wide range of credit market participants were affected by overall credit flows. My model took into account not only data on the sources and uses of funds for nonfinancial corporations but also changes in the portfolios of pension funds, insurance companies, banks, thrifts, and other suppliers of funds, all broken down by asset class (stocks, bonds, etc.). Approaching the problem in this way gave me a comprehensive view of the financial markets, one that allowed me to see how each of its key participants fit into the larger picture.

This approach yielded some intriguing insights. To begin with, it showed that overall increases in the effective demands for credit do not necessarily mean that interest rates are going to rise. Whether rates will rise or not depends much more on how close the economy is to full employment. Second, our model showed that under tight credit conditions major demanders of credit—such as the U.S. government and large business corporations—are far more effective in competing for loans than the typical household. Third, my analysis showed that the behavior and competitive position of financial institutions can change rapidly. Some leading institutions are influenced by business and credit cycles much more than others. Credit flow analysis also helped me spot shifts in the portfolio preferences of investors. There is, simply put, no constancy in the financial markets, but rather continual ebbs and flows, with occasional major structural changes.

Flow-of-funds analysis also gave me a better feel for the *direction* of interest rates, but not the *magnitude* of change. Credit flows depend a great deal on economic activity. Consumer spending, new construction activity, capital outlays by business, and spending by governments—all of these major economic activities require financing. With this in mind, I decided to test the financial viability of these economic demands by looking at a widely agreed upon economic forecast for the coming year and then adjusting that economic forecast according to what seemed financially feasible for the economy under the circumstances. In cases where there did not appear to be enough credit available from traditional financial institutions, I knew that individual investors would have to take up the slack. Large shortfalls put upward pressure on interest rates, whereas modest shortfalls indicated stable or falling interest rates.

The growing sophistication and complexity of credit flow analysis, in spite of its obvious benefits, has wrought new challenges for the practitioners of the craft. I use the word "craft" deliberately, for flow-of-funds analysis is not simply a matter of applying formulas in a logical and systematic way; it requires experience, intuition, and good judgment.

In fact, the challenges facing the forecaster never have been greater. One major reason is that financial markets have become increasingly blurred, both in their composition and in their institutional boundaries. Another problem is the chronic lack of relevant and complete data, a consequence of accounting procedures failing to keep pace with the latest financing methods and investment techniques. Still another perplexing trend for the economic and financial forecaster is the internationalization of financial markets, which makes it extremely difficult to link economic activity with credit flows. Inflows from abroad may come from private-sector investors or from foreign central banks—each with very different implications. Private foreign investors favor a strong U.S. currency, whereas foreign central bank purchases tend to occur when the U.S. dollar is weakening. Overall, however, America has become increasingly dependent on foreign sources of funds, albeit in an irregular pattern. The net increase in new foreign funds (as a percentage of net credit market debt financed in the American market) averaged 7 percent in the 1980s, and rose to an average of 15 percent in the 1990s.

Comments on Credit and Its Cousins

At first, my analysis and forecasts of monetary and fiscal policy, credit flows, and interest rates found a loyal audience within Salomon Brothers. On March 23, 1962, I issued the first in a series of weekly short commentaries on monetary and banking statistics (see Exhibit 8-1). These very modest weekly reports, then called "Comment on Weekly Monetary Statistics," were consumed by traders, salespeople, and partners throughout Salomon Brothers, some of whom mailed the reports to key clients. Soon these reports grew longer and more elaborate, and Sidney Homer suggested that I publish a more formal weekly report for external distribution. The result was *Comments on Credit*, launched in 1962, a periodical that attracted a wide readership in financial circles. On the first page of each issue, I usually summarized monetary developments from the previous week, and presented near-term expectations. The subsequent pages contained short and succinct commentary on new developments in the money and capital markets. This commentary, highlighted with tables and charts, covered a range of subjects, from specific developments in financial institutions, to patterns of finance among business corporations, to state, local, and federal finance and trends in interest rates.

March 23, 1962

Free reserves of member banks fell to $378 million during the past statement week. While this is the second time within the last three weeks that free reserves have dropped below $400 billion, the decline cannot be regarded as a reversal of monetary policy. Last week's decline is probably due to a Federal Reserve miscalculation in the size of the float. Because of tax payments, the Federal Reserve had in all likelihood estimated a larger increase in float than the $194 million reported on the weekly statement.

The policy of the Federal Reserve so far this year has been to supply reserves at a lower rate than a year ago, but insufficiently adequate to support the business recovery.

The first *Comment on Weekly Monetary Statistics*, reprinted (with permission of Salomon Smith Barney) above, ran a scant two paragraphs. Over time, the bulletin would evolve into the much longer *Comments on Credit*, with a readership of 25,000.

Exhibit 8-1

Researching and writing *Comments on Credit* was one of my most difficult and rewarding duties at Salomon. Even as my managerial responsibilities at Salomon grew to include supervision of all research activities and a place in the senior management of the firm, I continued to write the front page of *Comments on Credit,* while delegating the rest to newer members of our research staff, including Dick Johannesen and James McKeon, who assisted me in the flow-of-funds analysis. Sidney Homer occasionally contributed some wonderful commentary. Sidney also founded two other Salomon periodicals that achieved great success: *Bond Market Roundup* (a weekly) and *Bond Market Review* (which appeared monthly). These three publications— valued for their soundness, conciseness, and clarity of presentation— ultimately found an audience of some 25,000 key members of the investment community. Unrivaled in their day, they were a tangible example of the benefits of Salomon's decision to support fixed-income research.

Still another publication that we produced at Salomon—*Prospects for the Credit Markets*—also attracted a great deal of attention. Based heavily on flow-of-funds analysis, *Prospects* appeared each December. The popularity of this annual probably derived from its unique combination of useful data and cogent analysis. *Prospects for the Credit Markets* reviewed leading economic and financial developments, and—as its title suggested—provided sector-by-sector prospects for key financial markets. This kind of analysis was rare at the time, and— perhaps more importantly—the forecasts that we published in *Prospects* established a strong track record.

The hunger within the financial community for such analysis was demonstrated by the hoopla that, by the 1980s, greeted the publication of each new issue of *Prospects.* Although the topic of credit markets and interest rates might seem to be fodder for the driest esoteric journals, in fact Salomon presented these findings in what more closely resembled major media events. Typically, the firm would invite a thousand or so of its clients to a major presentation—usually at New York's Waldorf Astoria Hotel—where they were joined by a phalanx of financial news reporters. An international audience also shared the spectacle via telephone hookups to our out-of-town offices, where distant

clients listened in on the presentations. On occasion, television sta-
tions would broadcast the proceedings as far away as Australia.

Growing Salomon's Research Globally

As our research group gained recognition inside and outside of
Salomon, expansion followed. Among the early professionals whom
we recruited was Martin Leibowitz, who joined the firm in 1969. Some
initially doubted the hire. For one thing, Marty was a nephew of Sidney Homer, which may have raised questions about nepotism since
Marty knew little about the financial markets. For another, in his early
years in the firm, he seemed to take a passive role—perhaps because he
felt out of place in the organization. What Marty brought to the firm
was indeed unconventional at the time: a set of quantitative skills that
could be applied for analyzing fixed-income markets. He is a brilliant
mathematician, and I believed that the firm could benefit enormously
from the methodologies in which Marty was skilled. To support that
kind of work, we set up a small division called Bond Portfolio Analysis. Over time, that group dispelled the doubts about its value to the
firm; and Marty emerged as a recognized authority in his specialty,
with many publications to his name. It was a vanguard research group,
one that, for a long time, had no peer on Wall Street.

My own role in the firm expanded as well. Soon after I became a
partner in 1967, Bill Salomon asked me to take over as head of the
firm's faltering stock research unit. Although I had recently agreed to
take over the Bond Market Research Department—to fill the void created when Sidney Homer became a limited partner—I accepted the
second assignment as well. Now I was responsible for the firm's total
debt and equity research operations, which included 13 professionals
in 1970.

The next logical step was to build research capabilities to support
foreign operations. As Salomon enlarged its international presence,
first in London and then in Japan and Hong Kong, I moved ahead with
plans to establish an international fixed-income research unit. Finding
the right people to staff the new operation quickly emerged as the

biggest obstacle. Most applicants were interested in international and economic balance of payments research. But I wanted men and women who understood foreign money and capital markets. After some fits and starts, I recruited Jeff Hanna, who understood exactly what I was looking for, and he in turn helped me to recruit John Lipsky and Nick Sargen. Both men had very strong academic backgrounds—each held a doctorate from Stanford University—as well as excellent experience as practitioners. John had been with the International Monetary Fund, Nick with J. P. Morgan and Company. Just as we had been in the vanguard on the domestic side, our new international research operation—by focusing on fixed-income markets, monetary and fiscal policies, foreign interest rate structures, and credit flows—offered investors useful and hard-to-find data and analysis. Few of our competitors—certainly not the foreign operations in leading American investment banks—offered anything comparable.

The pattern continued: As Salomon diversified into new businesses, research moved along in lockstep. This occurred again in the late 1970s and the mid-1980s, when the firm entered the mortgage and real estate markets. Once again, in an effort to set Salomon apart from its competitors, I asked myself: What services did the market demand that our rivals were not offering? The answer, in this case, was several-fold. To begin with, recruiting first-rate talent was the key to success. Marty Leibowitz helped to recruit quants (the insider's term for those trained in quantitative methods) capable of analyzing the intricacies of mortgage prepayment patterns and the values and characteristics of different types of mortgage securities. In setting up our research effort in real estate, we hired Ken Rosen—a recognized academic authority in the field—as a consultant. Rosen, in turn, helped us recruit David Shulman, who headed the research effort in real estate.

All of this growing and building made for exciting times at Salomon. For those of us who had come on board in the early stages of this great expansion, the transition made an especially deep impression. None of us envisioned how robustly the firm would grow in the course of a single generation. The endpoints of my career at Salomon frame the dramatic story: At one end (early 1962)—as the firm's first Ph.D.—I joined the six-person, upstart research "depart-ment"; at the other (1988), I managed a research effort staffed with more than 450, of whom about 50 held doctorates and a much larger number held M.B.A.s.

Remarkably, throughout these decades of aggressive expansion, Salomon's senior management never imposed budgetary constraints on our research efforts. In large measure, this reflected the vision of Bill Salomon, who led the firm when most of the research functions were put in place. Both he and Charles Simon sagely recognized the vital role that research played within the firm. Admittedly, I also tried to operate with a tight research budget, one that produced valued and objective analysis.

My position at the helm of Salomon's burgeoning research organi-zation was ideal when it came to sharpening my skills and broadening my knowledge about financial trends. As part of our fixed-income research, I conducted special studies on banking, on the structure of the corporate bond market, on corporate financing strategy, on the dynamics of the U.S. Treasury and federal credit agency markets, and on the cyclical and secular patterns of interest rates, just to mention a few. Moreover, I was able to tap into industry developments, corporate sales trends, and capital spending patterns by interfacing with the equity security analysts.

More than that, my daily interactions with traders and salespeople on Salomon's vast trading floor gave me different, but no less valuable, kinds of information and insights. What was the composition of the trading? Who were the institutional participants? Were they shorten-ing or lengthening the maturity of their portfolios? Was the financing calendar growing, and if so, in what maturity? These questions were daily fare among the firm's hundreds of high-energy salespeople and securities traders.

Another often-discussed question was the Fed's activities in the open market. As a leading dealer in U.S. government securities, Salomon watched the Fed's open market operations carefully for hints about its interest rate leanings. Whether the Fed was buying or selling securities outright or through repurchase agreements, for example, was a clue to whether the central bank was leaning toward tighter or looser monetary policy. But in strategizing about such matters with our traders and salespeople, I had to stay mindful of our very different time horizons. Whereas they were oriented toward the very near term—it is not uncommon for a trader to begin the day bearish and end it bullish—I took a much longer perspective. For this reason, in my discussions with traders, I tried to winnow out the ephemeral information from that of more enduring significance. At the same time, I quickly learned, some traders are simply more perceptive and sure-footed than others.

Research and daily interaction with traders were indispensable parts of my practical education on Wall Street. But there was more. One of the most intriguing aspects of my job was the fact that it brought me into regular contact with leaders of major corporations, financial institutions, and governments throughout the world, as well as with key policymakers and monetary authorities. Often, I would meet with one of these individuals over a meal after having given a talk at his home institution. Although I was ostensibly the "teacher" on these occasions, I privately saw myself as a student as well, for I always took the opportunity to ask these leaders about their expectations and the developments in their fields of endeavor.

These discussions usually helped me sharpen my thinking; and even when they didn't, I still found them useful for revealing the biases of my hosts. This was especially important in the case of government officials, who tend to talk about what *should* be rather than what they think *will* be. This bias seems to be endemic throughout government circles worldwide. (For example, it is virtually impossible to find an official government document that forecasts a major business recession, or even a wide cyclical swing in financial markets or economic activity.) Nor, in these conversations with government officials, have I found them to be forthcoming about new policy directions. Nevertheless, I am convinced that my interactions with such officials—whether in high-level meetings or in telephone conversations—benefited all parties involved. They helped me sharpen my thinking about key policy issues, while bringing government officials closer to developments in the markets.

Unwitting Pundit

Scarcely a year after we launched the research effort at Salomon, our findings and forecasts began to attract attention in the wider financial community. As noted, the increasing popularity of *Comments on Credit* was one reason. Another was the fact that the business press began to call on Sidney Homer and me regularly to comment on interest rate trends and other late-breaking financial news. Following Sidney's retirement in 1971, I became head and spokesperson for Salomon's up-and-coming research effort. As my public profile increased, I became more reflective and deliberate in my public pronouncements, which in turn inspired me to begin sorting out my thoughts about major issues on paper.

By the mid-1970s I had begun to give lengthy, formal addresses to groups of economists, business leaders, policymakers, and academics. From Sidney Homer I had learned the value of writing out my comments before giving a speech, especially before a large audience. Not only did the writing process help me clarify and refine my thinking, but it also produced a text that I could then mail to our clients and to interested members of the media for quotation. In a growing number of cases, my speeches were published in their entirety in the pages of leading business periodicals.

In this way, I somewhat unwittingly found myself playing the role of financial pundit. The new role required some adjustment, and no small amount of additional work. For me, the writing of long memos and speeches is a painstaking process, one that is virtually impossible to do in the office, where interruptions and distractions abound. I therefore found it necessary to do most of my writing at home in the evenings and on weekends. Even with a well-conceived outline in hand, I normally have needed two full weekend days to compose a 40-minute speech. There were many years in which I wrote eight or more speeches, on top of the usual flow of long memoranda, editing the work of others, and so on.

Still, the rewards have been well worth the effort. Along with the obvious satisfaction of getting one's ideas out to appropriate audiences, frequent public speaking and publication imposed on me a discipline that has encouraged me over the years to delve into meaningful topics and to avoid repetition or sloppiness in my thinking. Most importantly, my speeches and writings serve as a clear record of my positions. As my views became widely known, this record proved to be invaluable—for my supporters as well as my critics!

In most cases, the media and clients have focused on my assessment of (1) the interest rate outlook, (2) the implications of that outlook for the economy and financial markets, (3) current fiscal and monetary policies, and (4) fundamental undercurrents or structural changes taking place in the financial markets. Demand for my views on the first subject was, of course, a direct outgrowth of my weekly writings in *Comments on Credit* as well as the annual release of *Supply and Demand for Credit*. When speaking about interest rates and credit flows, I strived to link those trends with broader real-world financial and economic developments.

The credit crunch of 1966 (which I describe in fuller detail in Chapter 13) was a turning point in my career as a credit and interest rate forecaster. So tight was credit during that squeeze—the first major crisis of its kind since the end of World War II—that 3-month Treasury bills were driven to their postwar high of 5.58 percent, while high-quality corporate bonds rocketed upward to 6.18 percent. I publicly predicted the 1966 credit crunch, as well as its consequences: a brief economic slowdown, followed by a rally in the fixed-income markets. By the end of the first quarter of 1967, the rally was over and I became bearish again. That episode convinced me of the value of credit flow analysis for anticipating prospective credit demands. It also bolstered my public profile on Wall Street as an interest rate and credit market forecaster.

Weighing the Variables

This is not to say that projecting interest rates and credit markets comes easily to me. Simply put, this kind of forecasting is no simple matter. There are many econometric models that promise to ease the task, but none (of the many that I have examined) delivers on that promise. Many forecasters mistakenly rely on past trends to project the future; they wrongly assume that business and financial trends repeat themselves. But that approach fails to take into account important structural changes that often shape business and financial activity. It also oversimplifies the highly complex dimensions of the economic and financial decision-making process, and thereby encourages a false sense of security. Finally, those who rely heavily on modeling too often are unwilling to scrutinize the quality and accuracy of their underlying data. They are so captivated by the elegance of their models that they don't question the underlying evidence and assumptions on which their models rest.

Rather, interest rate and financial market forecasting involves a constellation of variables that shift continually in relative importance. To begin with, it is important to examine the levels at which labor and capital resources are being utilized. If those are low, then an expansion of economic activity will likely have a modest impact on the credit markets. On the other hand, business expansion in the face of tight labor and capital markets normally will strain markets unless there are extraordinary gains in productivity, which is unlikely under such circumstances.

When rising economic activity leads to shrinking corporate profits, demand for credit intensifies. Businesses will increase their external borrowing and challenge the demanders of other borrowers. These conditions also cause business liquidity (as reflected on the asset side of the corporate balance sheet) to disappear, which further increases corporate dependence on external financing. To complicate matters still more, the low borrowing rate of corporations does not automatically lead to financial stability. In order for corporations to finance themselves by liquidating a large volume of their liquid assets, they must find buyers for those assets.

Another key variable to consider is the real estate market. As noted earlier, growing demand for household finance does not necessarily push interest rates higher. To the contrary: A robust real estate sector generally is a symptom rather than a cause of ample credit availability, which can accommodate a strong demand for housing credit.

Then there is fiscal policy to consider. Is it neutral, restraining, or stimulative? During periods of economic slack, stimulative fiscal policy will not immediately stimulate the credit needs of other demanders of credit. Indeed, on many occasions stimulative fiscal policy has failed to halt a decline in interest rates mainly because private-sector credit demands were weak, as they tend to be under such conditions. Still, the composition of deficit financing during periods of economic slack can influence the shape of the yield curve and retard private-sector reliquefication. If the government finances its debt heavily with longer maturities during a time of recession, for instance, such an action will hinder the ability of corporations to fund their liabilities—a move that helps set the stage for economic recovery.

Similarly, the general direction of monetary policy at a given time is not a sure-fire indicator of which way interest rates will go. A great deal depends on how good a job the Federal Reserve has done in assessing the condition and needs of the economy. Too often, monetary policy lags behind the rapidly evolving needs of business. A clear example of this occurred in the 1970s when rampant inflation caused a spike in nominal credit demands.

Sound forecasting about *American* credit conditions also requires a solid grasp of *foreign* economic and financial conditions. As long as the United States remains heavily dependent on foreign sources of funds, for example, high rates of growth here and abroad can be dangerous. By the same token, economic slack and easy monetary conditions throughout the industrialized world benefit the U.S. credit situation. It not only helps contain inflation, but also makes it easier for American firms and governments to attract foreign investment funds.

There are a host of other variables to consider when projecting future trends in financial markets. How will the liberalization of regulations affect the markets? What about the introduction of new investment and trading techniques? Are market participants becoming more or less willing to take risks? In the past, federally legislated interest rate ceilings limited the competition for funds, thereby holding down huge increases in interest rates when monetary policy tightened. This constrained the battle for a limited supply of funds. But whether or not the funds are allocated efficiently through this approach is a moot question. As I have suggested, these considerations simply cannot be captured by econometric modeling or by other quantitative analytical techniques.

The yield curve—that is, the range of interest rates from the shortest to the longest maturities—also can be a blunt indicator of interest rate trends. The conventional view holds that a positively sloped (or normal) curve points toward rising long-term interest rates, while an inverted curve suggests that long-term rates will fall in the future. But for forecasting purposes, these observations have very limited value. I have seen many instances when a negative shift in the yield curve has caused long-term interest rates to rise sharply, causing steep price declines in long bonds. Much depends on how long the curve will be inverted and when short rates will reverse their upward path.

In the postwar period, policymakers managed on several occasions to bring about an inversion of the yield curve—with the yield on 3-month Treasury bills above the yield on long bonds. In the future, however, this will be much more difficult. The reason is the extraordinary expansion of fixed-income leveraging. Because of the proliferation of hedge funds, along with proprietary traders within banks and financial institutions who readily dump their long-term fixed-income holdings whenever they face or even anticipate rising short-term rates, long-term rates often rise as sharply as short-term rates. The old relationship between the two has become an anachronism of economic history.

The art of financial forecasting can be understood through such general principles—but only in part. As I have suggested, forecasting is a matter of applying general principles to unique historical circumstances. For this reason, I now explore several examples of how I formulated forecasts—with varying degrees of success—from the 1960s to the 1990s. In the next chapter, I chronicle forecasting in action.

9

Forecasting and
the Great Bull Market

*Within a half hour or so of the release of my memo,
one of our traders called to report that the fixed-
income markets were rallying. . . . [That] trading
day—Tuesday, August 17, 1982—ended in record
territory. . . . the largest single-day rise in its history.*

Three recent episodes in postwar finance illustrate many of the general principles of forecasting that I outlined in the previous chapter. In the first case, I review the events leading up to the cyclical peak in U.S. bond yields in 1974. In the second, I discuss the fall 1981 reversal in the secular rise in interest rates. Then I consider the unusual combination of elements that explains interest rate patterns in the 1990s.

Forecasters not only must read a complex constellation of economic variables to "get it right"; those who work at private investment houses (as I did) often face pressures to shade or even withhold certain kinds of forecasts, as I discuss at the end of this chapter. In fact, there is a general bias against bearish forecasts (for reasons that I explore in Chapter 15), as I discovered when I was labeled "Dr. Doom" throughout the 1970s and 1980s.

When Yields Peaked in 1974

When U.S. long-term interest rates hit a cyclical peak in October of 1974, the business cycle did not hit bottom at the same time. In fact, long-term U.S. Government yields reached their zenith some 9 months into a business recession—an extraordinary, perhaps even unprecedented, delay by historical standards. According to conventional economic wisdom, these two events—the interest rate peak and the business cycle peak—should coincide closely. But in that 9-month period, the yield on 3-month Treasury bills rose from 7.43 percent to 9.22 percent, while the yield on U.S. Governments climbed from 7.10 percent to 8.70 percent. I did not become bullish about the bond market until October 1974, however, when long Governments were yielding 8.37 percent and declining, an irregular fall that would extend well into 1975.

My position on the bond market—which stood out from the mainstream of expert opinion—rested on several considerations. First, there was the inflation picture. Although the economy was lagging, inflation (and thus nominal growth) remained high. In the 3 months prior to March 31, 1974, the nominal rate of GDP—which then consisted entirely of inflation—had climbed a striking 10.2 percent, the highest level in the postwar period. During prior postwar economic cycles, the growth of GDP (in current dollars) had been very modest.

Meanwhile, corporate borrowing was running high in early 1974. Nonfinancial corporations were spending heavily on capital investment, and their working capital needs were running high as well. Thus, there was heavy demand for external funding, and to meet that need, corporations were borrowing heavily in both the short and long markets, and their position was deteriorating.

There was, to be sure, ample debt available. For their part, the thrifts were constrained by interest rate ceilings—which they bumped up against regularly during those inflationary times—and their growth was limited by disintermediation. The story was quite different for the commercial banks, which did not face interest rate ceilings. Moving aggressively to increase their corporate lending, they issued a vast wave of new negotiable certificates of deposit.

Then there was the larger global economic picture, with its prominent new trouble spot, the Middle East. The OPEC oil embargo that followed the 1973 Yom Kippur War was an economic wild card, one that surely would have profound yet difficult-to-predict consequences for the U.S. economy in general and for interest rates in particular. According to many experts at the time, the energy crisis, for all its disadvantages, would have the salutary effect of easing pressure on interest rates (especially on long-term bonds). But I disagreed. In an early 1974 address at the New School for Social Research in New York, I summarized my case in this way:

> The impact of the energy shortage on the economy differs sharply in its initial stage from the economic impact of monetary restraint. The shortage of energy at first reduces the effective capacity to produce that in turn must force a reduction in demand that tends to resist the rationing through bidding up the price of scarce items. Effective monetary restraint reduces demand without significantly curtailing the supply of goods and thus reduces inflationary pressures. If the energy crisis should become increasingly severe, the pressure on interest rates would abate only after substantial demands have been reduced. ("Economic Disarray," January 26, 1974)

As the months passed and the recession deepened, I watched with alarm as the economy continued to worsen (by all the standard measures). As troubling as this was, however, I knew it couldn't last. But when would the economy turn the corner? And more specifically—my constituency wanted to know—when I would become bullish on the outlook for bonds?

The dilemma dragged on, and the question continued to nag at me. Even as late as mid-1974, I could not find enough encouragement in the markets or in conversations with business leaders, portfolio managers, and governmental officials to change my stance. What ultimately inspired me to change my position were the fall annual meetings of the International Monetary Fund and the World Bank in Washington. Listening to the presentations of key finance ministers at those meetings, and speaking informally with some of them, was quite eye opening for me. These economic leaders were exceedingly pessimistic, in a few cases even distraught, about immediate economic prospects.

And so immediately upon my return to New York, I met with my staff to reexamine all the data we had at hand. And then I turned bullish.

To convey my new posture to colleagues and clients, I wrote a two-page memorandum entitled "The Coming Rally in the Very High-Grade Taxable Bond Market." To my surprise, the memo provoked a significant reaction in the markets as soon as the media released it. Just prior to its release, the long government bond yielded 8.49 percent. When news of my bullish stance broke the following day, yields fell 33 basis points, and the Dow Jones Industrial Average rallied 23 points, or 3.9 percent.

Fortunately, I had made a timely call. Long Governments hit their cyclical peak (8.6 percent) in August 1974.

October 1981: The Secular Peak in Long-Term Rates

Among the many forecasts that I have made publicly, none attracted more attention than my announcement in August of 1982 that—after holding out for months—I was turning bullish. It was an extraordinary time in financial history. In the early 1980s, the United States endured one of its most severe economic recessions in decades. Even so, a great many economic forecasters failed to anticipate either the downturn or the recovery. The chief reason, it seems to me, is that their forecasts were based on formulaic econometric models or on overly simplistic methods.

In that instance, as in so many, long-term trends in interest rates provided valuable clues to the larger economic picture. It is now understood that postwar cyclical declines in interest rates have been short-lived, while cyclical *increases* have been both longer and of greater magnitude. Thus, by the mid-1970s, a secular rise in long-term interest rates had lifted high-grade bond yields from a low of 2.5 percent in 1945 to 7.25 percent as the cycle neared its peak.

Such secular movements—which investors who are not historically minded tend to ignore—typically last many years. From 1899 to 1920, for example, a long secular rise carried high-grade bond yields from 3.20 percent to 5.27 percent, while the secular fall that followed drove yields down to 2.45 percent in 1946 (see Exhibit 9-1). True, such long trends have been interrupted by periodic counterdirectional

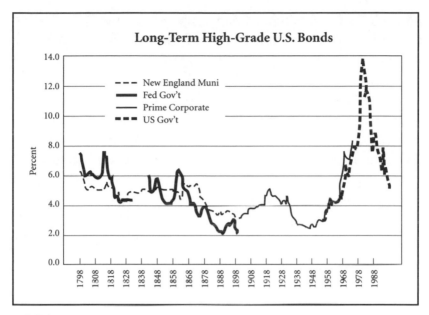

Exhibit 9-1

short-term moves. But the overall patterns are unmistakable, and investors who ignored them did so at their peril.

The same was true in the 1970s, when a great secular bear market was flourishing, and raising difficult analytical questions about when it might end. I expressed my concern about the uncertainties that lay ahead in testimony before the Joint Economic Committee of Congress in June 1978.

> I have concluded that our economy and financial markets are on a treacherous course. We are in the midst of a volatile economic recovery and a dangerously high rate of inflation. Unfortunately, there are no policies now in place that will readily curb the growing economic and financial excesses. Whatever direction policies will take from here on will be painful to some sectors and most likely for the economy as a whole.

In fact, several forces lay behind my increasingly bearish stance. Inflation, like interest rates, had moved from a cyclical to a long-term pattern. In examining the five cyclical lows and highs in the inflation rate in the post-World War II years, I found that the *lows* had moved progressively *higher*—from an actual contraction in the price level in the third quarter of 1949 to an increase of 4.7 percent in late 1976. At the same time, I discovered that the cyclical *peaks* of inflation had moved progressively *higher* as well (excluding the Korean War–inspired spike of 1951). Many analysts seemed to have been misled by the sharp increase in energy prices due to the Arab oil embargo of 1973–1974. Certainly, the embargo had had an inflationary effect; but I was convinced that the inflation problem was more broadly based, which in turn had serious implications for the financial markets. One way or the other, as a general principle, inflation enlarges the demand for credit.

There was a less apparent factor behind my bearishness as well. It had become increasingly clear to me that structural changes in the financial system were dulling the normally restraining effect of rising interest rates. The pressure that rising interest rates normally exerted on financial institutions had been eased by a series of recent changes, most notably by the government's liberalization of Regulation Q ceilings on time and savings deposits, by the spread of floating interest rates, and by growing access to foreign funds. With these kinds of changes, financial institutions no longer felt powerfully and immediately restrained by rising interest rates. By failing to consider these structural changes, many forecasters seriously misjudged interest rate prospects in the mid-1970s. And the trend was only beginning. In later years, the levels at which final demanders of credit—from corporations, to governments, to households—were actually restrained by higher interest rates were readjusted upward.

It was not just the increase in inflation that fueled the demand for credit in those days of the 1970s. Conservatism in borrowing by households and business had declined dramatically. Consumer and even mortgage funds were available, assuming the borrower was willing to pay the prevailing rate. Banks were eager to lend money, and were devoting considerable financial talent to the task, encouraged in part by the huge transfer of wealth brought on by the sharp rise in oil prices. In spite of the bankruptcy of the Penn Central and the travails at several other leading financial institutions, the short-term lending sector was going strong.

The quagmire in which fiscal and monetary policy was caught in the 1970s also troubled me. Despite the need to curb the federal budget in the face of high inflation and the high utilization of real resources, fiscal policy remained expansionary. When a new cyclical economic expansion began in late 1975, many experts claimed that the federal government's expansionary fiscal policy was being largely offset by state and local government surpluses. I didn't see it that way. Looking at the data for the first 3 years of that expansion, I found that the *combined* public-sector budget deficit for that period was much greater than in comparable periods of economic recovery. Clearly, government spending was still having a stimulating net effect.

There were problems on the monetary side throughout the 1970s as well. The Federal Reserve was achieving only limited success in its efforts to hold the growth of the money supply within official long-run targets. That was serious enough, but I saw an even bigger problem: the Fed's inability to curb the massive creation of debt. The Fed did not seem to appreciate some of the important dynamics at work in the 1970s' economy: the new inflationary psychology, the private sector's greater willingness to incur debt, and the impact of the structural changes in the financial markets on interest rates. All these trends, it seemed to me, suggested that the financial system was being liberalized from frictional impediments. With the weakening of such impediments, the Fed would be forced to boost interest rates higher than it would have when frictional forces acted as a restraining force on monetary creation. All this led me to conclude that interest rates had much higher to go before some demanders of credit would withdraw from the market. And even then, households and marginal business borrowers, rather than sounder businesses or the federal government, would be the first to retreat from the credit markets.

But how high would rates need to climb before this happened? How high was high? That was the vexing question for me. From their cyclical low of 7.6 percent at the close of 1976, long U.S. Governments had risen to 8 percent in 1978 and reached nearly 9 percent by the start of 1979. Meanwhile, short-term rates, as reflected by the yield on 3-month U.S. Treasury bills, climbed to 4.5 percent at the end of 1976,

6.04 percent in 1977, and 9.25 percent in 1978. Yet in spite of these large increases, I concluded that much higher interest rates were still to come. Inflation was still mounting, credit demands remained robust, and the dollar was weakening in many currency markets. Borrowers willing to pay the going rate—and there were many—got the money. The yield levels in several fixed-income markets were approaching new secular highs.

As we entered the fall of 1979, the drama in the markets intensified. Even though the pace of economic activity seemed to be slowing, the inflation rate was not. For its part, the Federal Reserve was struggling to slow the growth of the money supply. M2, for example, galloped ahead at an annual rate of 15 percent. Bank credit was growing even faster than it had the year before. Households and businesses were borrowing at near-record levels. And as pressure on the U.S. dollar intensified, foreign leaders began to openly criticize our failure to take corrective action.

The issue came to a head October 7, 1979, when Paul Volcker announced that the Federal Reserve was adopting a strict monetarist approach. Henceforth, he explained, the Fed would set a target for the growth of money, and let interest rates float as demanders for credit bid for the limited supply of funds. It was a bold move for Volcker, who inherited a very precarious economic and financial situation when he was appointed Fed Chairman a few months earlier. To be sure, a handful of economists had been urging the Fed to adopt this monetarist position, most notably Milton Friedman. But these were isolated voices. What Volcker did took extraordinary insight and courage. The new policy—designed to painfully wring inflation out of the economy—was hardly popular with the Carter Administration. Even within the Fed itself, there was resistance to the new monetarist strategy, because many regulators feared major disruptions in the financial markets.

On that score, they were right. Soon after the Fed launched the new policy, interest rates shot up. The 3-month Treasury bill rate, which stood at 7.98 percent in late September, climbed to 12.53 percent by the end of the year and hit 14.93 percent by March of 1980. But to the grave disappointment of the Fed, long-term interest rates continued to rise. Long Governments, which stood at 9.23 percent in late September, finished the year at 10.08 percent and reached 12.27 percent by the end of March 1980.

Nevertheless, in *Comments on Credit* I strongly endorsed the Fed's new strategy, which I deemed a landmark decision. It would take time, it seemed to me, for the new policy to have its desired effect; inflation had persisted for so long that inflationary expectations were deeply embedded in the financial markets and in the larger economy. But the Fed was clearly committed to reversing the nation's pernicious inflationary trend, and eventually investors and savers would change their behavior accordingly.

Still, until the Fed's new stance began to prove its worth (when the inflation rate plummeted from 14 percent in late 1979 to 9.7 percent in mid-1981), Volcker endured scathing criticism for the economic slump that accompanied the monetary tightening. On one occasion in 1980, I visited him in his Washington office, only to find the outer office filled with construction bricks. Naturally, I asked about them, for there didn't appear to be any renovations under way. I was told the Brick Layers Union had sent over the piles of bricks, along with a message that they were no longer needed—a pointed reminder that economic malaise can be very painful.

For taking a bold—even courageous—stance and sticking with it, Paul Volcker stands out as one of the great central bankers of the twentieth century. It is easy for a central banker to be popular during euphoric financial times. But the political perils are severe when tough measures are needed—measures that extract a high short-term toll in the interest of longer-term economic health—as they were in the late 1970s. That is why the Federal Reserve must remain free of political influence. But even that is not enough; strong leadership is needed as well.

In the first quarter of 1980, as credit markets continued to deteriorate and inflation rose to 14.6 percent, a frustrated Carter Administration put forward a new anti-inflation program. First, the administration promised to reduce the budget deficit in the next fiscal year. Second, it decided to restrain the growth of credit by limiting consumer credit and by increasing marginal reserve requirements on large short-dated negotiable certificates of deposits, on Eurodollar borrowings, and even on repurchase agreements against U.S. Governments, federal agencies, and Fed funds borrowed from nonmember institutions. Money market mutual funds were constrained as well; such funds were now required to maintain a 15 percent deposit with the Fed on their increase in assets.

It was an ambitious program, but one about which I had serious misgivings. For that reason, I declined a White House invitation to attend a public unveiling of the program. Unfortunately, as I had anticipated, the new program caused a short-lived recession in the second quarter of 1980. When the 3-month rate for U.S. Treasury bills reached 15.6 percent and the prime rate hit 15.27 percent, I issued a special memorandum in which I declared that the peak in short-term interest rates probably had been reached. But I was premature. Treasury bills actually peaked at 17.25 percent in 1981, and the prime rate rose to an astonishing 21.5 percent in 1981.

My record was stronger when it came to long-term yields and markets in 1981. With GNP estimated to rise 11 percent nominally—but only 1.5 percent when adjusted for inflation—and with the possibility of modest economic recovery, I anticipated that new net credit demands would be pushed to record levels. From my perspective, the Fed would have to cope with a quick resumption of borrowings, with large gains in bank credit and money supply, with large demands from the federal government, and with even greater borrowing demands from business corporations.

Long-term interest rates rose for most of the year, and in October the yield for long-term Governments hit an extraordinary 15.25 percent. For a while, as bond yields continued to hover around 15 percent (their October high), I became increasingly concerned about my forecast. By mid-1982, long Governments were hovering around 14 percent. It appeared as though we had already passed the secular peak in the bear market that began in 1946, when long Governments yielded 2.5 percent. That turned out to be the case.

As my wife and I vacationed in Europe during late July and early August, I couldn't help dwelling on the interest rate situation. My wife sensed that I was distracted, as I continually mulled over the reasons for my bearish interest rate outlook. There were indications that conditions might be changing, and I became more and more uneasy about my forecasts. This feeling continued after I returned to work in New York. So after catching up on some urgent business at Salomon, I called together my associates to review the data on the current interest rate situation.

After doing so, I concluded that a significant interest rate decline lay ahead. What had changed? To begin with, the economy was stalling, which was likely to moderate inflation. Second, financial blockages and intense international competition were straitjacketing the economy. Businesses were coming under intense pressure to refurbish their balance sheets. At the same time, financial institutions no longer were enjoying conditions favorable to aggressive lending and investing. Another factor that was restricting lending—domestically and internationally—was the huge burden of international debt.

With all this in mind, I decided to become bullish. Over the weekend, I began to compose a memorandum for clients, which I finished Monday evening. Salomon's Executive Committee was scheduled to meet the next day at the Waldorf Hotel. As my driver dropped me off at the hotel for the meeting, I handed him my hand-written memo and told him to deliver it to my secretary, Helen Katcher. During the meeting, I left to take a call from Helen, who read to me the final draft of the typed memo. The text was fine, so I told her to release it to our salespeople and traders, as well as to the press (see Exhibit 9-2). When I returned to the meeting, a few of my partners seemed a bit annoyed by the interruption. John Gutfreund asked, "What was that all about?" I told him about my now public declaration that a significant interest rate decline was ahead. My colleagues seemed stunned at the revelation.

As it turned out, so were the financial markets. Within a half hour or so of the release of my memo, one of our traders called to report that the fixed-income markets were rallying in advance of the stock market's opening bell that morning. By 10 a.m., both the bond and the stock markets were swept up in a massive rally. With the growing excitement and confusion, John terminated our meeting at the Waldorf, and we all rushed back to the office. Trading volumes were enormous, and the atmosphere on our trading floor was charged with energy.

Bond Market Research

Memorandum to
Portfolio Managers

Salomon Brothers Inc

One New York Plaza
New York, NY 10004
(212) 747-7000

August 17, 1982

Henry Kaufman

The Prospects for Interest Rates

Recent events in the economy and financial markets necessitate a fresh look at the prospects for U.S. interest rates. These events suggest that the present decline in interest rates will continue, although irregularly, with perhaps some dramatic interruptions. The decline in interest rates, and the length of time such a decline will take, will largely be determined by both the extent to which the U.S. credit structure has been impaired and the level of interest rates that will rejuvenate sustained economic activity. In this context, conventional cyclical benchmarks are no guide. On balance, some interest rate benchmarks for the next 12 months are as follows: long-term U.S. Government bonds now yielding 12¾% will fall into the 9%-10% range; the Federal funds rate now at 10% will decline to a low of 6%-7%.

A smart recovery in economic activity in the second half of this year is not likely to materialize. This removes the immediate threat to long-term interest rates. Consumer spending, although holding at a high plateau, has failed to respond to tax initiatives, while the rest of the economy is straitjacketed by financial blockages and fierce international competition. Generally, poor economic prospects also make businessmen less confident that the economy will be able to support substantially higher prices. Thus, inflation expectations will erode gradually. Significant economic expansion will require further declines in interest rates and considerable time to unwind the major financial impediments.

The refurbishing of business balance sheets and the rekindling of profitability are now overriding priorities of corporate management. These priorities cannot be quickly set aside. The corporate financial structure has become extremely fragile: corporate debt is top-heavy, resulting in widespread credit quality deterioration; and corporate profits have been waning since 1979. This shift in priorities has resulted in efforts to reduce inventories and, more recently, to cut back capital outlays. These measures will contribute not only to a stagnant economy, but also to a sharp contraction in business external financing. In the past, reduced business borrowing has been an important contributing factor to the fall in long-term interest rates.

Major financial institutions are not in any position to implement aggressive lending and investing strategies. A fall in interest rates will encourage thrift institutions to improve their liquidity and to minimize the risks in their long-term assets. Therefore, no new boom in housing activity is likely. Also, commercial banks are hamstrung by a thin capital base as well as by substantial non-earning assets, which may actually increase if the economy does not rebound rapidly. Even insurance companies are forced to cope with unprecedented cash flow and profitability problems.

The massive international debt overhang restricts the stimulative capacity of both domestic and international financial institutions. Stagnation here and abroad is self-reinforcing. The strength of the dollar, despite falling U.S. interest rates, will probably mean that American goods and services will become less competitive in international markets, and this, in turn, will cause more credit problems.

Exhibit 9-2

Interruptions in the decline in interest rates in the months ahead will depend upon a number of critical considerations. First, there is the extent to which monetary policy reverts to the enforcement of monetarism. It will be difficult for the Fed to discern whether spurts in the money supply are due to technical factors or to new underlying demands from a growing economy. A prompt response by the Fed will temporarily push the funds rate up, stalling the funding of liabilities and the general reliquefication needed to bring the economy out of the doldrums. A significant lift in short rates will interrupt the rally in long bonds, causing a narrowing in the sharply sloped positive yield curve. However, this interruption is likely to be temporary because the reliquefication needs of the economy will also be stymied.

Second, the huge budget deficit is another factor that will periodically interrupt the bond rally. Signs of business recovery and large new U.S. Treasury issues will induce investor cautiousness because they will bring about fears of crowding out. Large Treasury deficits will also limit the ability of the Fed to follow a consistently easier policy. For the foreseeable future, there will be a massive supply of high-quality U.S. Government securities.

* * * * *

Exhibit 9-2 (*Continued*)

The trading day—Tuesday, August 17, 1982—ended in record territory. The Dow Jones Industrial Average gained 38.81 points (4.9 percent), the largest single-day rise in its history (see Exhibits 9-3 and 9-4). With a near-record 92.86 million shares changing hands, ten stocks closed higher for every one that closed posting a loss. In the bond markets, the bulls ran wild as well. Long-term Treasury bond prices jumped $40 (per $1,000 of face value), and most short-term interest rates tumbled by more than half a point.

The business press worldwide attributed the rally to my interest rate forecast. Even though, as the *Washington Post* reported, White

"Well, my adviser is H. Kaufman, and when H. Kaufman talks, everybody STAMPEDES!"

Exhibit 9-3

Permission of Paul Rigby. THE NEW YORK POST, August 19, 1982.

House spokesman Larry Speakes "suggested that the president's address to the nation Monday night may have had some impact on investors," the newspaper concluded that the bull market was driven by "an optimistic forecast by Wall Street Analyst Henry Kaufman." Other papers agreed, including the London *Financial Times,* which blared the headline: "Wall St surge as Kaufman predicts interest rate fall."

I was as surprised as others by the market response to my forecast. After all, we had passed the secular peak months earlier—although, to be sure, yield levels had not declined much since their October peak. And on other occasions I had made what I thought were more prescient and insightful remarks about aspects of the economy and financial markets. But, obviously, the conditions were ripe for a major reaction. In all likelihood, my forecast of falling rates catalyzed a widespread but still tentative belief that the great secular bear market of the post-World War II period had truly turned the corner.

The Brave New World of Interest Rates in the 1990s

In the early 1990s, the U.S. economy hit a peak and then began to descend into recession. But this cyclical downturn differed from earlier down cycles in several important ways. Many of the nation's deposit institutions—banks and thrifts alike—were wounded, some of them

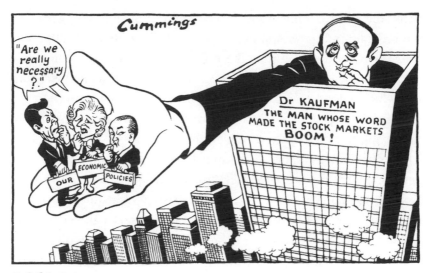

Exhibit 9.4

© EXPRESS NEWSPAPERS LONDON 0171-922-7902. Permission granted.

fatally. They had sustained heavy loan losses with inadequate loss reserves, which left their capital reserves seriously depleted. Bank stock prices plummeted sharply, with the share prices of some of the nation's largest institutions falling below $10. The already high rate of failure would have been even higher had regulators strictly enforced their requirements.

Many business corporations were overly leveraged as well. Much of this was a consequence of the junk bond market that had so entranced investors in the 1980s. Heavy leveraging constricted the operating flexibility of many business corporations, whose managers became caught up in a continual struggle to refurbish their firms' balance sheets, often to the detriment of other aspects of the business. Not surprisingly, credit quality yield spreads in the corporate bond market were extraordinarily wide. This was especially glaring for issues that involved the most prominent banks. For example, Chemical Bank had bonds outstanding that yielded 400 to 600 basis points more than comparably maturing U.S. Governments, and had equity market values at a large discount from their book values.

These were not the only interest rate features that were impeding economic recovery. Struggling to bolster their thin capital positions, banks did not lower the prime loan rate in proportion to the easing of the Federal funds rate. And in spite of the Federal Reserve's efforts to spur the economy by cutting the Fed funds rate 130 basis points (1.3 percent) in 1989, the yield curve in the early 1990s remained virtually flat, which did not offer lenders strong incentives to lend. (In contrast, a positively sloped yield curve—in which short-term rates are lower than long-term rates—encourages the creation of credit because lenders can borrow short-term funds below the cost of intermediate and long-term funds.) Given all this, I concluded that the Federal Reserve would have to lower interest rates sharply and quickly in order to achieve a more positive yield curve. Otherwise, small Fed actions would rapidly be arbitraged out through the many new credit instruments used by market participants. And while some thought that the emergence of a positively sloped curve might suggest a rekindling of inflationary expectations, I disagreed. Without decisive action, too many handicapped debtors and ailing institutions would be denied access to the financial markets for too long, with damaging consequences for the economy.

More than this, the federal budget—which had been highly stimulative for much of the 1980s—was losing its economic impact. But its financial legacy remained. Whereas the federal budget deficit had averaged $26.5 billion dollars per year (or 2.2 percent of GDP) in the 1970s, in the 1980s it climbed to $156.6 billion (3.9 percent of GDP). In view of this massive deficit explosion, it seemed very unlikely to me that policymakers would endorse another burst of deficit spending. Given that, the burden of economic recovery would fall squarely on a more accommodating monetary policy.

I also noticed that one key component of federal outlays, defense expenditures, was beginning to slow, forcing many defense contractors to scramble into other activities. On top of all that, international interest rates were too high to suggest a global economic resurgence anytime soon. As the 1990s began, short- and long-term interest rates in Canada, the United Kingdom, France, and Japan were well below the prevailing U.S. rates—short rates in Japan stood at 6.8 percent, 10-year Governments at 5.7 percent—while German interest rates were slightly lower than their American counterparts.

Meanwhile, I remained convinced that the economy could not be quick-started and that any economic recovery would be tepid, at least initially. The impediments—weak deposit institutions, an overleveraged business sector, and intense international competition—were overpowering. With fiscal policy crippled by staggering debt, the nation now depended on an easier monetary policy. When the Fed finally stepped up monetary accommodation in 1993, interest rates fell sharply; the yield on long U.S. Governments dropped to 5.97 percent by October, down from 8.76 percent at the start of the business recovery. But the bond market was far from stabilized. Long bond yields rose again to a high of 8.08 percent in November 1994, fell to 4.68 percent in the fall of 1998, then climbed again to just above 6 percent by the summer of 1999. These ups and downs reflected, among other things, overshoots in expectations, the increasing market participation of highly leveraged investors with short time horizons, and the uncertainties of financial crises such as the Russian bond default and the travails at Long Term Capital Management. All caused investors to prefer liquidity.

Amid the 1990s' interest rate gyrations, one feature stands out. In the long economic expansion that followed—the longest in the postwar period—interest rates fell significantly from their levels at the beginning of the recovery. This unusual pattern was largely a result of the fact that inflation has been held in check, in spite of the fact that unemployment rates have fallen in recent years to levels that ordinarily would re-ignite inflation. In that first leg of the 1990s expansion, the fixed-income markets benefited enormously from blockages that required business and financial institutions to restructure, improve operating efficiency, and strengthen balance sheets.

American financial markets also benefited in the 1990s from the sluggish pace of economic activity in Europe and from the long and deep business recession in Japan. That environment, by making it difficult for American firms to raise prices, helped contain inflation. It also attracted a large volume of foreign funds to the United States, which helped compensate for the low volume of households' savings. Foreign competition simply would not allow price increases to stick. And inflation was further held in check by the much-talked-about strides in American technology, from advanced computer networks, to miniaturization, to more efficient inventory management techniques.

Another special feature of the U.S. economy in the late 1990s has been the reduction of the federal budget deficit, followed by large budget surpluses. These dramatic fiscal achievements have fundamentally altered the pattern of credit flows since the start of the decade. As the growth of federal debt slowed and then contracted in the 1990s, both business and household debt at first slowed as well, but in recent years have risen sharply. Part of the heavy business borrowing has gone toward stock repurchasing, while household borrowing has been used to buy stocks and bonds alike. But if the federal government were to begin racking up large deficits again, the financial assets in which so many are now heavily invested would likely lose much of their value.

Such are the linkages between fiscal and monetary forces, between public and private investment, and between domestic and international conditions—linkages that make economic forecasting at once a fascinating and complex task.

The Challenge of Preserving Objectivity

These episodes in my career as a financial forecaster highlight some of the difficulties in making judgments about the future, even in the economic and financial arena, with its patina of quantitative precision. For even there, projections rest on imperfect information.

But an even greater challenge for the financial forecaster is the problem of preserving objectivity. My experience as both a forecaster and a manager of hundreds of economists and stock and bond analysts has taught me that many pressures—from many different directions—work to undermine the objectivity of the financial forecaster.

The act of going on the record with a forecast is itself intensely political. Before a prediction is tested, it is subject to debate. And even if it proves to be correct, the forecaster can be subjected to continuing criticism and even ridicule. For that reason, many forecasters play it safe by sticking with the consensus view. By echoing the prevailing opinions of their professional colleagues and peers, they minimize the chances of drawing fire. But this is not what forecasting should be about.

Another tendency in forecasting is to stay on a trend line. This generally works out to be a safe course because business and finance trends rarely change direction very radically. But the real value in forecasting lies precisely in predicting those discontinuities, however difficult and risky that may be. I have always believed that fundamental or structural changes can only be anticipated by examining a wide range of trends and forces, a methodology that does not lend itself to quantification. Furthermore, this kind of work can be extremely useful and gratifying.

In one instance, for example, I concluded that as the regulations governing how deposit institutions could bid for liabilities were liberalized, competition for funds would intensify during periods of monetary restraint, which in turn would drive interest rates higher than expected. In this case, regulatory change had a direct impact on interest rate behavior. Then there was the time when—observing the rapid growth of proprietary trading at traditional financial institutions, along with the advent of hedge funds—I predicted increased volatility in financial asset values. In that instance, I had to look at shifts within Wall Street firms for clues about macro phenomenon.

Even if done well, financial forecasting can lose its potency if presented poorly. Too many analysts and economists, including some whom I have supervised, bury their conclusions in long reports laden with historical data. I have always advocated putting major conclusions right up front, and presenting statistical information in ways that enable the reader to draw conclusions easily. But the financial markets are still awash in a flood of raw statistics on firms and the economy. This overabundance of data seems designed to impress clients with the comprehensiveness of the research rather than to serve any practical purpose. Now that computers are universally available for data retrieval, analysts should—as their name suggests—*analyze* rather than simply disgorge data.

But the greatest challenge facing analysts and economists who work for sell-side institutions (such as securities firms and banks) is maintaining objectivity. And it is now an open secret that many fail to meet the challenge. On the one hand, forecasters must spend considerable time conducting research and enlarging knowledge. On the other hand, they are continually queried by investors and corporate finance clients. A good sales staff—as it tries to squeeze every bit of knowledge out of an analyst—will urge him or her to meet often and for long hours with the firm's key clients. Sometimes, the researcher is pushed beyond his or her analytical abilities. It is therefore important that the analyst or the head of research place limits on such demands.

A researcher's objectivity is threatened more seriously when the analyst is called upon to help consummate a trade, or underwrite a new offering, or solicit a new investment banking client. Regrettably, this problem is hardly new. I have commented on this problem for some time. The Mexican financial crisis of 1994 is a vivid example. I noted in a *Wall Street Journal* article that apart from a few academics, none of the key participants in the global financial structure, especially those in the U.S., spoke of potential problems in Mexico. This is astonishing, considering the number of banks, securities firms, and mutual funds involved—each staffed with a small army of economists, analysts, and corporate finance specialists whose job it was to evaluate the Mexican situation.

It seemed to me that the source of this enormous failure was twofold. First, it showed the bias of many financial institutions to favor near-term over long-term profit opportunities, and to utilize their researchers in this pursuit. Second, it demonstrated that structural changes in financial markets were encouraging investors—not all of them sophisticated—to take on greater and greater risk. Enticed by the lure of high profit margins, many financial institutions geared up their operations to funnel vast sums of capital into Mexico and other developing countries. Few analysts warned about the potential volatility in their emerging market portfolios if liquidity problems were to develop. It was an investment environment that compromised the objectivity of a great many analysts and economists, who were drawn into their employers' broader marketing, underwriting, and distribution efforts. Even those with the best intentions were caught up in the excitement of closing a large deal or distributing a large block of securities.

For their part, the governments of the major industrial countries and the key multilateral financial institutions—the International Monetary Fund and World Bank—were conspicuously silent. They failed to caution either the Mexicans or the investor community about possible financial problems. If they had any reservations about Mexico's monetary, fiscal, or foreign exchange rate policy in 1993 and 1994, they certainly did not voice them in public. None of the leading officials made even a mild statement suggesting that investors think twice about investing in Mexico.

In a remarkable address to the Economic Club of New York in October 1999, Arthur Levitt, Chairman of the Securities and Exchange Commission, put this problem on the line—the first time a leading government official was so forthright about the matter:

> Our review of the relationship between companies and the analysts who follow them indicates that analysts, all too often, are falling off that tightrope on the side of protecting the business relationship. Analysts are a fixture on business pitches and investor road shows—doing their bit to market their own firm's underwriting talents and to sell a company's prospects.
>
> What's more, analysts' compensation is increasingly based on the profitability of their firm's corporate finance division, and their contribution to the deals to which they are assigned. In many respects, analysts' employers expect them to act more like promoters and marketers than unbiased and dispassionate analysts.
>
> An all-too-candid memo from a leading Wall Street firm's corporate finance department couldn't have framed the conflict more plainly: "We do not make negative or controversial comments about our clients as a matter of sound business practice . . . the philosophy and practical result needs to be 'no negative comments about our clients.' "

While I was at Salomon, analysts and forecasters did not need to compromise the objectivity of their research. My own experience at Salomon Brothers suggests some of the ways that financial research can be kept independent from the often-corrupting commercial pressures of the firm.

This was not a concern when I first joined Salomon. Our research group had to prove its value to the firm before the dealers and salespeople would take much of an interest. Nor did we feel pressure to conform to the consensus view on Wall Street, for the simple reason that there *was* no identifiable consensus view in financial forecasting during the early 1960s. Only a handful of Wall Streeters made forecasts, and the annual projections that came out of the government's Council of Economic Advisers were viewed with some skepticism.

Within a decade, however, our department had gained considerable stature. The key to our independence then became my appointment to the firm's Executive Committee in 1972. There, I was able to confront directly the occasional attempts to compromise the objectivity of a researcher. Usually, I headed off such problems before they ever reached the researcher. In 1984, for instance, Tom Hanley, our highly regarded stock analyst, was quoted on the front page of the *New York Times* reacting very negatively to the news that John Reed had become Chief Executive of Citicorp. "The horse race is over," Tom had said. "I can't believe it. I'm shaking. I'm in shock" (*New York Times,* June 20, 1984).

The day Tom's impolitic statement appeared in print, Salomon's Executive Committee convened. All agreed that Salomon needed to maintain a strong relationship with the powerful bank, and a few hinted that Tom should be fired. As Tom's supervisor, I told the Committee that I was not going to fire him because he was entitled to his own opinion, though I promised to speak with him about his choice of words. If Salomon fired Tom, I argued, the reputation of research at Salomon—and perhaps of the firm itself—would be seriously compromised. In another instance, Jules Maldutis, our airline analyst, wrote a negative report on Boeing. Our investment bankers were dismayed because they were not told about the report before it was released, and—more to the point—they preferred to have no such report in the first place. I explained that negative reports were as instructive as positive ones, but promised that in such cases our department would notify the corporate finance specialist covering the account before we mailed the report.

In my own forecasting, I followed a very specific routine. I always expressed my views on directional changes in writing. They might appear in the weekly *Comments on Credit,* or in a special memorandum to portfolio managers, or perhaps in the text of a speech. No advance copies were given to sales and trading personnel. Not surprisingly, this procedure did not sit well with everyone at Salomon. Occasionally, Salomon traders would phone me to complain that my comments had contributed to their losses (when they were either short or long on the wrong side of my forecast). But no senior partner at the firm ever put such a complaint to me.

In later years, however, I detected some subtle shifts in the attitude of certain senior partners toward research. Some questioned the extent to which research contributed to the profits of the firm. To this kind of comment I would respond rather jokingly that research accounted for about one-third of total profits. The typical rejoinder to this claim was, "Prove it," to which I would respond, "Disprove it." Some wished to internalize more of our research to strengthen proprietary trading and investment activities. In the years before I left, it was also suggested (not by John Gutfreund directly but with his approval) that someone else take responsibility for the daily administration of the research department. Sensing that this was an effort to loosen the controls over research in order to bring research closer to the sell-side effort, I stonewalled such efforts.

Nevertheless, a larger force was at work: the increasing impersonal relationship between investment bankers and their clients. Close relationships were being pushed aside by the increased volume of transactions in the open market, and by the profit that could be captured by trading, underwriting, and merger activity.

The well-publicized events at Salomon since my departure in 1989 have only reconfirmed my conviction that the best safeguard for research objectivity is strong leadership. To be strong, the head of research must serve at the highest managerial levels in the firm. More than that, top management must give its outspoken support to honest and objective research, even if that puts near-term profit opportunities at risk. Otherwise, researchers lose their credibility, and thus their value to their firm and to its clients.

The Origins of Dr. Gloom (a.k.a. Dr. Doom)

As my analyses gained widespread media attention in the late 1970s and 1980s, some members of the media began to refer to me as "Doctor Doom" or "Doctor Gloom" (see Exhibits 9-5 and 9-6). Around the same time, Albert Wojnilower—First Boston Corporation's highly regarded and influential chief economist—unwittingly earned the moniker "Doctor Death." Al has been a friend of mine for many years. We share a common heritage: Whereas my family had fled Nazi Germany, Al's escaped from Austria. Our careers intertwined when we put in overlapping stints at the New York Federal Reserve, he as chief of one of its divisions, and I as an assistant chief. A year or so after I joined Salomon Brothers in 1962, Al joined the First National City Bank (now Citicorp). Later, at First Boston Corporation, he too was quoted regularly in the business press. Al has tended to emphasize macroeconomic

"His name is Henry Kaufman and God knows he's gloomy, but he's not the gloomy Henry Kaufman."

Exhibit 9-5

"ISN'T HE A LITTLE YOUNG TO BE QUOTING ADAM SMITH AND HENRY KAUFMAN ? "

Exhibit 9-6

Reprinted from *Harvard Business Review* (Nov./Dec. 1987) by permission of D. Reilly.

factors, whereas I assigned greater importance to credit market developments and (during the 1980s) to the federal budget deficit. Still, we often came to similar conclusions, even if we arrived at them from different directions. Al is an insightful economist, and his speeches are models of clarity.

Al and I have kept in touch over the years, thanks in part to a regular luncheon he organized called "the Foursome." We would gather every other month or so to talk informally about economic and financial developments. There was never an agenda, and the conversation would range across a broad array of topics. Along with Al and me, a third original member still attends the luncheons: Leonard Santow (now a partner at Griggs & Santow), whose nitty-gritty knowledge of the Fed and U.S. Treasury has impressed me for decades. The fourth original member was Paul Volcker. When Paul left for the U.S. Treasury, his position was filled by Jack Noyes, then head of research at J.P. Morgan and previously head of research at the Fed's Board of Governors. After Jack retired, he was followed by Charles Sanford, head of Bankers Trust Company, and Rimmer deVries, the head of international research at J.P. Morgan. The Foursome has always held a special place in my professional life, a place where the free exchange of ideas supersedes politics and personalities.

I was dubbed Dr. Doom and Dr. Gloom because I often expressed concern about financial excesses that periodically swept through the financial community, and about the failure of regulators to take steps to prevent such excesses from recurring. For reasons I discuss in Chapter 15, most analysts are reluctant to acknowledge bad news or issue warnings about the future. But I have always thought that truth and accuracy are preferable to political expediency and wishful thinking. For that reason, I am often a lone bearish voice in a choir of stock market or interest rate bulls.

The troubling developments that I warned about—in *Comments on Credit* and in special memoranda—have included the dangerous rise in the rate of inflation in the 1970s, the excessive zeal of financial institutions and their often excessive pursuit of entrepreneurial finance, the overleveraging by business corporations, and the periodic ineptness of official policies. Rising inflation always has been a red flag to me. This concern dates back to my formative years when I listened to my grandfather describe how inflation ravaged Germany, and it has been reinforced by years of reading in financial history, with its many examples of societies being torn apart by the debasement of their currencies.

10

The Fed's Rise to Dominance

*I can never forget the powerful lesson from child-
hood about how the debasement of money and the
credit structure can wreak havoc on the social and
economic structure . . . money matters, but credit
matters more.*

Today, central banking enjoys a level of notoriety that is un-
matched in modern times. Whereas monetary policy, like economics itself, has long been considered a "dismal science" (to borrow a
phrase from John Maynard Keynes), Fed watching has become a popular spectator sport among not only market professionals but also a
large segment of the general public, which is fed a steady diet of up-to-
the-minute news about the central bank's moves. Recent Chairmen of
the Federal Reserve have commanded a level of celebrity normally
reserved for Presidents, sports superheroes, and rock stars. According
to public opinion polls, the current Fed Chairman is widely regarded
as the second most powerful individual in the country behind the
President, and thus more powerful than any member of Congress or
the U.S. Treasury Secretary. Indeed, in a 1996 survey, 41 percent of the
204 top CEOs polled by *Fortune* magazine considered Fed Chairman
Alan Greenspan as important as or *more* important than President
Clinton.

This was not always so. In fact, the prominence of monetary policy
is a fairly recent feature of postwar economic life. When I worked at
the Federal Reserve Bank of New York in the late 1950s, Bill Martin,
then Chairman of the Fed Board, was well respected by the immediate
Wall Street community but was hardly a household name like Alan

Greenspan is today. Whereas Martin toiled away in near obscurity as far as the public was concerned, Greenspan regularly makes headlines. His appearances before Senate and House committees draw near-perfect attendance, and his official utterances are broadcast to financial markets worldwide, where they often cause dramatic bullish or bearish reactions. According to the authors of a recent book about this phenomenon, "Greenspan's words and actions fill the daily financial news. He speaks and markets move. The thickness of his briefcase on a given day is taken as a sign of Important Things. He dodges knots of reporters and outthrust microphones like the hottest of rock stars. By any rational measure, the Greenspan phenomenon has spun slightly out of control" (Sicilia and Cruikshank, 2000, p. 14).

The Fed's path to prominence has been a winding one beset with potholes and even an occasional roadblock. At the end of World War II, the Federal Reserve faced the daunting task of reestablishing its effectiveness as a central bank. It has navigated shifting economic policy waters dominated at various times by fiscally oriented Keynesians or money supply–oriented monetarists. It has struggled to define and redefine key policy trigger thresholds such as inflation, unemployment, and monetary aggregates. And the postwar Fed has faced a variety of financial crises, some of an unprecedented nature. In spite of its stolid exterior—the Federal Reserve has long occupied an imposing, block-long, neoclassical edifice along downtown Washington's Constitution Avenue—the institution has evolved rapidly in recent decades. The many twists and turns in the Fed's postwar journey are keys to understanding the institution's role and influence in present-day economics, business, and finance.

Reestablishing Authority and Focus

The Federal Reserve emerged from the Second World War enmeshed in a web of constraints and obligations, and took years to reestablish its independent authority and clarify its postwar mission.

During the war, not surprisingly, monetary policy was completely subordinated to the economic demands of the war effort. To pay for the war, the federal government—as it had during previous wars—relied on a combination of taxation, borrowing, printing money, and confiscation of resources. The Roosevelt Administration boosted taxes until they supplied some 40 percent of federal revenues (versus 33 percent in World War I), but also borrowed aggressively through a series of bond drives. These drives created $157 billion in new debt, mostly through bond sales to nonbank investors. One major reason that the bond drives were so successful was that the Federal Reserve and the Treasury Department cooperated to hold 3-month T-bills and bond yields at fixed levels (⅜ percent and 2½ percent, respectively). To support those yields, the Fed made large-scale purchases of the government securities at those levels.

After the war ended, however, the Federal Reserve—then headed by Marriner Eccles—tried to break free of its obligation to support bond prices, while the U.S. Treasury (Under Secretary John Snyder) insisted that the practice continue. The result was a series of fierce, headline-making clashes between the two institutions. When Eccles's term expired, President Truman did not reappoint him; yet Eccles remained on the Fed Board. That kind of lame-duck persistence is difficult to imagine in today's environment.

Finally, in 1951, the Fed was released from its obligation to support bond prices, and promptly defined a modest role for itself. Its open market operations were confined to U.S. Treasury bills, based on the theory that the short-dated nature of bills would encourage market participants to express their own maturity preferences when the Fed supplied new funds or drained them from the banking system. This approach reflected the Fed's strong desire to operate behind the scenes. But it came to an end in 1961, when the Federal Reserve announced that its Open Market Account would purchase government notes and bonds of varying maturities in the open market, even those beyond 5 years.

That action reflected the Fed's twofold desire to support relatively low long-term interest rates in order to encourage the domestic economy, while keeping short-term interest rates high to retard the outflow of funds to foreigners. The shift went largely unnoticed by the public, but it certainly caught the attention of economists and professional investors. Indeed, an essential part of my early job as a Fed watcher was to forecast when the Federal Reserve might supply reserves outright through the purchase of Treasury bills or coupon issues. Today's Fed watchers try to answer the same question.

In that early post-World War II period, the Fed's policies were shaped by the economic travails of the preceding decades: overspeculation in the 1920s and the Depression in the 1930s. Ordinary citizens and some policymakers believed that the Fed, in the first instance, had failed to burst the speculative bubble, and in the second, did not do enough to end the Depression (or, according to another popular view, had actually exacerbated the economic calamity).

In any case, in the postwar period the Federal Reserve was still adjusting to the new regulatory regime that had been put in place during the 1930s. From the separation of commercial and investment banking to the creation of the Securities and Exchange Commission, the 1930s were a turning point in financial history. For a time, the new regulations—many of which segmented markets and restricted the lending and investment activities of banks—made it easier for the Fed to work unobtrusively yet effectively.

Therefore, when the Federal Reserve again became active as the central bank, it had to reconsider its mission and strategy. This was not as easy as it might seem at first glance. The Employment Act of 1946 had committed economic policymakers "to promote maximum employment, production and purchasing power," but made no explicit mention of the Fed. The Humphrey Hawkins Act of 1978 was clearer about the Fed's role, or rather dual role: to help achieve full employment as well as price stability.

But these twin goals often are at odds with each other when it comes to specific policy actions, and in pursuing them the Fed frequently has been forced to make critical compromises—and political enemies. Quite a few politicians and economists have emphasized the full-employment goal. Some within the Fed have agreed with that central goal, but for the most part the Fed has focused on managing money and credit to encourage growth with price stability.

Interestingly, the two most powerful central banks in the years since World War II—the Federal Reserve and the German Bundesbank—have evolved out of two very different crucibles. Whereas the U.S. central bank was restructured and redefined during a period of deflation and high unemployment, Germany's central bank was shaped by that country's hyperinflation in the 1920s. A central bank historian has noted, "the [German] bank's abiding nightmare—exaggerated as it might often seem—remains the hyperinflation of 1923. 'Never again!' is the Bundesbank's rallying cry. It knows that one sure way to lose its reputation is to err on the side of pecuniary laxity" (Marsh, 1992, p. 12).

The Federal Reserve's postwar readjustment included the slowly dawning realization that there need not be a trade-off between inflation and unemployment. At least two developments brought about this change. One was simply the passage of many Depression-free years. After the war, many policymakers (like the majority of Americans) assumed that another major economic slump would come as America returned to a peacetime footing. But by the late 1950s it was clear that the opposite had happened. Second, the anti-inflation attitude of central bankers was strengthened over time as they came to fully appreciate the distorting effects of rising prices on economic and financial behavior.

The 1970s carried important lessons for central bankers as well. While the U.S. Fed was trying to expand demand and money to avoid economic recession, Germany and Japan—whose central banks pursued a more conservative monetary policy—turned in far better economic records. The lesson seemed clear: Central banks should have a greater degree of independence. Accordingly, the central banks in America, England, and Japan were granted more independence. And later, when the European Monetary Union was formed, it featured an independent European Central Bank.

On Keynesianism and Monetarism

The proper role of the Federal Reserve was an issue debated fiercely by proponents of the two leading schools of economic thought in the postwar period: monetarists and Keynesians (the latter named for

British economist John Maynard Keynes). The central tenet of monetarism is that inflation is caused by an overabundance of money, and
that control of the money supply rests with the Federal Reserve. The
matter is not that simple, although a large number of less orthodox
monetarist economists believe that inflation cannot endure over a long
period of time (with "long" seldom defined) without a rapidly growing
money supply. Keynesians, on the other hand, argue that inflation
often is caused by nonmonetary developments such as wage increases
and high import prices. They advocate a flexible approach to fiscal
measures such as taxation and government spending to achieve sustainable economic growth. They believe, in other words, that demand
for goods and services can be managed through flexible fiscal policies.

Keynes's theories actually had both fiscal and monetary components. Although he had a great deal to say about monetary policy, he
became best known for his theory of fiscal intervention during periods
of depression. During a major economic slump, he said, the quantity
of money in circulation was no longer very important; the self-
correcting dynamic of the business cycle would break down. For
example, consumers would become so fearful about their future
income that they would refrain from spending even as prices fell. The
only way to break the stalemate and revive the economy, Keynes said,
was for the government to spend, even if that created budget deficits.

For their part, monetarists have argued that the Great Depression
would have been mitigated if the Fed acted more vigorously to increase
the money supply. More generally, monetarists postulate that good
growth is not a trade-off between inflation and unemployment; rather,
low inflation fosters low unemployment. This view prevails today.
After a half century of dominance, the Keynesian view—at least on this
critical question—gave way to the monetarist view beginning in the
late 1970s.

Keynes's most influential work was *The General Theory of Employment, Interest, and Money,* which appeared in the depths of the Great
Depression (1936), but did not gain a following until after World War
II—itself a massive Keynesian experiment that seemed to prove the
economic virtues of heavy government spending. In the 1950s and
1960s, many policymakers advocated an oversimplified form of Keynes-

ianism, which attributed the economic health of the nation almost solely to fiscal measures. In that view, the government did not need to concern itself with long-term monetary trends because it could spend itself out of any jam. Keynes wielded enormous influence for decades, not only through his voluminous writings, but also through his activism in government circles. He represented the British Treasury during the Paris Peace Conference following World War I, and played a major role in the establishment of the International Monetary Fund and the World Bank.

Whereas Keynes became (somewhat unwittingly) the father of fiscal activism in the postwar period, Milton Friedman was the most influential monetarist. Friedman gained influence as the key synthesizer of monetarism in the post-World War II period. Like Keynes, he first gained prominence by publishing an important book, in his case *A Monetary History of the United States, 1867–1960*, which he coauthored with Anna Schwartz in 1963. Unlike Keynes, Friedman has remained on his academic perch, perhaps a reflection of his general disdain for the governmental process. Nevertheless, his voice and writings have profoundly influenced late twentieth-century economic thought and practice.

The Keynesian-monetarist debate is nicely summarized by Marjoric Deane and Robert Pringle in their fine book on central banking: "[T]he continuing divide is mainly over the monetarist assumption that, left to itself, the economy will find its own equilibrium with no involuntary unemployment (except that caused by unnecessary state intervention), while Keynesians believe it suffers from so many 'rigidities' in key markets, especially labor markets, that disequilibrium can persist for years" (Deane and Pringle, 1994, p. 114). Monetarists, therefore, want the Fed to stick to a constant money growth rate target, while Keynesians would give the Fed leeway to adjust the growth of money in order to meet the economy's near-term needs.

As a student of economics and economic history and as a practicing economist, I have never aligned myself strongly with either of these schools of thought. As a graduate student, I saw merits and weaknesses in both positions, a view that was only confirmed after I joined Salomon Brothers. My ambivalence about becoming a devotee of either side was heightened in 1968, when I attended a much-publicized debate between Milton Friedman and Walter Heller, who—as former Chairman of the Council of Economic Advisers when President Kennedy cut taxes in the early 1960s—represented the Keynesian viewpoint. Sponsored by Salomon Brothers, the event was held in an auditorium at NYU's Graduate School of Business Administration, which was jammed to capacity with business and financial leaders and economists, so popular was the Keynesian-monetarist debate in those days.

Walter Heller, who spoke first, gave a talk entitled "Is Monetary Policy Being Oversold?" Milton Friedman followed with "Has Fiscal Policy Been Oversold?" It was exhilarating for me to watch the two giants of economics. Each was an articulate and passionate speaker, although Friedman worked at a disadvantage that day. The lectern had been raised for Heller, who is a very tall man, but it became stuck in place when the much-shorter Friedman took the podium. We could only see the top of the second great economist's head that day. But his speech was powerful nonetheless.

My main problem with both theories had to do with their rigidities as tools for dealing with the practicalities of business and financial life, which often are quite unpredictable. Neither theory provides variables for anchoring a forecast that would have a reasonable chance of remaining accurate a year or so into the future. In the economy, the time gap between changes in the money supply and the behavior of the economy has no consistency. Shifts in fiscal policy also have disparate effects on business and financial markets. These and other variables made me suspect that strict adherence to Keynesian or monetarist theory would weaken my effectiveness as a forecaster and as an observer of the economic and financial scene.

In an advanced industrial society, the role of government never will be as passive as monetarists would prefer, and perhaps it never should be. Given the imperfections inherent in our business and financial structures, we need an attentive state as we strive for economic progress. At the same time, I can never forget the powerful lesson from childhood about how the debasement of money and the credit structure can wreak havoc on the social and economic structure. All of this led me to conclude: Money matters, but credit matters more. This is especially true in our dynamic financial world, where the linkage between money and credit is looser than economic theory suggests.

So as I sat listening to Walter Heller and Milton Friedman in 1968, I thought about how my real-world experience challenged the Keynesian position as well. A flexible fiscal policy—that is, one that supposedly would be in correct alignment with the needs of the economy—was problematic. At its heart, the Keynesian approach rests on the rather naïve assumption that fiscal discipline can be brought to bear on economic imbalances as needed. Such is not the case. For example, the much-heralded Kennedy tax cut, in which Walter Heller had played a key role, reflected the pleasant side of fiscal activism. But the other side of the Keynesian equation—the unpleasant *disciplining* side of fiscal activism, which entails the timely raising of taxes and pruning of federal expenditures—failed miserably in the 1960s. Neither President Johnson nor the Congress advocated a Keynesian policy of fiscal tightening when the Vietnam War scaled up dramatically in the middle of the decade. Although a number of Keynesian economists called for such measures, Congress and the President stonewalled attempts to raise taxes.

When Congress finally passed a surtax for 1969–1970, it was too little, too late. The day the surtax was passed, I was sitting with Arthur Okun, Chairman of the Council of Economic Advisers, in his office. When Arthur received a call from Capitol Hill informing him that the surtax had passed, he was obviously elated. He then turned to me and said, "Now we have to push the Fed to lower interest rates," suggesting there was an immediate *quid pro quo.* And the Fed *did* lower the discount rate—a grave mistake. Inflation continued to heat up and, after a brief pause—as anxiety continued to mount in the financial markets—interest rates rose again.

Flexible fiscal policy as a means of stabilizing the economy was discredited further in the 1970s. Following the financial collapse of the Penn Central Railroad, economic policymakers became fiscally and monetarily expansionist. Inflation picked up, and the dollar came under attack in the foreign exchange markets. Then conservative Republican President Richard Nixon did the unthinkable: He imposed wage and price controls and floated the dollar in the foreign exchange markets. These radical decisions brought only temporary relief, however. As soon as the President's program moved from Phase I to Phase II, inflation resumed its march. Meanwhile, the floating of the dollar and its devaluation (as part of the Smithsonian Agreement of December 1971) did not quickly improve America's international trade balance, as hoped, nor did foreigners pour money back into the United States.

The Search for an Elusive Monetary Target

Monetary policy did not distinguish itself during this period either. The monetarists, however, made considerable headway, especially as inflation defied all attempts by the Keynesians to contain it. In the early 1970s, the Federal Reserve adopted a policy that, over the long-term, aligned its objectives with the growth of the money supply and bank reserves, yet did not completely abandon interest rates as a key variable in monetary policy. This approach was followed a few years later by what was called "practical monetarism," in which the Federal Reserve publicly announced the setting of interim targets for the growth of selected monetary aggregates, and defined a range for the Federal funds rate. At the same time, the Fed established quarterly targets for monetary growth, which stretched forward for a year from the current quarter.

These new monetary policies gradually ushered in a new kind of monetarism. For much of the postwar period, the Federal Reserve relied mainly on interest rates to manage the financial system. The principal monetary indicators were short-term interest rates and free reserves (excess reserves less borrowings by member banks from the Fed). This approach, it seems to me, served the Fed quite well in the early postwar years. When the Federal Reserve boosted short-term rates (particularly its discount rate) moderately in the 1950s, for example, the private sector responded to the cautionary signal.

Fed officials therefore began to search for new policy tools to influence the behavior of the new breed of business and banking practitioners. This search, which continues today, is far from easy. Control of the money supply, which monetarists favor so strongly, is difficult at best. The definition of money itself has broadened considerably. Originally, the Fed defined money as demand deposits and cash in circulation. The definition now includes time deposits and other near-term assets. Adding to the complexity of monetary policy, the Fed has redefined these aggregates many times in the past four decades. Since the early 1960s, new aggregates defined by the Fed have included M1, M1A, M1B, M2, M3, M4, M5, M1+, L, and M1B–shifted.

When the above-mentioned problems of defining money supply began to surface in the 1970s, I concluded that the linkage between the economy and the growth of money was flawed because of changes in the financial markets. The liberalization of financial markets appeared to me, as I have said, to give credit a more pivotal role than money. Simply put, the Fed had lost control over the debt-creation process. This began in the 1960s when the central bank instituted policies that automated the process of debt creation, particularly in the banking system. It gained momentum when the government removed most of the Regulation Q ceilings for larger-denominated certificates of deposit, a step that not only encouraged banks to bid for liabilities, but also gave them reason to acquire assets with floating rates of return based on a spread over the cost of bank liabilities.

The resulting elimination of money rate risk from banking transactions ignited a wave of debt expansion and sharp increases in loan commitments. The Fed no longer could control the money supply with traditional means (that is, by setting growth targets for the monetary aggregates). In effect, this transformation—the automation of the debt-creation process in the U.S. and abroad by removing lender money rate risk—transformed financial institutions from fiduciaries of temporary funds and savings into financial entrepreneurs.

While that was happening, the Federal Reserve did not concern itself with the rapid growth of debt. Instead, it tried to monitor and control the growth of the money supply (M1), a rather small component of the American debt structure and of economic activity. I believed that the time had come to consider the obsolete aspects of the Fed's money supply approach, and to find a new and more appropriate monetary target. The money supply, which consists of demand deposits plus currency outside the banking system, had become a much smaller percentage of gross national product than it had been a decade or two earlier. It had drifted apart from GNP. A variety of money substitutes were available, and high interest rates had produced great efforts to reduce cash balances to bare minimums. In addition, money supply growth no longer was leading overall economic activity in any consistent way. The lead time was at times quite long, and it varied considerably from cycle to cycle.

In a talk before the Annual Meeting of the Society of American Business Writers in May 1975, I proposed a new target for monetary policy: debt creation. I elaborated that proposal when asked to testify before the Committee on the Budget of the House of Representatives in February 1975, and again at a meeting with the members of the Board of Governors of the Federal Reserve Board, including then Chairman Bill Miller. My proposal gained some additional support when Professor Ben Friedman of Harvard University published an extensive study of credit aggregates in which he favored targeting nonfinancial debt.

My plan called for the targeting of total debt, which I believed could be measured reasonably well (and with only a small lag time) by using a proxy that encompasses a greater financial base than the money supply. This debt proxy would consist of credit market instruments and deposits held by the private domestic nonfinancial sector (households, businesses, and state and local governments). Historically, the relationship between the debt proxy and GNP (current dollars) had been remarkably close from the early 1950s through 1977. The debt proxy had moved contemporaneously with GNP through previous business cycles and periods of inflation and widely fluctuating interest rates, thus giving considerable validity to the stability of the relationship. In short, the level of the debt proxy was virtually equal to, and in exact alignment with, GNP. Regression analysis of quarterly changes of both series also showed great consistency.

In 1983, the Federal Reserve—heeding the recommendations from myself and others—finally began to set a monitoring target for the growth of total domestic nonfinancial-sector debt. To my dismay, however, even the new, more encompassing measure of the U.S. capital market proved to be inadequate. Among other things, the timeliness of the availability of data has been insufficient for enforcing policy. More importantly, the continued rapid changes in the money and capital markets have produced new instruments and additional credit creation that have not been captured by this aggregate. Accounting and reporting deficiencies, for one thing, have prevented the capturing of the increasingly large off-balance-sheet activities of financial institutions such as the use of financial derivatives.

In the late 1970s, my ongoing concern about the ineffectiveness of our economic policies grew. (See Exhibits 10-1 and 10-2.) In early 1979, I could see only the fast approach of policy paralysis. Policymakers, including the President, were becoming exasperated as well. America's faltering economic and financial performance, especially on the inflation front, prompted President Carter to change the leadership at the Fed. In early 1978, he had appointed business executive William Miller as Chairman of the Fed. Neither a banker nor an economist, Miller brought no monetary experience to the job. When I heard of Bill's appointment, I worried about how successful he could be in the very complex, new setting. I had spoken with him several times, mainly at Salomon Brothers luncheons, while he was still CEO of Textron, a diversified conglomerate.

He had all the bearings of a CEO, but not of a central banker. This made me wonder: How quickly would he learn the intricacies of central banking? With no central banking experience, how beholden would he be in his policy positions to the President who appointed him? Would he be able to objectively evaluate the strengths and weaknesses in the monetarist and Keynesian arguments? I also doubted his capacity to lead and persuade other members of the Federal Open Market Committee, who were well seasoned and trained in monetary matters. That distinguished and experienced group included Henry Wallich and Lyle Gramley—both Board Governors—as well as Paul Volcker, who held two powerful positions: Vice Chairman of the Federal Open Market Committee and President of the Federal Reserve Bank of New York.

My concerns grew as Miller's Fed emerged as a house divided. Whereas key Board members favored monetary tightening, the new Chairman voted to maintain the status quo. On one occasion, Treasury

> Unfortunately, there are no policies now in place that will readily curb the growing economic and financial excesses. Indeed, official pronouncements that inflation is now the number one national problem are hardly reassuring. They can only be regarded as a failure in the recent past to perceive correctly the challenges that confronted us. If the inflation problem had been perceived correctly and countered with preventive measures, no such admission of failure would be necessary today. Of course, recognizing correctly the current problem is a step in the right direction. However, considering the complexity of the current economic and financial situation, I know of no easy or simple solution. Whatever direction policies will take from here on will be painful to some sectors and most likely for the economy as a whole. It is dismaying to me to find that we have learned so little from the trying economic and financial experiences which began in the mid-1960's. As a consequence we again are confronted with serious imbalances.
>
> ---
>
> Henry Kaufman, "Economic Excesses and Financial Constraints," statement before the Joint Economic Committee of the Congress of the United States, Washington, D.C., June 28, 1978.

Exhibit 10-2

Secretary Michael Blumenthal diminished my confidence in the new Fed Chairman during our informal conversations. "Henry," Blumenthal remarked to me on one occasion, "I am probably the only Secretary of the Treasury whoever urged the Chairman of the Federal Reserve Board to tighten, but the Chairman refused." With all of this—and considering the precarious state of the nation in the late 1970s—Miller's ouster in mid-1979 was long overdue. (He became U.S. Treasury Secretary.)

His replacement was Paul Volcker, a well-seasoned central banker. Volcker acted quickly to overcome the policy paralysis. In a historic statement issued Saturday evening, October 6, 1979, Volcker's Fed announced a series of tightening decisions and policy actions that promised to usher in a new era of strict monetarism at the Fed. These included sharp increases in the discount rate and reserve requirements,

The U.S. Government is rapidly losing its effectiveness in dealing with the serious inflation problem. Indeed, from the point of view of effective, prompt action and public confidence, stabilization policies appear to have stalled. To some extent, this paralysis reflects some uncertainty about the underlying resiliency of the economy and a hesitancy in making difficult and perhaps painful official decisions.

Each of the three major policy arms of our Government seems to be lacking in intent and effectiveness in dealing with the inflationary problem. The voluntary incomes policy program instituted at the end of October has not had a meaningful impact in slowing the dangerous rise in inflation. Fiscal policy over the remaining six months of this fiscal year is mandated. Instead of a sharp slowing in Federal expenditures they are growing at close to 10%. Similarly, monetary policy lacks decisiveness. The authorities are apparently caught within a monetarist web and betray ambivalence about current national economic priorities.

Nevertheless, the leadership for fighting inflation will eventually have to be assumed by the Federal Reserve, since monetary policy is far more flexible than either incomes or fiscal policy.

Henry Kaufman, *Comments on Credit*, March 1979.

Exhibit 10-2

and greater control over bank reserves (which would now allow greater fluctuations in the Federal funds rate over shorter time periods).

Volcker had been in Belgrade, attending the annual meetings of the IMF and World Bank, but left the meetings early to return to the United States. Some claimed that the central banker had left Belgrade early after foreigners expressed their deep concern about the weakness of the U.S. dollar. Volcker's own explanation was far more mundane: There was little left to do in Belgrade.

In my view, Volcker's bold announcement (if not his early departure from Belgrade) was inspired by his quick realization that he faced a grave situation as the new Fed Chairman. And his strategy announcement proved to be a shrewd and timely move. Needless to say, pure monetarists and politically conservative politicians were overjoyed by the Fed's new direction. For their part, liberal economists hardly were in a position to raise strong opposition to the new regime, given the discredited state of Keynesianism at the time. Still, it is important to recall that Volcker did not advocate closing the monetary valves altogether, but rather supplying a steady but moderate flow of new money.

Nevertheless, it was a dramatic moment in modern economic history. A Democratic President with Keynesian leanings had appointed a central banker who briefly turned monetarist—a fact perhaps no less startling than Richard Nixon's enactment of wage and price controls. Desperate times seemed to call for unconventional measures.

Once again, however, the Fed's strict adherence to monetarism was short-lived. It was derailed by a severe recession in the early 1980s, by additional financial innovations that produced volatility in the money stock, and by pressure from supply-side economists, who garnered the political clout—following the election of President Ronald Reagan—to engineer large tax cuts and spending increases. The pressure to conform to Reagan's economic vision was strong. Chairman of the Council of Economic Advisers Martin Feldstein, hardly a Keynesian himself, nevertheless stated in the CEA's 1983 report: "I conclude, therefore, that monetary policy should be one of rules tempered by discretion. This is not a neat solution but the world is, unfortunately, too complex for neat solutions" (*Economic Report of the President*, 1983, p. 25.) Feldstein would soon run afoul of the Reagan program and resign the CEA chairmanship before completing his term.

The central bank continued to set targets for the various monetary aggregates, but never again were they the key variables that triggered policy responses. Instead, the Fed Governors determined policy on the basis of judgments about the current and prospective state of economic and financial behavior. It was an approach reminiscent of the Federal Reserve of the 1950s and 1960s, although the analytical tools at the Fed's command had become far more sophisticated since then.

And while strict monetarism had reigned for only a short while, monetary policy nevertheless had become the dominant and most powerful economic arm of the federal government. Where fiscal policy had failed to halt the virulent inflation of the 1970s, monetary policy, under the strong leadership of Paul Volcker, had succeeded.

The 1990s buttressed the dominance of monetary policy. By the early 1990s, when the nation slid into recession, fiscal countermeasures were no longer available. The staggering federal debt accumulated in the 1980s made sure of that; the United States no longer had the option of cutting taxes or boosting spending to stimulate the economy. In earlier periods, politicians and economic policymakers had lacked the will to make Keynesian policy work (by raising taxes and cutting spending during good times). In the early 1990s, outsized budget deficits and a behemoth national debt wrapped a tourniquet around fiscal policy. In any case, the consequence was the same: The task of bringing the economy out of recession fell to the Federal Reserve.

Seen in this way, the triumph of monetary over fiscal policy in the last 50 years is a remarkable turnaround, one that few could have imagined in the 1950s. It is all the more remarkable when we consider some of the ambiguities in monetary policy and its major failings in the postwar period, which I discuss in the next chapter.

11

Shortcomings of Fed Policy

*At no time in the post-World War II period has the
economic well-being of the U.S. and the rest of the
world hinged so importantly on the performance of
the American stock market.*

Despite its rise to dominance since World War II, Federal Reserve
policy has had some significant shortcomings that contributed
to the periodic financial mishaps and to the volatility of the financial
markets. This is not to belittle the accomplishments of the Fed. It has
been an important positive factor in the second half of this century.
While there have been some business recessions, they have generally
been short-lived. Monetary policy certainly has played the key role in
ending these recessions and in achieving economic expansions of
much longer duration. There has been no repeat of the kind of economic depression that left such deep scars in the 1930s—an achievement for which monetary policy can surely claim some credit. And it
was monetary policy that broke the back of the virulent inflation of the
1970s, and that has facilitated the extraordinary economic expansion
of the 1990s.

Lagging behind Structural Changes

One of these shortcomings has been the Fed's inability to recognize
early on the impact that structural changes in the financial markets
have had on financial behavior, and the significance of these behavioral changes on the conduct of monetary policy. The structural

changes in banking are a case in point—specifically, the gradual lifting of the Regulation Q ceiling on time deposits to the point where banks were freed from this restraint by the 1980s. In response, banks adopted more flexible asset and liability management practices and floating-rate financing.

The banks accomplished this by breaking down the segmentation of the financial markets. Before then, commercial banks had been restricted mainly to financing businesses and were allowed to offer demand deposit facilities as well as individual savings and time deposits. Indeed, until the 1970s, commercial banks had a monopoly on the checking account business. The thrifts, on the other hand, provided mortgages and individual savings accounts. Banks were also constrained geographically. Branch banking, for example, was prohibited in some states. In others, banking franchises were limited to specific regions.

Such market segmentation offered the financial institutions a number of advantages. By limiting competition, it sheltered their profit margins. Banking customers, on the other hand, did not receive under this structure the lowest cost of borrowing or the highest return on their deposits. As for the Federal Reserve, segmentation made it easy to enforce monetary policy because the legal constraints on banking functions sharply reduced the market's capacity to oppose or wiggle out of tightening actions by the central bank.

So there were arguments to be made—especially on behalf of customers—for opening up the banking system to greater competition. Generally, the market is an efficient allocator of resources, and efficiency is desirable. Still, there are meaningful differences between the efficient allocation of *goods and services* through intense competition, and intense competition among *financial* markets and intermediaries. In the nonfinancial world, intensive competition encourages innovation and improved delivery of goods and services. In the financial world, intensive competition encourages lower profit margins for intermediaries, along with the search for investment and lending opportunities with higher profit margins—opportunities that typically entail greater risk, which can endanger not merely the banking institutions but the well-being of the larger society. This is because financial markets and institutions deal in a very essential and fungible commodity—money and credit—that cannot be copyrighted or patented.

As banking was beginning to open up to greater competition in the early postwar period, the Federal Reserve failed to recognize the significance of the change. No one in authority stepped forward to address the unleashing of entrepreneurial forces, or the shifting balance of fiduciary responsibility among financial institutions. Nor were there early warnings by the monetary authorities that the lowering of legal and regulatory limits would produce much higher interest rates in periods of monetary restraint.

In fact, the Federal Reserve generally underplayed the impact of these banking changes on the enforcement of monetary policy. With great flexibility in how they managed their assets and liabilities, financial institutions had become intermediaries, in the sense that they no longer had to bear the money rate risk. As long as these institutions could maintain a favorable spread between the cost of liabilities and the return on their assets, it no longer mattered how high interest rates were pushed by the monetary authorities. Moreover, banks quickly became quite confident in their ability to make sound credit judgments—a confidence that often proved to be ill-founded. In their competitive zeal, many made weak loans and poor investments that eventually had to be written off.

Belatedly, the Federal Reserve began to perceive these problems when it investigated the adequacy of bank capital. More importantly, the central bank failed to appreciate for some time how high it would have to raise interest rates to achieve a restraining effect on the less regulated banking sector.

This new dynamic had serious long-range consequences. Because the relationship between the availability of funds and the demanders of credit had changed, interest rates now had to be driven up to extraordinary heights for the central bank to achieve a restraining effect. That, in turn, has weakened marginal demanders of credit and strengthened their financially strong counterparts. Such winnowing is, of course, a function of the markets. But in extreme form, it will disrupt the smooth functioning of a democratic economy, and possibly encourage support for social democracy, which I believe would be a step backward.

The Fed also was slow to recognize the implications for monetary policy of an important related development: securitization. By and large, the central bank supported and encouraged the spread of this technique for turning nonmarketable credit instruments (such as mortgages) into marketable ones. Once again, the Fed welcomed an innovation that promised to increase the efficiency of financial markets, but did not put into place safeguards against potential abuses. In this case, the problem with securitization is that it tends to lower the standards for the granting of credit.

Consider the situation several years ago in South Korea. The Asian nation had made commendable progress toward transforming itself into a first world country. It was an export powerhouse. The government did not run a large budget deficit, and outstanding external government debt was moderate. Credit ratings were extremely high; in fact, as late as October 1996, Korea had a higher credit rating than IBM! So bankers in Japan, Europe, and the United States were willing to lend large sums for short-term maturities to Korea, assuming that they could securitize those credits at will. They gave little thought to the possibility that the borrowers might be confronted with a liquidity crisis, one that would slam the door shut on access to the purportedly "open" credit markets. That, of course, is precisely what happened.

Like securitization, derivatives—which also multiplied rapidly in recent decades—encourage a more relaxed set of credit-granting standards. With derivatives, higher-rated corporations can arbitrage their credit standing to lower their cost of funds by issuing long-term fixed-rate debt and then swapping the proceeds against the obligation to pay at a floating rate. Meanwhile, lower-rated corporations that ordinarily would be squeezed out of the bond market as the credit cycle matures can use derivatives to lock in long-term yields by borrowing short and swapping into the long-term maturity obligation. For their part, the bankers in the middle—who make markets and trade in these obligations and who hold pieces of custom-made derivatives—see their role as relatively risk-free. In fact, it is not.

From a broad economic policy perspective, securitization has far-reaching consequences. The degree of credit restraint in operation at any particular time cannot be measured by standard money supply or bank credit indicators. Other time-honored rules of thumb—such as the notion that financial intermediaries are in the business of borrowing short and lending long—are being turned on their heads as well. Financial institutions engaged in active securitization may be borrowing long and lending short, while hedging their exposure to interest rate movements through a series of transactions in financial futures and options. In this new environment, surges in credit demand have not had the conventional effect of flattening the yield curve; the impulses are quickly transmitted up and down the yield curve though the actions of the new lending originators. In this way, greater volatility is transmitted to the intermediate and long-term bond markets, with corresponding effects on equity markets.

Some believe that the emergence of a burgeoning open credit market diminishes the capacity of the central bank to affect economic and financial decisions through conventional monetary policy actions, because the multiplicity of credit channels easily meets the credit demands of hopeful borrowers. At first glance, this view—which last year was articulated by Professor Benjamin Friedman—seems quite logical. He noted three important developments to support his conclusion. The first is the drop in the demand for bank money and the rise in substitutes such as "smart cards." Second is the sharp increase in nonbank credit cards. Finally, Professor Friedman pointed to the likely decline in the use of central bank reserves as a means for settling interbank deposits because of the increase in private clearing mechanisms (B. Friedman, 1999).

It is important to remember, however, that the Federal Reserve operates at the margin of credit availability. Variations in interest rates have a powerful impact on market behavior. Credit channels provide the financial lubrication for the near-term-oriented, highly leveraged entrepreneurial portfolio managers who take positions that contribute to the kind of exceptional volatility that has become more and more common in the financial markets. In that sense, the central bank's influence on the markets is potentially magnified. The least bit of unexpected easing or tightening can touch off powerful and possibly cumulative effects on the markets. But increased volatility of asset values may have important—and difficult-to-measure—consequences for economic fundamentals such as consumption, business fixed investments, home building, and so on. Economic modeling is of little value in addressing this question, for it is based on historical data from an era when financial markets were simpler—when, for example, the leverage provided by financial derivatives simply didn't exist.

The Federal Reserve failed to incorporate in its strategy the shift from a setting in which credit creation was halted quickly (by tighter money and market segmentation) to a more innovative and deregulated setting in which fierce competition spawned higher interest rates and greater deterioration in the credit quality of borrowers and of financial intermediaries. Albert Wojnilower stated this change very succinctly in 1980 in an excellent and very perceptive paper published by the Brookings Institution:

> Cyclically significant retardations or reductions in credit and aggregate demand occur only when there is an interruption in the supply of credit—a "credit crunch." Such interruptions may be promoted, intentionally or accidentally, by the destruction of lenders' incentives through regulatory rigidities . . . or the emergence of serious default problems in major institutions or markets. Following such episodes . . . the authorities . . . and the private markets . . . have deliberately reshaped the financial structure so as to prevent the recurrence of that particular form of credit supply interruption. (Wojnilower, 1980)

The Federal Reserve's slowness in perceiving the implications of these structural changes has led to some financial crises in recent decades. The Fed has mistakenly assumed that the discipline of the market would sufficiently limit large problems from erupting. This was certainly true when derivatives began to spread rapidly. The central bank embraced the recommendations of the Group of 30, which had promulgated a series of steps that institutions should take to promote reasonable behavior by participants in the derivatives market. In spite of their widespread support, these recommendations failed to accomplish their purpose. Ironically, some of those very institutions whose senior heads coauthored the Group of 30 plan suffered large losses in financial derivatives.

Perhaps the most glaring breach of the Group of 30 rules occurred in 1998 when Long Term Capital Management suffered catastrophic losses from derivatives. In spite of the fact that LTCM's actions clearly violated the Group of 30 guidelines—this newcomer to the financial scene had obligated itself to derivatives with a notional value of $1.4 trillion. Clearly, the system of self-imposed discipline proposed by the Group of 30 was not working.

The global financial upheavals of 1998 severely damaged not only financial markets but many national economies as well. The extent of the damage was portrayed vividly by William McDonough, in his presentation at the IMF–World Bank meetings in September 1998. He showed statistically the sharp widening of credit quality spreads that had taken place in just a few months in three key sectors: mortgages, the emerging market, and high-yield (junk) bonds. Yield spreads had widened even between newly issued and seasoned U.S. Governments of nearly comparable maturity. McDonough emphasized that new-issue financing in some sectors had virtually come to a halt, and that some market makers were finding it difficult to finance their inventory. Overall, market liquidity was drying up. This financial crisis, according to McDonough, had the potential to become the worst in the post-World War II period.

Fortunately, that didn't happen, in part because the Fed acted decisively to contain the spread of the crisis. But that does not excuse the central bank for failing to discover the rising tide of abuses in the credit markets to begin with. Where were the bank examiners from the Fed and the Comptroller of the Currency when the problem began to surface? Did the monetary authorities lack the needed information flows for early detection? And what about the senior managers at the institutional lenders? Were they aware of the magnitude of the risks their institutions had undertaken? The Federal Reserve must keep abreast of structural changes in the financial markets if we are to avoid major calamities in the future.

"Lender of Last Resort"—for Whom?

Another challenge facing the Federal Reserve is the need to clarify its "lender-of-last-resort" responsibilities. Traditionally, this meant that the Fed provided funds to banks in times of serious financial trouble. But securitization and globalization have broadened this responsibility. To cite a few examples: The Fed played a key role in restructuring the Franklin National Bank in 1974, and helped bail out both the First Pennsylvania Bank of Philadelphia and the Continental Illinois Bank of Chicago in 1984. Later (in the 1990s), the Fed came to the rescue of several of America's largest banks (by not enforcing capital requirements and write-offs on loans that were in arrears and classified as nonperforming assets).

The Fed also helped resolve the silver crisis in 1980—a lender-of-last-resort activity that did not involve the injection of liquidity. Bache, Halsey had loaned more than $200 million to the Hunt brothers, who had cornered the silver market. The Hunts put up their silver holdings to collateralize the loan. When the price of silver collapsed, so did the collateral value of the loan. Of course, Bache had financed its loan through bank loans. Thus, the credit value of the Hunt loans now endangered the financial sanctity of several large banks. The Fed did not provide any credit to quell the crisis, but Fed Chairman Paul Volcker pushed the lending banks very hard to reach an accommodation with the Hunts. Paul Volcker believed that this situation posed a systemic risk, but others—including several Fed Governors—disagreed. In a similar and more recent case, the Fed, this time under the leadership of Bill McDonough, took the lead in negotiating an agreement between moribund Long Term Capital Management and its large banking, investment company, and insurance company creditors. Again, in playing this role, the Fed claimed to be heading off a larger threat to the financial system. That was probably true, although questions remain about whether LTCM got off easy in the settlement.

Even in the international arena, the Fed has been inching toward a role as lender of last resort when major financial calamities arise. In the Mexican crisis of 1994, the South Korean crisis of 1997–1998, and the Brazilian crisis of 1998, the Fed worked cooperatively with the U.S.

Treasury to put together rescue packages. To be sure, the Treasury took the lead in these efforts; but these efforts could not have succeeded without the Fed's participation. More than this, the Federal Reserve's *domestic* policies are increasingly shaped by *international* considerations. This is not problematic per se; in fact, it is unavoidable, given the increasingly global character of economic relations today, with the United States the dominant player. But we must recognize that a U.S.-dominated global economic system means a greatly enlarged role for the Federal Reserve.

Therein lies a dilemma. It was the power of America that rescued Mexico, Brazil, and South Korea from falling into a financial abyss—facilitated by the IMF and World Bank. But both international institutions are dominated by the U.S. Other countries were brought along in these rescue missions, some voluntarily and others by U.S. persuasion. However, the U.S. has not been able to assert the same leadership in its monetary relations with other major industrial blocs, especially Japan and the European Monetary Union. But those relationships will be most important in the future, because economic cycles are bound to shift so as to cause a slowdown in U.S. economic growth and stronger growth in Europe and Japan. That, in turn, will shift capital flows out of the U.S. Moreover, developing nations will always suffer when the economic and financial behavior of the industrial countries goes astray. These imbalances could be even greater in the years ahead, when an economically unified continental Europe may set wrong policies in motion.

Two other unresolved challenges confront the Federal Reserve that are worth mentioning, because both involve the Fed's role as lender of last resort. One is the question of how far the Fed should spread its safety net? This is a nagging and rather messy issue in this rapidly changing financial world. The generally unstated assumption in years gone by was that the safety net should extend to the largest commercial banks that, after all, are the traditional wards of central banks. Whether there should be a lender of last resort for other types of financial institutions in order to avert a devastating shock to the financial system at large is not settled. Central bankers, of course, vehemently deny any such mandate in their public utterances.

Still, it is hardly far-fetched to suspect that Fed officials have ruminated seriously behind closed doors about the sorts of circumstances that might compel them to broaden the Fed's lender-of-last-resort role to nontraditional clients. As noted earlier, they have broadened the safety net in recent years on some occasions. Even in dealing with those traditional wards of central banks—the commercial banks—the issue has become very complicated. Commercial banks, in the traditional sense, are not commercial banks anymore; investment banks are not investment banks; and insurance companies are not insurance companies.

Large encompassing financial institutions have rather quickly come on to the financial scene. Citigroup—perhaps the most visible among them—has under its umbrella a bank, an insurance company, an investment banking concern, and a finance company. And as more such institutions are organized, more will be considered "too big to fail." If so, the declining portion of the market that would be allowed to fail under this new setting will have to experience the real brunt of monetary restraint. Unfortunately, the institutions that are allowed to fail will enhance the market position of those that are too big to fail. This is yet another example of the fact that the central bank has not thought ahead strategically about how the enlargement of its lender-of-last-resort responsibilities might affect the functioning of an economic democracy.

Stock Prices and the Wealth Effect

The other challenge that confronts the Federal Reserve is the role that the sharp increase in financial wealth should play in determining monetary policy. Wealth effects are now recognized to be powerful influences on the evolution of the economy. Not too many years ago, the Federal Reserve (along with most other central banks) was somewhat skeptical about the potency of wealth effects. But today, more and more households recognize how their financial net worth is affected by movements in asset values, and adjust their expenditures on goods, services, and housing accordingly. Business corporations modify their investment decisions in part in response to what is happening to their share prices. Business formation is subtly influenced by the level of the stock market, too, because a strong market allows individuals to take risks that they would shun at lower asset prices. International capital flows, and thus the value of the dollar, also are affected by the value of financial assets—and by expectations about future asset price movements. Because these effects have become an important transmission mechanism from the financial sector to the real economy, they deserve careful consideration by the Fed's monetary policymakers.

The constituency of today's U.S. financial bubble is very broadly based. Households now have 30 percent of their financial wealth in stocks, double the percentage a mere decade ago. Quite a few have even become day traders. Some observers believe that households are long-term investors, who therefore would not alter their economic decisions because of a sharp sell-off in stocks. This is a naïve observation. Households are a heterogeneous group. Young participants may well be long-term investors, but older investors —the fastest-growing demographic segment—probably are not, because they lack future earning power, and sharp declines in stock values would quickly endanger their standard of living. Moreover, quite a few households in all categories have borrowed funds that they have invested in stocks. They have no staying power.

In addition, the rise in stock values has had a pervasive influence on economic and financial decisions that will be endangered when the bubble bursts. Quite a few of the mergers—which helped to drive up equity values in the first place—would not have been consummated. The bubble has contributed to the rapid growth of the financial infrastructure. And because investors tend to emphasize the market value of businesses, the bubble has concealed the highly leveraged position of business. Stock options have become an important form of compensation for senior management of established corporations and for the seeding of new enterprises.

By the mid-1990s, I had become concerned about what impact the growth of financial wealth would have on the behavior of the economy, and how that might in turn influence monetary policy.

Unfortunately, the Federal Reserve did not become openly concerned about the "wealth effect" until late in the decade, when Chairman Alan Greenspan began to warn that a major stock market correction could spark a recession. (Millions of householders could become reluctant to spend following a sharp decline in the value of their stocks.) As in former periods of extraordinary financial exuberance, forecasts abound about further very sharp increases in the value of financial assets. There is talk of having entered a "new era" of unbroken economic and financial strength. Some say that the relationship between rates of return on stocks and on bonds has changed fundamentally. But this is nothing new. Financial history has been punctuated periodically by such predictions. In fact, the appearance of these kinds of statements should themselves serve as a warning that we are in a period of exuberance rather than one of rational financial behavior.

The Federal Reserve has responded to the stock market bubble ambiguously. In a speech in December 1996, Alan Greenspan talked about the Fed's concern with rising stock prices. He asked: "But how do we know when irrational exuberance has unduly escalated asset values, which then become subject to unexpected and prolonged contractions as they have in Japan over the past decade? And how do we factor that assessment into monetary policy?" That expression—which got wide attention, and was criticized by many—wasn't even a declaratory sentence. It was a rhetorical question.

There is no mandate for any central bank to take into consideration financial asset prices explicitly or even otherwise in the formulation of monetary policy. Years ago, many households had large savings deposits, and therefore benefited when the Fed raised interest rates. Today, they fear higher interest rates, which may endanger the value of their stock holdings. Business corporations generally do not favor a tough monetary stance. It tends to blunt sales and profit growth. Concurrently, in the political arena, neither the most conservative nor most liberal are favorably disposed to Federal Reserve tightening.

Financial bubbles are not new; history is replete with them. In its formative years, the Federal Reserve had to deal with the most devastating bubble in the twentieth century—the boom of the late 1920s. At that time, the Fed became increasingly concerned about the speculation in the stock market. But consider the key events and how the Fed reacted to them. The Dow Jones Industrial index of common stocks rose by

29 percent in 1927, 48 percent in 1928, and another 29 percent to its peak in September 1929. Wholesale prices actually fell somewhat from late 1928 through 1929. Meanwhile, commercial banks significantly enlarged their role in investments, creating affiliates that underwrote and distributed many different types of securities. One historian summarized the scene by writing, "Selling securities was a highly lucrative activity, so much so that competition among investment bankers and the investment affiliates of major banks took the form of searching out potential issuers of stocks or bonds. The intensity of the bankers in the scramble for 'deals' suggests the spirit of the Oklahoma land rush but in pursuit of intangible rather than real wealth" (Degen, 1987, p. 52).

In response to these developments, the Fed raised the discount rate in a series of stages from 3.5 percent in 1928 to 6 percent in 1929. Loans by brokers fully collateralized by securities had interest rate costs as high as 12 percent. A debate broke out within the Federal Reserve about how the Fed should deal with the financial speculation. On the one hand, the Federal Reserve Board itself favored a selective credit intervention. It might, for example, pressure member banks to restrain securities lending at the risk of losing their privilege of borrowing at the Fed's discount window. The Board wanted to distinguish between productive loans that would encourage economic activity and securities loans that would encourage speculation. On the other hand, the individual Federal Reserve Banks, especially the powerful New York Fed, led by the very influential Benjamin Strong, favored broad restraining measures such as increases in the discount rate. In the end, the Fed raised interest rates and used moral suasion to restrain lending on securities. The dominant approach clearly was to restrict the overall availability of money and credit.

There are some striking similarities between that period and recent years. Stock prices as measured by the Dow Jones Industrial Average have risen by 196 percent in the last 5 years (to their peak in August 1999) as compared with 214 percent in the 5 years ending in 1928. In the economy, the inflation rate has been well contained. Comments about a new economic era and a new productivity paradigm have been proliferating, inspired in part by ubiquitous computer applications, technological improvements, and globalization.

While loans collateralized by securities have increased in recent years, they have not been the real driving force behind the dramatic gains in stock prices this time around. Instead, there have been large share buybacks by corporations, huge shifts to equity investments by households, and the advent of day trading. Alan Greenspan, just like Benjamin Strong, does not favor a selective intervention in the marketplace.

Again, consider the historical parallels. In 1927, Strong's forceful leadership resulted in an easing of U.S. monetary policy, largely for international reasons. The Fed lowered the discount rate and made large purchases of securities. The gold standard was in trouble. In the second half of 1927, easing by the Fed was expected to make money cheaper in the U.S. and encourage some gold to flow back to Europe. In the second half of 1998, the Fed also eased monetary policy to ease international tensions when Russia defaulted a bond issue, and when Long Term Capital Management experienced serious liquidity in its highly leveraged portfolio, which raised the possibility of a global systemic financial debacle. Some historians have criticized Strong's action in 1927, and a few now consider the magnitude of the Fed's easing in 1998 as too much.

Of course, the two periods are not precisely the same. Contextual changes from one period to another usually cloud the similarities. Nevertheless, the present stock market boom should not be ignored in the deliberations of the Federal Reserve. At no time in the post-World War II period has the economic well-being of the U.S. and the rest of the world hinged so importantly on the performance of the American stock market.

In reflecting on the current state of the stock market, Alan Greenspan stated in his July 1999 Humphrey-Hawkins testimony:

> Should an asset bubble arise, or even if one is already in train, monetary policy properly calibrated can doubtless mitigate at least part of the impact on the economy. And, obviously, if we could find a way to prevent or deflate emerging bubbles, we would be better off. But identifying a bubble in the process of inflating may be among the most formidable challenges confronting a central bank, pitting its own assessment of fundamentals against the combined judgment of millions of investors.

The statement suggests that he may be hoping to repeat what he did in previous times of sharp market declines. From its peak in August 1987 to its trough in November 1987, the Dow Jones Industrial Average dropped nearly 1,000 points, or 36 percent. Following the precipitous 508-point drop on October 19, 1987, the Federal Reserve declared its commitment to pump money into the system, and lowered interest rates substantially. Again, in 1998, when stock prices fell 20 percent, the Fed also eased monetary policy substantially. Some, of course, may say that the easing was insufficient. In more recent times, despite the massive easing in monetary policy and fiscal stimulation, Japan is still trying to overcome the bursting of its own bubble in stock and real estate values.

But even if such a successful rescue of the stock market could be accomplished by the Fed the next time around, the central bank would be faced with a difficult policy conundrum. It would have established in the minds of market participants an asymmetrical approach to market behavior. Over time, central bank successes at restoring market stability will encourage a new attitude among all types of investors, a kind of analogue to deposit insurance, whereby they count on the central bank to bail out the market. And that will lead to a far more asymmetrical financial world. Greater risk taking will become the norm. Interest rate reductions will tend to be sharper and predicated on major reductions in household net worth. Interest rate increases to combat inflation will be more tentative and protracted because the central bank naturally will fear that premature, hasty, or unexpectedly forceful increases in officially determined short-term interest rates will precipitate a sell-off in the markets and a major erosion of asset values.

Indeed, the main lesson from the Japanese experience—that overly tentative easing of monetary policy in response to the financial fallout from the collapse of an asset bubble is a recipe for frustration or even for failure—will further accentuate this trend. The basic problem with bailing out markets and holding up prices is that such an approach does not remove the underlying problem: overstated financial values. If an economy is to move ahead efficiently, they must be wrung out of the system.

Thus, a full evaluation of the achievements and failures of the Fed in the second half of the century is not yet possible. We have avoided a depression for the last 45 years, and Fed policy surely can claim some of the credit. In the late 1970s, the Fed broke the back of a very dangerous bout of inflation. For that, Paul Volcker always will be enshrined as the determined Chairman who stuck to it in the face of many near-term obstacles. To enforce the discipline to rein in inflation was probably the most difficult task a central banker has faced in these 45 years.

No one volunteers for discipline, certainly no child, adult, or constituency of society. Alan Greenspan has presided over the longest U.S. economic expansion in history. His insights into the structural changes in our economy, new technology, and their linkages to the rest of the world have been a major factor influencing monetary policy in the 1990s. Most of the time during his leadership, Fed policy has been one of accommodation. How he will be enshrined as a monetary policy leader, however, will very much depend on whether the stock market bubble will be handled without major economic and financial mishap. It is a formidable task.

An Agenda for Change

While monetary policy continues to evolve in its formulation, procedures, and implementation, the process is rather slow. Therefore, the chances are that monetary policy will not keep pace with the requirements of managing a volatile financial market and thus promote sustainable growth. Let me state clearly some of my own views on monetary policy.

To begin with, I believe that the primary objective of a central bank should be to maintain the financial well-being of society in the broadest sense. That means establishing stable financial conditions by exercising careful oversight over financial markets, institutions, and trading practices; anticipating potential problems; and taking remedial action *before* those problems can do widespread damage. For that, the Fed must pursue monetary policy actions that will, over time, lay a foundation for the successful achievement of sustainable economic growth with minimal inflation, and with minimal risks of financial shocks that could disrupt the economy.

There is no longer any reliable analytical guidepost on which to direct monetary policy. The vast structural changes in the financial system that I have described make it impossible for any central bank to anchor policy to any monetary or credit target. There is no alternative but to fall back on judgment. But judgment exercised toward what objective? There are currently significant differences of opinion about basic objectives of monetary policy, especially among politicians, academics, and financial market participants, although perhaps less so among central bankers themselves.

In my judgment, monetary policy will need to take into much greater account the impact of financial market developments on changes in the value of financial assets and on the net worth of the private sector. In the past, the central bank was able to formulate monetary policy around what might be called the "output-income-inflation nexus." Whether by targeting short-term interest rates or by targeting some version of the money supply, the Fed's goal was to achieve a relative balance between the aggregate supply of goods and services in the economy and the aggregate demand for goods and services. Supply was constrained by resource availability—essentially by the size and utilization of the capital stock and the pool of unemployed workers. Demand for goods and services was constrained by income and by access to credit. Monetary restraint was called for when demand started to press upon supply, create bottlenecks, absorb unused resources, and threaten higher inflation. Monetary accommodation was called for when incomes faltered, access to credit was somehow constricted, or business and consumer confidence was shaken by an exogenous event such as an oil price shock. Central bankers did not ignore variations in net worth, particularly at times of sudden changes, like the 1987 stock market crash. But it is fair to say that these considerations received only intermittent and normally subordinate attention. After all, most individuals in times past did not directly hold many financial assets other than what they kept in the bank. To them, happenings in the equity and bond markets held only a remote importance to their lives.

Therefore, I do not agree with those who maintain that the central bank should have only the most single-minded of objectives—specifically, the pursuit of price stability, perhaps defined as a target range for the inflation rate. In my view, the logic for enshrining such a narrow objective—namely, that an environment of low inflation is both a necessary and a sufficient condition for economic growth and financial market stability—is flawed, and in practice such a price-stability objective will rarely, if ever, be faithfully pursued.

Indeed, I would argue that this objective is deceptive, because it fails to give precedence to maintaining the financial well-being of society. Why? First, low inflation, for all of its virtues, is no guarantee against the emergence of financial excesses. History proves this conclusively. The classic case for the United States was the decade of the 1920s, when inflation remained low, while financial excesses developed both in the equity market and in commercial real estate.

More recently, we have the vivid example of the 1980s. Inflation performance was exemplary; the rise in the consumer price index in 1986 was one of the lowest in the entire postwar period. But within the fabric of our financial markets there developed some of the worst financial excesses of this century, a process that would eventually lead to massive financial failures, huge taxpayer costs, and a largely unforeseen credit crunch that would aggravate the business downturn and constrain the subsequent economic recovery. Arguably, low inflation is a necessary condition for financial well-being. But it is not a *sufficient* condition for financial well-being. That requires a more complex set of economic and financial circumstances, grounded not only by a central bank's monetary actions, but also by its role as the institution entrusted with assuring the safety and soundness of the financial system as a whole.

Second, an obsession with achieving low inflation at all costs carries other risks. Long-lasting economic stagnation can bring about a potentially large and highly undesirable redistribution of wealth. That approach can, over time, undermine public support for free markets, which may be reflected in a swing toward a narrowly nationalistic posture on international trade—a damaging development.

Third, the alternative to a sole central banking objective of low inflation is not indifference to the rate of inflation. Central banks that have acquiesced in, or abetted, high inflation are practicing a form of financial corruption that eventually destroys national unity and leads to financial ruin. But a central bank that has built up a reputation of integrity and devotion to stability can look beyond the inflation situation at any particular time and anticipate how the inflation rate will evolve in reaction to changing economic circumstances. Such a central bank will be able to pursue an accommodative monetary policy, even in the face of a lingering rate of inflation that is higher than the expected rate that will eventuate over a long time period. This ability to craft a policy on the basis of sound analysis of future trends, rather than moving in lockstep with available data that necessarily record only what has already happened, is the hallmark of sensible, effective monetary control.

As I see it, the proper responsibility of the central bank—assuring the financial well-being of society—requires an intimate involvement in financial supervision and regulation. In fact, I have long believed that it is only the central bank—among the various regulatory agencies that share responsibility in this area—that can represent the perspective of the financial system as a whole. This should be the central organizing principle behind any comprehensive reform of financial regulation and supervision in the United States.

There is no mandate at the present time for any central bank to take into consideration financial asset prices explicitly in the formation of monetary policy. Nevertheless, the bubbling in the American financial market is an untenable situation. The way events are unfolding now, one of several events will extinguish the exuberance. One is a corporate profit squeeze more pronounced than the one now beginning to emerge. Another would be a further sharp deterioration in the Japanese economy that would weaken Japanese financial institutions even more. With these institutions so closely linked globally, financial problems are bound to occur elsewhere. Still another problem will confront us if Japan and Europe stage strong economic recoveries. This would end the surge of foreign funds to the U.S., and also would increase inflationary pressures.

My concern about the bubbling of the American financial markets was heightened in August of 1999 as I sat in the audience listening to Alan Greenspan talk about the problem of correctly assessing large

increases in financial asset values, during a symposium, "New Challenges for Monetary Policy," sponsored by the Federal Reserve Bank of
Kansas City at Jackson Hole, Wyoming. I was not reassured when he
said, "History tells us that sharp reversals in confidence happen
abruptly, most often with little advance notice." He then went on to
say:

> These reversals can be self-reinforcing processes that can compress siz-
> able adjustments into a very short time period. Panic market reactions
> are characterized by dramatic shifts in behavior to minimize short-term
> losses. Claims on far-distant future values are discounted to insignifi-
> cance. What is so intriguing is that this type of behavior has characterized
> human interaction with little appreciable difference over the generations.
> Whether Dutch tulip bulbs or Russian equities, the market price patterns
> remain much the same.
>
>   We can readily describe this process, but, to date, economists have
> been unable to anticipate sharp reversals in confidence. Collapsing confi-
> dence is generally described as a bursting bubble, an event incontrovert-
> ibly evident only in retrospect. To anticipate a bubble about to burst
> requires the forecast of a plunge in the prices of assets previously set by
> the judgments of millions of investors, many of whom are highly knowl-
> edgeable about the prospects for the specific companies that make up our
> broad stock price indexes.

Nor was I reassured by his concluding statement:

> We no longer have the luxury to look primarily to the flow of goods and
> services, as conventionally estimated, when evaluating the macroeco-
> nomic environment in which monetary policy must function. There are
> important—but extremely difficult—questions surrounding the behav-
> ior of asset prices and the implications of this behavior for the decisions
> of households and businesses. Accordingly, we have little choice but to
> confront the challenges posed by these questions if we are to understand
> better the effect of changes in balance sheets on the economy and, hence,
> indirectly, on monetary policy.

I came away uneasy for two reasons. One is that the Fed did not know how to deal with a bubble. The other is that the Chairman was of the opinion that the Fed could undertake ameliorating actions to alleviate the negative consequences of a sharp decline in asset values. This is based on the assumption that lower interest rates will accomplish this purpose. But this is far from certain, although the Fed intervened successfully in the fall of 1987 and again in the fall of 1988. Much of that success, however, depended on a favorable set of domestic and international circumstances at the time. And it is also important to recognize that a Fed easing that quickly reverses markets to a new upward trajectory does not eliminate the bubble but extends it. Financial reasonableness can only turn to the market after excessive values have been eliminated.

From my perspective, the question is not *whether* any one or more of these will happen, but *when* and from what level of the market. After that, I suspect a chorus will rise for a more definitive monetary strategy, one that takes into account financial behavior.

I have made these observations about the shortcomings of monetary policy with at least a touch of hesitation. The Federal Reserve is not an impersonal, machine-like institution, but rather a human organization composed of many highly dedicated and extremely talented individuals. Neither the Fed's leaders nor its many professional staff members live in isolation. Like the rest of us, they are influenced by the norms and larger forces that shape the larger society. The behavioral biases that affect other kinds of economic decision making also affect the making of economic policy. Still, in spite of such imperfections, the Federal Reserve comes closer to being an independent and objective arbiter and policy body than any other institution in our economic democracy.

12

The Urgent Need for Regulatory and Supervisory Reform

If... Microsoft were indeed permitted to acquire Citibank.... [there] would emerge a virtually unassailable corporate elite honeycombed with conflicts of interest... that would be difficult to dislodge, and surely would erode economic efficiency.

In the late 1960s, I watched with growing alarm as scores of corporate borrowers—in an effort to circumvent regulatory lending constraints—piled into the commercial market as issuers. The trend continued, and culminated in the collapse of the Penn Central Railroad.

The crash of the Pennsy was one of the more dramatic examples of a trend that has occupied and troubled me for three decades: the unwillingness of official supervisors and regulators to come to grips with threats to the sanctity of the financial system that have grown out of structural changes. As the pace of change has quickened, regulators have found it increasingly difficult to keep abreast of evolving technologies, markets, and financial institutions. But we can—and must—do better.

The official regulation of financial markets and financial institutions ordinarily is a topic reserved for specialists. The subject can entail a great deal of terminology and technicalities of little interest to outsiders. Yet regulation touches everyone involved in the financial markets at many levels, as demonstrated by the highly publicized scandals that have rocked the financial community in recent years—the collapse of the savings and loans; the BCCI scandal; the turmoil at Long Term Capital Management; the mismanagement of the bailout money given to Russia by the IMF; and Nicholas Leeson's crippling unauthorized speculation at Baring Brothers—among others. In each of these cases, investors, depositors, or taxpayers lost billions of dollars, and many industry experts pointed accusatory fingers at regulators for failing to head off the calamities.

The continuing high volatility of financial markets also has raised questions about the behavior of certain market participants, and about the influence of new types of financial instruments and computer-driven trading techniques, all of which—say some industry experts—are operating without proper official oversight. While some of this criticism may be off target, it seems to me that official institutions and supervisory practices have not kept pace with financial innovation, nor with the greater financial freedom encouraged by the deregulated market environment of the 1980s and 1990s.

Financial innovation and formal deregulation have had many consequences, some good, some not so good. But one effect is incontestable: These forces have drastically increased the availability of credit, particularly to borrowers who earlier had been considered high credit risks. The result has been occasional lending binges of unprecedented dimensions, as entrepreneurially driven financial institutions have been spurred on by competitive exhilaration, the lure of high fees, inept credit judgments, overly optimistic economic assumptions, and sometimes even outright fraud and criminality. This lending binge was centered in commercial real estate and land, but extended as well to highly leveraged corporations, to the household sector, and to loans and investments abroad. As economic assumptions proved to be faulty, many of these loans went sour, while still others remain at high risk. Not surprisingly, many lenders clamped down in reaction to the overindulgence, leading to a credit crunch in the early 1990s.

In spite of these problems a decade ago, we have seen in recent years a resurgence of this same kind of liberal investment and lending practices. Americans have loaned huge sums to and invested in developing countries in Latin America, Asia, and elsewhere. The junk bond market has flourished again. Households have encumbered themselves with heavy debt. And, as will be noted later, corporations have not improved the credit quality of their outstanding bonds, even though their profitability has improved a great deal.

The managers of failed or troubled financial institutions do not bear sole responsibility for the recent volatility and crises, although they deserve the lion's share of the blame. Flawed regulatory structures and practices are culpable as well. This is not to say that we should expect regulators to micromanage our financial institutions. But financial regulators can and should be held accountable for not taking account of the risks that were being collectively loaded onto the financial system through the rapid, overconcentrated growth of credit by financial institutions as a whole. Indeed, it is fair to ask: Who besides those responsible for identifying and limiting systemic risk are in a position to assume a "macro" point of view?

Crises in recent years have proved that our present system of financial regulation is incapable of averting a powerful shock to the financial system, the effects of which were contained by a safety net funded by understandably disgruntled taxpayers. We also should have reason to doubt that our current system of financial regulation is adequate to deal with new mishaps arising out of the new world of "high-tech" finance—the somewhat shadowy and untested area of immense off-balance-sheet exposures that lurk in the form of swaps, options, futures, and their many permutations.

Basic Precepts for Sound Regulatory Reform

The soundness of any specific proposals for reforming U.S. and international regulatory systems—including those I propose later in this chapter—depends on the fundamental precepts on which they rest. Unfortunately, a discussion of basic principles often gets lost in the welter of details, or drowned out by the more strident voices during discussions of regulatory reform among experts. But if we have learned anything from the unhappy experience of trying to reform financial regulation, it is that no consensus is likely unless there is a good-faith effort to reach common ground on matters of principle.

The **first precept** of sound financial regulation is that nations face a choice between regulated and deregulated financial markets—but most try to avoid making the choice. In regulated markets, authorities bear some responsibility for the mistakes and misfortunes of the financial institutions that they oversee. Market discipline plays a role, but one normally limited to smaller institutions. For institutions that are "too big to fail"—a category that unfortunately often includes some not-so-big but politically connected institutions—effective market discipline is foreclosed. Whenever this kind of favored institution gets into trouble, some sort of formal or informal safety net kicks in.

In contrast, a true system of deregulated markets permits losses as well as gains, and even the failure of sizable institutions. Market discipline is taken seriously. No firms are too big to fail. The threat of runs on financial institutions is supposed to act as an ever-present restraint on the entrepreneurial juices of management. There is little need for elaborate capital requirements painstakingly negotiated by regulators and financial institutions because—without strong balance sheets and unquestionable financial strength—an institution would not long survive the rigors of competition.

Today, the regulation of financial institutions and markets in virtually all of the advanced economies is less intrusive than it was a generation ago. At the same time, no nation possesses a true system of deregulated financial markets. What we see instead is an uneasy amalgam of some formal regulatory controls coexisting side by side with more informal, judgment-based official oversight, with large patches of economic activity that escape regulation or supervision altogether. It is an often-confusing and internally inconsistent way to configure an economy.

This leads to my **second precept** for sound financial regulation: Comprehensive deregulation is impractical, and its true consequences are intolerable even to the governments that espouse the virtues of free-market capitalism.

Once again, the too-big-to-fail phenomenon is instructive. In the real world, financial authorities possess powerful incentives to safeguard the payments mechanism, whatever their ideological commitment to market discipline. It is widely known that depositors incur minor costs when they abandon an institution. Moreover, most large depositors are fiduciaries—such as corporate treasurers or investment advisers—who are legally mandated to avoid all risk on short-term assets. They must therefore shift funds from institutions that show the slightest hint of possible failure to banks of unquestionable financial strength. More than that, the payments mechanism can't function if there is a major institution in the chain of settlements that is thought to be financially insecure. All of these factors compel financial authorities to intervene when signs of serious trouble emerge at a leading financial institution.

Given these realities, the only condition under which a nation can embrace market discipline without compromise—and abandon the too-big-to-fail doctrine—is when all large financial institutions are too *strong* to fail. And that, in turn, depends on close, ongoing official oversight. Stated another way, deregulation without close supervision of financial institutions must rely on an *explicit* pledge to bail out institutions thought to be too big to fail. This apparent paradox is inherent in the special characteristics of financial institutions that distinguish them from other kinds of business organizations, especially their interdependence on each other (through the payments system) and their public utility–like function in the economy, where they serve as a crucial component of the infrastructure.

The logical corollary is that the more free-market-oriented an economy, the greater its need for official supervision of financial institutions. This is because a truly market-oriented economy poses the highest risk of business failure, and correspondingly high risks to the balance sheets of financial institutions that lend to the business sector. A deregulated financial sector without close supervision would be correspondingly more vulnerable to market pressures in times of economic stress. Improved supervision does not mean more intrusive regulation. It means, rather, that official supervisory authority must become far more knowledgeable about the diversity of operations in which financial institutions are engaged. This includes the full range of its risk-taking activities, the quality of its risk modeling, and the impact that off-balance-sheet activities can have on the institution's well-being.

The **third precept** for regulatory reform—following closely on the second—is that in a world of increasing financial consolidation, leading financial institutions must adhere to an unusually high code of business conduct. They must take into account not only their narrow private interests, but also their considerable public responsibilities.

Consolidation essentially demands that the largest financial institutions be thought of as less like ordinary business enterprises and more like public utilities in their economic functions and importance. Without a recognition of their awesome role and responsibilities in the larger society, financial institutions will capture through consolidation far too much influence over the direction of nonfinancial corporations. That, in turn, will undermine the competitive dynamics of the marketplace. As Adam Smith recognized more than two centuries ago, market competition can prevail only in an economy composed of many independent small- and medium-sized institutions. Of course, Smith could hardly envision the emergence of the kind of gigantic financial institutions we have today—institutions so large that their individual successes and failures redound throughout the larger economy and society.

The **fourth precept** of sound financial regulation is that financial market participants will always push risk taking to the marginal edge, unless prevented from doing so. This is because the marginal edge holds special appeals, for it is there that competition is least, profit margins are greatest, fees are most lucrative, and ancillary business is easiest to line up. In largely deregulated markets, the regulatory structure does not provide a safe haven for the making of relatively secure profits. Rather, deregulated financial institutions face intense competition in their core businesses, and therefore feel greater pressure to move toward the marginal edge.

In contrast, regulated markets create protected segments, havens where average financial institutions can earn comfortable profits without stretching. To be sure, some institutions will always stretch, and those most conscientious in following official rules will at times be enticed to make marginal loans and investments. But regulated financial markets rarely attract the kind of high-risk-taking entrepreneurs who are inevitably drawn to deregulated environments.

The **fifth precept** is that regulatory responses to new financial methods and instruments tend to be desultory. The historical evidence of this regulatory lag is abundant. The emergence of negotiable certificates of deposit and asset-liability management in the 1960s, of large syndicated credit in the 1970s, and of new forms of derivatives in the 1980s—all initially evoked tepid responses from market participants and regulators alike. Regulators failed to grasp the technical complexities of these new tools, instruments, and techniques, or to comprehend their broader significance for the financial system.

There is an institutional dimension to this problem. The discrepancy between the salaries paid to regulators and those paid to leading market participants is proportionately much greater than the earlier gap between the pay of examiners and loan officers. It is therefore difficult for regulatory agencies to attract and retain the best talent in these areas. Clearly, higher pay scales are needed.

More than this, today's new financial businesses cut across traditional institutional lines. For instance, the market leaders in interest rate swaps include a few commercial banks, several investment banks, and even a small number of insurance companies. This institutional overlap poses new challenges for regulators. So does the problem of evaluating systemic risks, because many of today's transactions are cleared and settled without going through the traditional payments mechanism.

The **sixth precept** of sound regulatory reform is that financial deregulation and innovation complicate the tasks, not only of the regulatory agencies themselves, but also of monetary authorities. Stated differently, it is more difficult to stabilize markets through monetary policy adjustments in a deregulated system than in a regulated one.

The tremendous growth of interest rate swaps is a prime example. In the expansion phase of the business cycle, easy access to interest rate swaps keeps marginal participants in the credit structure longer, thereby diluting the impact of monetary restraint. Without access to interest rate swaps, marginal borrowers would be forced either to accept the risk of borrowing at floating rates or to cut back on their credit demands.

But when there is financial distress—as there normally is during a recession—the central bank's efforts to revive the economy by encouraging faster growth in money and credit will be thwarted to some degree by the existence of interest rate swaps. That is because the weaker credit typically is the counterparty borrowing at a variable rate but paying a fixed fee. Recessions squeeze the cash flows of weaker credits, making it more difficult to service fixed-rate obligations. Besides, the weaker credit in these circumstances does not benefit from the decline in short-term interest rates or the emergence of a positively sloped yield curve. From a cyclical perspective, therefore, a financial innovation (the interest rate swap) that is ostensibly neutral when it comes to monetary policy actually reduces the effectiveness of monetary adjustments throughout the cycle.

The **seventh precept** of financial regulation is that the present system overregulates minor matters—especially at the level of the individual institution—while paying insufficient attention to broader, systemic weaknesses. This unfortunate bias is an artifact of our financial history. Regulatory regimes tend to persist; that is, laws and institutions change more slowly than markets and technologies. Thus, regulations imposed for what seemed like good reasons at the time become difficult to discard in later years when they become archaic. There is a bureaucratic dimension to the problem as well: Regulatory agencies are populated by lawyers, so that much of what gets regulated is that which attorneys (as opposed to financial experts) feel most comfortable dealing with.

In the United States, the problem is compounded by the fragmented structure of financial regulation. We have, for example, overlapping federal-state bureaucracies for banking and securities regulation, but no federal presence in the insurance industry. The U.S. also regulates banking on a consolidated basis, at the level of the holding company, but does not apply the same approach in regulating securities firms, where the corporate parent may be an insurance company or even a nonfinancial institution. Thus, in many important cases, no single regulatory agency is looking at the whole picture, which includes some sprawling, multifaceted organizations.

The **eighth precept** is that the international dimension of financial institutions is growing, and will be increasingly difficult to oversee effectively without greater global harmonization of regulatory, accounting, disclosure, and trading standards and practices. All of the major participants and instruments in today's capital markets are integrated. But we are far from developing a single set of standards and practices, apart from a few notable successes such as capital requirements. Supervisory and auditing standards and relationships are simply inadequate, as demonstrated by a series of major international scandals over the last two decades: Herstatt, Franklin, Banco Amrosiano, BCCI, and Banca Nazionale del Lavoro, among others. And with regulatory regimes falling farther and farther behind the innovation curve each year, we can only expect more such calamities in the next two decades.

Reforming International Regulation and Supervision

While financial excesses and their hurtful economic consequences never can be eliminated completely, they can be limited through improved supervision and regulation of financial institutions and markets.

The modern, globalized financial structure is based on innovation and risk taking. Formal regulations and barriers to financial activities have been lowered, and over time they will come down further. Paradoxically, however, it is the more open, freewheeling financial environments that require the most astute and sophisticated supervision and regulation. In such systems, risk takers require discipline that is at once more intensive and better informed than in less market-oriented environments—the kind of discipline that is only possible with plenty of information about risk exposures.

But oversight—whether by official institutions or by the market itself—has been uneven at best, and frequently is tardy. There has been, quite simply, far too little sharing of information among official organizations, and far too little dialogue between regulators and private lenders and investors. Furthermore, many emerging markets have been hobbled by weak regulatory regimes, with little or no informal supervision and oversight to take up the slack.

To improve global financial architecture, I have long proposed the reorganization of the IMF and the World Bank, and also a more ambitious measure: the creation of an entirely new institution, which I will provisionally call the Board of Overseers of Major Institutions and Markets.

More than 50 years have passed since the IMF and the World Bank were created. The challenges they faced in the immediate aftermath of World War II were far different from the ones they now confront in our global markets. These two official institutions have failed to prevent major international financial conflagrations. At best, they are outmatched firefighters. But fire fighting is not enough—because international markets have become more perilous, and because no major industrial nation is willing to unleash the full force of its market discipline. What is urgently needed, therefore, is another major international accord on the scale of the Bretton Woods agreement, one that will either undertake a major overhaul of existing institutions or put in place entirely new ones.

In the wake of the Mexican crisis of 1995, the government heads in the major industrial nations, spurred by the Clinton Administration and hoping to avoid a recurrence, attempted to install an early warning system at the IMF and World Bank. The effort failed. And because of that, the official international financial institutions were largely unprepared to isolate the Asian financial crisis and thereby keep it from spreading.

Why? Because in a world of securitized credit and open credit markets, nations resist any attempt to interfere with their access to credit. Nor were any of the industrialized nations willing to exercise firm leadership to contain the financial disarray. Japan was encumbered by its own severe financial problems, and in any event has precious little experience (or credibility) playing the role of orchestra leader for financial bailouts. The United States—which had taken the lead in Mexico—viewed the Asian turmoil as more complex, and therefore not susceptible to the kind of program it engineered in Mexico. For their part, the Europeans saw Asia as a faraway region in which they exercised marginal power and influence. In any case, they were preoccupied with the lead-up to the establishment of their common currency, the Euro, and so were disinclined to take on broader responsibilities.

Once the Asian financial turbulence spread, market participants began to reconsider what it would mean for the world. The conclusions were sobering. It became increasingly clear that financial systems throughout Asia were far more fragile than previously thought, and that financial systems in the other major industrial economies were far more exposed than previously believed as well.

It also is now clear that the IMF—as presently constituted and managed—is poorly equipped to meet the heavy burdens placed upon it by its board of directors, the governments of the major industrialized nations. Even when the IMF is well aware of imbalances that threaten the stability of a member country, it lacks either the leverage to prod an errant nation into making timely adjustments in policy or the will to apply that leverage. In short, it is effectively stymied by the realities of the modern financial world of securitized flows of private capital.

Moreover, the IMF is handicapped by weaknesses in the national and international structures for regulating and supervising financial institutions. Many emerging markets lack independent banks or bank supervisory authorities with either the mandate or the power to confront institutions that are acting recklessly by taking on too much risk. To the contrary, these institutions often are prevented from detecting abuses such as excessive lending to insiders, to affiliates, or to politically connected companies.

Therefore, my plan for a new Board of Overseers of Major Institutions and Markets is designed primarily to put teeth into the current, largely ineffective system. The new Board would focus on three central tasks. First, it would set forth a code of conduct for market participants in order to encourage reasonable financial behavior. Second, it would supervise risk taking, not only by banks and other financial institutions that have always been subject to regulation and official supervision, but also by important new participants in the global markets. Finally, acting on behalf of member governments, the new Board would work to harmonize minimum capital requirements, to establish uniform trading, reporting, and disclosure standards, and to monitor the performance of institutions and markets under its purview.

Over time, this new international regulatory body would rate the credit quality of the market participants under its authority. Institutions that failed to abide by member standards would be sanctioned. Those that chose not to join the system would be subject to criteria and controls different from those of members. For example, lending to banks in nonmember nations would be subject to higher capital requirements and limitations on maturities. Nonmember nations also would not be allowed to sell new securities in the equity, bond, and money markets of members as freely as members themselves. The new Board would not enact specific regulations to control flows of capital internationally, but instead would visibly raise the bar for those wishing to take advantage of capital markets. In these and other ways, the actions of the Board should dramatically reduce risks in the system, although it could not hope to eliminate them entirely.

This kind of institution would also be well positioned to perform a variety of other vital tasks. It could supervise finance companies and other institutions that are in effect unrelated. It could improve international oversight of securitization. It could help forge international agreements on the investment powers of universal banks, and help oversee potential conflicts of interest as more financial institutions play the dual roles of lender and shareholder. All the while, it would continue working to bring together banking, securities, and insurance regulators to reach agreement on standards—accounting standards, disclosure standards, and trading standards. Today, there are large differences from one nation to the next. Accounting standards for financial institutions range from strict to lenient, disclosure standards from transparent to opaque, and trading standards from permissive to regimented.

To supplement and reinforce the work of this kind of Board of Overseers, we also need to institute some long-overdue reforms at the International Monetary Fund. In recent decades, the IMF has lost its focus and effectiveness in the face of a changing international financial environment. Like the present-day IMF, the revamped IMF that I have in mind would be responsible for organizing and partially funding emergency lending operations to protect the safety and soundness of the global system when member governments face serious balance of payments problems and are shut off from normal sources of external financing. And the new IMF would be responsible for setting policy conditions that borrowers must follow in order to qualify for emergency loans.

But *unlike* its predecessor, the reformed IMF that I envision would be proactive; that is, it would be responsible for anticipating problems and for pressing member governments to take timely preventative actions. It would be responsible for rating the economic and financial strength of its members. It would evaluate their fiscal and monetary deficiencies of the kind that could lead to excessive inflows of short-term capital from abroad, or that might compromise the health of the domestic banking system. Detecting such weaknesses, the new IMF would then demand remedial action. And if member governments refused to act, the reorganized IMF would make public the noncompliant nation's newly reduced credit rating. Because that kind of publicity would dramatically shrink the recalcitrant nation's access to credit in the open markets, it would serve as a powerful incentive to cooperate.

To be sure, rating the creditworthiness of sovereigns is a difficult job. But an appropriately staffed IMF would have a far better chance of doing the job effectively than would private credit rating agencies, which would not be privy to the kind of detailed and timely information available to the IMF.

Finally, reform of international financial supervision and regulation should include the revamping of the Group of Seven (G-7) leading industrial nations. The need for G-7 reform grows directly out of the recent creation of the European Monetary Union and its common currency, the Euro. It is imperative that the new European central bank begin a dialogue with the central banks of the United States and Japan on how to better harmonize monetary policies across the oceans. No longer can these banks operate in relative isolation; each must take into account the global implications of its actions. If, for example, the actions of the central banks create an overabundance of global liquidity, that in turn would pose a threat of worldwide inflation or of excessive growth of global credit. On the other hand, a shortage of global liquidity would threaten economic growth.

It is probably too much to expect that such attempts to harmonize the efforts of the leading central banks should include the goal of minimizing huge swings in currency rates like those that have plagued the international monetary system in recent years. Still, the world's central bankers should at least attempt to discuss the implications of outsized currency movements for the global trading system. Existing forums such as the Bank for International Settlements in Basel, Switzerland, hold some promise, but are too informal to undertake a systematic approach to the problem. The best candidate therefore seems to be a reformed and revitalized G-7.

The kind of international regulatory system I am advocating— whether composed of a combination of old and new institutions or of entirely new ones—would affirm the basic precepts that I outlined earlier in this chapter. Its financial institutions would be independent in their ability to exercise objective credit judgments. They would weigh their fiduciary duties against their legitimate desire to make a profit while fully disclosing their financial positions on the basis of realistic, prudent accounting standards. These institutions would operate under strict but reasonable regulatory standards developed to conform with both domestic and international market conditions. The reformed system would be designed to buttress the real economies of member nations, to facilitate noninflationary growth, and to support business enterprises during periods of temporary stress.

Recent initiatives do not go far enough in addressing the fundamental changes that have transformed the structure of international finance in recent years. One proposal, put forward by the G-7 at the Denver Economic Summit in 1997, called for loose cooperation and improved information exchange. Public officials cannot continue to depend on rigging up ad hoc support packages through the existing institutions when crises strike. In the end, inertia is the greatest risk to international finance. Ironically, the longer the present financial exuberance goes on, the harder it will be to maintain a sense of urgency about reforming the system for the day when exuberance turns into panic and disorder.

Proposals for Domestic Reform

Just as the nineteenth century closed with one of the great merger movements in American history—among industrial firms—the twentieth century has come to a close with a giant merger movement in banking. Bank of America's merger with Nationwide, Deutsche Bank's acquisition of Bankers Trust Company, and Banc One's purchase of First National Bank of Chicago are among the many notable consolidations. Because many of these mammoth mergers cut across traditions, they hold enormous implications for the structure of official supervision and regulation of financial institutions.

The entire structure of overseeing large, complex institutions needs to change accordingly. The Federal Reserve, which regulates bank holding companies, should retain its broad responsibilities, alongside the other agencies that are part of the U.S. regulatory cocktail: the Comptroller of the Currency, the FDIC, the state banking agencies, the SEC, the CFTC, and so on. The problems posed by giant banks are not new; the giant money centers and superregional banks raised the same sorts of issues.

But if we enter a new phase of widespread amalgamation in banking and insurance, then we must refashion our national regulatory system accordingly. Today, insurance companies are regulated at the state level but not at the federal level. This system has become increasingly outmoded as insurance firms have branched out from coast to coast. But it has worked, because the state insurance commissioners reached a modus operandi that has been broadly acceptable to the industry. However, the combination of banking and insurance would render that system inoperable. One way or another, official supervision of the insurance industry at the national level must come, even if it is done as a cooperative effort undertaken jointly by the various state insurance commissioners.

Gigantic financial conglomerates also increase the potential for conflicts of interest. When a major insurance company is combined with a large commercial banking operation, the newfound size and power on the asset management side of the business holds enormous potential for abuse. After all, achieving economies of scale through consolidation is one of the primary motivations behind many of these mergers. The message to clients is hard to miss: "Borrow from us or issue securities with us and we will make sure that if push comes to shove our asset people will find a good reason to buy the paper." In this way, independent credit judgments are subordinated to the vaunted "customer relationship." But there are serious moral and practical questions to be raised about this kind of financial relationship. For one: Who is going to umpire the process at close hand?

Finally, megamergers that join banks with other financial institutions should compel regulators to face once and for all the insidious "too-big-to-fail" doctrine. Consider the recent Travelers-Citicorp merger. Can the new behemoth enterprise be considered anything but too big to fail? Its financial sinews will reach into virtually every city and large town in America, and into every nation abroad as well. It will be intertwined with households, businesses, financial counterparties, and governments. It will reach into every phase of financial life: securitization, lending, derivatives, and asset management. Tens of billions of dollars will cross its books each day, involving transactions in foreign exchange, securities, and almost every other imaginable financial business that might fit under its sprawling institutional roof. How could the financial system as a whole cope with the side effects of a failure of the new Citigroup? It could not.

In cases like this, it will be necessary to make such immortal giants "too *good* to fail." This cannot be done without an expansion of official supervisory capacity that many will find unpalatable. Even so, our political economy has regulated public utility monopolies aggressively for more than a century. It is time we acknowledge that our giant financial institutions are "affected with a public interest" much like those utilities.

Regulatory Paths to Avoid

Proposals abound for the reform of the U.S. financial regulatory system. Unfortunately, many of these schemes are based more on political or ideological considerations than on a sound understanding of the dynamics of modern finance. One of the most troublesome of these is the proposal to lift the long-standing prohibitions against nonbanking businesses owning banks.

This suggestion is brought before Congress with troubling regularity. The proponents of this idea have offered various arguments over the course of the last couple of decades. During the Bush Administration, when banks were financially strapped, the merger advocates suggested that commercial banks could take over the struggling banks and infuse them with much-needed cash, thereby relieving the taxpayers of a potential burden.

But banks became quite profitable again in the 1990s, so the arguments shifted. These days, proponents of nonbank ownership of banks (among them, many Treasury officials) are making a kind of fatalistic argument. They say that nonbanks should be officially permitted to own banks because the marketplace already is mixing commercial and financial institutions. As Peter Wallison argued in the pages of the *Wall Street Journal* (July 29, 1997), "The separation of banking and commerce is as outdated as a 10-cent first-class stamp. After all, competition is the dominant theme in banking today." Should Microsoft therefore be allowed to acquire Citibank? No problem, says Wallison.

This reasoning is fallacious on several counts. To begin with, it assumes that banks are like any other ordinary business, and thus subject to the same venerable free-market precepts. They aren't. Banks are heavily regulated—but then, so are many other industries. What really sets banking apart is that it is undergirded by heavy taxpayer subsidies in the form of cheap government-supplied deposit insurance and a unique safety net provided by the Federal Reserve System's discount window. To be sure, the FDIC is funded by the premiums from member banks. But these premiums do not come close to paying for the insurance that banks receive in return: the backing of the full faith and credit of the United States. Such advantages are not attainable under normal competitive conditions.

Because taxpayers must foot the bill for bank failures—a potentially enormous bill, as we discovered in the 1980s—the question of banking ownership and control should not be left to the impersonal forces of the marketplace. Rather, to protect the taxpayer (and, ultimately, the larger society) this peculiar industry warrants a unique structure of laws, regulations, and supervision. And for these legal and regulatory projections to have any legitimacy, the long-standing separation between banking and commerce must remain intact. That separation helps to safeguard against potential abuses and dangers—ranging from abusive lending and investment practices and conflicts of interest to the excessive concentration of economic power.

Consider the possible range of abuses available to the new bank and commercial conglomerate. It could use its bank to extend credit to those who would benefit the whole organization. It could attract low-cost funds through insured deposits, and then use them to finance retailers, jobbers, manufacturers, and others in the firm's product distribution chain. It might even withhold credit from those who are—or might become—competitors to the parent in its non-banking businesses.

Why would a successful commercial business want to own a bank in the first place? The rate of return on invested capital is higher in most industrial businesses than in banking, and most carry far less debt in proportion to shareholders' equity on their balance sheets than the typical bank. If a commercial enterprise has amassed too much cash from its core business, then the sounder strategy would be to use that excess cash to buy back more of its own stock or, better still, pay it out to shareholders through larger dividends, leaving them the choice of what to do with the capital—including, perhaps, investing it in banks.

That gangsters bought banks in the 1920s and that drug lords do so (through intermediaries) in our own time should serve as a cautionary reminder. In these extreme cases, banks are used for criminal activities, especially for the laundering of profits from illegal activities. But these kinds of criminally motivated mergers are nevertheless driven by the profit motive: The bank is acquired to serve the interest of the "business." In doing so, it also provides some legitimate services to honest customers and clients. The same symbiotic relationship would come into play when a legitimate nonbanking firm acquired a bank. It would serve outsiders, but its central mission inevitably would be bent to the demands of its owner. That would all be a matter of competitive business strategy were it not for the fact that taxpayers were assuming much of the risk and, if need be, absorbing large losses.

It is easy to envision the cascading effect that would ensue if, following Wallison's advice, Microsoft were indeed permitted to acquire Citibank. In short order, many of the Fortune 100 industrial and commercial firms would own the nation's leading banks. This would undermine one of the fundamental characteristics of a healthy economy: the ability of lending officers to make objective judgments about the creditworthiness of potential borrowers. Hobbled and overburdened as it already is, our financial regulatory system would not be able to stem the tidal wave of preferential lending, in spite of existing prohibitions and the best intentions. Out of this would emerge a virtually unassailable corporate elite honeycombed with conflicts of interest—some apparent, others more obscure to the public—that would be difficult to dislodge, and surely would erode economic efficiency.

Another argument sometimes raised in favor of legitimizing bank and nonbank mergers goes like this: What about in cases of ailing and failing institutions? What harm would there be in allowing commercial and industrial firms to buy a defunct institution that otherwise would be shuttered by the FDIC, at considerable taxpayer expense and at the cost of many jobs? It is a seductive argument.

But it, too, is flawed. The takeover of a faltering bank is extraordinarily difficult. The management responsible for the calamity must be replaced. And by that time much of the franchise value of the institution typically has been lost, only to be restored through painstaking effort, if at all. Experienced banking executives would find the task daunting. Therefore, how likely are the managers of a commercial or industrial business, with no relevant banking experience, to engineer such a turnaround?

More than that, the money that might be saved in the short run through such a nonbank bailout will be far overshadowed in the longer run by the potential financial liability to the public that will emerge as the new commercial or industrial parent is able to slip in under the federal safety net. For this reason, nonbanking firms in trouble are likely to be more interested in acquiring banks than their soundly managed counterparts. Would the public have been better off if Pan Am, or LTV, or Federated Department Stores had been able to acquire an ailing and failing deposit institution in the 1980s?

Offsetting these damaging effects of banking and nonbanking mergers, I see few if any benefits. Banks need not be owned and controlled by large commercial and industrial firms in order to attract new capital. What they *should* do is rebuild investor confidence in their financial health and profitability over the long term.

Regulation to Balance Profit and Responsibility

Throughout the modern history of the United States, a debate has raged between two opposing camps when it comes to the question of disciplining financial institutions. One camp holds that financial institutions have a crucial public responsibility, one that sets them apart from other business enterprises. They are the custodians of our savings and temporary funds. By their very nature they are leveraged heavily, and for them to survive and succeed, they must *balance* their fiduciary responsibility with their entrepreneurial drive. According to those who hold this view—myself among them—this balance is virtually impossible in the absence of government supervision and regulation.

The other school believes that the best way to discipline institutions—regardless of any broader public responsibility—is through the open market process. According to this perspective, financial institutions are no different from other kinds of nonbanking enterprises. Banks and thrifts—and certainly securities firms, insurance companies, and other financial corporations—therefore should be permitted to prosper or fail, just like any other business enterprise. Proponents of this approach claim that despite the deregulation of recent decades, we haven't gone far enough in removing controls over the financial sector. More deregulation is required, they say, and with it a growing tolerance for failures, small and large.

By encouraging financial entrepreneurs to test the marginal edge of risk taking, deregulated markets exaggerate the credit cycle and the business cycle. This was brought home vividly in the 1980s, first with the overleveraging in the energy sector following the second energy crisis, and then with the worldwide real estate lending boom. The common denominator in both cases was a community of interests that linked together the motives of both borrowers and suppliers of credit.

The astonishing growth of floating-rate financing and interest rate swaps—innovations at the margins of traditional finance—clearly has fostered credit and business volatility. These instruments enable a marginal credit to stay in the market longer, which in turn permits projects that would have been denied at an earlier stage of a business expansion to go forward, thereby stimulating economic growth and prolonging the upswing in the cycle. Similarly, a downturn in economic activity will affect assets more adversely, thereby magnifying the severity of the contraction.

It is commonly agreed that the problem with regulated markets is that they rely on the sudden interruption of credit flows to achieve monetary restraint. Advocates of deregulated markets have long hoped that adjustments would take place more smoothly and with less disruption to the real economy. Such has not been the case, however.

But extreme deregulation is dangerous, as demonstrated by how much our financial fabric has been weakened and torn during the same years that the deregulation movement has taken hold. When it comes to deregulation, the fundamental difference between financial and nonfinancial businesses has made all of the difference. Competition outside the financial sector normally leads to cost reductions, product innovations, and lower costs for consumers. In the financial markets, however, the typical result of sharp-edged competition is that institutions begin to seek higher profits by engaging in speculative lending and trading practices and by leveraging their already thin capital structures even more.

Overregulated financial markets pose risks to the financial health of an economy as well. Most importantly, there is the danger of bureaucratic inertia, with its menacing potential to magnify economic and credit cycles. Whenever there is a system of either formal or informal credit allocation, the decision makers of the regulatory institution are likely to make procyclical judgments of their own. Bureaucratic dynamics being what they are, civil servants find it exceedingly hard to be contrarians. Their natural tendency is to question new lending in areas with a history of problems, but to readily bless lending in areas that are growing rapidly under presently favorable conditions. The outcome of these biases is exaggerated credit cycles and losses to the financial institution over the longer term.

Why do official policy responses so often lag far behind structural changes in financial markets? There are several reasons. To begin with, officials commonly underestimate the potency of a new structural change. And by the time it becomes obvious that something significant has happened, the market adjustment triggered by structural change no longer can be easily brought under the existing regulatory framework. This is because structural changes often do not fall within the neat categories normally used to delineate official institutions. For example, when financial derivatives emerged as a major component of modern finance, there was considerable confusion about which regulatory umbrella should cover them. (For a detailed discussion of the regulation of financial derivatives, see Chapter 4.) That uneasiness has persisted, even as the market has been buffeted by several derivatives-related mishaps in recent years.

Regulation also lags behind structural change because the impact of the latter is difficult to quantify in the early stages. Consider, for example, the public's heavy investment in the equity markets through mutual funds. It took quite a while for U.S. financial officials to appreciate that this trend might generate a significant wealth effect among millions of households. Now that wealth effect addiction is widespread, policymakers are beginning to understand that the level of consumer expenditures on goods, services, and housing ultimately is related to the strength of the stock market—and, therefore, that there might be considerable withdrawal pains for the larger economy if the stock market suffers a severe setback.

Internationally, official policy responses to structural change have been handicapped by those and other shortcomings. For example, vested interests in the official international financial institutions needing reform may feel threatened by proposed changes, and at times voice their opposition to reform. For their part, the sovereignties themselves generally find it difficult to give up any independent control, even though financial markets and economies are integrating globally at a rapid clip. It seems, for instance, that the U.S. government supports overall reform of the current international system of regulation only reluctantly. This may be out of concern that any comprehensive reform might require the United States to relinquish some of its dominance over these institutions. If true, this would be shortsighted leadership, for the U.S. would realize no permanent benefit in being the most powerful member of an institution with eroding credibility and authority.

Developing nations seem to oppose international regulatory reform because they are afraid that improved scrutiny of financial institutions and markets would jeopardize their access to funds in the private markets. More specifically, they may be concerned about the consequences of having to increase the transparency in their domestic banking system or bring to light financial problems that otherwise might remain concealed. This is an egregious misconception. Ensuring access to credit for less-than-creditworthy institutions only exaggerates the financial and economic cycle, as several Asian nations now painfully realize. It is, in fact, in the great interest of developing economies to reduce extremes in the financial cycle, because doing so helps produce a steadier and less interruptible flow of private funds.

Financial excesses eventually impoverish the marginal borrower and, for a while at least, tend to strengthen the bargaining position of the strongest participants in the credit system—namely, the governments, financial institutions, and business corporations of the major industrial nations of North America and Europe. That is the clear message that comes out of the financial wreckage in Asia. Unfortunately, this narrow advantage is merely a transitory benefit, since ultimately we all become losers as financial crises fan out from their centers of origin. It is therefore worth pondering in the United States whether we can truly escape damage to our own economy in the absence of a much stronger and more up-to-date international regulatory system.

In recent years, the United States has managed to remain fairly well isolated from the financial upheavals that have engulfed nearly half the economies of the world. One result has been an imbalance between the economic performance of America and that of much of the rest of the world. And one effect has been highly competitive product markets. But it is easy to envision the unfolding of a different scenario. Once business activity picks up outside American borders, leading to shrinking liquidity and tightening credit, the expansive global marketplace will be strained. At some point, the dynamic, securitized, globalized marketplace in which confidence has been running so high will face heightened risks. But it would be foolish to wait until then before modernizing our systems of international and domestic financial regulation and oversight.

This is not to belittle the efforts under way to improve risk management. For example, the New York–based Counterparty Risk Management Policy Group, headed by E. Gerald Corrigan and Stephen G. Thieke, has made some important recommendations. These include improving credit risk estimation methods, setting stronger internal limits, tightening collateral margins, making internal risks more transparent to senior managers and regulators, and improving the sharing of information between counterparties. Nevertheless, there are no enforcement powers behind these recommendations. And just like the Group of 30's recommendations about derivatives in the early 1990s, these guidelines are likely to be ignored in the competitive struggle for profits and markets.

At the end of the day, many of the chronic shortcomings that plague official financial supervision and regulation stem from its strong propensity for *incremental* adaptation and change. Too often, regulators act like the proverbial boy at the dike who struggles to plug one leak after the next. It is certainly difficult for regulators to take a proactive stance, to anticipate change and refashion strategies and tactics accordingly. By their nature, supervision and regulation are reactive; they will never keep pace with the headlong rush of financial innovation. Still, incremental change sometimes is simply not enough; a fundamental overhaul of the system is needed. Given the pervasive structural changes in financial markets that have come about since World War II, the time for such an overhaul is long overdue. What would the regulatory system look like if it were designed from scratch today? If we are to break the cycle of regulatory and supervisory shortcomings and foibles, then regulators must ask themselves that question—and act on the answer.

13

Learning from Financial Crises

It is not uncommon for one crisis to induce behavioral changes that contribute to the next crisis. In this sense, crises always teach lessons—though not always the right ones.

Financial crises are frightening and often devastating events. The crises I have witnessed firsthand from Wall Street and studied academically have convinced me that financial panics and upheavals have a powerful, shaping influence on both financial fundamentals and the progress of the markets themselves. This is because crises induce behavioral changes and responses in the private sector as well as in the public policy arena. A major crisis can leave scars that last for a full generation or more, shaping financial behavior in ways that are not always obvious or even constructive. In fact, it is not uncommon for one crisis to induce behavioral changes that contribute to the next crisis. In this sense, crises always teach lessons—though not always the right ones.

The Depression Legacy

When I began my career in 1949, two recent, major world events still held a profound influence over the financial world. One was the unparalleled crisis of the 1930s—the Great Depression—the aftereffects of which continued to shape economic and financial behavior in all sorts of ways for years to come. The other was World War II, which had a different but also powerful, lingering effect on economics and finance in the early postwar period.

The Great Depression was, of course, an immensely devastating episode in modern world history. The enormity of the collapse can readily be captured by a few statistics. In the American economy, the peak in 1929 to the trough in the 1933 contraction resulted in a drop of 30 percent in gross national product, 48 percent in manufacturing production,* and 45 percent in personal income. Unemployment increased nearly 800 percent, as the unemployment rate spiraled from 3.2 percent to 24.9 percent. In the financial markets, stock values plummeted 85 percent from their 1929 peak to their 1932 trough. By the end of 1932, nearly 22 percent of all the commercial banks in business at the end of 1929 had failed.

The Depression shaped the behavior not merely of those millions of Americans of all walks of life who suffered through "the great collapse." It also affected millions in the next generation, who listened to their friends and relatives recount vivid stories of uncertainty, struggle, and hardship. My own experiences with the Depression were a mixture of firsthand experience and oral renditions. As noted earlier, I often listened to my grandfather's recitation of the German hyperinflation of the 1920s—how it contributed to the rise of Nazism and thus forced us to flee Germany. I also carried into adulthood vivid memories of how hard my parents worked to earn a living during our early years in the U.S., when the scars of the Depression were still clearly visible.

Franklin Roosevelt's Administration responded to the crisis with a dizzying array of new laws and programs—the so-called "alphabet agencies" of the New Deal. The financial sector was one of FDR's prime targets, and soon after taking office he spearheaded legislation (the Banking Acts of 1933 and 1935) that instituted stricter controls over financial institutions and investors. The newly created Federal Deposit Insurance Corporation reversed the panicky withdrawal of bank deposits across the nation by insuring bank deposits (initially, up to $2,500 per depositor). Banks were prohibited from paying interest on demand deposits. Commercial banks, in particular, were prohibited from engaging in underwriting or trading corporate or other private

---

*This figure compares 1929 and 1932, when this index hit its low point.

securities. This separation of commercial and investment banking (through the Glass-Steagall Act of 1932) was intended to insulate bank deposits from the kind of speculative risk taking that had played such a large role in the bull market of the late 1920s.

Roosevelt's banking reforms also invested the Federal Reserve System with new power: to set maximum interest rates that banks could pay on time and savings deposits, and to set margin requirements on security loans. The New Deal also established the Securities and Exchange Commission to supervise trading on organized exchanges and over-the-counter securities markets. Now, issuers and underwriters of public securities had to meet strict standards of disclosure.

The Second World War proved to be a boon for the nation's economy and financial system. The rapid and full-blown mobilization of the economy for war pulled the country out of the Depression. On the financial side, the federal government placed additional constraints on credit creation through the imposition of down payments on consumer credit and restrictions on mortgage financing. This strengthened the credit structure, so that by the end of the war, American financial institutions were highly liquid, and interest rates and stock prices were low. Nevertheless, the Depression mentality—job insecurity, the desire for a financial nest egg, a reluctance to consume—lingered on, fostering a general conservatism in business and personal financial behavior.

In these and other ways, the economic and financial environment that I entered as a young professional in the 1950s and 1960s was hardly typical. The United States stood without peer, politically or economically, lending support to Henry Luce's claim that "the American Century" was dawning. The war-ravaged economies of Europe and Japan were just beginning to recover. Here at home, there was new confidence that economic policymaking could be handled scientifically. The newly established Council of Economic Advisers (1946) gave professional economists a more direct voice in macroeconomic policymaking. There were, to be sure, cyclical swings in the economy, with recessions occurring in 1948–1949, 1953–1954, 1957–1958, and 1960–1961. But these recessions were quite mild compared with those in the interwar years, lending credence to the notion that experts could "fine-tune" the economy. Overall, real GNP grew at a robust 2.8 percent annual average between 1951 and 1960, while unemployment and inflation remained in check.

In the financial markets, the Federal Reserve emerged from its World War II cocoon. The Fed-Treasury Accord of March 1951 removed the 2.5 percent peg on the long government bond (enacted to aid war financing) and allowed the Fed to pursue a flexible monetary policy. A few years later, the Fed—in an effort to lessen its interference in the credit market—took the major step of limiting the open market trading of Treasury bills. The bond market during the 1950s experienced three cyclical swings. In these periods, yields on Governments rose on average 42 percent and (during the rally) fell 16 percent, a modest pattern judging by subsequent events. In contrast, stock prices rose irregularly, with the Dow Jones Industrial Average starting at 200 and closing at 679.

Meanwhile, commercial banks returned to the business of commercial lending. Some merged to consolidate stronger positions in the market, but there was nothing like the merger mania in financial institutions that would erupt in later decades. In the open credit markets, corporate bonds began to gain in popularity, with a few of the new series featuring 100-year maturities (a phenomenon that would not recur until the 1990s). By and large, risk taking in the financial markets of the early postwar years was moderate. The Great Depression and World War II were continuing to shape the culture of money, from Wall Street to Main Street.

Still, there were hints of change. In retrospect, one event in particular heralded the less restrained and more volatile times to come. For a brief time in 1959, interest rates climbed to surprisingly high levels by the norms of the day. The U.S. government issued a 5-year note with a 5 percent coupon. The issue soon became known as the "Magic 5s," because the bonds attracted individual (as opposed to institutional) investors in very large numbers. I recall seeing a long line of people lined up in the lobby of the New York Federal Reserve Bank, waiting to fill out subscription papers for the new offering. In retrospect, the

Magic 5s was a harbinger of things to come—of a future investment environment in which small, household investors participated alongside professionals in a quest for higher returns.

By the middle of the 1960s, following two decades of unprecedented economic stability and prosperity, the notion of "financial crisis" had lost much of its meaning. Memories of the Great Crash, of the Depression's hardships, and of the upheavals of war had begun to fade. Economists and financial experts were beginning to employ new tools—such as econometric modeling and early computers—for collecting and analyzing data and monitoring economic performance. Many economists spoke confidently and convincingly about meeting bold growth objectives. Some even came to believe that the economics profession had tamed the business cycle once and for all.

The 1966 Credit Crunch

In the financial arena, the credit crunch of 1966 was the first major mishap of the postwar era. The result of a unique confluence of events, the crunch nevertheless originated with a typical cyclical upturn: the economic buildup that followed the recession of 1960–1961. With the recovery, capital spending by business at first began to gain momentum slowly, but then rose sharply going into 1966. A driving force was the recent heavy escalation of the Vietnam War, which spurred a sharp rise in defense spending. As the year unfolded, unemployment inched below 4 percent; and by the third quarter of 1966, inflation (as measured by consumer prices) was running at an annual rate of 3.8 percent—markedly higher than the 1.5 percent or so that had prevailed over the preceding 3 years.

At the same time, high-ranking economic policymakers were relying more and more on fiscal controls in their efforts to regulate the economy and sustain growth. This reflected the widespread acceptance of the theories of British economist John Maynard Keynes—or at least a popularized version of these theories. (See also Chapter 10.) Writing during the Great Depression, Keynes had argued that heavy government spending was needed to pull an economy out of a major slump—even if large budget deficits were a result.* During the war, it was abundantly clear that the explosion of federal spending ushered in the economic recovery, apparent proof that the Keynesian approach worked.

In the postwar period, the economics profession increasingly came to see flexible fiscal policies—the timely raising and lowering of taxes, on the one hand, and spending, on the other—as the chief way to assure sustainable growth. Advocates of the new fiscalism wielded some very seductive, scientific-sounding rhetoric: They spoke of "fine-tuning" the economy, of "mid-course corrections" and "rolling read-justments," and of bringing the economy in for a "soft landing." Such was the thinking behind the Kennedy tax cuts, which came at a time when there was no federal budget surplus but the pace of economic expansion had begun to flag.

The theory had merit, but it ran into trouble when applied in the real world. To begin with, as Keynes's approach was popularized, it was oversimplified. The British economist had advocated monetary controls during normal times, with deficit spending to be reserved only as radical surgery to resuscitate a dying patient. Now, Keynesian surgery was being used as a cure for economic colds and flu. More than this, the approach used by policymakers typically was lopsided. Not surprisingly, political leaders found the expansive side of the Keynesian model—the tax-cutting part—much more agreeable than the restraining side. Even when the economy was running hot, politicians tried to avoid tax hikes at any cost. It was a clear case of short-term political expediency winning out over long-term consistency.

My suspicions about this kind of macroeconomic management were heightened during the scaling up of the Vietnam War in 1965. It seemed to me at the time that the surge in defense spending would

---

*Although the New Deal, with its heavy spending on public works and other ambitious programs, seemed an embodiment of the Keynesian approach, Roosevelt was unfamiliar with the economist's theories. He was more interested in providing a modicum of relief for newly impoverished members of the middle class. And he remained dedicated to balancing the budget, which he attempted to do at the first signs of recovery in 1937, ushering in the so-called "Roosevelt recession."

eliminate any fiscal drag in the federal budget, and probably boost deficit levels higher than officially projected. I cautioned that such a fiscal approach would increase pressure toward inflation and higher interest rates. Unfortunately (for the nation), my warnings proved correct. President Johnson rejected the advice of his economic team— which recommended asking Congress for a tax increase in early 1966—marking the end of the period's flexible fiscal policy. The result of the heavy "guns and butter" spending without counterbalancing new tax revenues was the beginning of what became know as the "great inflation" in modern American history.

The unhinging of fiscal restraint certainly made the Federal Reserve's job more difficult in 1966. But monetary policymakers also contributed to the credit crunch in their own way. A key development came in 1962, when commercial banks began to issue negotiable certificates of deposits. These new money market instruments fundamentally altered the structure of financial markets, for they allowed the banks to bid for liabilities in the open market for the first time. Whereas before a bank depended on the wealth of its local community, now it could buy deposits in order to increase its loans and investments, and thereby enlarge its role as a financial intermediary. Few industry experts in 1962 recognized the long-term significance of the negotiable CD. Many saw it merely as a technical modification.

In short order, it became clear they were wrong. As loan demand picked up in 1966, the dynamic new structure in commercial banking quickly came to the fore. Banks began to bid for funds aggressively, driving open market rates above the maximum interest rates allowable for small time and savings deposits. This prompted thousands of small, individual depositors to withdraw large portions of their household savings and to shift them into U.S. government bonds and other open market investments. Some individuals even borrowed against the cash surrender value of their life insurance policies and invested the proceeds in open market obligations. This phenomenon—the shifting of funds from deposits and insurance policies into open market investments—came to be known as disintermediation.

By the summer of 1966—when the market hit the maximum allowable interest rate on large-denomination CDs—the credit crunch was in full swing. For financial insiders, it was an extraordinary and scary event, especially given the placid rhythms that had prevailed since the end of the war. The dramatic tightening of credit had enormous ramifications for the housing market (by forcing a wave of loan denials), and for businesses that began to turn from banks to the open credit market to finance expansion. Major financial institutions of all kinds—but especially the thrifts—were liquidating bond portfolios at a rapid clip.

Salomon Brothers felt the squeeze on several fronts. Traders began to widen the spreads between buy and sell prices. Salespeople found it harder and harder to place new offerings. And the firm's own inventory of securities became increasingly expensive to finance.

Each day seemed to bring new—and more unpleasant—revelations. Three-month U.S. Treasury bills climbed to the lofty height of 5.58 percent, a rate not unusual now but unheard of at the time. Southern California Edison, a stalwart utility, issued a long bond that yielded up to 6.19 percent in the secondary market. Many thrifts came under increasing pressure from deposit withdrawals. Large commercial banks, which began to experience problems in rolling over maturing certificates of deposit, scrambled to recoup by acquiring Eurodollar deposits and by issuing commercial paper through bank subsidiaries and affiliates.

Government action helped quell the crisis. In late August, the Federal Reserve issued a letter to the nation's commercial banks urging them to slow the growth of business loans and the liquidation of securities. It also indicated that it would tighten lending through the use of the Fed discount window by member banks. Around the same time, President Johnson called on federal credit agencies to curtail their financing and promised to trim the federal budget.

The key interests in business, finance, and government drew differing lessons from the credit crunch of 1966. Business corporations sought ways to avoid being constrained in the same way in the future. Many entered the market as new issuers of commercial paper domestically and of bonds in the Euro market. Financial institutions such as banks and thrifts clamored for an easing of the Regulation Q restrictions (which set a ceiling on allowable interest rates). For their part, individual investors began to reconsider their investment options. The credit crunch, by introducing thousands of small-scale investors to alternatives to ordinary passbook savings, provided the first glimpse of the dramatic democratization of investments that was about to dawn.

It is important to note that throughout this crisis, credit quality remained high. In that significant respect, the 1966 crisis differed from subsequent postwar financial upheavals, in which credit-quality deterioration would figure prominently. The reason was that in 1966, the denial of credit came quickly. Interest rates were halted from escalating even further by financial market segmentation, by interest rate ceilings imposed on banks and thrifts by the government, and by competition with the capital markets themselves.

Still, the upheaval of 1966 left an indelible mark on American finance. And it added a new term to the finance lexicon: "disintermediation." As this word began to gain currency, Sidney Homer and I tried to substitute a less cumbersome term. We called on the readers of *Comments on Credit* to suggest something more elegant. But as the suggestions came in—"unbanking," "circumfiduciation," "redepositing," "de-de-mediation," "nonconduitivity," "revesting," "transbonding," "retromediation"—it became clear to us that the alternatives were even worse than the original. Disintermediation stuck.

The Collapse of the Penn Central

A credit crisis of a different sort materialized in 1970. Like the 1966 upheaval, this one had some cyclical underpinnings. Inflation had been on the rise. The Vietnam War continued to drive up military spending. Corporations were turning more and more to external sources of funding, a common signal that business expansion had entered a late phase. Against this backdrop, the Fed was tightening monetary policy. (See Exhibit 13-1.)

The banks were feeling the squeeze. Because the Fed refused to raise the Regulation Q ceiling, there was a large runoff of negotiable CDs. In an effort to offset these constraints, banks began to borrow more heavily from overseas branches and from the Eurodollar market.

A national growth policy implemented by a faulty guidance
system breeds inflationary expectations. The most surprising
aspect of the inflationary pressures during the last few years was
not the sharp increases in wholesale and consumer prices during
1965 and 1966. This reflected, of course, the usual cyclical phenomena associated with rapid expansion. It was the continuation of inflationary expectations following the credit crunch in
the Fall of 1966. It is true that the price rise abated but expectations did not. Official policy virtually assured the resumption of
the inflationary spiral through large dosages of spending,
through monetary injections, and through failure to enforce
wage and price discipline.

Henry Kaufman, "The Market Implications of Poor Official Policy Timing," a talk delivered before the Municipal Finance Forum, Washington,
D.C., February 20, 1968.

Exhibit 13-1

They also issued commercial paper through their holding companies
and borrowed by consummating repurchase agreements. With these
and other measures, they struggled mightily to avoid the conditions
that had wreaked such havoc in 1966. Meanwhile, corporations also
tried to avoid the sins of the recent past. Recalling their difficulties in
obtaining ready access to bank loans a few years earlier, they began to
issue commercial paper on a larger scale.

In 1969, I began to detect simmering problems in the credit markets, and discussed the growing likelihood of a major disruption with
Sidney Homer. Sidney suggested that we communicate our concerns to
Arthur Burns, the recently confirmed incoming Chairman of the Federal Reserve. Burns had not yet assumed his new post, so we met him at
his office in the State Department, where he was finishing out a stint as
special adviser to President Nixon. Sidney Homer had known Arthur
Burns for years, and in time I also came to know him well. Our get-
togethers, though infrequent, were always thoroughly enjoyable to me.

Although Arthur Burns was of medium height and had a somewhat high-pitched voice, he had an imposing presence. His shock of

white hair parted in the middle, the pipe he usually clenched between his jaws, the slow and measured cadence of his speech—all conveyed an air of gravitas. Undergirding his demeanor was Burns's impressive credentials: Columbia University professor, expert on business cycles, former Chairman of the Council of Economic Advisers. In short, he was a recognized authority, and acted like one. (Even so, as the next 8 years would demonstrate, the Burns chairmanship hardly marked the finest hour for modern monetary policy. Among other foibles, he underassessed the significance of the energy crisis of 1973, supported Nixon's wage and price controls, and tended to overextend monetary ease.)

Our meeting with Burns took place on the Thanksgiving eve of 1969. Armed with reams of data, we emphasized the sharp rise in the volume of outstanding commercial paper that—in combination with a sizable increase in bank loans—was eroding corporate credit quality. The amount of commercial paper outstanding, we pointed out, had climbed from some $10 billion in June 1965, to $32 billion by the end of 1969, to a staggering $40 billion by May 1970. The trend might well cause some corporate insolvencies, we suggested.

Burns understood our analysis, but I sensed that he thought we were overstating the urgency in this situation. Nor was he well positioned to act. Even had he been Chairman at the time, he had no experience in dealing with a financial crisis as the nation's central banker.

The crisis hit in May 1970. The precipitating event was the financial collapse of the nation's behemoth railway system, the Penn Central Railroad. The Pennsy had been pulling a trainload of commercial paper—some $200 million worth—due to mature in 3 months. But it found itself unable to roll over the maturing notes, nor to secure new paper. As news of this debacle hit the Street, the Penn Central's share price plummeted.

Signs of a broader crisis were popping up elsewhere as well. Credit-quality yield spreads began to widen sharply. When two major finance companies—Commercial Credit and Chrysler Financial—also failed to roll over their maturing notes, apprehension spread throughout the commercial paper market.

At the height of the Penn Central crisis, Bernard "Bunny" Lasker, Chairman of the New York Stock Exchange, requested a meeting with

me. Lasker was about to meet with President Nixon to discuss strategies for coping with the crisis, and he wanted my advice. During my
meeting with Lasker, which took place the day before he was to meet
with the President, I made several suggestions.

To begin with, I advised that he enter the White House unobtrusively. Press coverage of Lasker's visit would only serve to incite further
instability in the markets. Second, I said, try to meet with the President
alone. This would give Lasker an opportunity to communicate his concerns less formally and more directly than if others were in the room.
My specific recommendations on policy were that the President
should encourage the Fed to ease monetary policy and to lift some of
the ceilings on time deposits so that the banks would be in a more liquid position to ease the pressure in the commercial paper market.

Lasker seemed to take my advice to heart, and told me that, as a
personal friend of President Nixon, he should be able to arrange a private meeting with little difficulty. We departed on a note of optimism.

But these best-laid plans went awry. Upon his return from Washington, Bunny informed me that the press had gotten wind of his visit
to the White House, and that many of the President's advisers had sat
in on the meeting. Because of the presence of so many others, Lasker
had presented only watered-down versions of the recommendations
that we had discussed.

Even so, the Fed did ease monetary policy in June, which had a pronounced positive effect on the credit markets. It also suspended the interest rate ceiling that banks could pay on large-denominated CDs with a
maturity of 30 to 89 days. As I had suspected, financial conditions began
to ease soon thereafter. Meanwhile, the banks issued a large volume of
CDs. The amount of commercial paper outstanding fell sharply, so the
banks expanded their loans to offset a large portion of this contraction.
With all of this, however, the economy began to slide into recession.

Unlike the 1966 credit crunch, the 1970 crisis involved a serious
deterioration in credit quality, one severe enough to precipitate a
major bankruptcy (the Penn Central) and to bring several other major
corporations to the brink of disaster. Unfortunately, credit-quality
deterioration was to become a common feature of financial crises
throughout the remainder of the twentieth century.

American corporations emerged from the turmoil surrounding the collapse of the Penn Central determined to avoid a similar fate. Thus, they scrambled for more bank lines of credit to back up their maturing commercial paper. Increasingly, commercial banks made loans with floating interest rates, and financed those loans with deposits and borrowings of comparable maturity. This meant that, in effect, commercial banks were becoming spread bankers.

The redefinition of the commercial banking business posed new risks, however. The first clear demonstration of this came in 1974, with the failure of the Franklin National Bank. Franklin had been an aggressive issuer of negotiable CDs and federal funds, and also was a large borrower in the Eurodollar interbank market. But the credit quality of its loans was poor, and the bank had suffered large losses in the foreign exchange market. The latter, in turn, caused the failure of Herstatt, a private bank in West Germany. Herstatt's collapse caused yield spreads between Treasury bills and CDs to widen dramatically, and ushered in a period of disarray in the foreign exchange and Eurodollar markets.

These developments highlighted the new instability that had been infused into the banking system with the growing popularity of spread banking. Less obvious at the time, but quite significant in retrospect, were the corrective steps taken by the Federal Reserve to contain the reverberations from the Franklin National and Herstatt episode. As the crisis began to unfold, the Fed loaned money to Franklin National in an effort to protect financial markets—especially the market for CDs—and thus stabilize Eurodollars and foreign exchange. In this way, the Fed had extended the scope of its operations as a lender of last resort into the international arena for the first time in the postwar period. It would not be the last.

The Oil Crises and Their Hidden Effects

The year 1973 was a watershed in American economic history. After a generation of unprecedented economic expansion, the economy suddenly entered a period of much slower growth and even stagnation (depending on the index one considers). Now, for the first time since the end of the war, the U.S. economy suffered a perplexing and damaging combination of high inflation, high unemployment, and slow growth. Traditional economic models came up short in explaining this phenomenon; unemployment and inflation were supposed to counterbalance each other, not emerge at the same time. So unprecedented was the union of stagnation and inflation that a new term was coined to describe it: "stagflation." (See Exhibit 13-2.)

There were, to be sure, structural and cyclical forces driving the new stagflation, including, as we have seen, the pernicious inflationary pressures unleashed during the Johnson Administration. But there was an immediate precipitating cause as well: the oil shock of 1973–1974. During the Yom Kippur Jewish holiday in October 1973, Egypt drove tanks across the Suez Canal into Israel-occupied territory. In the fierce but brief war that followed, the United States supported Israel. In reaction, the Arab exporting nations joined forces with leaders from other exporting nations to transform the weak Organization of Petroleum Exporting Countries (OPEC) into a strong and militant cartel. The result was an effective oil embargo—and a surge in the price of crude oil from $3.70 per barrel in 1972 to more than three times that amount 18 months later.

Eventually, persistent inflation increases economic and financial concentrations, encroaches on private freedom and withers away the disciplines required to preserve a well-functioning democratic society. The true economic liberals of our day are those who urge strong anti-inflationary measures. Their philosophy assures the survival of economic and political democracy and sustainable economic growth. Economic stimulation through policies of permissive inflation must be labeled the philosophy of the economic reactionaries. Their philosophy has all the ingredients of future economic and financial shock.

Henry Kaufman, "Inflation, Credit Flows and Interest Rates," a talk delivered before the Association of American Railroads' Treasury Division Convention, Phoenix, Arizona, October 23, 1973.

Exhibit 13-2

Few economists and policymakers failed to perceive the direct consequences of this huge surge in crude oil prices. Higher transportation costs would ripple through the world economy, driving up prices of all goods shipped by truck, train, car, and plane. Moreover, oil was the raw material feedstock for billions of tons of petrochemical products manufactured each year, including the leading mass-produced plastics. And the United States, which consumed the majority of the world's oil, most of it imported, surely would feel the brunt of the oil embargo the hardest.

While all of this was true, it was merely part—the most obvious part—of a far more complex picture. The early 1970s energy crisis also had an enormous impact on the structure of world finance. But few experts or policymakers perceived these dynamics at the time. In that sense, American leadership during the travails of the mid-1970s came up horribly short.

The first oil crisis (another would follow in 1979) had three very important implications for the financial markets that were not properly understood at the time. First was the essential importance of the American dollar as the vehicle that made a huge international transfer of oil wealth possible. Second was the fact that the United States possessed enormous *potential* power to limit the size and negative consequences that massive flows of capital were likely to have on world economies and markets, particularly in the developing world. Finally, U.S. policymakers sacrificed our powerful position for the sake of immediate political objectives, apparently oblivious to the larger negative repercussions. Such were the views that I expressed in 1973–1974, and I believe the passage of time has only strengthened their validity.

At the heart of the problem was a tension between the interests of the U.S. economy generally and the more narrow interests of leading financial institutions that handled the flow of petroleum wealth. For these banks, particularly a handful of large U.S. banks, the business of handling the flow of oil money represented a tremendous opportunity. It all seemed quite simple. Oil consumers would pay boycott-inflated higher prices to the producers, who in turn would redeposit the funds in large Western banks. The banks would then use these redeposits to finance the oil consumers. This elegant circulation of capital, rather than the larger implications of the arrangement for the American economy, captured and held the attention of U.S. government and financial leaders during the oil crisis.

The problem was that two vitally important aspects of this transaction structure were practically ignored. First, greater and greater reliance on the U.S. dollar and on this network of international banking relationship facilitated the rapid climb in the price of oil. After all, without this kind of international financial system for purchasing oil (with U.S. dollars through international banks), the OPEC nations would not have been able to make markets in their plentiful product.

The second problem emerged from the fact that the wealthy oil producers became large creditors of the banks, which eagerly attended their every need. This led to the channeling of credit to borrowers of lower credit quality. The oil producers were owed money by large money centers, which in turn were owed money by nations and corporations with deteriorating credit quality. Still, Wall Street encouraged the trend, for oil capital represented an enormously attractive financing and investment opportunity. Week by week, the finance ministers and central banks of the oil-producing countries gained prominence and desirability. Before long, the airplanes to Riyadh and other Middle East capitals were crowded with Western bankers and portfolio managers. And both Wall Street and Washington failed to recognize the wider importance of this shift in financial resources.

My chief concern at the time was that the aggressive involvement of the banks ultimately would lead to trouble—not only for the banks themselves, but also for the U.S. dollar and for financial markets in general. I expressed these views at a conference (sponsored by the London *Financial Times*) in April 1976, in a talk titled "Will the Banker Need to Adjust to a Harsher Climate over the Longer Term?" I noted in particular that the rapid growth of bank assets and liabilities had not been accompanied by a reasonable increase in bank equity capital. I also concluded that banks would be required to disclose more information, and that they were likely to encounter tougher and more conservative accounting standards in the future as well as more intensive official supervision.

Because my talk received considerable attention in the press, it came to the attention of the senior management of Citicorp, who invited me to lunch to challenge my observations. Citicorp was led by Walter Wriston (President and CEO since 1967, Chairman since 1970), the most influential banker of his day, and probably since. Walter is a tall and rather lanky man, with an intense bearing and a dry wit. Economically and politically conservative, he had close ties to the Republican political leadership in his day. His speeches were a model of clarity, and usually garnered wide coverage in the press.

As our reputations grew in the financial community, it was quite apparent that we held sharply contrasting views about the proper role of banking. For me, that role is special and unique, and should be bound within certain confines. As repositories of large pools of savings, banks (and indeed many other financial institutions) possess an awesome fiduciary responsibility—one that should temper the institutions' entrepreneurial drive.

In contrast, Walt Wriston championed entrepreneurship in banking. He believed that banks should set growth targets. At Citibank, he admonished managers to grow profits by an ambitious 15 percent per year. (In my view, such pressure on lending and investment officers leads to compromises in credit standards that eventually imperil the institution.) But Wriston's influence in the industry was without parallel, making him a kind of Pied Piper of commercial banking at the time. Following his views, many others pursued aggressive liability management practices.

Wriston's entrepreneurial banking philosophy is captured in his famous assertion that "banks fail, but countries do not fail." The suggestion that nations always pay their debts has, of course, no historical foundation. Yet Wriston's widely known view encouraged institutions and investors to participate in loan syndications that channeled vast sums of capital to developing nations without the proper degree of scrutiny. The result was a massive wave of defaults in the 1980s, with disastrous consequences for third world economies, for global financial markets, and for Citibank itself.

When we used to greet each other, Walter frequently would tweak me about our philosophical differences. (In contrast to Wriston's swashbuckling reputation, I had become known—as we will see in the next chapter—as "Dr. Doom.") "Is the world coming to an end yet, Henry?" he would jibe, to which I would respond: "Not as long as Citicorp has access to the Fed's discount window." Phillip Zweig records in his exhaustive biography of Wriston that Citibank's economists saw me as their "nemesis" and often "sniped at [me] in public and in private":

> While Citibank was forecasting a decline in rates, Kaufman was predicting a continuation of record long-term rates. But no one seemed to pay much attention to Citibank. When Dr. Doom spoke, the markets listened—a fact that caused great angst at [Citibank headquarters]. "There was a lot of competitive jealousy," admitted former Citibank economist Harold van Buren Cleveland. . . . (Zweig, 1995, p. 748)

Walter also resented the role of the securities firms. A decade later, when the *Wall Street Journal* asked him to review my 1986 book, *Interest Rates, the Markets, and the New Financial World,* the scathing review—12 paragraphs of harsh criticism against two sentences of praise—opened with this sarcastic line: "For Henry Kaufman, a senior officer of Salomon Brothers with a clear view of its trading floor, to deplore the creation of excess credit is like the piano player in the fancy house protesting that he didn't know what was going on upstairs" (Wriston, 1986, p. 748).

Walter seemed especially incensed in the review by what he characterized as my "unseemly attack on commercial banking." Unseemly or not, I had much to say in that book, as I do in this one, about the excesses of freewheeling, Wriston-style financial practices, whether in commercial banking or in other institutions. And in the end, the decade of the 1980s provided no better example of the risks of such excesses than Citibank under Wriston. In spite of its many accomplishments, the New York financial powerhouse (as Zweig has documented) pushed hard to dismantle rather than repair America's ailing financial regulatory system; helped flood the economy with billions of dollars in easy consumer and real estate debt; and, most unfortunately, led the charge in making billions of dollars of bad loans to the third world.

My luncheon meeting with the senior management that day in 1976 was very cordial, but it wasn't long before the conversation came around to some of my comments at the *Financial Times* conference. I was told that I overstated the need for bank capital because I did not take into account recent changes in the nature of banking. Most notably, continued the Citibankers, banks had become highly competent liability managers. Rates of return on assets now floated at a spread over the cost of bank liabilities. In this way, banks no longer had to assume money rate risks. As for the credit risk in banking transactions, the Citibank senior managers explained to me that such was the real business of banking, a business in which they had a high level of expertise.

I was not persuaded. To begin with, I responded, the historical record in finance challenges their assertions. Declines in a bank's credit quality typically have increased its money rate risk; and the past is littered with erstwhile creditworthy loans that turned out to be bad risks. And if bank capital becomes a smaller and smaller proportion of total assets of a bank, why then should there be privately owned banks? Someone might reasonably ask: "Why should such a small equity base of private stockholders have control over such a vast amount of assets?"

My views on these matters have not changed since that luncheon at Citibank—nor, do I suspect, have Walter Wriston's.

But a quick review of yet another postwar credit crisis—the upheaval of 1981–1982—belies the notion that banks could escape money and credit rate risks. At the heart of that crisis was a battle among demanders of credit for a limited supply of funds. That was not so remarkable. But what had changed in the financial market was that many interest rate ceilings had been raised significantly or removed altogether.

The credit squeeze itself was in large measure an outgrowth of Federal Reserve policy. Following the appointment of Paul Volcker as Chairman in November 1979, the Fed began to restrain excesses in the economy—particularly high inflation and less restrained banking practices—by holding the growth of reserves to the banking system to very moderate levels. It was the beginning of a much more monetarist policy regime. During the worst of the credit crunch that followed, interest rates escalated to 21.5 percent for the prime loan rate, 17 percent for mortgage rates, and 15.25 percent for long U.S. government bonds. With this, lending to finance housing activity plummeted, and the thrift industry—saddled with billions of dollars in low interest rate, long-term mortgages—hemorrhaged red ink.

Meanwhile, lending to less developed countries also evaporated as one after another LDC found it impossible to meet its obligations. For Mexico, the crisis was especially acute. The nine largest U.S. banks had made loans to Mexico totaling $13.4 billion, or an astonishing 50 percent of their capital. After Mexico temporarily closed the foreign exchange markets and declared that all foreign currency bank accounts in Mexico would be convertible only into pesos, the banks agreed to a debt rescheduling. They had little choice.

The lack of prudence on the part of leading American banks showed up elsewhere at the same time. In Oklahoma, Penn Square Bank collapsed under the pressure of a large portfolio of loans to energy companies. Continental Illinois, a large Chicago bank, also got into trouble through its aggressive lending, much of it to energy companies.

In spite of the seriousness of these problems, however, American banking didn't detect the right signals—or learn the right lessons. For soon after the debacles of 1980–1982, the financial markets embarked on a near-decade-long period of reckless finance that, as I explain in the next chapter, fostered the worst crisis in American finance since the Great Depression.

14

Learning from the Financial Excesses of the 1980s and 1990s

From my vantage point, junk bonds often played the role of disguised equity substitutes for institutions restricted from buying equities directly. The junk bond market collapsed in the latter part of the 1980s—and with it, Columbia Savings and Loan.

The 1980s saw an amazing explosion of debt creation. My analysis showed a clear and troubling pattern: Debt was growing much more briskly than economic activity. In the 1960s and the 1970s, the growth of nominal GNP had remained in quite close alignment with the growth of domestic nonfinancial debt. But that alignment fell apart in the 1980s. As the decade unfolded, I devoted more and more of my speeches and writings to this unwholesome trend.

The debt explosion was driven by several underlying factors. To begin with, there was an attitudinal change, as the Depression-borne conservatism about saving and spending (which I discussed earlier in this book) dissipated. Even during the financial crises of the 1960s and 1970s, some of which I have reviewed here, few institutions actually failed. The widespread security and prosperity among financial institutions, businesses, and households alike fostered a culture of confidence—even complacency—and risk taking. The shift in attitude within the household sector was demonstrated by the fact that fewer and fewer Americans celebrated what once had been a great milestone in the prewar and immediate postwar period: paying off one's home mortgage. Instead, 1980s householders often stepped up their borrowings.

Corporate attitudes toward debt changed as well. Moving away from past practices, corporate financial officers saw the differences between money and credit, and between liabilities and liquidity, as less and less significant. Banks and thrifts became such liberal lenders and investors that many were insolvent by the time the credit binge ran its course at the end of the decade.

Burgeoning Government Debt and Its Consequences

The third major underlying factor contributing to the 1980s debt explosion was the financing needs of the U.S. Government. As is well known, it embarked on a huge wave of budget deficits through tax cuts and sharp increases in defense expenditures. The discontinuity is striking. In the 1960s, federal debt grew an average of 2 percent per year, compared with nearly 7 percent for the growth of GDP; in the 1970s, federal debt grew 9 percent on average per annum, GDP by 10 percent. In the 1980s, U.S. debt surged an average of 13.2 percent per year, while GDP increased only 7.5 percent. Stated differently, the budget deficit stood at roughly a quarter of GDP at the end of the 1960s and 1970s, but had climbed to about half of GDP by the end of the 1980s.

The federal government's burgeoning debt was the combined product of higher military spending, expanded social spending (on Social Security, Medicare, and Medicaid, the largest and most politically untouchable programs), and deep tax cuts. The latter had been espoused by a small but very vocal cadre of economic "supply-siders," including economist Arthur Laffer, Senator Jack Kemp, and *Wall Street Journal* columnist Jude Wanniski. The theory (it was no more than that) rested on the assumption that tax rates were so high that they were stifling work and capital investment. The supply-siders argued— and convinced the Reagan Administration—that heavy tax cuts would spur economic growth so much that the net result would be an increase in federal tax revenues.

Unfortunately, the exact opposite occurred. As tax rates fell, tax revenues plummeted. Recent data from the National Bureau of Economic Research shows that the Reagan Administration's key tax law (the Economic Recovery Tax Act of 1981) subtracted roughly $100 billion from total annual tax revenues in the early 1980s, and more than $200 billion per year beginning in 1987. (The other three tax acts had either neutral or small effects one way or the other.)

Watching this debt crisis unfold, I became increasingly disturbed—and outspoken. Testifying before Congress in 1984, I stated:

> I am convinced that if there had been much smaller budget deficits in the past few years, then a much lower level of interest rates would have resulted. With lesser deficits and with modest private credit demands that are usually associated with recessions and the early phases of business recovery, monetary policy would have had to step up its effort to restimulate the economy much more so than it did under the actual fiscal policy that prevailed.

A study released by the U.S. Treasury Department shortly after my testimony reached the opposite conclusion. It saw no correlation between changes in government borrowing and changes in interest rates—a conclusion based on the observation that when deficits are large in economic recessions, interest rates still fall; and, conversely, when deficits are small in economic expansions, interest rates still rise. I countered by pointing out that the 1980s deficit was far overshadowing the growth of the economy in proportional terms. I asked, "How much lower would interest rates have fallen if the deficit had been smaller?"

One of my chief concerns was the mounting budget deficit's distorting influence on private finance. I shared the widespread apprehension about the growing competition for investment capital between public and private borrowers caused by the mounting federal debt. But my concerns ran deeper. As the government increased its issuance of longer-dated debt, corporations and households tended to shift their borrowing in the short maturity sector or to floating-rate financing. The immediate costs of this debt structure were usually lower, to be sure; but because refinancing costs were unknown, the effect on the private sector was to increase interest rate risk taking.

My views on U.S. fiscal policy did not please everyone. Secretary of the Treasury Donald Regan claimed that my views were slanted against the Reagan Administration because, he believed, I was a Democrat. The fact is, I have been an independent voter, and supported Republicans and Democrats alike, depending (mainly) on the soundness of their economic policies. No party has a monopoly on wisdom.

I drew criticism during a meeting with senior Republican Congressional leaders in the early 1980s. The meeting was arranged by Peter Flanigan, a former assistant to President Nixon, who invited in several senior Wall Streeters for a discussion of the President's budget. Congressman Bob Michel, the House Minority leader, was there, as well as Barber Conable, a highly respected Congressman from upstate New York, who would later head the World Bank. All were familiar with my concerns about the ballooning budget, but I nevertheless gave a brief summary of my position.

Their response took me off guard. I was told in no uncertain terms that because Wall Street now had an administration that supported business and the financial markets, I should support the Reagan Administration in my writings and pronouncements. I responded by elaborating my views further. They were not convinced, nor did I heed their admonition. Although no minds were changed that day, oddly enough I left Capitol Hill with an intense sense of patriotism. After all, where else could I have exercised such freedom of expression, even in the highest ranks of government? Certainly *not* in the National Socialist Germany of my youth.

Rethinking the Crash of 1987

Many of the financial excesses of the 1980s became more glaring—and intolerable—as the decade headed to a close. The most dramatic upheaval, of course, was the stock market crash of October 19, 1987. This 508-point freefall in the Dow Jones Industrial Average was the largest single-day percentage drop (20.4 percent) in Wall Street history. The stock market already had sustained a 500-point decline that began in late August. The combined losses in the 2-month period exceeded $1 trillion.

In the months leading up to the crash, I grew alarmed by a severe tightening in the credit market and the apparent discord between

American and European officials regarding both the weakness of the American dollar and the ballooning U.S. budget deficit. Under these circumstances, the strength of the bull market puzzled me, although my analysis was not focused on the question of when and by how much the market would sell off. Even so, the subject came up during the question-and-answer session following a speech I gave at an institutional conference in Florida on Thursday, October 15—4 days before the crash. I told the audience that the underlying economic and financial conditions suggested a high degree of financial volatility that made a 150- to 200-point drop in the Dow Jones Average likely, although I did not suggest when this might happen. The following day, the Dow dropped 108 points, setting the stage (we later realized) for a huge drop on the following Monday.

Sunday, October 18, I appeared on *Meet the Press*. Not surprisingly, the journalists pressed me to prognosticate about what the market might do the next day. I tried my best to sidestep such questions by pointing out that there was no analytical way to forecast an extraordinary event such as a crash a mere 1 day in advance. The large setback on Friday already had investors on edge, and I had no intention of adding to the turmoil with my remarks. For this reason, I sounded more vague and reassuring about the situation than I really felt.

Secretary of the Treasury James Baker, who was questioned by the panel after me, did not mimic my tactic. When asked about some of the signs that seemed to indicate a deterioration in international monetary and foreign exchange matters, he replied, ". . . we will not sit back in this country and watch surplus countries jack up their interest rates and squeeze growth worldwide on the expectation that the United States somehow will follow by raising its interest rates." The remark surprised me, and after the program I said to the Treasury Secretary: "Jim, that was quite a candid statement. The market may not take it the way you may have meant it." I'll never forget his firm reply: "Henry, some things need to be said."

The next day—the day of the crash—was dramatic and traumatic, to say the least. There were trading breakdowns in all markets related to stock. The volume of sellers was overwhelming. The crash spread to stock markets in other countries. And as the market broke through the floor, questions naturally arose about whether borrowers would be able to meet margin calls, and whether lending institutions would reduce lending commitments to securities firms. Rumors about likely failures in the financial markets began to spread.

When I walked through the trading floors at Salomon, I witnessed two contrasting scenes. On the fixed-income trading floor, traders and salespeople were watching the monitors that exhibit pricing trends in money and bond markets. Many were gossiping about the events taking place in the stock market. Overall, the atmosphere was tranquil.

But on the floor below, where stocks and stock-related instruments were traded, bedlam reigned. Telephone lights were flashing everywhere, with most seeming to go unanswered. Many of the young traders and salespeople were so awestruck by what was happening that they didn't know what to do. It was mostly the older and more experienced people who manned the phones in an attempt to relate information to clients and take orders, hoping that at least some of them would be executed. It was a tumultuous scene.

The Federal Reserve broke the panic the next afternoon by flooding the market with reserves. Alan Greenspan, who became Fed Chairman a mere 9 weeks before the crash, calmed investor jitters by announcing that the Fed would "serve as a source of liquidity to support the economic and financial system." To be sure, some later criticized Greenspan for helping to bring on the crash to begin with—by raising the bellwether discount rate on September 4 from 5.5 to 6 percent, the first hike in 3½ years—but his handling of the crisis was generally applauded. For its part, the Reagan Administration encouraged corporations to announce large-share repurchase programs.

After the '87 crash, explanations flew like trade slips on the Exchange floor. But several fundamentals were clear. Earnings had been under pressure; price-earnings ratios were on the rise; and inflation—after falling in 1986—was on the resurgence. In the financial markets, interest rates were moving up sharply, with long U.S. Governments reaching nearly 10 percent in early October. As noted, the Fed raised the discount rate 50 basis points in September; and the dollar was under pressure in the foreign exchange market. Yet in spite of all of this, the stock market had climbed 44 percent between January and its August peak.

The stock market boom had been fueled by several factors. One was the merger-and-acquisition movement of the 1980s. Because most of this activity was financed by debt, the movement had the effect of siphoning a large volume of stocks out of the market. As credit markets tightened and credit yields widened, it became harder to finance these issues. Moreover, their absence during the uncertain period surrounding the crash contributed to its severity.

A technique known as "portfolio insurance," developed not long before the crash, also accentuated the downturn. The idea was simple enough: The participant sold stock futures when stock prices fell to limit or insure his portfolio against large losses. The problem arose when index arbitragers tried to benefit from lower future prices by buying futures and selling in the stock market in New York. Thus, portfolio insurance initially encouraged its users to increase their holdings of equities. But its breakdown added selling pressure in the market, thereby exacerbating the crash.

Corporate Debt and Merger Mania

The crash of 1987 was a symptom of some of the weaknesses in financial markets during the 1980s. There were other weaknesses with less dramatic symptoms that were no less serious. One of the most significant was the loading up of corporate debt—a trend I called "the decapitalization of American corporations" in a speech before the National Press Club in Washington in early 1989.

The magnitude of the trend was startling, and manifested itself in several ways. First, there was a staggering substitution of new debt for outstanding equity. During the 1980s, the debt of U.S. nonfinancial corporations surged by a colossal $1,557 billion, compared with a $552 billion increase in the 1970s. At the same time, nonfinancial corporate equity contracted by $267 billion, in contrast to its $341 billion expansion in the 1970s. As corporate debt soared, interest payments by U.S. nonfinancials also skyrocketed—to 30 percent of internal cash flow by the end of the decade. To put these numbers in perspective, these payments preempted more internal cash flow than during the recessions of 1974 and 1982, when the ratio was 19 percent and 22 percent, respectively.

The 1980s corporate leveraging explosion was accompanied by a severe drop in corporate credit quality. For eight consecutive years, downgradings in corporate credit ratings outpaced upgradings. As a result, by the end of the 1980s, the number of major American corporations rated A and AA was down markedly, and only a handful managed to hold on to a triple-A rating.

This corporate debt binge was driven by a merger-and-takeover mania that swept across the American corporate landscape, itself aided and abetted by a boom in junk bond financing. As is true today, many participants in the M&A and LBO wave of the 1980s had strong vested interests in its continuation. Buyouts often present top managers with attractive opportunities to cash out their stock options at a high premium. And many of the management buyouts of the 1980s rewarded existing managers with strong equity positions in the new corporate entity. For their part, stockholders typically played a passive role in the reorganizations, reaping instant financial benefits as bidders paid high premiums for their shares, then investing their capital elsewhere.

In conclusion, the rapid growth of debt is one of the most pressing problems facing the United States today. It cannot be solved by fine tuning monetary policy to narrow money growth targets. In addition, it cannot be redressed solely by reducing the Federal budget deficit, although such action would be a helpful and essential measure. What is required is a comprehensive program encompassing a clear-cut definition of the role of the credit market in our society and measures that will blend the best of deregulation and reregulation. To accomplish such a feat, however, we will have to subordinate many vested interests for the sake of preserving the integrity of credit—an absolute essential for the preservation of a democratic economic society.

Henry Kaufman, "Dangers in the Rapid Growth of Debt: The Need for a National Policy Response," a talk delivered before the National Press Club, Washington, D.C., January 16, 1985.

Exhibit 14-1a

Others benefited from—and therefore supported—the M&A and LBO craze as well. Commercial and investment banks profited handsomely from all the loan and bond financing. Lawyers earned stratospheric fees. The equity market at large also reaped immediate benefits, because the withdrawal of large numbers of shares tends to boost market prices elsewhere higher than they would have been otherwise. Given these rewards, it was difficult for the various participants in the merger and LBO game of the 1980s to be very objective about the social and economic benefits of these transactions.

It was not so difficult for me. I strongly opposed what I considered to be the excessive use of debt by corporations in the 1980s. (See Exhibit 14-1.) Among other things, I believed that highly leveraged firms ran a good chance of reporting higher-than-normal losses during a cyclical downturn in the economy. Quite a few would find their

---

But it is the prolonged, and highly undesirable, shift away from equity towards debt financing by many business corporations that is especially worrisome now. This shift has accelerated in recent years as a result of the corporate merger, acquisition, and leveraged buyout mania which, in a number of ways, has heightened the disregard for capital. I believe that unless something is done to forestall excesses that are almost inevitable in this area, the health of the free enterprise system in the United States will be endangered.

Now, I would not go so far as to assert that all highly leveraged corporate restructurings are unwise. Some may well yield positive economic effects. But taken too far, the decapitalization of American corporations will cause future financial stress. Ultimately, it will put the Government into the business of business through bailouts that will move our system closer to a social, and away from an economic, democracy.

Henry Kaufman, "The Decapitalization of American Corporations," a talk delivered before the National Press Club, Washington, D.C., January 10, 1989.

Exhibit 14-1b

> We are entrusted with an extraordinary responsibility—
> other people's money. Financial institutions have huge liabilities,
> made up of the financial assets of households, businesses and
> governments, and usually only a small percentage of total foot-
> ings is their own capital. Hence, we cannot escape public
> scrutiny. We are not independent of the world outside of finance.
> Otherwise, all would be pursuing occupations in financial mar-
> kets and abandoning everything else. The fact is that no matter
> how ingenious we are or have been in financial markets, we did
> not invent the wheel, the computer or the electron microscope.
> We make critical judgments, however, that join money and
> credit with myriad economic activities. This is a singular and
> crucial responsibility. To carry it out successfully requires objec-
> tivity and a sense of the public trust.
>
> ---
>
> Henry Kaufman, "Financial Opportunities and Responsibilities," a talk
> delivered before The Wharton School of the University of Pennsylvania,
> Philadelphia, Pennsylvania, February 9, 1987.

Exhibit 14-1c

cash flow inadequate to service their newly acquired debt, leading to an inevitable string of reschedulings—or worse. For corporate failures, it seemed to me, were likely to become a fairly common feature of the next recession. And that, in turn, would raise the political issue of whether the nation was prepared to accept the full discipline of the marketplace in order to exorcise these excesses of leverage.

The proponents of the M&A and LBO mania dismissed my concerns. Debt poses no real burden, they contended, because if economic adversity ensues, debt can be restructured easily. They called attention to the higher debt-equity ratios of European and Japanese corporations, which had been showing very good performance records. Some even asserted that managements of companies would find it easier to pursue long-term strategies when they do not have to be subservient to the short-term time horizons of the stock market.

The junk bond market—a major financial vehicle that financed the LBO and M&A boom of the 1980s—grew geometrically in that decade.

Opening the decade at $30 billion (or 13 percent of the total corporate bond market), junk bonds spiraled upward to $211 billion, or 27 percent of the total value of corporate bonds, by the end of the 1980s.

The Wall Street firm that popularized junk bonds in the 1980s and dominated that market was Drexel Burnham, which was led in this endeavor by Michael Milken, whose leading role in the junk bond market in the 1980s has been well recorded, as has his fall from power. I have never met Mike Milken, and have spoken with him only once on the telephone. But, for me, it was a pivotal phone call.

After I left Salomon Brothers in 1988, I organized my own money management firm (Henry Kaufman & Company, Inc.). As part of that effort, I wanted to establish a closed-end, high-grade bond fund. Jack Kugler, a former partner of mine at Salomon, who was managing the U.S. Government desk at Drexel, suggested a meeting with Fred Joseph, the senior member of the firm. Drexel was very receptive to my venture, and expressed a strong interest in marketing a $500 million closed-end bond fund. We were only a few weeks away from signing off on the transaction when I received a telephone call from Mike Milken. He said that he had heard from Fred Joseph that "We were going to do business together." He was delighted at the prospect, he said, and hoped that we would meet soon—especially since our views differed on junk bond financing. That evening I left on a business trip to Japan. But my brief conversation with Milken stuck in my mind throughout the trip— especially his emphasis on doing business together. It bothered me terribly. I had serious reservations about junk bonds in general and Milken in particular, even though he had not yet run into legal troubles.

When I returned from Japan, I called Fred Joseph and asked him to put the financing on hold. There were plenty of reasons why my decision seemed illogical. I myself was confident that Drexel would have made an all-out effort to launch our high-grade bond fund successfully, especially in view of the questionable reputation it was getting in the high-yield bond market. Charles Simon, with whom I discussed the financing, told me I was foolish to scuttle the arrangement. After all, he said, mine was a high-grade bond fund, and not a very low (junk) grade offering. And turning it down probably meant the loss of about $2 million in annual net income.

But I called off the deal anyway. And within a year, Drexel got into financial difficulty, while Mike Milken ended up paying more than $1 billion in fines and serving jail time. To his credit, Milken became a large supporter of cancer research and other benevolent causes after his release from prison, which has helped rehabilitate his reputation in recent years. But his legal travails certainly did little to help the image of Wall Street in the 1980s.

Trouble in Banking

The financial excesses of the late 1980s reached beyond the stock market and the corporate board room to destabilize two other key financial institutions: thrifts and commercial banks. The thrifts, in particular—once the epitome of financial strength and security—were badly damaged. The reason, simply put, is that in the 1980s they engaged in speculative real estate lending. The government played a role in this story, since the Garn–St. Germain Act of 1982 permitted thrifts to buy junk bonds (which securities firms underwrote in increasing volume). And some thrifts—encouraged by the aggressive marketing efforts of underwriters of these obligations—became large buyers of junk bonds.

One of the leaders of this trend was the Columbia Savings and Loan Association of Los Angeles, led by Tom Spiegel. Ambitious and aggressive, Spiegel was convinced that a large junk bond portfolio would produce hefty earnings for his institution. After discussing these matters with Spiegel on several occasions, I became concerned by the naïvete of what he was doing. He apparently believed that junk bonds provided a kind of marketability lacking in conventional mortgages; that junk bonds were easier to service than mortgages (with junk bonds, you simply clipped the coupon, whereas mortgages demanded that the lender collect monthly interest and amortization payments); that it was easy to learn how to make sound credit judgments on bond offerings (and besides, lots of good information on issuers of junk bonds was available from Wall Street firms); and that the wide yield spreads between high-grade and junk yields were likely to narrow as the junk bond market became more seasoned.

From my vantage point, junk bonds often played the role of disguised equity substitutes for institutions restricted from buying equities directly. The junk bond market collapsed in the latter part of the 1980s—and with it, Columbia Savings and Loan.

The thrifts were enticed into reckless lending and investing in the 1980s, not only by the proliferation of junk bonds and the lifting of the ceiling on maximum interest rates payable on deposits, but also by the lowering of net worth standards. Minimum net worth requirements were lowered early in the decade, and in some instances the Federal Home Loan Bank Board allowed thrifts to report asset values higher than what was permitted by standard accounting practices. By the end of the decade, the stark fact was that the tangible net worth of FSLIC-insured thrifts had fallen to just 0.8 percent of assets, compared with 5.3 percent in 1980. Thrifts began to fall like dominos, and the federal government had to rescue millions of depositors.

The commercial banks, too, made a large number of commercial real estate loans that failed to withstand the weak side of the business cycle. Worse, they were involved in loan syndications for LBOs, part of which remained in their portfolios. Bank capital was hit hard by write-offs, while loan reserves were inadequate. At the height of the credit debacle, bank shares had fallen dramatically from their peaks in the 1980s. Some of the nation's most prominent banks saw their shares fall into the $10 to $20 range, or in some cases even lower; and many suffered credit-quality downgrades. By the time it was all over, not a single major U.S. commercial bank retained a triple-A bond rating. It was a devastating erosion, considering the fact that in the mid-1970s 15 U.S. banks were rated AAA. Now, many of the nation's largest banks had outstanding bonds that sold in the market some 500 to 600 basis points above the yield on comparably maturing U.S. Governments. Banks and thrifts increasingly seemed to be the dinosaurs of the financial markets.

Not surprisingly, the broadly based upheavals and failures in the financial markets contributed to a business recession at the end of the

1980s. Strictly speaking, the recession was relatively short-lived. But recovery from the slump was sluggish, compared with the quick revving up of the economy that followed most other postwar recessions. The pervasive financial fragility of the early 1990s proved to be a powerful obstacle to a speedy economic recovery.

The Upheavals of the 1990s

As it turned out, financial recuperation and rehabilitation took several years. After all, what kind of financial institution possessed a strong enough asset base and capital position to finance a robust business recovery? At the end of 1990, according to the Office of Thrift Supervision, out of the universe of 2,452 savings and loan associations with $1.1 trillion of assets, 594 institutions with assets of $237 billion were classified as not well capitalized or profitable, and did not meet or were not expected to meet capital requirements. Billions of dollars' worth of junk bonds and highly leveraged transactions had to be written down and exchanged for equity.

Furthermore, the challenges associated with restoring the nation's starved equity capital base in the very early part of the 1990s were daunting. Financial institutions in particular discovered that issuing new shares often was quite difficult, given the low price their shares commanded and the pervasive concerns about financial institutions on the part of investors. Many banking institutions either reduced or eliminated dividend payments, while a large percentage of nonfinancial corporations watched their profits—and thus their capacity to retain earnings—dwindle away. In large measure, historically high leveraging was to blame.

From 1990 to early 1993, the American credit markets went through a period of convalescence. This occurred, as I have noted, within the context of a mild recession followed by moderate economic growth. Several factors helped usher in the recovery. Flexibility in the labor market and pressures on firms to improve efficiency and performance played important roles. To their credit, economic policymakers did not attempt to force-feed a quick and powerful rebound, which probably would have diminished the projects of a sustained business recovery—as well as the rehabilitation of the markets.

The federal government eventually bailed out some financial institutions and liquidated many others. In some cases, regulators kept open those financial institutions that were deemed too big to fail; the strict regulatory requirements that were applied to small institutions were waived for the wayward giants. The official supervisory and regulatory authorities also prodded many institutions to write off bad loans and investments more quickly than usual, and to enlarge their capital by issuing new stocks and bonds. For its part, the Federal Reserve—at first reluctantly and then more aggressively—engineered an expansionary monetary policy. By the end of 1993, a stronger financial framework was in place that gave the economy the wherewithal to move ahead vigorously.

Even so, the financial excesses of the 1980s had not burned a deep enough scar into the financial community. In spite of the widespread damage, and the arduousness of the rehabilitation and recovery that followed, speculative financial practices returned remarkably quickly in the 1990s. Mexico in 1994, the Asian developing nations in 1997, Russia in 1998, Brazil in 1998, and the near collapse of Long Term Capital Management—all were scenes of extreme financial turmoil.

These trouble spots, although quite diverse, shared a common denominator: The upheavals were played out in the open credit markets. In Mexico, the financial culprit was huge short-term borrowings in the form of marketable paper denominated in U.S. dollars. In Asia, many of the faltering economies suffered not only from weak banking practices, but also from huge debt incurred in the international marketplace. The same was true in the Russian crisis. Long Term Capital Management's problems centered on leverage so excessive that it could not be unwound in a manageable fashion without endangering key institutions involved in open market financing.

The fates suffered by these debtors—plunging equity markets and sharp declines in the prices of their fixed-income obligations—have brought into focus some key weaknesses in current financial practice. One is the limited power of quantitative risk modeling, upon which many institutional lenders and investors relied as they funneled funds into these sectors. Another revealed weakness is the dubious value of marking to market. The practice may hold when markets are reasonably stable (although even then the transaction price will depend on a variety of factors such as size of the outstanding issue, maturity, and credit quality). But when markets become volatile, the last quoted price of a security is indicative of next to nothing.

Another troubling feature common throughout the world's financial crisis points in recent years is the failure of open market investors to perform due diligence. (Commercial banks similarly came up short in this regard in their loans to foreign and other borrowers.) As noted in an earlier chapter, the Mexican crisis of 1994 is a clear example. Apart from a handful of academics who voiced concern, the research community in Wall Street was upbeat about Mexico right up to the onset of the crisis.

The breakdown of due diligence can be traced to new pressures in the business of finance. The decision of many financial institutions to emphasize near-term over longer-term profit opportunities certainly is an important influence. So are the structural changes in financial markets that have been encouraging investors—not all of them terribly sophisticated—to become greater risk takers. As mutual funds have become popular, for example, many investors have given scant consideration to the risks posed by liquidity problems to their portfolios.

Many of the financial difficulties that have plagued markets in recent years reflect generational differences in the investment community. The crisis at Long Term Capital Management (LTCM) is a case in point. The individuals involved in LTCM's recent travails are not engaged in traditional financial businesses. They are of a new vintage: trained in arcane mathematical techniques, prideful of quantitative risk analysis, and not outward-going in demeanor. But like the buccaneers of old, they are eager risk takers, willing to employ huge leverage to succeed.

I know quite a few of the senior people at Long Term Capital, some of whom were associates of mine at Salomon, where they first got an opportunity to apply their financial talents. Most were unassuming and introverted, and worked very closely as a group. I sensed that they would prefer to internalize the firm, to diminish client relationships, and to increase the volume of proprietary activities. I certainly underrated John Meriwether's leadership strength in attracting such a cadre of very strong analytical people. The tactics he employed in marketing LTCM also showed exceptional shrewdness. Many investors obviously could not resist the sales pitch from the LTCM group, which included two Nobel Prize winners and a former Vice Chairman of the Federal Reserve Board.

In spite of all its resident talent, LTCM nevertheless got into deep financial trouble. Surprisingly, the firm's analytical wizards apparently did not take into account some financial market fundamentals. They failed to understand, for example, that sizable positions in individual securities cannot always be liquidated quickly, especially when the obligations are of weaker credit quality. And they misconstrued the complexities of convergence trade.*

Perhaps the most startling aspect of the LTCM problem was the failure of the lending institutions to pursue effective due diligence, which would have avoided the market disruption in the fall of 1998. One has to wonder: When institutions pride themselves in knowing their clients, how could LTCM—with an equity base of a few billion dollars—have built up balance sheet footings of more than $100 billion, and hold outstanding commitments in financial derivatives with a notional value of some $1.4 trillion? My experience on Wall Street tells me that deficiency reflected the triumph of the trading and sales personnel over the individuals responsible for evaluating the financial strength of clients. Think of this conflict as follows: LTCM did a huge volume of trading with banks and securities firms. These trades were probably quite profitable. The granting of credit to finance these trades often was collateralized, although (I suspect) over very thin margins. That large volume of very profitable trades was like an addictive elixir,

---

*An example of a convergence trade is one involving two securities with an identical maturity date where one security has higher credit quality and lower yield and is sold short, while the other one has a weaker credit rating and higher yield and is bought long. This requires the capacity to stay with the trade—difficult to do in the period leading up to the maturity of both obligations, when credit spreads could widen further and financing costs could increase significantly.

one that the involved institutions did not want to give up, and that overwhelmed the less powerful credit people.

The financial crises of the 1990s also demonstrated the extraordinary power and influence wielded by the United States in containing the financial flare-ups, primarily through its strong influence over the policies of the International Monetary Fund. The U.S. led the bailout of Mexico in 1994, as well as efforts to alleviate the financial upheavals in South Korea and Brazil. In these cases, the United States used its economic and financial muscle to overcome the objections of those who opposed the rescue packages. It should be noted, however, that American financial intervention and financial support were often motivated as much by strategic political considerations as by a desire to quell financial turbulence.

Crises have a profound influence on financial behavior. They typically inspire a shift in attitudes and behavior from exuberance to conservatism, followed by a renewed spirit of economic and financial participation and then another cycle of excess.

Each crisis is a unique historical event, never to recur in quite the same way. Yet a few commonalities are worth noting. One is that large-scale crises have long-lingering aftereffects. The healing of economic and financial wounds takes time, sometimes years or even decades. Such was the case following the Great Depression. This is to be expected. If there were no penalty for misbehavior, perhaps we would all be sinners. Financial crises can serve as clear, albeit stern, reminders that financial markets, like all kinds of human societies, cannot function well without widespread adherence to sound codes of conduct.

Another common characteristic of financial crises is that most market participants fail to anticipate them. If they did, the crisis wouldn't materialize, for the majority of market participants would take countervailing actions that, collectively, would mute the developing turmoil. Only a few see the storm approaching. The vast majority—after contributing to the making of the crisis in the first place—are caught off guard when the tempest hits, and suffer the consequences accordingly.

The fact that so many fail to anticipate major financial disruptions points to the limitations of analytical techniques for predicting crises, especially the timing of their onset. Economic and financial modeling alone cannot forecast major financial upheavals. Nor is history a reliable guide; there are simply too few historical benchmarks, and crises vary greatly from one to the next. Past patterns can provide some guidance, but only if wedded to an understanding of the unique features of a current situation.

For policymakers, the recent history of financial crises throughout the world carries a tough lesson: The potential for credit crunches and broader crises remains. It did not vanish with the removal of interest rate ceilings, with the dismantling of financial market segmentation, with the globalization of credit markets, or with the extension of broader lending and investing powers to financial institutions. I suspect this reality has come as something of a disappointment, especially within the academic community, which generally has supported these financial innovations in the hope that more open, flexible credit markets would permit smoother reactions to modest changes in credit conditions and thereby improve monetary control. For their part, regulatory authorities continue to underestimate the potential for credit crunches, mainly because they continue to believe that new products, markets, or trading techniques have had only limited effects, or have even reduced the danger of credit crunches.

The history of financial crises also suggests that official supervisors, regulators, and monetary authorities have yet to appreciate many of the long-term consequences of their actions or of several key market developments. Deposit insurance, for instance, provided a safety net for depositors, but it also removed market discipline from deposit institutions. The lifting of interest rate ceilings on deposits seemed like a minor step when the liberalization began, but—when combined with floating-rate financing—it fundamentally transformed relationships among financial intermediaries. Program insurance for portfolios spawned problems that were not truly examined until the crash of 1987. Financial contagion, a cause célèbre in the past decade, captured the attention of officials and market observers only *after* it contributed to a series of crises. Clearly, foresight has been missing.

We cannot rid the financial markets of excesses. Nor should we try, for such a system would not encourage the kind of risk taking that also

helps meet legitimate credit needs. Too little credit creation is as harm-
ful as too much. But in many respects, the present system—and the
direction in which it is heading—poses unwarranted and unnecessary
risks to financial markets and to national economies. What is needed
for the future is improved supervision over markets and institutions in
order to limit, if not eliminate, the kinds of excesses that have caused
such pain and disruption in the past.

15

The Role of Bias
in Economics and Finance

*The propensities and biases of human behavior in the
financial markets also have exacerbated one of the
defining trends of our time: increasing volatility.*

Those of us who work in the financial markets spend most of our
time in the realm of rationality. Whether trying to evaluate industry or company earnings prospects or to project the outlook for interest rates, the economy, or monetary policy, we rely on the presumed
objectivity of rational analysis. At the same time, however, we are
inevitably drawn into another kind of analysis, one that is no less
important but seldom considered fully in the financial world. That is
the analysis of both temporary and long-term *behavioral* changes that
can exert great influence over the economy and the financial markets.

In approaching this problem, experts tend to follow one of two
principal approaches. One is a competitive, market-based view. Here,
the allocation of resources is purely and simply a consequence of the
interplay of market forces. It is important to recognize that this seemingly abstract concept actually rests on a foundation of assumptions
about human nature: that man is rational, ever striving to maximize
returns in the marketplace; and that individuals and firms that do well
will prosper, whereas those that fare poorly will suffer losses and even
fail unless they modify their behavior and improve their efficiency.
This is the world of unfettered, rational capitalism—the world
described by Adam Smith in 1776, and recapitulated, in somewhat
modified form, in modern neoclassical textbooks.

The chief problem with this view is that no industrial economy in the world is purely laissez-faire. Pure competition is a mental construct devised by economists to understand and illustrate certain principles. But nowhere is it a reality. The governments of capitalist nations everywhere recognize that major economic and financial disruptions can endanger the well-being of the larger society, and therefore intervene—to a greater or lesser degree—in the operation of the market.

This points to the second common view of how investor behavior is shaped: government activism. There are many kinds of techniques, laws, and regulations that alter competitive behavior from what it would have been in a "pure" market. Government activism can range from direct ownership of some economic activities, to explicit control, to trade and labor practice restrictions, to limits on who can own what or what they can do with their property, to a variety of "dos" and "don'ts" for financial institutions and for the origination and trading of securities. These state interventions into the workings of a market economy at the micro level—the subject of endless debate—have far-reaching effects, some good, some not so good.

However, governments and central banks have an even more profound effect on economic and financial behavior on the *macro*-economic level. Such policies are aimed at moderating extremes in business and finance, and at sustaining a rate of economic growth that is steady and moderate without unleashing inflationary pressures. There is no denying that our skills at analyzing, evaluating, and to some extent controlling the modern economic and financial system have improved tremendously in the postwar period; and we have achieved some success in steering the economy toward steady growth with low inflation. Even so, the process has been fraught with missteps and considerable controversy. Modifying economic and financial behavior through macroeconomic policy is an imperfect, complex, and difficult process.

It seems to me that the greatest achievement in the domain of economic and financial management in the last 60 years is something that has *not* transpired: a business depression of the magnitude of the 1930s debacle. To be sure, we have not eliminated the business cycle. There have been nine cyclical swings since the Great Depression, with recessions lasting from 6 to 24 months, and with business expansions extending to 90 months or—in the case of the 1990s economic expansion—even longer. This is hardly a poor record, although experts will disagree about how much of this economic record can be ascribed to prudent and timely monetary and fiscal policies and how much to the self-regulating properties of an essentially sound market economy.

As I have observed the efforts of policymakers to modify economic and financial behavior on the macro level over the past four decades, I have seen the difficulties, even internal inconsistencies, inherent in the process. And I have concluded that fiscal policy has turned in the poorest record of success—a judgment that admittedly contradicts much of the conventional wisdom.

Biases That Shape Fiscal and Monetary Policy

In the early postwar period, the fiscal policy record was very positive. There was widespread agreement among policymakers about the need to employ flexible fiscal measures to stabilize the economy; and influential economists exhibited great confidence in their ability to fine-tune the economy with fiscal levers.

What was forgotten by the devotees of fiscal activism is an important behavioral bias: the preference of individuals and governments alike for accommodation rather than for discipline and restraint. This asymmetry is especially glaring—and potentially dangerous—in the political arena. Tax cutting is invariably popular, whereas raising taxes or reducing government expenditures directly reduces voter income. There is seldom if ever a strong political constituency that favors tax hikes, or spending cuts, or even the forgoing of tax cuts.

Compounding this problem is the fact that fiscal policy excesses—fostered by the inherent behavioral bias against restraint—have distorting and retarding effects on society that often take a long time to manifest themselves. Those with political power know this and tend to manipulate fiscal policy accordingly.

The global business recession in the early 1990s is a case in point. Every major industrial nation except Japan came out of the prior business expansion with large budget deficits and with a large volume of outstanding government debt. These were the unhappy legacies of government officials who were no longer in power. As a result, fiscal policy was immobilized nearly everywhere in the industrialized world. And by default, the task of reviving economic growth fell to monetary policy. That state of affairs surely irritated unrepentant fiscal activists. But for those of us who see the embedded biases in fiscal policy, the greater reliance on monetary policy was preferable to further manipulation on the fiscal side.

Greater emphasis on monetary policy also helped address some of the problems associated with the excessive leveraging of the 1980s. In the early 1990s, both businesses and households needed to lower their debt burdens, a task aided significantly by the lower interest rates that resulted from more aggressive monetary policy. As interest rates fell, more and more borrowers were able to refinance their higher-cost long-term debt. At the same time, the cost of new short-term borrowing fell. More than this, aggressive monetary accommodation has the special virtue of being easily reversible—in stark contrast to fiscal accommodation. With the revival of economic activity, the central bank can gradually move from accommodation to restraint without grave political consequences.

To be sure, fiscal policy has played an important—and peaceful—role in adjusting political claims, and not only at the hands of the poor or government employees. But the potency of the budget-making process has been undermined by behavioral biases—weaknesses inherent in us all. For that reason, monetary restraint has played the leading role in stamping out inflation; and monetary accommodation, more than fiscal adjustments, has resuscitated the economy from slumps. None of that would have been possible without the acquiescence, silent or otherwise, of the society as a whole. After all, no central bank is an island unto itself.

Even monetary policy is shaped, and in some ways constrained, by behavioral biases. One is the strong desire for order and predictability. This often takes the form of a search for golden rules for implementing monetary policy. Many central banks, for example, have embraced a doctrine of targeting certain officially defined money supply ranges in order to achieve steady economic growth. As noted earlier in this book, however, the problem with this approach is that structural changes in the financial markets have made it increasingly difficult to both define and target money.

Countervailing against the desire for order is an apparently even stronger human impulse to escape discipline. Consider the explosion of new financial instruments and institutions that operate outside the direct control of monetary and regulatory authorities. Mutual funds have become bank substitutes. A huge volume of financial transactions that incorporate leverage go unrecorded on balance sheets. Linkages with foreign financial markets have multiplied. Much financial innovation in recent decades—including these examples—has contributed to a move by monetary authorities away from classical or traditional patterns. They now see that simple rules for conducting policy are no longer effective; a more judgmental, conditional approach is needed.

A central irony in current monetary policy is that—in spite of the sweeping transformations in markets and financial institutions—many economists and central banks continue to believe that monetary tightening or easing should be done as unobtrusively as possible. This is wishful thinking, for it fails to come to grips with either the intent of monetary policy or the realities of human behavior. Let's remember that the chief intent of monetary easing is to raise the value of financial assets, and vice versa. What limits the continuing erosion of asset values from monetary restraint is the correct judgment on the part of markets that restraint will be followed by monetary ease, thereby making the restraint powerful enough to cause pain for a large number of individuals, corporations, and financial institutions. But a behavioral bias on the part of many market participants and analysts often undermines this mechanism. That is their demonstrated predisposition to proclaim that the *latest* move toward monetary restraint will be the *last* move—even when financial markets continue to signal relatively high levels of business and investor optimism.

Biases in Financial Forecasting

The financial markets are shaped by behavioral biases in a variety of ways, particularly when it comes to the complex (and poorly understood) process of economic and financial forecasting. To begin with, most predictions fall within a rather narrow range that does not deviate from consensus views in the financial community. In large measure, this reflects an all-too-human propensity to minimize risk and avoid isolation. There is, after all, comfort in running with the crowd. Doing so makes it impossible to be singled out for being wrong, and allows one to avoid the envy or resentment that often inflicts those who are right more often than not. As Barton Biggs of Morgan Stanley has observed: "On an investment committee, it is almost better to be wrong with the group than to express a contrary view, even if it is right, because if by chance you are both wrong and a dissident, you are finished as a functioning member of the committee or firm" (Biggs, 1999). And as a practical matter, few are ever able to anticipate big shifts in economic and financial behavior. If a large number of market participants were able to do so, they would act accordingly, heading off the dramatic changes in the first place.

Forecasting is also shaped by the weight of history. Many projections—whether of an individual corporation's earnings or of standard macroeconomic indicators—are based on an assumption that past cyclical patterns will repeat in the present. This bias has been reinforced by statistical averaging, which has become easier and easier to do, thanks to advances in computational power in recent years. This widespread impulse—to believe that the future is grounded in the past—is understandable, but should be viewed with great caution and skepticism. To be sure, there are repetitive patterns in the broad pattern of economic and financial change. But the critical ingredient in making good projections often is a matter of identifying what *differs* from the past.

The dangers of relying too heavily on historical trends in forecasting became abundantly clear from the early 1970s through 1981, when interest rates in the United States rose to unprecedented heights that surprised and baffled most observers. Why were so many caught off guard?

Because they failed to take into account profound structural changes in the financial markets that ushered in a new period in the credit markets. Up until then, moderate increases in interest rates squeezed many would-be debtors out of the market. But in response to the credit crunches of 1966 and 1970, a series of structural shifts—especially the corporate movement toward large contractual lines of credit, the coming of floating-rate financing at banks, and the government's lifting of interest rate ceilings—opened up the credit markets to a greater and greater number of participants. Forecasters who looked to past patterns, but who failed to take full account of recent structural changes, failed to predict the extraordinary interest rate surge of the 1970s.

The business recovery of the early 1990s is another case in point. Why was it so lethargic? It later became clear that interest rates had to be much lower, and sustained for a much longer period of time, than was called for by conventional forecasts. And the reason, again, was a new set of conditions that defied the traditional models—in that case, debt overload, failures of financial institutions, and excesses in the real estate market. Before the economy could return to a firm footing, those obstacles had to be overcome.

Some biases in the forecasting process are chronic. One of the most profound is the clear bias against negative predictions, either about the financial markets or about the economy. From the President's Council of Economic Advisers—which rarely if ever sees recession on the horizon—to individual business corporations and financial institutions—which assiduously avoid talk of near-term difficulties—good news and neutral news both push out bad.

There are many reasons for this bias. On the most general level, people are inclined to optimism as a way of coping with the often-harsh realities of life. According to one anthropologist, optimism has been a key biological mechanism for the survival of our species (Tiger, 1979). The human bias toward optimism has been documented quantitatively, from studies that show that most people believe they are better than average and more likely than others to escape misfortune, to an intriguing survey of British drivers, 95 percent of whom claimed to be better than average at the wheel. In the marketplace, Denis Hilton has observed, "buyers and sellers in zero-sum markets presumably believe that they have the edge over the other party in the transaction: otherwise the market would not exist" (Hilton, 1998, p. 5).

The realities of the workplace also tend to mute pessimistic prognostications. And, of course, negative forecasts make for bad politics. They can cut short the careers of political leaders, interfere with the aspirations of business managers, and imperil the performance records of financial managers. Even so, negative forecasts often are accurate forecasts.

Throughout my professional career, I have encountered the fallout that comes to those who make negative predictions. In the 1970s, I repeatedly warned of pernicious high inflation rates and the attendant sharp rise in interest rates. In the 1970s and 1980s, I was one of a very few to make unwelcome predictions about the damaging effects of the debt explosion and of the poor supervision of financial institutions. Such admonitions (as noted in Chapter 9) earned me the sobriquet "Dr. Doom." Even so, I never wavered from the conviction that accuracy is better than false hope in financial forecasting.

Even if one could deliver an absolutely correct—albeit dire—forecast of impending crisis, who really has the capacity to take advantage of it? Among the ranks of large business organizations—the central, wealth-creating institutions in our economy—few are able to make good use of bad news. Top managers rarely have the power to reverse an expansionary course. Large corporations are pressured by internal constituencies and external stakeholders to push for continued growth. Their people, their machinery, their procedures—all are geared to build market share and to expand.

When contraction or crisis forces corporate restructuring, seldom is the process managed with vision. It is normally undertaken under duress, when the very survival of the firm is threatened. The behavioral bias toward growth blinds many managers to the frequent need to manage the downward slope of the business cycle with the same attention they give to expansionism. Ironically, when downsizing does come, the resulting write-offs—certainly a reflection of earlier management errors—often are heralded by the market. The lack of intellectual honesty in such situations extends to the accounting treatment of the losses as well, since tax laws allow the write-offs to be taken as a one-time charge against earnings, thereby insulating them from the firm's operating earnings. A more authentic approach would force the firm to go back and restate the overly cheerful operating earnings of the past in order to distribute the losses from the unprofitable activity over its entire lifetime within the firm.

Optimism can have, ironically enough, its downside. Consider the widespread belief in investment circles that equity prices are likely to continue rising indefinitely. In the United States, it has become almost an article of faith, a kind of mathematical certainty, that returns on stock holdings will reliably persist at somewhere between 9 and 12 percent. This is utter nonsense. To be sure, the average annual rate of return for those holding a basket of American stocks has remained in that range over the past 50 years, making it good sense to invest a portion of one's personal assets in the stock market. According to one report, "The Institute of Psychology and Markets found in a recent survey that the average mutual fund investor expects an 18.1 percent annual return on his investment over each of the next ten years" (Faber, 1999, p. 1). But no one can predict what will happen over the next 10 years, let alone the next 50, as a matter of either economic logic or common sense.

On that score, it is worth keeping in mind just how anomalous the last 5 years have been on Wall Street. During the 5 years ending August 1999, the Dow Jones Industrial Average posted cumulative gains of 196 percent, and that came on top of a 73 percent cumulative gain in the previous 5 years (August 1989 to August 1994). Only one 5-year period in business history showed a higher return: the great bull market of 1924–1928, when the Dow climbed an astounding 214 percent. But that surge came after a preceding 5-year return of only 13 percent. And what followed the late 1920s boom is notorious: a 5-year, 67 percent decline in the Dow. The Dow's recent performance surely is remarkable. But neither is it inevitable, nor does it portend the end of the business cycle.

Biases Affecting Investor Behavior

The propensities and biases of human behavior in the financial markets also have exacerbated one of the defining trends of our time:

increasing volatility. The fact that today's financial markets are much more institutionalized and securitized than those of 15 or 20 years ago has important implications for the behavior of market participants.

To begin with, it means that a growing number of investment managers have become risk averse; that is, they have become centrally concerned with protecting the survival of their institutions by insulating them from unexpected events. Among very large institutional investors, this strategy often takes the form of approximating market averages. There are two reasons for this. First, performance around the average rate of return of a standard market index reduces the risk of client loss. Second, over the longer term, huge investment pools move in sync with trends in the general economic system in which they reside.

There is, however, a central irony to this quest to avoid risk. The more that large portfolios are invested to replicate the movements of the larger market and economy, the more *susceptible* that market will become to sudden shifts and to the investment intentions of the dwindling number of active managers. Stated more simply, as the number of market followers grows, so does the influence of a shrinking number of risk-taking investors. The result is greater volatility—quite the opposite of what the majority of institutional investors desired in the first place.

The institutionalization of investment over the last generation also has constrained the behavior of investment managers in key ways. For one, they have come under increasing pressure to meet precise performance measurements—and these criteria have been calibrated over shorter and shorter time horizons. The growing preoccupation with short-term results often causes investors to neglect attractive long-term profit opportunities. And, of course, short-term investing is inherently more volatile than a longer-term market orientation.

At the same time, structural change in the markets in recent decades—securitization—has interacted with the behavioral bias of aversion to risk to foster greater volatility. Securitization has encouraged the notion among investors that the market prices for a very large share of society's financial assets are attainable at any time. Prior to their securitization, home mortgages, bank loans, and private placements were not readily marketable, and therefore not considered to have a continually available market price. But securitization does not mean continuous marketability, and the belief that it does has led—in yet another way—to the ironic fact that the desire to avoid risk has fostered greater volatility. This is because more and more institutional investors who cluster around market averages, and who are subject to ever-more refined performance criteria, have turned to securitized assets. Unfortunately, many securitized assets have proved to be highly illiquid when market conditions sour. Under such conditions, it becomes impossible to mark to market, and thus impossible for the risk-averse investors to operate within their precise performance criteria.

The growing emphasis on short-term performance has led to a growing interest in financial derivatives and other exotic investment instruments. More and more end users—from corporate treasury departments, to insurance companies, to small- and medium-sized depository institutions, to mutual fund managers, and even to a number of public agencies such as state and local governments—have been seeking exceptional gains through futures, options, swaps, structured notes, and other combinations of leveraged instruments.

But the more these instruments are created and traded, the more volatile the underlying financial markets may become. This, in turn, encourages demand for more so-called "risk management" products, in a self-reinforcing cycle. Unfortunately, many investors and end users remain unaware of the true risks involved in these financial instruments. And such knowledge can come at great cost. Sometimes it takes a shock to the system—with large losses for many participants—to expose the shortcomings of these products, from their lack of liquidity, to the mystery of their price movements under dramatically changing market conditions, to the difficulty of marking them to market under the best of circumstances. In the case of derivatives and exotics, new is not necessarily better.

False Assumptions and Fallacies

Behavioral biases are not the only obstacles to reasonable financial behavior. Many investors and clients are also captive to *fallacies* about money and markets that mislead or corrupt their actions. One of the most common is the odd notion that "the market" itself has human characteristics. We can see daily references in the news that "the market thinks so and so" or "the market concluded such and such" or—the biggest fallacy of all—"the market knows best." The latter assertion might mean that if equity prices are rallying, then (because "the market knows best") the rally is based on a careful assessment of the prospects for the economy and for corporate earnings growth. But that is rarely the case. Just as often, the market is going up because it is going up; many investors are following the lead of some, who may or may not have done their homework. The fact is, "the market" is an abstract concept. It is the sum total of thousands of largely uncoordinated decisions, many of which are based on little or no analysis. To anthropomorphize the market—that is, to see it as a human actor—is to make a grossly false analogy.

Another fallacious belief that stands in the way of rational financial behavior is the notion that risks are knowable, that they can be calculated precisely based on historical data, and that they can be diversified. This view, although it has become quite popular lately, is deeply embedded in the framework of many of our financial institutions. As noted earlier, the proliferation of new econometric techniques and the coming of powerful, inexpensive computers have encouraged greater reliance on quantitative risk management methods. More than a few financial institutions have made a business out of providing data and methodologies for these risk management systems. But all of this reinforces the illusion that risk can be dissected and predicted with a high degree of precision, much like a physicist or chemist can predict the behaviors of subatomic particles and molecules. In the case of financial risk, however, all of the exactitude lies in the formulas and calculations, not the current risks and future events themselves.

Another dubious concept that nevertheless influences financial behavior is the assertion that markets are efficient, liquid, and symmetrical. What does this imply? To begin with, it suggests that an investor can mark an existing holding to market based on the previous marketplace transaction price. It also means that selling is as easy as buying. These propositions have some validity in normal times, at least for the principal equity, bond, and currency markets. But in troubled times—such as we encountered in the late 1990s—this logic no longer holds.

Consider, for example, how the recent financial disruptions in Indonesia challenge widely held assumptions about market liquidity and balance. As the financial crisis in Asia unfolded in late 1997, a holder of Indonesian bonds would not have been able to evaluate their worth on the basis of the previous trade. Nor did price quotations from dealers hold much value; they would have been indications only, hardly valid for making an actual transaction. In fact, in the fallout of the Asian crisis, any portfolio manager who tried to trade out of an Indonesian bond position would have discovered the harsh reality that market liquidity had virtually dried up. He could certainly *buy* as much as he wanted; but he couldn't *sell* much of anything.

In the midst of that crisis, some of the very large mutual funds found that their methods for calculating net asset values no longer worked, thanks to the intense volatility of the situation. Unable to mark a portion of their holdings to market, they had to retreat to the much less appealing method of *estimating* fair market value without reference to actual market conditions—which, of course, were in disarray. The use of "fair market value" during very volatile conditions probably places some mutual fund investors at a disadvantage. One thing is certain: It exposes the precept that markets are always liquid as an illusion.

Rational decision making in financial markets also is undermined by the often-hidden ties and conflicts of interest between Wall Street analysts and the firms or governments whose performance and prospects they are reviewing. As noted in an earlier chapter, quite often the firms that employ such analysts are trying to build lucrative business relationships with several of the institutions on which they report to the larger financial community. This conflict of interest hardly is new, nor is it ever likely to be resolved, given human nature and the exigencies of a competitive financial industry. But it nevertheless points to the fallacy—held by many leading academics—that market prices embody all available information. Rather, we can only be sure that market prices embody the information that companies, governments, and analysts have found it convenient to provide; and even then, much crucial data are often impossible to bring to light in a timely fashion. In these and other ways, rationality is limited by information imperfections.

A related fallacy is that the credit quality of companies or governments is measurable in precise and timely ways, either by lending institutions or by the credit ratings institutions whose judgments strongly influence investor decision making. With growing volatility and securitization in financial markets, accurate credit evaluation is more essential than ever. That is because, in the new financial world, even small changes in prospects can lead to very sharp movements in asset prices. When, for example, the prices of existing bonds drop abruptly, the price of new credit accordingly becomes far more costly. In earlier years, credit resided mainly on the balance sheets of financial institutions, and was not continually marked to market. There was thus a buffer between possibly ephemeral developments and the borrower's credit position.

Now, in contrast, the prospects of a company or country are sensitively dependent on its credit standing. Everything has speeded up. And there is much greater tension between, on the one hand, the need of participants for what has become known as "transparency" (timely and dependable information about an institution's financial condition) and, on the other hand, the understandable desire on the part of borrowers to delay publishing bad news—revelations that almost certainly would cast doubt on their credit quality and thus increase the cost of borrowing.

The Asian crisis—one of the major financial events of this generation—reminded world markets that financial behavior should have a strong element of conservatism. That attitude has faded along with the memories of the Great Depression, and is quite foreign to those whose only experience has been an extended period of what can only be characterized as "financial bliss." In the current environment, those who have pointed out that certain asset values were overextended, and that investors were taking enormous risks—myself included—often have been branded as old fashioned and out of date. We did not understand, according to these "modern" critics, the modalities of the New Paradigm, in which inflation never rises, growth never pauses, and asset prices are destined to climb forever.

Here in the United States, many financial soothsayers have been churning out articles that tout the New Paradigm. They talk about why U.S. stocks could not be too high: because millions of new investors are eager to get into the market to secure the lofty long-term returns that are bound to materialize. They argue that American stocks could not be overvalued: because investors are all too willing to pay extraordinary premiums relative to firm book values in order to take advantage of the "intangibles" that enable corporations to exploit presumably limitless global opportunities. They suggest that record low dividend yields are irrelevant: because investors prefer capital gains to dividends for tax reasons. And they assume that companies stand ever ready to produce high capital gains by using cash flow to buy back their own shares.

This kind of reasoning, faulty when applied to the domestic scene, is just as flawed when used to explain international flows of equity and debt capital to the emerging markets. It is one thing to call attention to the long-term potential of many of these national economies. But it is quite another to interpret large-scale flows of funds into the emerging debt and equity markets as *proof* that these nations are somehow immunized from economic and financial problems. This false assumption ignores the fact that when access to credit becomes too easy, excesses normally follow. Since we have seen this happen time and time again in the developed world, it is fallacious to expect that the pattern will not hold in the emerging markets. But politicians the world over are loath to take the kind of difficult steps needed to head off excesses. They simply do not want to bear the onus of stifling growth or precipitating financial difficulties. This explains why nothing was done to avert the recent crisis in Asia. And yet the startling chain of financial upheavals—originating in Southeast Asia and soon destabilizing financial markets around the globe—has served as a wake-up call for investors worldwide. Whether in developed nations or emerging markets, it is no longer so easy to be sanguine about the New Paradigm.

16

Neglected Financial Lessons

Today's financial community is suffering from a bad case of amnesia. Most Wall Streeters are unaware of or have forgotten about the damaging effects of irresponsible behavior in their rush to "innovate" and profit.

———————

The years since World War II have been an extraordinarily eventful and highly inventive period in financial history. Along with the unprecedented growth and innovation have come a number of disturbing financial mishaps, scandals, and credit crunches. What should we have learned from this remarkable period in financial history?

For those caught up in the press of everyday events, it is often difficult to step back and reflect upon what the recent past has to offer in the way of useful lessons. Such is my endeavor with the 17 lessons that follow. They range from the implications of broad transformations—securitization, globalization, major regulatory shifts, and the like—to observations about much narrower market phenomena, such as marking to market, modeling, and the impact of rallies on asset values.

For Policymakers

Lesson 1: *The United States has not sustained a proper balance between financial conservatism and financial entrepreneurship.*

A good starting point to approach this question is the fundamental and long-standing tension between two broad financial groups.

These two groups have stood at opposite ends along the spectrum of continuity and change.

At one end of the spectrum have been the financial conservatives. Such individuals favor preserving the status quo in the marketplace, and generally are predisposed to question the merits of financial change. They hold in high esteem the traditional values of prudence, stability, safety, and soundness.

At the opposite end have been financial entrepreneurs—risk takers restlessly searching to exploit anomalies and imperfections in the market for profitable advantage. Their credo is market efficiency, profitability, and expanded choice. And these entrepreneurs have few second thoughts about disrupting existing institutions, for such "creative destruction" (to borrow a phrase from Joseph Schumpeter) is inherent in the capitalist system. They consider existing laws and regulations to be fair game, ripe to be tested and challenged, especially when they can claim to have produced enough public benefit through their creative destruction to keep the regulators and prosecutors at bay.

A sound and dynamic financial system should embody characteristics from both ends of this spectrum. But the best system should maintain a wise and delicate balance between the two antipodes. That is because when the financial system swings far in one direction or the other, serious problems for the larger system often result.

Financial conservatism, if taken to an extreme, can stifle economic growth and renewal as well as social invigoration. It is difficult for fledgling enterprises to take root and grow in an environment of excessive conservatism, which favors and supports existing institutions to the detriment of those that may be more efficient and more promising. By dulling the aspirations of risk takers, a society heavily dominated by financial conservatism ultimately will pay a stiff price, weakening the very core of its economic democracy.

At the same time, financial entrepreneurship can become excessive—and damaging—as well. Unfettered entrepreneurialism often leads to serious abuses, whether in the form of reckless lending, exploitation of the public safety net, or trampling of the basic laws and morals of the financial system. Such abuses weaken a nation's financial structure and undermine public confidence in the financial community.

For a variety of reasons, America has too strongly condoned—even encouraged—financial entrepreneurship. Over time, this chronic imbalance has led to two damaging sets of consequences for our financial system. To begin with, the dominance of financial entrepreneurship has both created and been a consequence of a less-than-robust regulatory system. Understaffed, underfunded, and badly fragmented, this system has been slow to recognize some of the more serious abuses wrought by rampant financial entrepreneurship. It is a system in dire need of reform (see Chapter 12).

More than that, weakly restrained entrepreneurship has carried a social price. Damaging tears in our financial fabric have extracted huge losses from American taxpayers forced to bail out failing institutions. (The multibillion-dollar savings and loan debacle of the 1980s is merely one of the more notorious of these failings.) Weak regulation also has spawned a series of major and costly financial scandals, both here and abroad. And the lack of strong oversight of the most aggressive entrepreneurs has fostered a debilitating level of overleveraging—of our business enterprises, our households, and our government itself.

The inability or unwillingness of U.S. regulators to balance financial entrepreneurship and financial conservatism did not emerge overnight. Nor did it begin with the strong deregulation ideology of the Reagan regime in the early 1980s—although the ideological fervor of that Administration surely skewed the balance even further in the direction of laissez-faire. Rather, America's weak regulatory system is an outgrowth of a larger imbalance, with deep roots in the American past, between the power of the state and the power of business. In the middle of the nineteenth century, the United States—unlike the industrialized nations of Europe—did not possess a large state bureaucracy or a strong civil service tradition. In fact, at the federal level, the rise of state power in America came largely in *response* to the emergence of big business in the late nineteenth century. The first federal regulatory commission—the Interstate Commerce Commission—was created in 1887 to control abuses in the nation's first big business—the railroads. Even then, the ICC's powers were quite limited (initially, it possessed no powers of enforcement), and were supplemented by new legislation over the course of decades.

In the financial area, the United States had no regulatory apparatus to speak of prior to the New Deal banking and securities reforms of
the 1930s. As noted in Chapter 13, those measures, supplemented by
new legislation in World War II and in the early postwar period, made
for a highly predictable and reasonably well-supervised financial sector—at least by American standards.

But the pendulum began to swing back in the direction of looser
financial oversight in the early 1960s. Two key innovations were the
negotiable certificate of deposit, which gave large banks access to
wholesale sources of funds, and the emergence of an essentially unregulated Eurodollar market, which together permitted the virtually unre-
strained growth of assets by large banking institutions. A new concept
was born—"liability management"—to serve the new culture of
aggressive, entrepreneurial growth with little governmental oversight.

The problem is that when financial institutions become strongly
growth-driven, they run the risk of losing their capacity to assess risk
adequately. Rather, they become focused on the goal of finding assets
that promise to yield at a rate higher than the cost of deposits. The risk
inherent in this kind of interest rate arbitrage was reduced still further
in the 1960s by the advent of floating-rate financing. As rates began to
float, the financial institution that originated a new loan was left only
with the credit risk associated with the asset; no longer did its managers need worry about getting caught in an interest rate pinch.

But entrepreneurial bankers—as opposed to the silent majority of
more orthodox bankers who continued for the most part to lend out the
money that was deposited in their banks—pushed the boundaries of
practice still further. They began to preach that even asset risk could be
minimized: through loan syndication with other banks and—as textbook mathematics seemed to dictate—through diversification into a
range of new financial services. In this new financial world, the banking
entrepreneurs viewed bank equity as unimportant. All that was really
needed, they said, was to retain access to wholesale sources of funding,
which in turn could be assured by continual growth and—no less important—by the continuing security of the government's official safety net.

For their part, the financial authorities—especially the Federal
Reserve and the U.S. Treasury—at first watched the coming of nego-

tiable CDs, floating rates, and the new style of banking with a degree of uneasiness. It was clear that these developments would *magnify* the expansion of credit, which at times would conflict with the aims of federal monetary policy. But in the end, Fed and Treasury officials decided to endorse the rise of entrepreneurial banking, and abetted the transition by raising and ultimately abandoning the Regulation Q ceiling on interest rates for wholesale deposits. Other restrictions were loosened as well. In order to help U.S. banks to compete more heartily with foreign banks in the Eurodollar market, regulators began allowing them to establish shell branches that were virtually unregulated. And the requirements for capital-to-loans ratios were made more liberal.

This new policy direction gained momentum in the wake of the two oil shocks of the 1970s, when high-growth banking proved to be a convenient adjunct to U.S. foreign economic policy. Increasingly, global economic activity was supported through bank loans, and as a result, there were fewer demands for official financial support from the industrialized nations as well as from developing countries hurt by the sharp rise in oil prices. Rarely did U.S. financial or monetary officials voice concerns about whether the new wave of bank loans would be repaid. Meanwhile, the entrepreneurial bankers took for granted that borrowing nations would make good on their loans because countries weren't supposed to go bankrupt. This blind spot—for bankers and regulators alike—proved to be an expensive mistake. All of the major borrowing nations went into default, with costs that far exceeded any benefits from diversification.

In the final analysis, the tilt toward unbridled—or at least loosely constrained—financial entrepreneurship has exacted economic costs that often far outweigh their economic benefits. Only by improving the balance between entrepreneurial innovation and more traditional values—prudence, stability, safety, soundness—can we improve the ratio of benefits to costs in our economic system.

Lesson 2:   *What is off balance is perhaps as important as what is on the balance sheets.*

This is only logical. When leverage is generated off the balance sheet, the standard accounting numbers do not begin to describe the full extent of exposures. Korea, for example, was supposed to have had more than $30 billion in official foreign exchange reserves when its problems began in late 1997. But these reserves disappeared quickly because of outstanding commitments in the forward market that the authorities had undertaken in previous months to covertly defend the currency before the financial problems broke out in the open. To take another example, in the summer of 1998, LTCM was reported to have had commitments in the various financial derivatives markets of about $1.4 trillion that dwarfed the data reported on its conventional balance sheet.

The lesson is painfully clear: Without a full-scale modernization in the collection and dissemination of all relevant financial data, including off-balance-sheet information, potential investors are largely in the dark about the true creditworthiness of their counterparties.

Lesson 3:   *Policymakers need to take behaviorial biases into account.*

My review of behavioral biases and other barriers to reasonable financial behavior in the previous chapter focused on fallacies and blind spots common among market participants and their expert advisers. But the irrational attitudes that shape world financial markets—especially as brought to light by the Asian-born global crisis—carry important lessons for policymakers as well.

As a starting point, policymakers should not assume that reasonable financial behavior is the norm. To the contrary. During times of market prosperity—when asset values are advancing and when market analysts and government officials are extrapolating good times ahead—cautionary words are ignored at best, ridiculed at worst. In such conditions, asset values easily can rise to unwarranted heights, risks can be underplayed, and credit-quality spreads can be compressed far below levels that adequately compensate investors for their risk taking. In prosperous times, lenders let down their guard, making it easy for businesses to overextend. But even when the bubble bursts and investors take flight, modest changes in policy—changes that under ordinary circumstances would effectively dampen an overenthusiastic rally—now have virtually no impact in restoring market confidence. Thus, reasonable financial behavior is compromised on the upside of a market swing as well as on the downside.

Recent adventures in Brazil provide an illuminating example. Had the Brazilian authorities tried to implement stern fiscal discipline prior to the crisis—when money was pouring into the Brazilian market—rather than in the midst of the crisis, the market would have responded much more positively. Such a policy would have signaled a determined and forward-thinking government, rather than a reactive one. But the fiscal discipline came too late, and the crisis roiled on.

The irrationalities of financial behavior also hold important lessons for today's International Monetary Fund (IMF). As it is presently constituted and managed, the IMF is ill equipped to meet the heavy demands placed upon it by its directors: government representatives from the major industrial nations. The IMF's involvement in Thailand clearly shows why. The IMF (along with many others who study the economic and financial conditions in emerging nations) has long been aware of imbalances that threatened Thailand's stability and prosperity. And it watched for at least 2 years the danger signals that led to Thailand's financial crisis in the late 1990s. But the IMF was unable to induce the Thai government to take corrective policy actions, because it was stymied by the realities of the modern financial world, in which securitized private capital flows freely across national borders.

More than this, the IMF is handicapped by the weaknesses in both national and international structures for regulating and supervising financial institutions. Many emerging markets, for example, lack independent central banks and bank supervisory authorities with the mandate and the power to control institutions that are taking on too much risk. To the contrary, such institutions often are discouraged or prevented from detecting or reporting excessive lending to insiders, affiliates, or politically connected companies. It has been several years since the heads of government of the Group of 7 (G-7) nations responded to the Mexican financial crisis by instructing the IMF to improve the quality of data collected from IMF members. Yet that admonition remains unfulfilled, leaving market participants with incomplete data about the financial conditions and health of domestic banking within the IMF member nations.

The dilemma is that when foreign capital inflows cease, central banks have no policy options that will not jeopardize key financial institutions within the nation. If the central bank tries to tighten monetary policy to stabilize the economy and to prevent a run on the currency, the ensuing economic slowdown will cause insolvencies and increase the pressures on an already weakened banking system. But if the central bank stands back and lets the currency depreciate sharply (the alternative forced on the authorities of nearly every Southeast Asian nation in that crisis), the local companies that had borrowed heavily in foreign currencies—in the mistaken belief that the exchange rate would hold—end up sustaining huge losses. And the failure of those enterprises further weakens the domestic banking system. Until the IMF and its members recognize the instabilities that may result from large-scale capital movements in a world of globalized, securitized financial markets, crisis spots are bound to erupt—and spread—with growing ease.

The behavioral bias toward inflated asset prices (reviewed above) also holds important implications for America's central bank, the Federal Reserve System. It will always be the case that the basic objective of monetary policy is to balance sustainable economic growth with price stability. But most associate price stability with the stability of goods and services. There is, however, another key dimension: the prices of real *assets* such as housing and commercial property on the one hand and the value of financial assets on the other hand. To what extent should the Federal Reserve take into account inflation in asset prices when formulating monetary policy? There is a political dimension to this difficult question, for the simple fact is that inflation in asset prices is quite popular, whereas inflation in the prices of goods and services typically hurts the average individual or family in very tangible ways.

Still, excessive inflation in financial asset prices sets in motion a series of forces that over time can undermine the foundations of a stable economy. For one thing, it stifles the incentives to save. In the 5 years prior to December 31, 1998, for example, the financial net worth of Americans had gone up by $9.8 trillion, while fresh savings out of current income had amounted to $664 billion. Excessive inflation in financial asset prices can breed excesses in business investment, can contribute to undue economic and financial concentration, and can encourage questionable flows of funds into risky markets at the hands of inexperienced investors.

The Federal Reserve's historical record when it comes to changes in financial asset values has been asymmetrical. The record shows that when asset values have fallen suddenly—as they did during the October 1987 crisis—the Fed has eased monetary policy to provide greater liquidity to the financial markets in a time of stress, and perhaps also to counteract the decline in domestic spending that might result from the loss of financial wealth. But when asset prices have advanced strongly, escalating financial wealth, the Federal Reserve generally has not responded by tightening monetary policy.

This asymmetry has given rise in the market to an expectation that faulty investments will be bailed out by the central bank. And political support for this policy approach is growing. Householders have become so keen on the stock market as a source of wealth creation that millions see monetary tightening as a direct threat to their financial well-being. This stands in stark contrast to the earlier, long-standing practice among householders to put most savings in simple bank deposits. In those days, many risk-averse people, especially among the elderly, preferred high interest rates. But in recent times we have seen a growing antagonism—on both sides of the political spectrum and among savers and investors of all stripes—toward prudence in fiscal or monetary policy.

This reality raises a fundamental issue, one that lies at the heart of our economic democracy. If we truly desire an economic and financial system based on a free market, then our central bank and government financial authorities must pursue *symmetrical* policies when it comes to financial asset prices. Following this logic, the Fed would ease monetary policy to check sharp declines in asset prices—but only to the degree that sharp *advances* in asset prices were resisted by monetary tightening. To be sure, the complexities of our social and economic system and its strong ties to the international scene will at times demand an asymmetrical policy approach. But the central bank and other financial authorities need to recognize the moral hazard in such an approach.

Monetary authorities can and should do more to discourage extremes in financial behavior, and to encourage reasonable financial behavior. A good starting point for defining a code of conduct for market participants is to recognize the many biases that shape financial behavior in often unacknowledged ways. Otherwise, we will face more episodes that prove that there is no such thing as high-return, low-risk investing—and that deviations from reasonable financial behavior often end in disappointment and pain.

For Financial Institutions

Lesson 4: *People in finance are entrusted with an extraordinary responsibility: other people's money.*

This basic fiduciary duty too often has been forgotten in the high-voltage, high-velocity financial environment that has emerged in recent decades. With financial assets extraordinarily mobile, with growing corporate access to debt financing that is perceived to be just as secure as the liquid assets actually owned by the firm, and with the absorbing excitement of the trading floor—which for some becomes a sort of game, an end in itself—the notion of financial trusteeship is frequently lost in the shuffle.

The shabby events of the recent past demonstrate that those of us in the business of finance neither cannot nor should not escape public scrutiny. After all, the huge liabilities of our leading financial institutions are derived from the assets of millions of individual households, businesses, and governments. Only a small percentage of the total footings of financial institutions represent their own risk capital. For this reason, we in finance are hardly isolated, insulated, and independent from the external world. (If we were, finance might quickly become the world's most popular profession!) It is our job to make critical judgments about how to channel money and credit into a broad range of economic activities. To carry out this singular and crucial task properly requires objectivity and a strong appreciation of the public trust in our hands.

When this responsibility is not carried out faithfully, what is the source of the laxity? Some would say that regulations have not been tough enough; but maintaining the public trust is not solely, nor even primarily, the government's job. Others wish to heap all of the blame on the so-called "yuppies of Wall Street." To be sure, some Wall Street upstarts—commanding powerful new information and trading technologies, and riding the 1980s and 1990s bull market—have become cocky and arrogant. But I wonder if their lack of a sense of proportion is entirely their own fault. After all, many were never taught as part of their university or business school curricula either business ethics, or the values and responsibilities inherent in prudent financial behavior, or the lessons of financial history. And today's highly competitive markets surely are a poor teacher of such lessons.

To a surprising degree, the responsibility for lapses of proper conduct in the markets rests with the members of my generation who have occupied powerful positions in senior management. This generation—having witnessed the dramatic transformations in the postwar years—should understand the lessons of financial history, should see their relevance for today's marketplace, and should have assumed the responsibility for passing along this knowledge to today's young traders and financial managers.

Senior management, more than any other group in modern American finance, must hammer home the central truth about financial behavior: Breaking the rules is not merely a breach of ethics and the law—it is poor business. To be engaged in questionable financial dealings may well cost a financial institution millions of dollars—immediately! And it will surely imperil many client relationships, and along with them the future of sales and profits.

Trust is the cornerstone of most relationships in life. Financial institutions and markets must rest on a foundation of trust as well. Otherwise, the huge volume of financial transactions that take place each day could never be consummated quickly, efficiently, and relatively cheaply. Conversely, mistrust would lead to exorbitant transactions costs. When financial buccaneers and negligent executives step over the line, the damage is inflicted on all market participants. That is why the large majority of ethical and responsible market participants must not tolerate the transgressions of the few abusers. And regulators and leaders of financial institutions must be the most diligent of all.

Lesson 5:   *Securitization does not eliminate the important role of commercial banks in the buildup of risks.*

The Japanese, European, and American banks that had increased their short-term lending in Asia vastly magnified the risks to bond investors, most of whom had acquired their bondholdings at a time when bank lending was mostly subdued. They figured that the bankers were out of the business and would not return. This assumption proved wrong. Despite the sorry experience of the 1980s, the bankers believed that short-term loans could be securitized at will, because the ratings were so high. None foresaw obstacles to funding risks, which then would lead to lowered ratings.

For Investors

Lesson 6:   *Even lightly leveraged market participants lose access to position financing in a disorderly market.*

This was particularly acute in the emerging debt markets in the past couple of years. Under normal market conditions, dealers are more than willing to finance their customers as a way of encouraging a greater volume of transactions. But a harsh lesson has been learned by many of them. Investors cannot count on normal business relationships with dealers when conditions turn turbulent. They step back from making markets, and bid-offer spreads swell. They also scale back or entirely stop providing financing even for longtime customers. This contributes greatly to the contraction of liquidity that sets the stage for sharp movements in asset prices. It also impedes stabilizing purchases of assets that are declining sharply in price. For example, those who might have stepped in as contrarians after prices on emerging market debt fell sharply were incapacitated—which of course helped guarantee that the momentum of price decline would persist.

Lesson 7:   *Good times breed the illusion of boundless liquidity.*

To state this lesson from postwar financial history more fully: Markets that blossomed during the pleasant days of escalating equity prices, modest yield spreads relative to U.S. Government bonds, and slender bid-offer spreads (in both equity and fixed-income markets) do not provide boundless liquidity in more turbulent times.

Liquidity is not something that can be measured with numerical precision. It has to do more with the "feel" of the market. When liquidity is relatively plentiful, buyers or sellers of stocks or bonds can rely on being able to execute a transaction for a relatively large sum without precipitating a significant movement in prices against them.

Liquidity tends to be more abundant in rallies than in setbacks because of the mutually hospitable nature of the phenomenon. Buyers in rallies are exuberant because they are participating in a favorable trend. Often, a self-reinforcing dynamic sets in, as the favorable trend reinforces the positive judgments of buyers on the likelihood of future advances.

Sellers in rallies are generally happy as well. They probably acquired the financial asset at a lower price, so they are cashing in for a profit. Even if they acquired the asset at a higher price, they are relieved to be selling for a much-reduced loss. They may also be disposing of only a part of a position. Thus, while they are displaying prudence by scaling back their holdings, they still have a stake in the upside potential for the asset that they are selling partially.

Most important, the dealers in the middle of trades during rallies are more than willing to take into inventory sell orders of their customers. Emboldened by the stream of buy orders that are pouring in, they are likely to set relatively modest spreads between their own bids and offers, in this way counting on good trading volume to keep generating profits.

During market setbacks, however, buyers and sellers are much less sanguine. Buyers become anxious that they are getting in too early. Sellers fear that they will not be able to unload as much as they would like. On top of this, margin calls sometimes force selling even by those who suspect the setback is temporary and would have held. Thus, asset prices have a tendency to fall back sharply even on modest volume—and sometimes without any trades taking place at all! In the process, market makers withdraw from making markets, for fear of tying up scarce capital by holding inventory.

Lesson 8:   *Marketability is not the same as liquidity.*

That many investors have falsely equated marketability with liquidity has been a chronic problem in recent financial history. How, then, is marketability different from liquidity? Liquidity is a characteristic of the markets, whereas marketability has to do with how easy it is to trade a particular security or class of securities. To illustrate, most stocks are more marketable when a country has a highly liquid equity market. But not every stock enjoys a high degree of marketability—even in an otherwise liquid market—because of negative developments specific to particular companies.

It is undoubtedly true that when financial assets are securitized, they become more marketable than before, when they were lodged on the balance sheet of some financial institution. But too often, securitizing financial assets can give the false impression of seamless marketability. The fact is, market activity varies considerably over a financial cycle. To see the point, we need only consider how readily large blocks of Brazilian bonds could be distributed as late as the spring of 1998, and then how difficult it became only weeks later to disgorge them from portfolios without acquiescing to huge price concessions.

Lesson 9:   *Marking financial assets to market is an imperfect process.*

Alongside the development of securitization, there has been a rapid expansion in the practice of marking to market. In years past, the procedure of reevaluating the net asset values of portfolios on a daily basis (to reflect changes in asset prices) was practiced mainly by securities firms. It was also done by a relatively small group of investment managers acting on behalf of large institutional investors (such as pension funds) and by a comparatively modest-sized mutual fund industry. Banks and insurance companies did not mark to market, and their regulators did not want them to do so. They mainly held securities on their balance sheets at book values. They did not recognize interim (or unrealized) profits and losses. They tended to buy and hold. The great bulk of their assets was not securitized, and was not amenable to repricing in an active secondary market.

But in recent years, the number of institutional investors that mark to market—most notably the mutual funds—has grown dramatically in size and importance. At the same time, changes in accounting guidelines and regulatory rules have encouraged an irreversible movement toward greater marking to market by traditional financial institutions. Securitization has undermined the key argument against marking to market—namely, that valid prices cannot be determined—while the passage of time has worn down both official and industry opposition to the practice.

Even so, it is important to recognize that marking to market is an imperfect process, especially under difficult market conditions. Generally speaking, it tends to *overstate* values and to offer investors a kind of false comfort. When market conditions deteriorate and liquidity seizes up, no one can really claim that the last quoted price in organized markets (such as the NYSE) or quoted by dealers in the over-the-counter market is the real market value—at least not without taking into consideration the size of an intended trade, the credit quality of the issuer, the activity of other market participants, and related dimensions of the transaction.

Lesson 10:   *Modeling risk has great limitations, including poor guidance for managing options exposures.*

Mathematics and the computer technology that permits financial market participants to exploit its power have a dark side. Up until the events of last year, there was a strongly held belief that financial risks are knowable, can be calculated with mathematical precision by massaging historical data, and can be diversified. These were always fallacies, but it took the near collapse of Long Term Capital Management, one of the most prominent users of mathematical model-based investing, to prove the point.

What we all know now is that historical trading patterns are a useful starting point for assessing risk, but only a starting point. Most instances of sudden deterioration in credit standing of a corporate or government borrower are not predictable. They reflect submerged weaknesses in underlying economic or financial structures that are not captured by the available data. Models are basically backward looking and are essentially useless when the underlying structure changes. One of the key structural changes is the loss of liquidity. In the case of managing elaborate positions of options and other complex financial derivatives, models that provide good formulas for conducting dynamic hedging under normal circumstances are of no assistance when transactions cannot be made without huge price concessions.

Lesson 11:   *Contagion is a major force in the modern globalized, securitized system.*

In recent decades, the rush to shed risk has spared no segment of the stock and bond markets. It certainly has not been limited to the emerging debt markets. Yield spreads have widened even for AAA-rated asset-backed securities, well-secured utilities, collateralized commercial mortgages, and corporate issuers with dependable cash flow.

Why is contagion so common and so frequently disregarded until it is too late? One reason is the nature of the information on which investors rely to make their decisions. Sudden declines in financial asset prices often are precipitated by new data that call into question the original analysis on which the decision to invest was grounded. What investors then do is to think probabilistically: If such and such a country is in worse shape than we thought when we got in, then other countries might also be facing similar problems. So they sell the obligations of governments, banks, and corporations in these other countries to minimize the danger that the infection might have already spread. But in so doing, they set off a chain of selling that creates the kind of contagion we have seen frequently in recent years.

Lesson 12:   *International diversification fails to provide much protection to the investor.*

This was true in 1982. It was true again in 1994–1995. It has been true in the past 2 years. Why do investors continue to believe in the perceived benefits of diversification?

Part of the reason is that the case for diversification is one of the most convincing of textbook formulations. Here is an intuitively appealing doctrine given a veneer of scientific inevitability through the use of elegant and reasonably accessible mathematics. All you have to understand is the elementary principles of variances and covariances, and soon you are convinced that the overall volatility of a portfolio can be less than the volatility of the individual components of that portfolio. So there is such a thing as a free lunch after all, the mathematics seems to be saying! When yearning seems to be supported by equations, it is hard to buck.

But the reality of markets intrudes. Take an investor with a portfolio of emerging market bonds. Let one of the issuers come under intense scrutiny. This is likely to be a rather thinly traded market in the best of times. At times of stress, liquidity will shrivel up almost immediately. Rather than sell at a gaping price concession, the investor is likely to do the next best thing, sell the bonds of another country, nearby geographically or with similar fault lines. The alleged benefits of diversification quickly evaporate in the real world.

Lesson 13:   *Investors cannot rely on sell-side analysts to alert them to bad news; they can't rely on government, IMF, or World Bank staff either.*

So many people have a vested interest in sustaining large flows of capital to the developing world that there is a conscious or unconscious suppression of leading indicators of problems. It is a kind of self-censorship. The risk assessments of sell-side analysts, in both traditional investment banks and commercial banks now operating in that manner, have to be viewed against the realities of the business in which their employers are in. Underwriting and distributing new issues of securities is a prominent source of earnings for most of these firms. Stern criticisms of a country, its economic policies, and the financial health of its banks and corporations often cause intense friction with clients and potential clients who do not take kindly to this sort of objectivity. They often threaten a loss of underwriting mandates to those firms whose analysts do not bury uncomfortable findings.

Moreover, in an ideal world, the IMF or World Bank could publish coolly objective appraisals of country prospects and policies. That is not today's world. But the multilateral lending institutions have sometimes gone down the path of being cheerleaders for emerging markets during the period when credit is flowing in liberally—and often excessively.

The lesson of course is that investors have to do their own research, but that is difficult because of the pathetic quality of much of the data provided by the governments of emerging countries. Transparency is worthless without a stern test of the veracity of the information released. But no one in a position of authority has been willing to take on that responsibility.

Lesson 14:   *Ratings agencies are not timely in their analysis but lag events. The credit risk in the high-octane world of finance has been systematically downplayed for a long time.*

The ratings agencies were overly generous toward Asian borrowers almost until the last second in 1997. Because high ratings put the Asian countries' dollar debt in the standard bond indexes, indexers, who do no independent credit evaluation, had to own the paper. Once the ratings were cut, indexers had no alternative but to sell, magnifying the collapse in asset values in the secondary market and making it that much more difficult to issue bonds to fund short-term bank debt. Once the indexers began to sell, yield spreads widened relative to U.S. Treasuries, and the ratings agencies took the widening in yield spreads as a sign that the situation was deteriorating further. So they continued to downgrade the credits, even after IMF programs were put in place. The ratings agencies have done a lot of soul searching subsequently. They have been more responsive to signs of improvement in economic and financial conditions, and have upgraded some of the same securities downgraded only months before, notably in the case of Korean obligations. But the lesson is clear: Investing by the ratings is dangerous, no matter how good a job the ratings agencies may do in the future.

Lesson 15:   *At times of turmoil, market participants can't rely on netting plus positions and minus positions with clients.*

Thus, gross exposures may be the true exposures.

Lesson 16:   *When default looms, securitization shifts power away from investors and toward borrowers.*

This was dramatically revealed in the case of Russia. Securitization meant that collectively lenders had less clout once conditions went badly wrong in August. The Russian government successfully was able to exploit that mismatch of negotiating position by its unilateral repudiation of domestic debt. It retains considerable clout in the ongoing negotiations over the disposition of the foreign currency–denominated debt left over from the former Soviet Union.

Investors must be wary of some of the ideas floating around in the U.S. Treasury for diminishing the standing of bondholders in negotiations over the rescheduling of emerging market debt. In the future, official creditors, such as the various export-import banks, will increasingly be in conflict with private lenders and unwilling to subordinate their interests. The superior position of bondholders cannot be taken for granted, notwithstanding the covenants in existing indentures.

Lesson 17:   *Rational analytical techniques cannot predict extremes in financial behavior.*

The modern quantitative and econometric techniques developed in the last generation have given investors and portfolio managers a new sense of confidence in the ability to forecast financial trends and behaviors. By compiling and analyzing historical data, and by building models that take into account current variables, econometricians often try to predict the movement of interest rates, stock prices, inflation, unemployment, and so on.

During times of financial euphoria and investor panic, however, these techniques become virtually worthless. The reason is fairly simple: The vast majority of models rest on assumptions about normal and rational financial behavior. But during market manias, logical and analytical minds do not prevail. The historical record is clear—few have been able to predict when a panic or raging bull will appear, and fewer still have known how far it would go. Such markets are driven more by hubris, elation, fear, pessimism, and the like—emotions that the current models do not, and perhaps cannot, compute.

History's Rhymes

Many of the distinguishing features of contemporary financial life have historical antecedents. A prime example: the difficulties that our financial institutions have been experiencing with their loans to developing nations. This problem is hardly new. International debt has been a recurring problem. Financial history is full of moratoriums, defaults, and confiscations. And in many of these cases, lenders took false hope in the notion that nations, as opposed to business corporations, were safe from insolvency.

A few illustrations over several centuries should make the point clear. In the fourteenth century, when Florence was the world's key banking center, its two leading banking houses collapsed because they had extended too much credit to Edward I, Edward II, and Robert Anjou, King of Naples. The lenders found it impossible to get the collateral that was put up to secure the loan. "Instead of being repaid," notes historian Benjamin Cohen (1986), "the lender was willy-nilly forced to lend more and more and to throw good money after bad in the hope of saving what he had already lent."

Much later, in the nineteenth century, England led the West in international finance. Its many initial successes were followed by serious debt problems, including numerous losses and defaults involving both financial institutions and nation-states. The Baring Brothers— one of England's preeminent banking houses—had to be bailed out by the Bank of England and by other institutions after overextending itself to a faltering Argentina in 1890. The early twentieth century brought similar foibles. The United States floated nearly $12 billion of foreign bonds between 1920 and 1932, a vast sum for its day. By 1935, nearly 40 percent of the value of foreign bonds listed on the New York Stock Exchange was in arrears.

The excessive use of leverage—an ongoing theme throughout financial history—contributed to the failure of 14 U.S. railroads during just one panic and to the collapse of 600 banks during another financial panic. The immediate predecessor to the current wave of leveraged buyouts and high-risk debt financing was probably the pyramiding schemes of the public utility holding companies in the 1920s. Many of those holding companies financed their acquisitions of independent operating units through the excessive use of debt. When financial problems surfaced at these companies, they often forced their subsidiaries to go into arrears on their preferred stock dividends and to halt common stock dividends. This, in turn, choked off the cash flow to the holding companies, which were struggling to meet their own heavy debt burdens and preferred stock dividends.

In their heyday, the public utility holding companies employed new techniques in finance with the same zeal as present-day issuers now use what we refer to as "innovative financing" or "financial engineering." The techniques employed in the 1920s to secure legal control over operating companies included (1) the issuance of a large volume of bonds; (2) the issuance of nonvoting preferred stock; (3) the issuance of different classes of preferred stock, with only one having controlling voting power; (4) the establishment of voting trusts with shares controlled by a small number of voting trustees; and (5) the issuance of large numbers of stock purchase warrants (or stock options) to the controlling interests. The parallels to our own time are clear—and so is the lesson: Heavy leverage controlled by a few is a recipe for trouble.

We should also not be surprised when financial heroes of the moment turn out to be villains who corrupt the financial markets. In the eighteenth century, John Law rose to fame in part by helping to stabilize a tottering financial situation in France by directing his own bank to redeem all of its notes in gold at a fixed rate. Yet he later fell into disrepute after devaluing the currency, manipulating the stock in his Mississippi Company, and other shenanigans. During the First World War, celebrated financier Charles Ponzi erected a towering financial pyramid—borrowing from new lenders to pay off old debt— which collapsed dramatically in the 1920s, wiping out the life savings of thousands of hapless investors. One of his contemporaries, Ivan Kreuger, the "Match King," amassed huge debts to finance his sprawling empire in matches. But he kept much of the vital information about his companies and their assets in his head, inaccessible to confidants, subordinates, banks, and accountants, who nevertheless raised few questions about his methods. When he committed suicide in 1932, he left behind what may have been the largest bankruptcy on record up to that point.

The public utility holding companies of the 1930s had their hero-turned-scoundrel as well: electric utility magnate Samuel Insull. A brilliant engineer and utility manager, Insull made the fateful mistake of launching a second career in the world of high finance. As with the other Icarus-like figures I have discussed, Insull experienced a meteoric rise, followed by a harrowing plunge. At the height of the bull market mania in the late 1920s, shares in Insull's two key enterprises— Commonwealth Edison and Middle West Utilities (MWU)—soared to dizzying heights. In the first 6 months of 1929, Commonwealth Edison stock rose from $202 dollars per share to $450, while the price of an MWU share shot up from $169 to $529. In the final weeks before the Wall Street crash—which also brought down Insull's house of financial cards—the value of total securities in Insull's various utility enterprises rose an average of $7,000 per minute, 24 hours a day. Insull's personal fortune also grew geometrically, from $5 million in 1927 to $150 million in 1929.

The Great Crash choked off the financial lifeblood that kept the Insull scheme alive: operating company dividends and the sale of preferred stock. On April 16, 1932, a group of Morgan bankers informed Insull that he could get no more credit to meet his looming June 1 payments. Knowing the end had come, a shaken Insull mumbled, "I wish my life on earth had already come to an end."

MWU, which soon fell into receivership, then controlled an astonishing 239 companies, 24 holding companies, and 13 subsidiaries that together supplied power to 4,471 communities in 30 states and Canada. So complex was the Insull financial web—one contemporary Wall Streeter called the holding company directors "wizards of financial chicanery"—that it is difficult to peg shareholder losses from the Insull collapse with any precision. But the sum was gigantic, with estimates ranging from $500 million to $2 billion in 1929 dollars.

Insull did not go down without a fight. In a saga that captured headlines for months, the erstwhile utility king was investigated and indicted, then fled to Greece, was captured off the Turkish shore, extradited to the United States, and finally put on trial in Chicago. A new phrase entered the lexicon of Depression-worn America—"from Insull to injury." More than any other individual of his era, Insull exemplified the financial excess and its damaging social and economic consequences.

All of this is not to suggest that the future may bring another Insull. In a strict sense, history does *not* repeat itself. Insull was a unique individual, and the whole context of his times—including government oversight of the financial markets and of the utility industry—has changed dramatically since Insull's day. The chances of someone executing the financial abuses that made Insull notorious are slim to none.

Still, although history does not *repeat* itself, as Mark Twain once said, sometimes it *rhymes*. We won't get Insull again, but we are very likely to see more Insull-like characters. The historical pattern strongly suggests as much. To be sure, these new characters will not use the same techniques for disguising and manipulating assets that Insull used; such methods will forever be outmoded and obsolete. But in our current environment, with its particular set of constraints and possibilities, overzealous financiers willing to push—or cross—the boundaries of the legal and ethical are sure to emerge.

Today's financial community is suffering from a bad case of amnesia. Most Wall Streeters are unaware of or have forgotten about the damaging effects of irresponsible behavior in their rush to "innovate" and profit. As I suggested earlier, the fault is not entirely their own. Our system of higher education rarely teaches financial history, or even business and economic history for that matter. Earlier this century, business majors at most colleges and universities were *required* to take courses in business and financial history, while the history of economics and economic thought was a staple in economics programs. This is no longer the case. In their entrancement with new quantitative methods, most business schools long ago abandoned their historically oriented courses, not merely as requirements, but as electives as well. Anything having to do with the qualitative side of business practice—ethics, business culture, history, and the like—was subordinated or eliminated as being too "soft" and "impractical." My deep concern about the eclipse of financial history inspired me to endow a chair in financial history at NYU's Stern School of Business.

But history is more important and useful during periods of rapid change—such as our own—than in relatively placid times. Only a long perspective can help us see long-term patterns and sort out what is lasting and salient from what is ephemeral and faddish. In finance, as in all human endeavors, history has valuable lessons to teach.

17

Financial Institutions
in the New Century

*[N]either improvements in technology nor the
growing use of the Internet is likely to reduce financial market volatility any time soon.*

I often marvel at the remarkable transformations in financial markets
during my half century on Wall Street: unprecedented growth, securitization, globalization, the explosion of new credit instruments, the
freeing of competitive restraints on institutions, wide interest rate
swings. The scale and scope of these changes, combined with the fact
that we have not seen a major depression in nearly half a century, are
both fascinating and encouraging.

It would be a mistake to conclude from this record, however, that
financial markets have matured to the point where there is little room
left for growth or change. Surely, the future will bring more growth,
volatility, and innovation. As I have suggested throughout this book,
structural changes have driven rapid expansion and rapid change in
financial markets over the last four decades, and I am convinced they
will continue to do so in the future.

Three institutional questions in particular deserve careful consideration. How will the conflict between the forces of devolution and the
movement toward economic and financial concentration be resolved?
How will the Internet reshape financial markets and institutions in the
next century? And what new challenges will the managers of financial
institutions face in the coming decades?

Recently, Congress and the President passed legislation that in effect repealed the Glass-Steagall Banking Act of 1932 by allowing mergers among insurance companies, banks, and investment firms. A more ambitious plan that would allow financial and nonfinancial firms to merge has not passed Congress, but it may in the next decade or two. The regulatory environment seldom has been more friendly to consolidation in the financial sector (and others) than in the last decade. That reality—along with the rapid diffusion of information technology networks through the financial world—is raising the stakes for tomorrow's investors and financial firm managers.

Devolution

A key challenge facing the financial markets is the conflict between devolution and the drive toward economic and financial concentration. Devolution rests on the premise that economic activity and governmental functions should be decentralized. Proponents of devolution advocate not only the decentralization of administrative tasks in the public and private sectors, but also the decentralization of authority and responsibility over economic, financial, and governmental decisions.

The pressures on central governments to devolve power vary from place to place. In some parts of the world, devolutionary movements have been a direct result of political upheaval. Most such cases, of course, are to be found in Eastern Europe and the former Soviet Union, where government authorities are engineering wholesale devolution in the face of great political ferment and transition. The process is happening in China as well, although there the impetus for change is driven at the local level. Already, the Chinese provincial governments and enterprises have acquired considerable autonomy (but not democracy as we understand it in the West), particularly in the rapidly industrializing regions.

The devolution of authority away from central governments is sweeping across much of the industrialized world as well. In many instances, bloated budget deficits and heavy debt burdens are behind the drive toward decentralization. No matter where we look, with the exception of Japan, central governments are hobbled by budgetary constraints. In the new Europe, the European Monetary Union tightly constrains deficit financing. Elected officials simply do not have the revenues needed to expand existing programs or launch new ones. Tighter budgetary limits are, in turn, eroding the appeal and popularity of central governments. At the same time, central governments are coming under greater pressure to find new ways to reduce budget deficits and to improve the efficiency of governmental activities.

As for financial markets, they are likely to see the continuing privatization of a growing array of activities and enterprises presently run by governments. And as privatization accelerates in many nations, credit demands will continue to shift from the public sector to private enterprises. At the same time, the decline of central government financing will leave the task of evaluating and accommodating credit demands to the financial markets. As a group, such demanders of credit will become more and more diverse in their needs and their risk levels—and thus pose higher risks than when their governments played a larger role.

To judge these credit obligations correctly, economies that embrace devolution will need to intensify their risk analysis. But there is no reason for private institutions to automatically embrace this priority. In fact, other aspects of devolution pull in the opposite direction—especially securitization, which fosters the devolution of risk taking within markets and institutions alike. At financial institutions today, debt and equity obligations are fractionalized into tranches that vary the level of risk taking. To enhance their short-term rates of return, investors rarely hold such obligations to maturity.

Consolidation and "Encompassing Institutions"

Widespread devolution in market instruments will continue to encourage massive consolidation among financial institutions. This trend is being driven by the confluence of several forces: advances in technology; changes in the needs and attitudes of investors, borrowers, and depositors; expansion of the open credit markets; and continuing deregulation of financial markets and institutions. Together, these changes may enable large institutions not only to exploit genuine economies of scale, but also to bear the heavy start-up costs of financial innovation. More than this, large institutions can more easily amass the large-scale capital needed to build and maintain dominance in the various capital markets. Charles Freedman and Clyde Goodet have succinctly summarized the reasons for the new wave of financial consolidations:

> First, given technological requirements, it will be extremely expensive in the future to maintain a competitive infrastructure for delivering financial services efficiently, and only large institutions can manage these costs. Second, there are economies of scale in some parts of the operation that can be realized only by very large entities. Third, a successful financial institution will have to be large enough to provide all or most types of services to its customers in a sort of financial supermarket, either because of demand or to take advantage of economies of scope (or "synergies"). Fourth, an international presence is essential for success, and only large institutions can compete outside the domestic market. Fifth, large amounts of capital will be necessary to handle the kinds of transactions and provide the kinds of services demanded by some customers in the future.
>
> These propositions imply that the successful financial institution of the future will be a very large conglomerate, operating in an international context, and providing all or most types of services to its customers in a technologically advanced way. (Freedman and Goodet, 1997, p. 18)

The daunting technological requirements that financial institutions will need to compete in the twenty-first century constitute an important factor driving financial consolidation. As the Internet speeds up the process of depersonalization in banking relationships (which I discuss below), financial institutions are trying to establish strong brand identity rather than build personal relationships with borrowers and savers.

Empirical work in this area has yet to demonstrate that large financial institutions can in fact exploit potential economies of scale,

especially since many unrelated functions and services can be out-
sourced or purchased from specialty boutiques. Historical data on this
matter may not hold validity in the future. First of all, securitization
has depersonalized the credit relationship within the marketplace.
Consumer loans and mortgages for households are being consummated through credit scoring procedures and not through face-to-face
contacts, as are a large volume of small business loans. But it is the
larger institutions, not the smaller ones, that possess the capabilities to
securitize the many obligations under this umbrella. Moreover, the
quantitative modeling of risk, whether correct or faulty, is also the
domain of large institutions, leaving smaller ones to depend on them
for guidance on risk assessment and risk measurement techniques.
The Internet will not end financial intermediation, but it will have
much to do with how credit is processed; nor will it reduce the need to
save for institutional risk taking and for the efficient allocation of
credit.

The United States is likely to see much more consolidation among
financial institutions in the early twenty-first century. This will come
on the heels of major moves in the last two decades. Consider some of
the highlights. In banking, the 1980s began with the top 10 banks holding 19 percent of the domestic deposits of insured commercial banks.
The percentage rose very slightly over the next decade, then climbed to
37 percent by the end of 1998. For the top 25 U.S. banks, this same
deposit concentration ratio rose from 29 percent in 1980, to 35 percent
in 1990, to 51 percent in 1998. As for mutual fund companies: In mid-
1999, the 5, 10, and 25 largest mutual fund organizations held (respectively) 34 percent, 46 percent, and 70 percent of all mutual fund assets.

In Europe, the pace of consolidation has quickened as well, especially following the establishment of the European Monetary Union. In
France, Germany, and Italy, a massive merger wave is under way in the
insurance and commercial banking sectors. Cross-border mergers and
acquisitions, once considered implausible, are beginning to take place.
The new banks and insurance companies created through such mergers
will lose their national identities; they will be seen as EMU institutions.
Meanwhile, Latin America and Asia are experiencing their own waves
of consolidations, but in many cases restructuring is driven by pressures

(often applied by central governments) to write off bad loans. Japan has been especially aggressive in this regard; in recent years giant mergers have melded the Bank of Tokyo with Mitsubishi, and the Industrial Bank of Japan with Dai-Ichi Kangyo Bank and Fuji Bank.

Out of this process of consolidation and conglomeration, at least in the United States, will emerge a new breed of financial institution that we might call an "encompassing institution." Such behemoths will conduct financial activities that cut across traditional institutional boundaries. The amalgamation of Citibank, Travelers Insurance, Salomon Smith Barney, and Commercial Credit Corporation into Citigroup will be emulated many times by other institutions. But encompassing institutions probably will not replicate full-fledged, European-style "universal banks," which combine financial and nonfinancial functions. American traditions—unlike those of Europe, where fear of centralized economic and political power is not as strong—suggest that we may not move for some time to allow banks and commercial corporations to merge.

Internally, encompassing institutions will face two principal challenges. First, they will be extremely difficult to manage, especially at the very senior level. In the next century, a larger proportion of middle managers will possess much greater technical know-how and autonomy as well as strong incentives to take risks—dynamics that I discuss in more detail at the end of this chapter. Second, high levels of concentration in the financial sector will increase conflicts of interest and force the central bank to extend its safety net under even more of our financial system.

More than this, consolidation is undermining competition in key segments of the financial marketplace. Encompassing institutions already are a powerful force in institutional asset management, and soon they will control large mutual fund complexes as well. As a result, they will be deeply engaged on all sides of the market *at the same time:* on the sell side as dealers and underwriters, on the buy side as institutional investors and portfolio lenders, and as financial advisers to their clients. Official regulators may insist on internal firewalls between these various functions, but such safeguards will be very difficult to monitor. For instance, if an institution is underwriting a sizable new issue that runs into an unanticipated squall in the marketplace, it hardly will need to demand *overtly* that its institutional asset management division lend a helping hand by acquiring a portion of the offering. The institution can depend on collegial ties to accomplish the result seamlessly, without breaching formal rules or even ethical norms.

Within encompassing institutions, maintaining objective research will become even more problematic than it is now. As I suggested in Chapter 9, researchers sometimes are torn between the desire to provide honest assessments of a company's or nation's prospects, the need to support securities sales efforts, and the need to uncover good investment ideas so that internal asset management can distinguish itself. Good senior managers try to shield their analysts from these potential conflicts of interest. But even with the best intentions in the world, firms sometimes will suppress, or at least fudge, undesirable research findings in the interest of retaining a piece of business. Certain clients simply don't want to read anything negative about themselves.

The problem will worsen in the future, and as it does, investors will have to tread even more warily than they do today. In the not-so-distant future, they will have to depend more and more on their own internally generated research and analysis, or on firms that specialize exclusively in research. Thus, in the markets of tomorrow, independent research with a reputation for high objectivity will command a premium.

The future challenges facing outside board members in highly diversified financial institutions are even more daunting than those that confront operating managers. I first realized the enormity of this task when I began serving on Salomon's board following our merger with Phibro. The outside members came in with diverse business backgrounds. With the exception of Maurice (Hank) Greenberg, none had strong firsthand experience in a major financial institution. How, then, could they possibly understand, among other things, the magnitude of risk taking at Salomon, the dynamics of the matched book of securities lending, the true extent to which the firm was leveraging its capital, the credit risk in a large heterogeneous book of assets, the effectiveness of operating management in enforcing trading disciplines, or the amount of capital that was allocated to the various activities of the firm and the rates of return on this capital on a risk-adjusted basis? Compounding the problem, the formal reports prepared for the board were neither comprehensive enough nor detailed enough to educate the outside directors about the diversity and complexity of our operations.

This problem is magnified as firms extend their global reach and their portfolio of activities. In recent years, quite a few major U.S. financial institutions have become truly international in scope. They underwrite, trade currencies, stocks, and bonds, and manage the portfolios and securities of industrial corporations and emerging nations. As noted earlier, some of the largest institutions contain in their holding company structures not only banks but also mutual funds, insurance companies, securities firms, finance companies, and real estate affiliates. The outside directors on the boards of such firms are at a considerable disadvantage when trying to assess the institution's performance. They must rely heavily on the veracity and competency of senior managers, who in turn are responsible for overseeing a dazzling array of intricate risks undertaken by specialized, lower-level personnel working throughout the firm's wide-flung units.

Unfortunately, the accounting profession has been of little help to outside board members. Few audit reports truly reflect a firm's range of risk taking. Reports on assets and liabilities would be far more meaningful if they were shown in gross terms instead of net figures. The off-balance-sheet activities most often cited in footnotes should be integrated into reports to reveal the total flow of activities and liabilities. Disappointingly, operating managements generally oppose conservative accounting rules when they are proposed by the FASB. This is because such rules tend to reduce stated profits and encourage conservative lending and investing policies, thus infringing on the stated profits. Over the long term, however, such rules will strengthen the institution's credit quality.

To function well, an outside board member needs to be prepared thoroughly before sitting down for his or her first board meeting. The financial institution should provide a comprehensive orientation program, one that includes (among other things) a detailed presentation on the firm's activities, advance copies of all reports to be discussed, guidance about how to judge the parameters of risk taking (including a comprehensive review of the quantitative risk modeling used by the institution), and a review of the institution's accounting procedures. More than this, a new outside board member should be required to meet with the official supervisory agency that oversees the institution, including (when relevant) the Federal Reserve, the Comptroller of the Currency, or the Securities and Exchange Commission. These officials can explain firsthand the nature of their responsibilities and how they see those of the director. Finally, the financial institution's in-house lawyer should discuss with each director his or her responsibilities and liabilities.

There are other important voids to fill as well. First, financial institutions find it difficult to recruit directors with valuable technical backgrounds—especially those with expertise in information technology, econometric modeling, and quantitative risk analysis. Second, the boards that govern today's largest institutions seldom dedicate enough time to the task. The complexities of the business typically demand that boards set up committees on finance, investments, human resources, credit, governance, and the like. To be sure, the role of an effective board should be to set policy, to represent the interests of the shareholders and lenders, not to operate the institution. But unless boards begin to devote enough time to handle their responsibilities, the industry may suffer even more upheavals, forcing government regulators to step in to remedy the situation.

Finally, on the broadest level, current and future concentration in the financial sector—along with parallel heavy merger activity in automobile manufacturing, telecommunications, airline manufacturing, petroleum, broadcasting, computers and software, and other core industries—poses problems for America's economic democracy. The conventional arguments in favor of large-scale mergers are that they reduce excess capacity and improve efficiency. This view certainly has some merit. Quite often, consolidation—among financial and nonfinancial firms alike—can lower the cost of doing business, leading to higher profits without price hikes. But costs cannot be lowered indefinitely in this way; at some point, *dis*economies of scale kick in. More importantly, as monopoly theory suggests, firms that become so dominant as to be unassailable have strong incentives (and few disincentives) to raise prices in order to boost profit margins. When that happens, there will be—theoretically, at least—opportunities for new entrants to unlock the monopolistic hold of encompassing institutions by introducing new products and services. But that seems unlikely. Although the established dominant firm or firms may be vulnerable on the product and service side, their enormous capital advantage allows them to simply acquire innovations, or copy them, outlasting their smaller rivals during the competitive phase.

As I have noted, today there is little popular, political, or governmental opposition to consolidation to compare with the contentious antitrust movement of a century ago. One reason is the devolution of power of national governments and the increasing power of the private-sector organizations that operate internationally. All too frequently, mergers are justified as a way of meeting international competition. According to this view, American firms must be allowed to achieve the same market standing as their foreign competitors in order to compete effectively. Politicians typically have little motivation to take on the "big interests," especially when, as noted, there is little public support to do so. As for "the public" itself—with so many ordinary householders invested in the stock market, and reaping the benefits of consolidation in the form of rising share prices and dividends—there is little chance of a modern "antitrust" movement emerging any time soon.

Ultimately, a high concentration in business and finance will exact a cost on society as a whole. This may evoke a political response; but with national governments losing their hold on international economic and financial developments, the response will have to come from either a return to nationalism (if international cooperation breaks down) or the creation of a new supergovernmental international institution designed to limit global economic concentration.

The encompassing institutions that I have described will—sometime within the next two or three decades—be functioning more like utilities than private corporations. Like utilities, they will be "too big to fail." In Europe, Latin America, Canada, and Japan financial asset concentration will force the authorities to allow very few institutions to fail. Over the longer term, much tighter supervision will circumscribe the activities of such institutions and thus limit their profit opportunities. But, again, why should the current management of financial institutions be concerned about such a distant event? After all, they will have retired long before that time. It will be someone else's problem.

The Internet and Financial Markets

There is no question that the Internet will continue to have far-reaching implications for the financial markets. Within a few decades hardly anyone will conduct financial transactions the way we do today. Very few will walk into a bank to deposit funds or apply for a loan. All regular banking customers will carry out their business on home and office computer workstations, which are becoming easier to use every day. Financial institutions and their clients no longer will have a personal relationship. At the same time, the Internet will become an increasingly important vehicle for arbitraging the cost of providing financial services to low-cost lenders. This does not mean that the Internet will usher in a new age of low interest rates, but rather that the differences in financing costs among providers of credit will shrink. Stated differently, banking fees will converge throughout the economy.

At the same time, although total profits in the financial sector may not shrink due to Internet banking, there will probably be some redistribution of profits among institutions. For example, financial institutions are currently rushing to become providers of "financial services" such as money management, household and business lending, and the securitization of debt. The process is bound to become highly standardized, and in the process, profit margins will be squeezed. But which market makers and investors will be required to assume the risks? This financial intermediation risk may well require a higher return.

One benefit of improved technology and increased use of the Internet is quite clear. Supervisory authorities and investors alike will have much more timely financial information. Company meetings with analysts will become a matter of open disclosure. Financial data will be released on the Internet in easily digestible formats. The task of the analyst will then be to analyze, not merely disgorge, data. For the official supervisory and regulatory authorities the new technology of tomorrow will allow the transmission of real-time information about the activities of financial institutions and of open market activities. This should be of immense help in improving supervisory understanding of financial developments. It will also speed the flow of important economic and financial information to the central banks. All in all, official supervision and monetary policy will have improved capabilities to make better decisions and thus limit financial excesses, a key prerequisite for sustainable economic growth.

Nevertheless, neither improvements in technology nor the growing use of the Internet is likely to reduce financial market volatility any time soon. For the time being, the flow of information combined with increasing securitization of assets will encourage quick market responses. The focus on near-term market performance of portfolios will not abate. Indeed, the enlarged universe of globally tradable instruments will likely increase this focus and keep volatility extremely high.

Challenges Facing the Managers
of Financial Institutions

In the early part of the post-World War II period, the job of managing large financial institutions was much more straightforward than it is today. Interest rates were not particularly volatile. For many years, financial markets were segmented. Banks made business loans; thrifts provided mortgages; insurance companies wrote insurance policies; mutual funds were a minor curiosity; and pension funds were inconsequential. The whole fabric of financial regulation and oversight was designed to ensure that financial institutions remained profitable most of the time.

This fostered intimate relationships between creditors and debtors. Institutional ties were ongoing. Commercial and investment bankers thought of themselves as serving and supporting their clients, even in troubled times. In return, bankers gained access to confidential information about corporate borrowers, and respected those confidences. For their part, corporate treasurers also felt that financial relationships should have a high degree of permanence. They held on to their lead bankers, and seldom shopped around for a more attractive proposition from a competitor.

The dazzling diversity of new financial instruments that I reviewed in Chapter 3—negotiable certificates of deposits, adjustable-rate loans, money market funds, credit card securitization, mortgage-pass-through securities, financial derivatives (all kinds of swaps, futures, and options), guaranteed investment contracts, zero coupon bonds, and endless varieties of asset-backed securities—have complicated the manager's task exponentially. So have the prodigious array of new types of financial institutions, most of them scarcely known or nonexistent 30 years ago: private pension funds, state and local retirement funds, government-sponsored mortgage entities (Fannie Mae and Freddie Mac), indexed funds, commodity pool operators, specialized finance companies, and all sorts of highly leveraged portfolio managers, including the now infamous hedge funds.

Out of this multitude of new instruments and institutions have developed a multiplicity of new markets and global interrelationships. The result is greater access to finance, greater ability to take risk, a relentless quest for short-term performance, and less permanence in financial relationships. We now live in a financial world in which older virtues—like knowing your customer, minimizing rather than merely managing risk, and learning how to turn down a promising but dubious deal—have been eclipsed and are even ridiculed as hopelessly out of date.

In spite of its many virtues, the new system does a poor job of nurturing effective managerial control within financial institutions, especially at the senior level. To begin with, senior managers seldom have much direct involvement in the day-to-day activities of the business. Instead, middle managers have become more powerful, because they stand on the front lines—originating, selling, and trading all these inventive financial instruments. For them, risk is a necessary ingredient in the search for higher rewards. Moreover, most compensation systems are structured to give middle management incentives to focus on near-term profits. Paradoxically, middle management specialists often earn more than their senior supervisors, thanks to profits from exotic financial derivatives and other new instruments. And that reversal of fortunes can undermine an organization's structure of authority.

In the new environment, middle managers are gaining greater autonomy through their technical prowess and global relationships than they could have commanded in an earlier era. Not surprisingly, when such managers aren't allowed to do what they do best—or what they think they do best—they are much more likely than their predecessors to jump to another institution that promises greater independence. Accordingly, middle-level managers in financial institutions need to continually urge top bosses to approve new propositions. At the same time, senior managers must look out for the long-term health of the institution.

But such interfirm tensions seem not to be waning, and with serious implications for the future of major financial institutions. A vivid example is the recent case in which major banks and securities firms made loans to several large hedge funds. The volume of trading activity was heavy, and the lending arrangements seemed to be quite profitable. The firm's middle managers wanted to forge ahead, and its senior managers couldn't bring themselves to turn down the business. In this case, as in so many others, the compulsion to keep the profit flow coming was inexorable, undermining risk considerations in the process.

The leaders of financial institutions need to recognize and combat the illusion in the securities markets that everything can be bought and sold. We now have a performance-driven system rather than one centered on institutions that buy and hold securities. Now, institutions are compelled to bring their holdings to market often. Yet it is the middle managers who typically control the process of marking to market. When liquidity is high and markets seem to be rallying indefinitely, risks seem remote. But when market conditions abruptly turn unfavorable and liquidity quickly dries up, middle managers often attempt to camouflage poor marketability as long as possible by simply marking to market on the basis of *indicative* prices rather than at the far lower prices at which genuine transactions could be made. By the time senior managers become fully aware of the deterioration in market conditions, it is usually too late to do much to save losing positions.

The growing importance and prestige of mathematics (especially quantitative risk analysis) in finance also is complicating the job of senior management. Like so much else in today's leading financial institutions, computer modeling is the purview of middle management. The ability to build models, enhanced by access to increasingly powerful and relatively cheap computers, creates the illusion of scientific exactitude. But the precision lies only in the calculation of the formulas. Models constructed from past data are capable of modeling the past. But they will invariably fail to predict the future when there are sudden shifts in the structure of the markets, as we have seen in recent years. Therefore, senior managers should be leery of putting their faith in models that worked profitably within an earlier set of structural relationships. The pace and complexity of changes makes certain rules of thumb obsolete. But replacing common sense with rigorous quantification is not the answer either.

Most middle managers possess little knowledge of past crises and failures. For that reason, senior and middle managers alike need to be skeptical of those who assert: "This time is different." Each generation of profit seekers tries to uncover a new paradigm, in which the trade-off between risks and return is supposedly better. But as we found out in the case of Russia, this can be patent nonsense.

Finally, senior managers must be tough-minded in the deployment of the firm's capital. It is their job to determine the true rate of return on capital—when a proper adjustment for risk is taken into account. They must look beyond what the models say about the measurement of credit risk. And they should be especially critical about whether risks are correlated across markets. Some of this can be monitored using data from the past, but senior managers must stand ready to assume outcomes that are far less favorable than the historical patterns.

18

Looking to the Future

I believe that sometime within the next few
years, the financial euphoria will be reversed. . . .
[P]erhaps an even bigger problem than the debacle
of Long Term Capital Management will surface
and kill the euphoric atmosphere.

Given my role as a forecaster of interest rates and other key financial trends, I would be remiss to end this book without some predictions about the future. So in the sections that follow, I consider some immediate risks to the U.S. economy and financial markets, what is likely to happen with interest rates in the early twenty-first century, and some of the promise and peril of a world economy with three dominant currencies (the Euro, the dollar, and the yen). I then conclude the chapter—and the book—by looking backward a century for a sense of perspective on the role of finance in the modern world now and in the future.

Near-Term Risks

In the past decade, the American financial markets have been supported by a strong economic foundation. The key economic indicators have turned in an exemplary performance: Real growth has been strong; inflation has been very low—especially for this mature stage in the business cycle; and employment has been rising. Many attribute the economy's rising efficiency (with contained labor costs) to the spread of information technologies and global competition—the two pillars of the so-called "New Economy."

But we should not forget that cyclical dynamics still reside in the economy and that structural changes continue to transform institutional arrangements in the financial markets. America's economic strength surely rests in part on the application of new information technologies. At the same time, however, the United States has benefited enormously from the poor economic performance in Europe and in Japan during the past 10 years. Excess capacity in the rest of the world has helped hold down inflation, while foreign economic and financial weaknesses have enabled the U.S. to attract an enormous volume of foreign funds, which has helped finance our own economic expansion. And that expansion (and the related prosperity) has made it possible for foreigners to sell a growing volume of goods to the United States, so that imports have outpaced exports at a faster and faster clip over time.

No one should assume that this nexus of events must necessarily endure. In fact, this unique set of conditions—so favorable to the United States over the past two decades—is beginning to fray. Japan is starting to emerge from its economic doldrums. One reason for this achievement, ironically, is that Japanese policymakers actually have been belatedly following much of the advice about how to cure their economic ailments given to them by U.S. policymakers and economic advisers. As Japan's banking problems are alleviated, its credit crunch will disappear. Concurrently, the European business recovery seems to have gained a firmer footing.

Could the U.S. live with European and Japanese success? The honest answer is: not very comfortably. A strong economy in Europe and Japan almost certainly would spark a tightening in world commodity markets and resurrect some inflationary fears. And it would stifle the outflows of investment capital from Japan and Europe, much of it currently going to the United States. These business recoveries abroad would dampen our ebullient fixed-income markets, driving up U.S. bond yields and driving down the value of the dollar. Already, the financial markets are registering some concern about the magnitude of the U.S. current account deficit.

Overriding this development is the uncertainty about the direction of the American stock market. I know of no time in the last 50 years in which the well-being of the American economy and that of the rest of the world have been so dependent on the strength of the U.S. equity market. Unfortunately, as I noted in an earlier chapter, there is no rational analytical technique that will enable one to correctly project the magnitude of extreme financial behavior. How high is high is always a magnitude difficult to quantify in periods of financial euphoria. On those occasions, rationales abound for why markets will still go higher, and why the extreme liberal relationships between stock prices and earnings will become even more liberal in the future. Many investors simply assume that the favorable economic and financial backdrop that contributed to the extraordinary performance of the market in this decade will not change. The quandary we all face is that at market peaks most of us have been caught up in the euphoria around us, with few remaining on the sidelines watching the casualties when the debacle takes hold.

I believe that sometime within the next few years, the financial euphoria will be reversed. The challenge to current market behavior may come from one of a number of directions. It may emanate from improved business activity in Europe, which likely would require higher interest rates here; or it may come from wage pressures that will squeeze profit margins and end the widely held expectations of continued improvements in corporate profits. With rising activity of all sorts in the financial markets, perhaps an even bigger problem than the debacle of Long Term Capital Management will surface and kill the euphoric atmosphere.

The next time that stocks fall sharply, several developments will increase the risk to the economy that official policymakers will have to evaluate carefully. One is the question of how average household equity investors will behave in a distressed market? As noted in Chapter 3, households have become heavily dependent on the appreciation of their equity holdings, and (lately again) on the rising value of their homes. This can be seen in the sharp drop in the personal savings rate in the late 1990s. Whereas Americans saved an average of 6 percent of their income in 1992, that proportion has fallen to only about 2 percent. Individual company stocks and stock funds have become the preferred method of "saving" for the nation's middle class. But many

Americans do not seem to understand that, unlike the days of the pass-book savings account, the principal on an increasing portion of their life savings is now subject to the risk of substantial loss.

Institutional groups that manage household portfolios claim that households are for the most part in it for the long haul—in part because much of this capital is invested in retirement plans—and therefore that householders would not sell into declining markets. I doubt that. Such investors have become so accustomed to generously rising equity values over the last two decades that they may be appalled by actual losses, much less lower rates of return.

Much will depend on the varying behavior of quite different demographic groups. Some mutual fund investors are naturally inclined to take the long view. Their investments may be part of a 401k or other tax-advantaged program, and they may be tolerant of even exceptionally sharp breaks in market prices. Even so, there is nothing to prevent householders from moving retirement funds out of stocks and into safer havens within their 401k or Keogh plans. Moreover, other groups of investors—the elderly who are reliant on stable asset values or the novice investor who has only an imperfect appreciation of how markets can fluctuate over the short term—may not be inclined to ride out a crisis. In addition, there are millions of investors in mutual funds who are aggressively seeking high rates of return, and who are capable of reacting to a market disturbance with every bit as much alacrity as a professional investment manager.

What happens during a correction, then, will reflect the dynamics of these various groups of investors, and the ensuing interactions among the different segments of the marketplace—domestic equities, domestic bonds, foreign equities, foreign bonds, and cash equivalents. I believe that in the face of an extraordinary market disturbance, there is the potential for very large departures from both equity and bond funds. That departure will not come in the initial stock market decline, which I believe will be led by the highly near-term-oriented leveraged investors, but rather after some delay when market prices threaten to go below the price at which households entered the market. There is currently no obvious alternative institutional investor group that would quickly step in to counterbalance such selling. On the contrary, institutional investors will be mesmerized by the spectacle of sizable mutual fund redemptions in much the same way that they would watch a multiple car accident on a crowded highway. Their natural reaction will be to wait until the dust settles. As a consequence, they will unwittingly accelerate not only the decline in stock prices but also the drop in consumer spending much more than econometric models now suggest.

When the equity markets come under attack, there will be days when price setbacks (in absolute terms) will match or even exceed the dramatic price spiral of October 1987. In percentage terms, however, these drops will be relatively much smaller because current price levels are much higher than in 1987. Therefore, it may turn out that the retreat in stock prices will come in moderate stages that cumulatively add up to a major contraction.

This kind of market pattern will only complicate the Fed's job by making it more difficult to judge when to intervene. After all, it is much easier for the Fed to lower interest rates sharply when there are severe breaks in the market—but much more difficult for the central bank to act decisively when a large decline unfolds haltingly over many months.

The other vulnerability is the increasing risk being taken by business corporations in their financial structures. This has been largely hidden by the long economic expansion of the 1990s and its accompanying financial euphoria, but it can be perceived in a number of key financial statistics. One is the relationship between the net increase in the equity book value of nonfinancial corporations and of their indebtedness. Exhibit 18-1 shows this trend for the period 1982–1999. Despite sizable increases in profits, the net equity position has been contracting again, while debt has picked up markedly. This is because corporations have used retained earnings (after the payment of taxes and dividends) and new borrowings to buy back large numbers of outstanding shares and to finance acquisitions.

How does this compare with prior periods? In the first 3 years of the 1990s, the credit-quality constraints on business forced corporations to increase equity and dramatically slow net new borrowings. Thereafter (through mid-1999) debt grew more rapidly than equity. In

---

Net Change in Equity Book Value and in Debt
of Non-Financial Corporations 1982–1999 ($ BILLIONS)

			Period		
	1982–83	1984–90	1991–93	1994–96	1997–99
Pre-Tax Profits	$291.4	$1,455.1	$781.5	$1,305.2	$1,516.6
Less:					
Taxes	$105.6	$606.2	$280.1	$415.6	$505.7
Dividends	$116.9	$587.6	$403.2	$551.8	$742.9
Plus:					
IVA	($19.1)	($74.7)	($12.1)	($39.8)	$3.4
Net New Equity	$21.9	($640.7)	$66.7	($167.4)	($731.2)
Net Change in Equity	$71.7	($454.1)	$152.8	$130.6	($459.8)
Net Increase In Debt	$186.1	$1,286.3	$46.9	$549.6	$1,036.0

Source: Flow-Of-Funds; Federal Reserve Board; 1999 Q2 Annualized.

Exhibit 18-1

the debt binge of the 1980s, the event that strangulated corporate finance strategy in the early 1990s, debt grew and equity fell sharply.

This pattern of corporate finance points to two related phenomena. First, major credit rating agencies are again significantly downgrading more issues than they are upgrading, although not yet at the rate they did so in the 1980s or early 1990s. Second, the composition of credit ratings of outstanding bond issues is shifting. Despite strong earnings performance in the last 5 years, note in Exhibit 18-2 the credit-quality decline in the composition of outstanding issues as compiled by Lehman Brothers. No American commercial bank—although their top managers would claim that they possess a strong capital base—have credit ratings today of AAA. In 1975, 15 large banks had this highest rating.

The shocking aspect of this credit-quality pattern mirrors the pattern of the 1980s. In that decade, the decapitalization of business was spearheaded by the many highly leveraged buyouts, which continued into the 1990s but were joined by large share repurchases. The excess leveraging of the 1980s had grim consequences for corporate America, from forced downsizing and outright failure to a slowed business recovery.

Market Value of Outstanding Corporate Bonds
Classified by Credit Rating
(% Distribution)

Date:	December 31, 1988	December 31, 1992	August 31, 1999
Credit Rating:			
Aaa–A	64.95%	64.42%	52.94%
Baa	23.47%	25.18%	22.93%
Bb and Lower	11.58%	10.40%	24.13%
Total	100.00%	100.00%	100.00%

Exhibit 18-2

It is unfortunate that we still do not fully appreciate the fact that corporate debt never can be a full substitute for equity. Because debt entails defined corporate obligations of interest payments and repayment schedules, it is a preemptive factor in corporate cash flow that may limit management flexibility. The abuse of the debt-creation process contributes to corporate failures; and for society as a whole it increases the risk of eroding the essence of economic democracy. Equity, in contrast, allows freedom of decision making and often reflects confidence in society and its political and economic institutions. If we diminish the role of equity, we invite the specter of business control shifting first to financial institutions and then inexorably toward government. This, in turn, encourages business concentration, and with it the chances of moving away from economic democracy.

Interest Rate Prospects

As we enter the next century, and as living standards rise and economies become even more globally integrated, financial markets will play a larger role in the average citizen's life. And interest rates will be a big part of the financial picture. Given my long and deep involvement with interest rate analysis and forecasting, it seems fitting that I offer some comments on interest rate prospects for the new century.

To begin with, the long-term secular decline in interest rates that began with high-grade bonds in October 1981 will continue for quite a few years to come. This secular decline has endured for 19 years, a shorter duration than the century's other secular rises and declines: the 35-year interest rate rise from 1946 to 1981, the 26-year decline from 1920 to 1946, and the 21-year increase from 1899 to 1920. The great variation in these historical patterns is clear; there is no consistency in time period, no clear average duration, and no uniformity in the spreads between highs and lows. The 1946-to-1981 rise—in which high-grade corporate bond yields rose by 1,112 basis points (454 percent)—dwarfs the other secular swings, and will not be repeated any time soon.

The sustained onslaught on the bond market was the product of a confluence of forces, most notably the federal government's out-of-control budget deficits, the oil price spikes of the 1970s, and the misguided willingness of monetary policymakers to finance excessive credit demands. Will we see a comparable oil shock in the early twenty-first century? Probably not, given the petroleum industry's improved techniques for finding oil and advances in the development of fossil fuel alternatives. Moreover, no matter what the shortcomings of monetary policy, bond markets will respond to inflationary pressures much more quickly than in the past. I believe that the secular decline in interest rates that began in 1981 will remain in force, despite some cyclical swings. It will reassert itself.

It is important to keep in mind that the cyclical behavior of interest rates during a secular bear bond market is quite different from the typical interest rate pattern in a secular bull bond market. In a secular *bear* bond market, cyclical interest rate declines are short-lived and increases are long-lived. During the great bear market from 1946 to 1981, cyclical rallies in long U.S. Governments lasted an average of only 12 months, while the setbacks averaged about 50 months. The opposite pattern holds for secular *bull* bond markets. For example, since the start of the current secular bull market in October 1981, yield declines have endured an average of 26 months, while the setbacks have lasted an average of only 12 months (see Exhibit 18-3).

I predict that in the next cyclical rally, long government bond yields will decline well below their previous cyclical and secular lows,

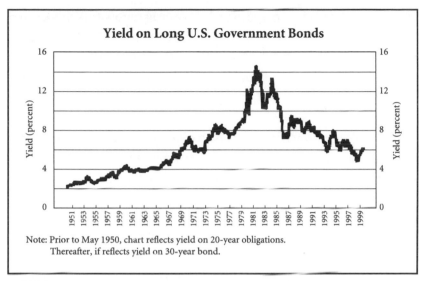

Yield on Long U.S. Government Bonds

Note: Prior to May 1950, chart reflects yield on 20-year obligations. Thereafter, if reflects yield on 30-year bond.

Exhibit 18-3

falling to around 4 percent. The reason: The Federal Reserve will need to lower short-term interest rates sharply in order to contain wider economic damage.

How will high-yield bonds—such as junk bond and the bonds of emerging nations—perform in this environment? Not very well. High-yield bonds are fair-weather investments. They thrive when access to the open credit market is exceedingly good, when economic activity in the industrial world is solid but not stellar, and when interest rates in the high-grade bond market are fluctuating moderately. When money is tight or economic conditions are poor among the advanced nations, the yield spread between high-quality and low-quality bonds widens. Even so, they continue to attract investors, sometimes in large numbers, whatever the economic climate. The reason is simple: In today's intensely competitive, deregulated markets, high-yield bonds offer the highest profit margins to financial institutions that trade and underwrite these obligations.

I am not suggesting that volatility has ended in the high-grade bond market, or that it will continue only in lower-quality obligations. With widespread securitization and related developments, the fixed-income market will continue to see periodic volatility. After all, securitization permits daily pricing, which encourages investors to focus on short-term performance. The truth is, long-term bonds are not purchased (as they once were) for the interest they will pay over the next 20 or 30 years. They are bought with the expectation of an upward price increase, and are sold in expectation of a price reversal. At the margin, the entire process is magnified by the increasing proprietary activities of traditional financial institutions and by the involvement of hedge funds. Both rely on short-term funding to finance their activities and cannot afford to withstand significant price declines in bonds.

In the next decade, securitized and globalized financial markets will sustain one of the past decade's most prominent interest rate patterns: the contagion effect. With the integration of financial communication and with the growing uniformity of analysis and portfolio behavior, world financial markets offer diminishing benefits for those who would build and manage international portfolios. Rather, the new environment favors investors who concentrate on high-quality obligations when credit-quality spreads are low, and on lower-quality obligations when credit spreads are high. The trouble is that it is quite difficult to know when to embark and disembark—especially when holding a highly leveraged portfolio.

The Euro, the Dollar, and the Yen

When the Euro came onto the financial scene at the start of 1999, warnings abounded about the serious challenge this new currency would pose for the dollar as the key reserve currency, and thus for America's leadership role in the financial markets. One of the strong advocates of this view has been Fred Bergsten, who bases this view largely on the fact the new Europe equals or exceeds the United States in many key economic measures and therefore will assert itself as a single voice on international economic and financial issues. But this view overstates the power of the new Europe. Its capacity to perform economically as flexibly as the United States is an open question. Of course, Europe will rebound cyclically from a high level of unemployment and huge excess capacity, but that does not mean the major

European nations necessarily possess the kind of dynamism needed to compete effectively in a globalized marketplace. When unemployment falls in France and Germany to about 6 or 7 percent, how will their economic performance fare? Will the rigidities in Europe loosen? The dominance of big business, national labor agreements, and big government—all need much greater economic reform before they can effectively challenge America over the next few decades.

Moreover, the United States holds the privileged position of being the world's sole superpower. Europe at best is an economic union— and nowhere near a political union. Its cultural and political divisions have deep historical roots. Along with America's standing as a superpower comes its status as a safe haven for investment, and its overwhelming influence in international economic and financial matters.

The biggest test for the Euro still lies ahead. It will come when one of the key countries gets out of sync with its partners. Since monetary policy cannot be targeted to meet the circumstances in any single member nation—and by definition, the renegade nation no longer will possess a national exchange rate policy—its sole remaining national policy instrument will be on the fiscal side. If such a country overheats, spawning an inflation problem, a fiscal tightening would be needed, and would likely garner widespread political support. All of this might be manageable by the Union. But suppose a nation is out of sync because it cannot sustain economic expansion and hence requires stimulus? Therein lies the real danger: a localized recession that the European Central Bank cannot or will not take steps to ameliorate. It is far from clear at present whether there will be enough latitude under the stability pact to ease fiscal policy.

Will the national government in question be able to resist public demands for stimulus? Will it even be able to hold onto political control? It seems to me that when a case like this materializes—as sooner or later it will—financial market participants will question whether that country will stay in the currency arrangement or seek to reestablish its own currency. There is no European-wide fiscal policy and therefore no systematic mechanism to transfer resources to members stung by economic downturns (unlike the situation in the United States, for example, where both automatic stabilizers and discretionary programs can fulfill that function). One way out of this problem would be for the stronger countries in the European Monetary Union to find informal ways to ease the fiscal constraint of the weaker ones. The stronger country would then be subsidizing the weaker one. Will such international altruism prevail? That remains to be seen. And the historical record raises doubts.

There is also confusion surrounding the issue of dethroning the U.S. dollar from its long-dominant position. To begin with, we should consider how the dollar might perform when the economic performance of the American economy is cyclically weaker than that of Europe. To be sure, when the American economy slows and the European countries concurrently move out of their economic doldrums, the new currency arrangements may put greater pressure on the dollar than under the more fragmented currency alignments of the past. This is not a one-way street. Strong economic performance in the U.S. will again rectify this situation. In fact, nothing else will.

With three major currencies in the world—the dollar, the Euro, and the yen—there is certainly the capacity to have very excessive fluctuations in the foreign exchange markets, fluctuations capable of destabilizing fundamental business and financial decisions and creating undue uncertainty. Examples of this abound. For instance, in just the past few years, the yen weakened from 110 to nearly 150, only to rally again to below 105. No fundamental development could be held responsible for such a huge variation over such a short period of time. Much of this swing reflected speculative capital flows associated with currency trades and other speculative activity that is now facilitated by new credit instruments, trading techniques, and very fluid financial markets.

I believe that these extremes can be constrained—but not by target zones as some advocate. Target zones for the three major currencies will encourage markets to push to either the upper or lower bands, forcing an official intervention or a resetting of the zones. The private sector has a huge capacity to press against the targets. The alternative is a formalized official working group, which would consist of specialists in international markets including traders and analysts who would continually track and evaluate market developments. Their work would include tracking currency of capital flows and communicating with major dealers in the marketplace on a daily basis. In this way, they would be able to gauge when to intervene in the market for maximum stabilizing effect.

This is not to claim that the Euro does not make a difference to the developments in the financial markets. The existence of a single currency will encourage the development of deeper and more tradable markets and securitization. The open credit market will grow more rapidly than traditional financial institutions. However, just as American financial institutions are becoming more encompassing in their activities, so will European institutions. Indeed, quite a few already have moved into universal banking. The conflicts of interest prevailing in these institutions will become even greater. With the devolution of political power as a result of the European Monetary Union, the private-sector economic and financial powers will increase significantly—especially as institutions unite across the individual country borders. It is an open question whether that next concentration of power in the private sector will be a force for an economic or a social democracy.

Tomorrow's Burgeoning Financial Markets

Regardless of the specific interest rate patterns in the twenty-first century, financial markets will continue to expand at a rapid pace. Over the longer term, there is every reason to believe that real economic growth will continue, and with it, rising standards of living around the world.

Early in this book, I told the story of how, in my early weeks at Salomon Brothers, I was asked to project the size of financial markets 10 years hence. But as startling as those projections seemed, they ultimately understated the realities of the postwar financial markets.

Having lived through one remarkable era, I now look ahead to the next, and pose the same questions I did 45 years ago: What will the future bring? What will financial markets look like 20 years from now? Or 50? It has been said that only one thing about the future is certain—

it will not become exactly what we expect. Still, the exercise can be entertaining, if not humbling.

First, a few ground rules. I base my projections on a nominal GDP growth rate of 6 percent, and on the further assumption that fixed-income markets expand at a somewhat higher rate than that because securitization will outpace economic growth domestically and, even more so, outside the United States. This approach indicates that the American bond market, which had outstandings of an estimated $12 trillion at the end of 1998, will grow to nearly $40 trillion in 20 years and to about $220 trillion in 50 years. The non-U.S. bond markets, which totaled $13 trillion at the close of 1998, will reach approximately $50 trillion in two decades and roughly $380 trillion in five. Meanwhile, the global equity market will grow large enough in 20 years to generate nearly four times the earnings of today's stock market. By mid-2050, another round of financial euphoria may well have engulfed the market.

Will the supply of credit keep pace with the demand? Judging from the stream of research monographs, position papers, and editorials, a great many experts are convinced that the answer is no. In the early 1990s, Morgan Stanley researchers published an article in which they estimated that total demand for capital could outstrip the supply by some $2.8 trillion by the year 2010, with an annual shortfall of savings relative to intended investment approaching 1 percent of the GDP of the industrialized Western world. Other analysts have come up with much smaller projections, a quarter or a third as large, but those too project very large shortfalls. To be sure, the anticipated global demands for capital are unprecedented in absolute terms. Historically, each new decade has generated capital demands that have exceeded those of the previous decade—as well as most reasonable *projections* from the previous decade. The reason is clear: Capital formation is an integral and essential part of economic growth.

In the next few decades, demand for capital surely will grow to immense proportions by today's standards. But estimates that the supply of capital will fall far short of demand should be viewed cautiously. For one thing, past projections of this kind have proved false; when the demand for credit is there, markets tend to produce a more or less adequate supply. Moreover, credit shortages are a normal part of economic life. Each day and in every country, enterprises postpone or reject potential investment projects because their expected rate of return lies below some hurdle rate. Those businesses are not economically optimal. But if those projects somehow did go forward, they would crowd out other, more productive ventures, and economic efficiency would suffer. It is virtually an iron law of economics and finance that a share of the total demand for capital will always be denied. And so it should be. Otherwise, the allocation of savings would be inefficient.

A Century's Perspective

As we look ahead to the next century, it is natural that we cast our gaze backward over the previous 100 years. Perhaps a measure of where we have come will give us some indication of where we might be headed. Of course, the passage of history is a story of both change and continuity. Certainly that has been true of Wall Street and the financial markets, although in that realm of modern life—compared with many others we might consider—change clearly has had the upper hand.

By the turn of the previous century, American economic life had taken on a decidedly modern cast, which is to say, a time traveler from today going back to 1900 would find much that was familiar. Giant industrial corporations were one of the most prominent features of that time, even though they had appeared fairly recently on the scene. In the middle of the 1800s, railroads and textile factories were the only big businesses, although none employed more than a few hundred people or a few million dollars in capital. At a major international exhibition in London in 1851, British industrialists confessed to being impressed with American technology for the first time—particularly the Yankees' new methods of making firearms and sewing machines with interchangeable parts. But it was not until after the Civil War— which stifled the nation's industrial progress—that America's industrial dam broke loose. Within a single generation, the United States emerged as the world's leading producer of iron, steel, petroleum, and other key products, and by 1900 it had more miles of railroad track than Europe and Russia combined.

In 1900, two-thirds of the nation's 76 million citizens still lived in rural communities, and only three cities had populations of more than 1 million (New York, Chicago, and Philadelphia). But that was changing rapidly (by 1920 more than half of all Americans lived in cities), thanks in large part to the explosive growth of manufacturing. At the turn of the century, already two-thirds of the nation's output (measured by value added) was in manufactured goods, even though manufacturing employed less than a quarter of the workforce. The average plant producing petroleum, iron and steel, and textiles (the three leading industries) had a capital investment of $1.4 million, $882,000, and $474,000, respectively, but those averages were belied by the behemoth factories built by the Rockefellers and Carnegies of the age. Carnegie, in fact, christened the new century by selling his sprawling steel interests to J. P. Morgan, who promptly assembled the $1.4 billion United States Steel Corporation in 1901, the nation's first billion-dollar enterprise.

Still, American manufacturing was then churning out a tiny fraction—roughly 1 percent, measured in constant dollars—of what today's cleaner and enormously more efficient plants produce. And only a foolish blue-collar worker of today would change places with his turn-of-the-century counterpart. In 1900, industrial workers toiled 10 hours a day, 6 days a week, and earned an average of $375 dollars a year. Worse than that, working conditions were typically unsanitary, unsafe, and often fatal, and there were very few protections—whether from unions (which had signed up a meager 5 percent of industrial workers), employers, or the government. Indeed, state and federal governments frequently trotted out their armed militias to help suppress striking laborers. Among American males of all occupations, whites lived an average of only 47 years, blacks a mere 33.

Even so, the nation's factory workers were enjoying rising real income, abetted by the *deflationary* price trend that dominated much of the late nineteenth century. And while no one could have known it at the time, the nation's middle class was about to embark on an educational revolution that would help boost incomes to unimagined levels over the next three generations. In 1900, a minority of the nation's children attended public school, and half of those who did dropped out before completing the eighth grade. More than that, the typical pupil attended school fewer than 100 days per year because of the demands of the farm and factory. Thanks to a public school movement in the early 1900s, however, both elementary and high school attendance rose dramatically, until by the 1960s a large majority of the nation's youth were graduating from high school. Along with the obvious benefits to these individuals, education yielded enormous social and economic returns. Economists have found universal public education in America to be one of the leading engines of economic growth.

Has technology changed as dramatically as education over the last century? Today, it is fashionable to ascribe the breathless pace of change in modern life mainly to "new technology." The Internet and the Web, biotechnology (from high-tech pharmaceuticals to genetic engineering), the miniaturization of electronics, "smart" weaponry—these are the kinds of examples some use to demonstrate that no generation in human history has seen more change. But a century's perspective on technological change can be humbling. As Norman Stone has observed, "In 1895 the novelist Henry James acquired electric lighting; in 1896 he rode a bicycle; in 1897 he wrote on a typewriter; in 1898 he saw a cinematograph. Within a very few years he could have had a Freudian analysis, traveled in an aircraft, understood the principles of the jet-engine or even of space travel." Are we, or the urban-dwellers of the Victorian Age, the braver expeditionary party across new technological terrain?

To return to the large corporation—how has the structure of American business evolved in the last 100 years? Earlier in this chapter, I suggested that business concentration was likely to be one of the most pressing issues of the new century. Interestingly, the same was true 100 years ago. As the nineteenth century drew to a close, the United States experienced the first great merger movement in its history (others would follow in the 1920s, the 1960s, and the 1980s). Between 1895 and 1904, 157 holding companies acquired some 1,800 firms, and at least a third of the newly created giants dominated their industries by controlling 70 percent or more of market share. These firms had total capitalization of approximately $4 billion—a sum four times greater than the total for industrial firms created between 1860 and 1893.

There are illuminating similarities and differences worth noting between that decade's merger movement and our own. A striking sim-

ilarity is that the financiers and managers in both periods were motivated chiefly by a desire to escape what they perceived to be intense or
"ruinous" competition. Most of the mergers of the 1890s involved
manufacturing firms that were suffering from overcapacity and were
cutting prices to hold on to revenues in order to meet their high debt
obligations. Merger seemed a much friendlier alternative, although
research has shown that the tactic seldom produced the hoped-for
monopoly rents (see Lamoreaux, 1985). In the 1990s, the manufacturing sector was responsible for only a piece of the merger activity; a
wide range of businesses—including financial institutions—were
swept up in the trend. But, again, the central impulse has been to
soften the rigors of competition, which is said to have intensified due
to technology-driven globalization.

What is strikingly *different* from one merger wave to the next is the
nature of public and political reaction. In the 1890s and 1910s, corporate consolidation inspired an enormous public outcry against the
"trusts" (a term used generically to refer to big business). Newspapers
overflowed with editorials deriding John D. Rockefeller, Andrew
Carnegie, Jay Gould, and other "robber barons," and for the first time
in American history the federal government stepped in to regulate big
business. First came the Interstate Commerce Act in 1887, which was
designed to limit discriminatory railroad rates, and then the Sherman
Anti-Trust Act of 1890—Congress's first attempt to constrain monopolistic practices. In practice, both acts proved to be weak against the
predominant power of big business. For decades, the courts in effect
made regulatory policy in how they interpreted and reinterpreted
these two key pieces of legislation. But during the Progressive Era of
the early twentieth century, the federal government took large strides
to regulate corporate America. Although a movement for national
incorporation laws failed, the federal government managed (among
other things) to break up several giant trusts (including the Northern
Securities Company, American Tobacco, and Standard Oil) and to
establish the Federal Trade Commission and the Federal Reserve.

In our own time, business consolidation is evoking no similar
reaction. Apart from Bill Gates of Microsoft, who has drawn fire from
the public and the Justice Department as much for his staggering

wealth as for his alleged anticompetitive practices, it is difficult to identify other targets of public scorn among the dozens of players involved in billion-dollar megamergers. The difference may lie in the economic backdrop: The great merger movement of the 1890s began during the severe economic depression that followed the Panic of 1893, whereas today's mergers are occurring in a time of economic prosperity and rising stock prices—with much of that stock held by ordinary citizens. The market for industrial securities was only just emerging in the 1890s, and its participants certainly did not include many members of the middle class. In that sense, too, the two centennial watersheds are markedly different.

One aspect of American life that has been transformed over the past 100 years is seldom included in historical retrospectives. But it seems to me that *financial markets* have evolved at least as dramatically as—perhaps more so than—manufacturing, work, technology, education, and business regulation since the turn of the previous century.

From today's perspective, the most striking feature of America's Gilded Age banking and financial markets is their lack of regulation. Wall Street was periodically upended by the often-successful attempts of colorful figures such as Daniel Drew, Jim Fiske, and Jay Gould to manipulate prices and corner markets. The only force countervailing against such panics was a handful of more responsible investors, most notably J. P. Morgan, whose every action was scrutinized by investors. Morgan engineered a successful rescue operation after the Panic of 1907 drove down GNP by more than 8 percent. That episode inspired Congress to begin formulating plans for a central bank. After all, Morgan couldn't live forever.

Financiers were held in disrepute by most of the nation's laborers and farmers, who believed that the "money changers" were producing no products of tangible value. Stock trading and bond trading were considered by many to be forms of gambling. But efforts to regulate commodity futures trading—then centered at the Chicago Board of Trade—were defeated by a Supreme Court ruling in 1905.

Banking was similarly unsupervised, apart from some weak state controls. The federal government made some efforts at regulation in 1900, by passing the Gold Standard Act, which allowed state banks to set up branches in small towns and ended the bimetalism debate by establishing gold as the only redeemable metal. Still, the vast majority of banks were local, single-unit operations, and access to capital and credit was becoming increasingly difficult as the nation's business enterprises expanded rapidly.

Quantitative measures of Wall Street's growth since 1900—when the total value of trades on Wall Street was $14 billion, and a mere 139 million shares changed hands the entire year—do not begin to convey the true importance of finance in American economic history. Simply put, richer nations have larger stock and bond markets than poorer ones, and the assets of their financial intermediaries are much larger in relation to GDP. Stated another way, an economy cannot grow and thrive without a strong commercial and investment banking infrastructure. Without the ability to create debt and equity instruments, the world's economies would not have advanced beyond their most rudimentary forms. Seen in this way, financial markets can be considered one of the great wonders of the world.

More than this, financial markets are in many ways a microcosm of the people and societies they serve. Though measured in sterile figures, they embody and reflect much of the drama of the human condition—from the quest for comfort, security, and wealth to the impulses to take risk and ensure the future and to compete and cooperate. The extremes of market movements reflect the extremes of human nature and human emotion—from optimism and elation to pessimism and despair. In the financial markets—as in life—rationality prevails *most* of the time.

With the ongoing growth of financial markets, with intensifying globalization, and with the continuing erosion of segmentation among financial institutions, the challenges faced by markets and institutions will mount. Against that backdrop, financial intermediaries will need to be ever-more diligent to balance their entrepreneurial impulses with their fiduciary responsibilities.

BIBLIOGRAPHY

Adams, James Ray, and Frantz, Douglas, *A Full Service Bank*. New York: Pocket Books, 1992.

Altman, Edward I., and Sametz, Arnold, eds., *Financial Crises*. New York: Wiley, 1977.

Bank for International Settlements, *Asset Prices and Monetary Policy: Four Views*. Basel, Switzerland, 1998.

Beckner, Steven K., *Back from the Brink: The Greenspan Years*. New York: Wiley, 1996.

Bennett, Robert A., "Citicorp Is Said to Choose Reid as New Chief," *New York Times*, June 20, 1984, p. A1.

Bergsten, Fred C., "America and Europe: Clash of the Titans," *Foreign Affairs*, March–April 1999.

Biggs, Barton M., "Groupstink," in *U.S. and the Americas Investment Perspectives*, Morgan Stanley Dean Witter newsletter, April 7, 1999.

Brooks, John, *Once in Golconda*. New York: Harper & Row, 1969.

Brooks, John, *The Takeover Game*. New York: E. P. Dutton, 1987.

Brownlee, W. Elliot, ed., *Funding the American State, 1941–1995: The Rise and Fall of an Era of Easy Finance*. New York: Woodrow Wilson Center Press and Cambridge University Press, 1996.

Cameron, Rondo, and Bovykin, V. I., eds., *International Banking, 1870–1914*. New York: Oxford University Press, 1991.

Carosso, Vincent P., *Investment Banking in America: A History*. Cambridge, Mass.: Cambridge University Press, 1970.

Chancellor, Edward, *Devil Take the Hindmost*. New York: Farrar, Straus, Giroux, 1999.

Chandler, Lester V., *America's Greatest Depression 1929–1941*. New York: Harper & Row, 1970.

Chernow, Ron, *The House of Morgan: An American Banking Dynasty and the Rise of Modern Finance*. New York: Simon & Schuster, 1990.

Cohen, Benjamin J., *In Whose Interest?* A Council on Foreign Relations Book. New Haven, Conn.: Yale University Press, 1986.

Counterparty Risk Management Policy Group, "Improving Counterparty Risk Management Practices," June 1999.

Dawson, John C., ed., *Flow-of-Funds Analysis*. Armonk, N.Y.: M. E. Sharpe, 1996.

Day, Kathleen, *S&L Hell*. New York: W. W. Norton, 1993.

Deane, Marjorie, and Pringle, Robert, *The Central Banks*. New York: Viking Press, 1994.

Degen, Robert A., *The American Monetary System: A Concise Survey of Its Evolution since 1896*. Lexington, Mass.: D. C. Heath, 1987.

Dodd, J. C., and Ford, J. L., *Expectations, Uncertainty and the Term Structure of Interest Rates*. New York: Barnes & Noble, 1974.

Douglas, Livingston G., ed., *Fixed Income Masterpieces: Insights from America's Great Investors*. Homewood, Ill.: Business One Irwin, 1993.

Douglas, Livingston G., *Yield Curve Analysis*. New York: Institute of Finance, 1988.

Dugan, Robert A., *The American Monetary System*. New York: Lexington Books, 1987.

Eichengreen, Barry, *Toward a New International Financial Architecture: A Practical Post-Asia Agenda*. Washington, D.C.: Institute for International Economics, February 1999.

Faber, Marc, "Trouble in Alan's Wonderland, but Hope for India," *The Gloom, Boom & Doom Report*, October 15, 1999.

Federal Reserve Bank of Cleveland, "Banking and Commerce: How Does the United States Compare to Other Nations?" *Monthly Review*, Fourth Quarter 1998.

Federal Reserve Bank of Kansas City, Symposiums Sponsored by the Bank:
Changing Capital Markets: Implications for Monetary Policy, 1993.
Monetary Policy Issues in the 1990s, 1989.
Maintaining Financial Stability in a Global Economy, 1997.
Restructuring the Financial System, 1987.

Federal Reserve Bank of New York, "The Role of the Credit Slowdown in the Recent Recession," *Quarterly Review*, Spring 1993.

Federal Reserve Bank of New York, *Intermediate Targets and Indicators for Monetary Policy*, July 1990.

Federal Reserve Bank of New York, "Broad Credit Measures as Targets for Monetary Policy," *Quarterly Review*, Summer 1979.

Federal Reserve Bank of New York, "Causes and Consequences of the 1989–92 Credit Slowdown," *Quarterly Review*, Winter 1993.

Federal Reserve Bank of St. Louis, "Money Stock Measurement: History, Theory and Implications," *Proceedings of the Eighteenth Annual Economic Policy Conference of the Federal Reserve Bank of St. Louis*, March–April 1994.

Ferris, Paul, *Gentlemen of Fortune*. London: Weidenfeld and Nicolson, 1984.

Fitzgerald, Terry J., "Money Growth and Inflation: How Long Is the Long-Run?" *Economic Commentary*, Federal Reserve Bank of Cleveland, August 1, 1999.

Freedman, Charles, and Goodet, Clyde, *The Financial Service Sector: Past Changes and Future Prospects*, Technical Report #82, Bank of Canada, 1997.

Friedman, Benjamin M., "The Future of Monetary Policy: The Central Bank as an Army with Only a Signal Corps?" Conference on Social Science and the Future, Oxford, England, July 1999.

Friedman, Milton, and Schwartz, Anna, *A Monetary History of the United States, 1867–1960*. Princeton, N.J.: Princeton University Press, 1963.

Friedman, Thomas L., *The Lexus and the Olive Tree*. New York: Farrar, Straus, Giroux, 1999.

Galbraith, John K., *The Great Crash*. Boston, Mass.: Houghton Mifflin, 1961.

Goldstein, Morris, *The Asian Financial Crisis: Causes, Cures and Systemic Implications*. Washington, D.C.: Institute for International Economics, 1998.

Grant, James, *Money of the Mind*. New York: Farrar, Straus, Giroux, 1992.

Greider, William, *Secrets of the Temple: How the Federal Reserve Runs the Country*. New York: Simon & Schuster, 1987.

Group of Thirty, *Derivatives: Practices and Principles.* Washington, D.C., 1993.

Guide to the Flow-of-Funds Accounts, Board of Governors of the Federal Reserve System, Washington, D.C., 1993.

Hilton, Denis J., "Psychology and the City: Applications to Trading, Dealing and Investment Analysis." London: Centre for the Study of Financial Innovation, April 1998.

Homer, Sidney, *The Great American Bond Market.* Homewood, Ill.: Dow Jones-Irwin, 1978.

Homer, Sidney, and Johannesen, Richard I., Jr., *The Price of Money.* New Brunswick, N.J.: Rutgers University Press, 1969.

Homer, Sidney, and Leibowitz, Martin L., *Inside the Yield Book.* New York: Prentice Hall and New York Institute of Finance, 1972.

Homer, Sidney, and Sylla, Richard, *A History of Interest Rates,* 3rd ed. New Brunswick, N.J.: Rutgers University Press, 1996.

Hyman, Sidney, *Marriner S. Eccles.* Stanford, Calif.: Graduate School of Business, Stanford University, 1976.

Kahler, Miles, ed., *Capital Flows and Financial Crises.* Council on Foreign Relations, New York, 1998.

Kaufman, Henry, *Interest Rates, the Markets, and the New Financial World.* New York: Times Books, 1986.

Keller, Morton, *Regulating a New Economy: Public Policy and Economic Change in America, 1900–1933.* Cambridge, Mass.: Harvard University Press, 1990.

Kindleberger, Charles P., *Mania, Panics and Crashes.* New York: Basic Books, 1978.

Kindleberger, Charles P., *A Financial History of Western Europe.* New York: Oxford University Press, 1993.

Krooss, Herman E., and Blyn, Martin R., *A History of Financial Intermediaries.* New York: Random House, 1971.

Krooss, Herman E., and Studenski, Paul, *Financial History of the United States.* New York: McGraw-Hill, 1952.

Lamoreaux, Naomi R., *The Great Merger Movement in American Business, 1895–1904.* New York: Cambridge University Press, 1985.

Leibowitz, Martin, *Investing, The Collected Works of Martin L. Leibowitz.* Chicago: Probus Publishing Company, 1992.

MacKay, Charles, *Extraordinary Popular Delusions and the Madness of Crowds.* New York: Bonanza Books, 1980.

Marsh, David, *The Most Powerful Bank.* New York: Times Books, 1992.

Matusow, Allen J., *Nixon's Economy: Booms, Busts, Dollars, and Votes.* Lawrence, Kansas: University Press of Kansas, 1998.

Mayer, Martin, *Markets: Who Plays, Who Risks, Who Gains, Who Loses.* New York: Norton, 1988.

Mayer, Martin, *The Greatest-Ever Bank Robbery: The Collapse of the Savings and Loan Industry.* New York: Scribners, 1990.

Mayer, Martin, *Nightmare on Wall Street: Salomon Brothers and the Corruption of the Marketplace.* New York: Simon & Schuster, 1993.

Mayer, Martin, "Is Everything Too Big to Fail?" *The International Economy,* January–February 1999.

Neikirk, William R., *Volcker: Portrait of the Money Man.* New York: Congdon & Weed, 1987.

Nocera, Joseph, *A Piece of the Action: How the Middle Class Joined the Money Class.* New York: Simon & Schuster, 1994.

Norton, Hugh S., *The Quest for Economic Stability: Roosevelt to Bush.* Columbia, S.C.: University of South Carolina Press, 1991.

Pecora, Ferdinand, *Wall Street under Oath.* New York: Augustus M. Kelley Publishers, 1968.

Perkins, Edwin, *Wall Street to Main Street: Charles Merrill and Middle-Class Investors.* New York: Cambridge University Press, 1999.

Plender, John, "The Bankers' Black Hole," London *Financial Times,* July 21, 1999.

Sampson, Anthony, *The Money Lenders.* New York: Viking Press, 1981.

Santow, Leonard J., *The Budget Deficit.* New York: New York Institute of Finance, 1988.

Seligman, Joel, *The Transformation of Wall Street: A History of the Securities and Exchange Commission and Modern Corporate Finance.* Boston: Northeastern University Press, 1995.

Sheridan, William A., *The Fortune Sellers.* New York: Wiley, 1998.

Sicilia, David B., and Cruikshank, Jeffrey L., *The Greenspan Effect: Words That Move the World's Markets.* New York: McGraw-Hill, 2000.

Sobel, Robert, *N.Y.S.E.: A History of the New York Stock Exchange, 1935–1975.* New York: Weybright & Talley, 1975.

Sobel, Robert, *The Last Bull Market: Wall Street in the 1960s.* New York: Norton, 1980.

Sobel, Robert, *Salomon Brothers, 1910–1985: Advancing to Leadership.* New York: Salomon Brothers, 1986.

Sobel, Robert, *Dangerous Dreamers: Financial Innovators from Charles Merrill to Michael Milken.* New York: Wiley, 1993.

Stein, Herbert, *Presidential Economics: The Making of Economic Policy from Roosevelt to Clinton.* Washington, D.C.: American Enterprise Institute Press, 1994.

Stein, Herbert, *The Fiscal Revolution in America: Policy in Pursuit of Reality.* Washington, D.C.: American Enterprise Institute Press, 1996.

Stewart, James P., *Den of Thieves.* New York: Simon & Schuster, 1991.

Stone, Norman, *Europe Transformed, 1878–1919* (Cambridge, Mass: Harvard University Press, 1984), p. 15.

Thomas, Dana L., *The Plungers and the Peacocks.* New York: Morrow, 1989.

Tiger, Lionel, *Optimism: The Biology of Hope.* New York: Simon & Schuster, 1979.

Vatter, Harold G., and Walker, John F., eds., *History of the U.S. Economy since World War II.* Armonk, N.Y.: M. E. Sharpe, 1996.

Volcker, Paul, and Gyohten, Toyoo, *Changing Fortunes.* New York: Times Books, 1992.

Wachtel, Paul, *Crises in the Economic and Financial Structure.* Lexington, Mass: Lexington Books, 1982.

Wallison, Peter J., "What if Microsoft Did Own Citibank?" *Wall Street Journal,* July 27, 1997, p. A14.

Warburton, Peter, *Debt & Delusion.* London: Penguin Press, 1999.

Waszkis, Helmut, *Phillip Brothers: The Rise and Fall of a Trading Giant.* Wiltshire, England: Metal Bulletin Books Ltd., 1987.

Weiher, Kenneth, *America's Search for Economic Stability: Monetary and Fiscal Policy since 1913*. New York: Twayne Publishers, 1992.

Well, Wyatt C., *Economist in an Uncertain World: Arthur F. Burns and the Federal Reserve, 1970–78*. New York: Columbia University Press, 1994.

White, Eugene N., ed., *Crashes and Panics*. Homewood, Ill: Dow Jones-Irwin, 1990.

White, Lawrence, J., *The S & L Debacle*. New York: Oxford University Press, 1991.

Wigmore, Barrie A., *The Crash and Its Aftermath*. Westport, Conn: Greenwood Press, 1985.

Wojnilower, Albert M., "The Central Role of Credit Crunches in Recent Financial History," *Brookings Papers on Economic Activity*, Vol. 2, 1980.

Wojnilower, Albert M., "Some Principles of Financial Regulation," Conference on Financial Deregulation Sponsored by Reserve Bank of Australia, Sydney, 1991.

Wojnilower, Albert M., "Business Cycles in a Financially Deregulated World," Conference of the International Economic Association, Trento, Italy, September 1997.

Wolfson, Martin H., *Financial Crises*. Armonk, N.Y.: M. E. Sharpe, 1994.

Wriston, Walter B., "Dr. Doom Takes a Dark View of Regulation," *The Wall Street Journal*, May 12, 1986.

Zweig, Phillip L., *Wriston: Walter Wriston, Citibank, and the Rise and Fall of American Financial Supremacy*. New York: Crown Publishers, 1995.

Speeches, Articles, and Published Interviews by Henry Kaufman
(listed in reverse chronological order)

"On Thin Ice? Why Henry Kaufman Is Worried [interview]," *Barron's*, November 8, 1999.

"Tax Cuts: Bad for the Market," *The Washington Post*, August 11, 1999.

"Protecting against the Next Financial Crisis," *The Journal of the National Association for Business Economics*, July 1999.

"A Conundrum: Near-Term Good Prospects against a Backdrop of Visible Fault Lines," address before the Warburg Dillon Read 1999 Global Bank and Financial Services Conference, New York, April 26, 1999.

"The Changing Dimensions of the Global Bond Markets," address before the Standard & Poor's Structured Finance Seminar, Palm Springs, Calif., April 12, 1999.

"Protecting against the Next Financial Crisis," address before the National Association for Business Economics 15th Annual Policy Conference, Washington, D.C., March 3, 1999.

"Too Much on Their Plate," *Financial Times*, February 4, 1999.

"The Recent Financial Turmoil: Lessons and Remedies," remarks on the occasion of the naming of the Henry Kaufman Management Education Center, New York University Stern School of Business, October 22, 1998.

"The New Financial World: Policy Shortcomings and Remedies," address before the Federal Reserve Bank of Boston 24th Economic Conference, "Beyond Shocks: What Causes Business Cycles," Chatham, Mass., June 26, 1998.

"The Passage through 'Bank Heaven,' " address before the UBS Securities Global Banking Conference, New York, April 28, 1998.

"The Global Influence of America's Imperfect Economic Democracy," address before a joint conference, sponsored by Mitsubishi Institute, Inc. and the Foreign Policy Association, Tokyo, Japan, April 23, 1998.

Remarks before an Extraordinary Ministerial Meeting of the Group of Twenty-Four, hosted by Banco Central de Venezuela, Caracas, February 7, 1998.

"The Need for a New IMF," *Time*, February 2, 1998.

"Preventing the Next Global Financial Crisis," *The Washington Post*, January 28, 1998.

"The Huge Asian Financial Bailout and the Inadequacies of the Official Financial Institutions," address before the Japan Society of Canada, Toronto, January 13, 1998.

"The Elusiveness of Reasonable Financial Behavior," address before the 16th Annual International Monetary and Trade Conference of the Global Independence Center, Philadelphia, November 20, 1997.

"The Yen, the Dollar, and the Euro," address before a Conference on Pressing Issues in U.S.-Japan Financial Markets, sponsored by the Institute of Fiscal and Monetary Policy, Ministry of Finance, Japan; Center on Japanese Economy and Business, Columbia University, New York; Japan Society, Inc.; and the Institute of Global Financial Studies (FAIR), Japan; New York, November 5, 1997.

"Key Developments in the Financial Markets and Their Implications," address before the 1997 Moody's Market Leadership Conference, Turnberry Isle, Fl., November 3, 1997.

"Successful Separation of Powers," *The New York Times* [Letters to the Editor], August 18, 1997.

"A Safe and Sound System," *Financial Times*, July 7, 1997.

"Keep Banks Out of Corporate Claws," *The New York Times*, May 18, 1997.

"Diminishing Financial Exuberance amidst Continuing Economic Growth," address before the UBS Securities Global Banking Conference, New York, April 29, 1997.

"The Exuberant May Soon Find Rationality," *The Los Angeles Times*, January 30, 1997.

"The Outlook for U.S. Interest Rates in 1997," address before the 11th International Interest Rate Forum, Frankfurt, Germany, December 2, 1996.

"Today's Financial Euphoria Can't Last," *The Wall Street Journal*, November 25, 1996.

"The Impact of Structural Changes on Financial Excesses," address before the 1996 BCA New York Conference, New York, September 10, 1996.

"Prospects for the U.S. Economy and Financial Markets," address before the 33rd Annual U.S.-Japan Business Conference, Tokyo, July 9, 1996.

"Bad News for Inflation Fighters [on inflation-indexed bonds]," *The Wall Street Journal*, June 19, 1996.

"The Challenge from Rapid Change and Depersonalization," address before the 1996 Haskins Partners Dinner, Leonard N. Stern School of Business, New York University, New York, May 9, 1996.

"Banking in the Prospective Economic and Financial Setting," address before the CS First Boston 1996 Annual Banking Conference, New York, April 24, 1996.

"Increased Financial Volatility: Implications for Markets and for Monetary Policy," address before Forum Analysis, Milan, Italy, February 2, 1996.

"Monetary Policy in the Changing Economic and Financial Environment," address before the Money Marketeers of New York University, New York, September 28, 1995.

"The Burgeoning Global Bond Markets: Issues and Implications," address before the Euromoney International Bond Congress, London, September 14, 1995.

"The Cyclical Trend and Economic and Financial Devolution," address before the CS First Boston 1995 Annual Banking Conference, New York, April 24, 1995.

Statement before the Committee on Banking and Financial Services, U.S. House of Representatives, Washington, D.C., April 5, 1995.

"A Paradox: Financial Gyrations during an Economic Upswing," address before the 92nd Street Y, New York, March 9, 1995.

"Why Alarms Didn't Ring over Mexico," *The Wall Street Journal*, January 26, 1995.

"Economic Forecast: Mapping a Course for the Future," *Pension Management*, January 1995.

"Financial Derivatives: Settled and Outstanding Issues," address before the North American Summit: Derivatives '94, Boca Raton, Fl., October 24, 1994.

"The Implications of Structural Changes in U.S. Financial Markets," address before the Japan Research Institute Seminar, Tokyo, October 17, 1994.

"Behavioral Biases in Economic Policy-Making and Investing," address before the Forum on Behavioral Economics for Financial Decision Makers, Cambridge Center for Behavioral Studies, Cambridge, Mass., October 5, 1994.

"The Kaufman Scenario," *Capital Market Strategies*, July 1994.

Statement before the Committee on Banking, Finance, and Urban Affairs, U.S. House of Representatives, Washington, D.C., June 23, 1994.

"Financial Derivatives and Structural Change in the Financial Markets: Current Issues and Future Prospects," address before a Price Waterhouse Executive Briefing, New York, June 13, 1994.

"Structural Changes in Financial Markets: Economic and Policy Significance," address before the CS First Boston Corporation Global Banking Conference, New York, April 25, 1994; and before the Board of Directors of the Federal Reserve Bank of Kansas City, Kansas City, Mo., March 9, 1994.

"A Bond Bull Takes a Bearish Turn [interview]," *The New York Times*, April 18, 1994.

"Financial Derivatives in a Rapidly Changing Financial World," *The Journal of Commercial Bank Lending*, April 1994.

"Dr. Doom Is Smiling [interview]," *Forbes*, January 17, 1994.

"A World in Which Frugal Capital Reigns," *Directors & Boards*, Winter 1993.

"Financial Derivatives in a Rapidly Changing Financial World," address before the City of London Conference on Derivatives, London, October 14, 1993.

"Opportunities and Challenges Confronting Monetary Policy," statement delivered before the Committee on Banking, Housing, and Urban Affairs, U.S. Senate, Washington, D.C., July 1, 1993.

"What Could Kill the Economy," *Fortune,* June 14, 1993.

"An American View of the Global Economy," address before the 35th Annual Congress of Association Cambiste Internationale, Helsinki, Finland, June 4, 1993.

"Beyond the Business Cycle: New Developments in Business and Finance," address before the Chapman University Economic Forum, Irvine, Calif., April 29, 1993.

"Cyclical and Structural Issues Facing U.S. Banks and Financial Markets," address before the First Boston Corporation Global Banking Conference, New York, April 28, 1993.

"Beyond the Business Cycle: New Forces of Business and Financial Change," address before the Executive Focus International 1993 Executive Forum, Orlando, Fl., February 11, 1993.

"The Monetary Path to Full Recovery," *The New York Times,* January 31, 1993.

"The Financial Markets Response to Expanding Global Capital Needs," address before the World Economic Forum 1993 Annual Meeting, Davos, Switzerland, January 29, 1993.

"Optimism from Dr. Gloom [interview]," *Management Review,* January 1993.

"Ten Reasons to Reform," *Euromoney,* November 1992.

"New Financial Risks," address before the Foro Barcelona, Barcelona, Spain, October 29, 1992.

"Fundamental Precepts Guiding Future Financial Regulation," address before the International Organisation of Securities Commissions, XVIIth Annual Conference, London, October 27, 1992.

"Toward a New Realism in Economic and Financial Policymaking," address before the World Development Congress, Washington, D.C., September 20, 1992.

"The U.S. Economy: On the Mend," address on the occasion of the establishment of the Henry Kaufman Chair in International Capital Markets at Tel Aviv University, Tel Aviv, Israel, May 19, 1992.

"Opportunities and Challenges in the Global Capital Markets," Walter Surrey Memorial Lecture, National Planning Association, Washington, D.C., May 1, 1992.

"Why America Needs Lower Interest Rates," *U.S. News & World Report,* April 27, 1992.

"Overcoming Our Economic Frustrations," address before the Sunday Breakfast Club, Philadelphia, April 1, 1992.

Written statement submitted to the Committee on Ways and Means, U.S. House of Representatives, December 18, 1991.

"A Durable Recovery," *The Washington Post,* December 18, 1991.

"Neglected Financial Lessons," address before the National Association of Business Economists' 33rd Annual Meeting, Los Angeles, Calif., September 23, 1991.

Statement before the Subcommittee on Telecommunications and Finance, Committee on Energy and Commerce, U.S. House of Representatives, September 13, 1991.

"Capital Scarcity and Capital Allocation," address to the International Monetary Fund, Osaka, Japan, June 4, 1991.

"How Treasury's Reform Could Hurt Free Enterprise," *Challenge,* May–June 1991.

Written statement submitted to the Committee on Banking, Housing, and Urban Affairs, U.S. Senate, Washington, D.C., May 15, 1991.

"Establishing an Improved Financial System," address before the North American Securities Administrators Association, Inc., Public Policy Day, Washington, D.C., April 18, 1991.

"The Prospect for Banking: Demise or New Vitality," address before the Bank & Financial Analyst's Association 21st Annual Banking Symposium, New York, March 27, 1991.

"How to Make Banks Safer," *U.S. News & World Report*, February 25, 1991.

"The Great Debt Overload Will Keep Recovery Feeble," *Fortune*, December 31, 1990.

"In Dire Straits [interview]," *Investment Vision*, November/December 1990.

"The Unfolding Crisis," address before the Edison Electric Institute 1990 Financial Conference, Coronado, Calif., October 29, 1990.

"International Interest Rates in Perspective," internal memorandum, May 1990.

"The Challenges of the 1990s [interview]," *IFR, The Journal of International Securities Markets*, Spring 1990.

"Why Interest Is Too High," *The Washington Post*, December 20, 1989.

"The 1990s: The Threat to Our Economic Democracy," address before the Money Marketeers of New York University, New York, November 16, 1989.

"Henry Kaufman: Corporate Debt Erodes Competition [interview]," *Business Week*, March 20, 1989.

Statement before the Committee on Ways and Means, U.S. House of Representatives, Washington, D.C., February 1, 1989.

"The Decapitalization of American Corporations," address before the National Press Club, Washington, D.C., January 10, 1989.

"Dr. Doom and Dr. Gloom," *Business Week*, October 17, 1988.

"Memo to the Next President," *The New York Times Magazine*, October 9, 1988.

"Past Blunders and Future Choices," Herman Krooss Memorial Lecture at the 35th Annual Business Conference, New York University Graduate School of Business Administration, New York, March 12, 1988.

"The Q&A . . . in Which Dr. Doom Is Something of a Cheersayer [interview]," *Business Month*, February 1988.

"Prospects for Financial Markets in 1988," coauthored with Jeffrey Hanna and R. S. Salomon, Jr., Salomon Brothers, December 9, 1987.

"Overview," presented at a symposium sponsored by the Federal Reserve Bank of Kansas City, "Restructuring the Financial System," Jackson Lake Lodge, Wyo., August 22, 1987.

"The Need for an Improved System of Financial Regulation," statement before the Committee on Banking, Housing, and Urban Affairs, U.S. Senate, Washington, D.C., July 30, 1987.

"Debt Relief for Developing Countries in a Volatile Financial World," address before a Global Debt Strategies Conference, sponsored by Euromoney and the Inter-American Development Bank, New York, June 25, 1987.

"Heightened Sensitivity of Financial Markets," address before the Opportunities in the International Capital Markets Conference, sponsored by Den Nordiske Investeringsbank, Stockholm, Sweden, June 9, 1987.

"World at the Brink [interview]," *Business Tokyo*, April 1987.

"The Risks in the World Economic Order," public lecture sponsored by the Nihon
    Keizai Shimbun (*Japan Economic Journal*) and New York University, Tokyo, Feb-
    ruary 24, 1987.
"Financial Opportunities and Responsibilities," address before the Wharton School of
    the University of Pennsylvania, Philadelphia, February 9, 1987.
Statement before the Board of Governors of the Federal Reserve System, Washington,
    D.C., February 3, 1987.
"Prospects for Financial Markets in 1987," coauthored with Jeffrey Hanna, Salomon
    Brothers, December 16, 1986.
"Debt in a Difficult-to-Control Financial System," address before the U.S. Congres-
    sional Summit on Debt and Trade, New York, December 4, 1986.
"The Great Bull Bond Market in Perspective," address before The Conference Board
    1987 Business Outlook Conference, New York, September 14, 1986.
"How Henry Kaufman Calls It Now [interview]," *Across the Board,* September 1986.
"Debt: The Threat to Economic and Financial Stability," address before a symposium
    sponsored by the Federal Reserve Bank of Kansas City, Jackson, Wyo., August 28,
    1986.
"Tax Reform Will Create 'Market Distortions' [interview]," *U.S. News & World Report,*
    June 30, 1986.
"In the Shadow of Financial Exhilaration," address before the National Press Club,
    Washington, D.C., May 6, 1986.
"The Federal Reserve and the Changing Financial Markets," address before a public
    policy dinner at the Federal Reserve Bank of Atlanta, Atlanta, Ga., March 13, 1986.
"The Significance of Heightened Market Responsiveness in 1986," address before the
    58th Annual Investment Seminar/Mid-Winter Meeting of the New York State
    Bankers Association, New York, January 30, 1986.
Interest Rates, the Markets, and the New Financial World (New York: Times Books, 1986).
"Prospects for Financial Markets in 1986," coauthored with Jeffrey Hanna, Salomon
    Brothers, December 18, 1985.
"Capital Market Implications of International Monetary Reform," address before the
    U.S. Congressional Summit on Exchange Rates and the Dollar, Washington, D.C.,
    November 12, 1985.
"Prolonging Economic Growth and Corporate Financial Risk Taking," address before
    the Chief Executive Officers' Dinner, *Business Week* Executive Programs, New
    York, September 10, 1985.
"Fallen Financial Dogmas and Beliefs," address before the Annual General Meeting of
    the Swiss-American Chamber of Commerce, Zurich, Switzerland, June 13, 1985.
"Key Issues in Financial Markets Today," address before the 1985 Convention of the Na-
    tional Council of Savings Institutions, New Orleans, La.: May 22, 1985.
"Who Runs America" (12th Annual Survey), *U.S. News & World Report,* May 20, 1985.
"Why Henry Kaufman Thinks the Recovery Faces a Showdown [interview]," *Chief Ex-
    ecutive,* Winter 1984.
"1985 Prospects for Financial Markets," coauthored with James McKeon and Nancy
    Kimelman, Salomon Brothers, December 11, 1984.
"Who Runs America" (11th Annual Survey), *U.S. News & World Report,* May 14, 1984.

Statement before the Committee on Ways and Means, U.S. House of Representatives, Washington, D.C., September 25, 1984.

"Interest Rates: The Remaining Discipline," address before the Texas Bankers Association's 100th Annual Convention, Fort Worth, Tex., May 4, 1984.

"Financial Developments of Significance to Corporate Finance," address before The Conference Board 1984 Financial Outlook Conference, New York, February 23, 1984.

"1984 Prospects for Financial Markets," coauthored with James McKeon and Steven Blitz, Salomon Brothers, December 14, 1983.

"Economic Expansion, Deficits and Interest Rates," address before the Boston Economic Club, Boston, November 16, 1983.

"Complexities of U.S. Stabilization Policies in an International Context," address before the Economic Policy Council (UNA-USA), Plenary Session, Washington, D.C., October 13, 1983.

"The Equity Market: A Long-Term View," address before the Robeco Jubilee Symposium on the Share in Future Society, Rotterdam, The Netherlands, October 7, 1983.

"Unusual Features in Today's Financial Markets," address before the Economic Club of Pittsburgh, Pittsburgh, Penn., May 25, 1983; and before the Midyear Economic Review Dinner, cosponsored by the University of Chicago and Salomon Brothers, Chicago, June 2, 1983.

"Financial Institutions in Ferment," *Challenge*, May/June 1983.

"Who Runs America" (10th Annual Survey), *U.S. News & World Report*, May 23, 1983.

"The Interest Rate Outlook," elaboration of comments made on the television program *Face the Nation*, Memorandum to Portfolio Managers, Salomon Brothers, May 15, 1983.

"Economic Recovery: Financial Prerequisites vs. Realities," address before the National Press Club, Washington, D.C., March 10, 1983.

"The Ferment in Financial Institutions," address before the New York Bankers Association 55th Annual Mid-Winter Meeting/Investment Seminar, New York, January 27, 1983.

"1983 Prospects for Financial Markets," coauthored with James McKeon and Steven Blitz, Salomon Brothers, December 6, 1982.

"The Wealth of the Nation [interview]," *American Heritage*, December 1982.

"Forces Affecting Near-Term Financial Behavior," address before the United States League of Savings Associations 90th Annual Convention, New Orleans, La., November 15, 1982.

"A Difficult Transition," address before Japanese government officials and financial and business executives, Tokyo, October 19, 1982.

"The Prospects for Interest Rates," Memorandum to Portfolio Managers, Salomon Brothers, August 17, 1982.

"Caution at the Start of Renewed Economic Growth: An Unusual Investment Posture," Investment Policy, Salomon Brothers, July 6, 1982.

"Sorting out the U.S. Mess [interview]," *Investors Chronicle*, July 2, 1982.

"Henry Kaufman: Market Mover Sounds a Warning [interview]," *Commodities*, July 1982.

"Why Interest Rates Are So High," address before the Association of International Bond Dealers' Conference and 14th Annual General Meeting, Venice, May 20, 1982.

"Who Runs America" (9th Annual Survey), *U.S. News & World Report,* May 10, 1982.

Meet the Press television interview transcript, May 9, 1982.

"Danger: Too Much Turbulence," *Challenge,* May/June 1982.

"Where Interest Rates Go from Here," *U.S. News & World Report,*" April 12, 1982.

"Continued Economic and Financial Uncertainties," Quarterly Investment Strategy Report, Salomon Brothers, April 7, 1982.

"The Urgency to End Our Economic and Financial Turbulence," statement [and transcript of questions and answers following the statement] before the Committee on the Budget, U.S. House of Representatives, Washington, D.C., March 16, 1982.

"Observations on the New Projections for the 1983 U.S. Federal Budget," Memorandum to Portfolio Managers, Salomon Brothers, February 10, 1982.

"The Challenge to Portfolio Management from the Economic and Financial Prospects of 1982," *The Investment Strategy Report,* Salomon Brothers, January 6, 1982.

"1982 Prospects for Financial Markets," coauthored with James McKeon and Deborah Jamroz, Salomon Brothers, January 4, 1982.

"Henry Kaufman, Market Mover," *Wharton Account,* Winter 1981–1982.

"The Many Faces and Implications of the Yield Curve," address before the New York State Bankers Association 32nd Annual Investment Seminar, New York, November 20, 1981.

"Banking in the Changing World Credit Markets," address before the Symposium on a Challenging Future for Banking, sponsored by the Institut Universitaire International, Luxembourg, and the European Investment Bank, Luxembourg, November 12, 1981.

"Catch 22 in the American Economy and Credit Markets," address before the Financial Executives Institute 50th International Conference, New York, October 12, 1981.

"The R$_x$ from Dr. Kaufman [interview]," *Newsweek,* September 21, 1981.

"Henry Kaufman Talks—," *Across the Board,* July/August 1981.

"The Interest Rate Gurus," *Financial World,* July 1–15, 1981.

"How Henry Kaufman Gets It Right," *Fortune,* May 18, 1981.

"The 100 Most Powerful People for the 80's," *Next,* April 1981.

"A Review of the Fed's Monetary Report for 1981," coauthored with Brian Fabbri and Robert V. DiClemente, Memorandum to Portfolio Managers, Salomon Brothers, March 9, 1981.

"National Policies and the Deteriorating Balance Sheets of American Corporations," address before The Conference Board 1981 Financial Outlook Conference, New York, February 25, 1981.

"The Crowding of the Municipal Bond Market," Salomon Brothers, 1981.

"1981 Prospects for Financial Markets," coauthored with James McKeon and David Foster, Salomon Brothers, December 8, 1980.

"Financial Challenges Confronting the New Administration," address before the New York State Bankers Association 31st Annual Investment Seminar, New York, November 21, 1980.

"New Precepts of Interest Rates," address before the Institutional Investor Bond Conference, New York, October 16, 1980.

"Credit Flow Developments at Midyear 1980," coauthored with James McKeon and David Foster, Memorandum to Portfolio Managers, Salomon Brothers, August 14, 1980.

"Kaufman of Salomon Bros.: When Henry Speaks, the World Listens," *Executive*, August 1980.

Statement before the Committee on Ways and Means, U.S. House of Representatives, Washington, D.C., July 30, 1980.

"Restoring Corporate Balance Sheets: An Urgent Challenge," coauthored with James McKeon and David Foster, Salomon Brothers, July 21, 1980.

"The Disregard for Capital," address before the Economic Club of Chicago, Chicago, May 1, 1980.

"Henry Kaufman, America's Interest Rate Guru," *Institutional Investor*, May 1980.

"A Tilt in Interest Rates," Memorandum to Portfolio Managers, Salomon Brothers, April 16, 1980.

"The New Anti-Inflation Program," Memorandum to Portfolio Managers, Salomon Brothers, March 17, 1980.

"Declare a National Emergency," *U.S. News & World Report*," March 10, 1980.

"The Interest Rate Cycle Challenge to Portfolio Management," Investment Policy, Salomon Brothers, January 8, 1980.

"1980 Prospects for Financial Markets," coauthored with James McKeon and David Foster, Salomon Brothers, December 6, 1979.

"Parameters for the American Financial Markets in the 1980s," address before the 1979 Annual Meeting of the American Council of Life Insurance, Chicago, November 26, 1979.

"The Difference Factors: Their Influence on American Credit Markets," address before the International Financial and Economic Outlook Conference, sponsored by The Conference Board of Europe, Frankfurt, Germany, October 23, 1979.

"Oil, Stagflation, and Interest Rates," Memorandum to Portfolio Managers, Salomon Brothers, July 2, 1979.

"The Wizard of Wall Street," *The New York Times Magazine*, May 27, 1979.

"The Implications of OPEC Price Increases and Domestic Decontrol," coauthored with several others, *Portfolio Strategy Bulletin*, Salomon Brothers, April 9, 1979.

"The Increasing Risks When the Economy Slips from its Moorings," Memorandum to Portfolio Managers, Salomon Brothers, March 19, 1979.

"Prospects for the American Financial Markets in 1979," coauthored with James McKeon and Peter Chapman, Salomon Brothers, December 12, 1978.

"Another Financial Crisis," address before the New York Bankers Association 29th Annual Investment Seminar, New York, November 17, 1978.

"A Dramatic Rise in Interest Rates," address before the American Bankers Association 1978 Annual Convention, Honolulu, Hawaii, October 25, 1978.

"Trouble Ahead from Continuing Credit Boom," coauthored with James McKeon, Memorandum to Portfolio Managers, Salomon Brothers, July 31, 1978.

"Economic Excesses and Financial Constraints," statement before the Joint Economic Committee of the U.S. Congress, Washington, D.C., June 28, 1978.

"The Future of the Dollar," address before the Council on Foreign Relations, New York, April 10, 1978.

Statement before the Committee on Budget of the U.S. House of Representatives, Washington, D.C., February 6, 1978.

"The Impact of Inflation on Interest Rates," address before the Inflation and Corporate Management Conference, sponsored by The Conference Board, New York, December 13, 1977.

"Prospects for the Credit Markets in 1978," coauthored with James McKeon, Salomon Brothers, December 1977.

"Financial Trends and Prospects," address before the 64th Annual Convention of the Mortgage Bankers Association of America, New York, October 24, 1977.

"Reflections on Economic Judgments," address before the Annual Meetings of the International Bank for Reconstruction and Development and Affiliates and the International Monetary Fund, Washington, D.C., September 28, 1977.

"Credit Market Prospects in the Coming Twelve Months," coauthored with James L. McKeon and Jeffrey L. Cohn, Memorandum to Portfolio Managers, Salomon Brothers, July 5, 1977.

" 'Practical Monetarism' and Its Impact on U.S. Interest Rates," address before the Management of Foreign Exchange Risks Conference, sponsored by the *Financial Times* in association with Forex Research Ltd., London, May 27, 1977.

"The Cyclical Setting and Trend for the Economy and Financial Markets," address before the 44th Annual Stockholders' Meeting of the Federal Home Loan Bank of New York, April 22, 1977.

Statement before the Joint Economic Committee of the U.S. Congress, Washington, D.C., February 7, 1977.

"Signs Indicate Economy Is Gaining Vigor," *Chicago Tribune,* December 27, 1976.

"Coping with Uncertainty about Inflation and Interest Rates," address before the Conference on Managing International Financial Relations in a World of Uncertainty, sponsored by the International Center for Monetary and Banking Studies, Geneva, Switzerland, December 2–3, 1976.

"Prospects for the Credit Markets in 1977," coauthored with James McKeon and Jeffrey Cohn, Salomon Brothers, December 1976.

"The American Credit Market: The Decade Ahead," address before the 27th Annual Investment Seminar, sponsored by the New York State Bankers Association in cooperation with the Graduate School of Business Administration of New York University, New York, November 19, 1976.

"Financial Prospects for 1977," address before the Los Angeles Area Chamber of Commerce Business Outlook Conference, Los Angeles, Calif., November 18, 1976.

Statement before the Committee on Banking, Housing and Urban Affairs, U.S. Senate, November 15, 1976.

"The Cyclical Outlook for Interest Rates," Memorandum to Portfolio Managers, Salomon Brothers, September 27, 1976.

"New Forces Affecting the Outlook for Business and the Credit Markets," address before the 1976 Annual Meeting of the School for Bank Administration, University of Wisconsin, Madison, August 5, 1976.

"Financial Crises: Market Impact, Consequences and Adaptability," address before the Conference on Financial Services, sponsored by the Salomon Brothers Center for the Study of Financial Institutions, Graduate School of Business Administration, New York University, New York, May 21, 1976.

"Will the Banker Need to Adjust to a Harsher Climate over the Longer Term?" address before the New York-World Financial Centre Conference, sponsored by the *Financial Times* of London, New York, April 30, 1976.

"The American Credit Markets Viewed from an International Perspective," address before the Lombard Association, London, March 9, 1976.

"Supply and Demand for Credit in 1976," coauthored with James McKeon and Jeffrey Cohn, Salomon Brothers, January 13, 1976.

"The Cyclical and Secular Trends of Interest Rates," address before the 26th Annual Investment Seminar, sponsored by the New York State Bankers Association in cooperation with the Graduate School of Business Administration, New York University, New York, November 21, 1975.

"Frustrations, Imperfections and Economic Financial Recovery," address before the Third Institutional Investor Bond Conference, New York, October 9, 1975.

"An Update on Economic and Financial Prospects," Memorandum to Portfolio Managers, Salomon Brothers, September 22, 1975.

"Needed: A Breakthrough in Economic Thought," Salomon Brothers, September 2, 1975.

"The Case for Business Tax Deductions," *The New York Times*, August 3, 1975.

"International and Domestic Challenges Confronting the American Business Corporation," Salomon Brothers, August 1975.

"Economic Recovery, Liquidity and Interest Rates," address before an executive briefing conducted by The Conference Board, Geneva, Switzerland, June 3, 1975.

"The Complexities of the Current Fiscal and Monetary Situation," address before the Annual Meeting of the Society of American Business Writers, Washington, D.C., May 5, 1975.

"Constraints on Business Management Strategy in the 1970s," address before Time Inc.'s Capital Investment Conference, Nassau, Bahamas, April 24–27, 1975.

"Supply and Demand for Credit in 1975," coauthored with James McKeon, Salomon Brothers, February 10, 1975.

"Financial Roadblocks to a New Economic Expansion," address before the 25th Annual Investment Seminar, sponsored by the New York State Bankers Association in cooperation with the Graduate School of Business Administration of New York University, New York, November 22, 1974.

"The Coming Rally in the Very High Grade Taxable Bond Market," Memorandum to Portfolio Managers, Salomon Brothers, October 7, 1974.

Statement before the Subcommittee on Economic Growth, Joint Economic Committee of the Congress of the United States, Washington, D.C., October 3, 1974.

"The Somber Visions of Henry Kaufman [interview]," *Financial World*, September 18, 1974.

"Credit Flows in a Troubled Economy," Memorandum to Portfolio Managers, Salomon Brothers, August 21, 1974.

"Forces of Change in the American Credit Markets," address before the *Financial Times* Conference, "New York as a World Financial Centre," New York, June 11, 1974.

"Inflation: The Disease Is Worse Than the Cure," address [delivered by Joseph P. Lombard] before the Boston Stock Exchange Conference, Boston, May 23, 1974.

"Supply and Demand for Credit in 1974," coauthored with James McKeon, Salomon Brothers, February 27, 1974.

"Economic Disarray and Disillusionment," address before the New School Conference, "Wall Street and the Economy '74," New York, January 26, 1974.

"Bond Yields: 'Attractive' and Rising; Interview with Henry Kaufman," *U.S. News & World Report,* January 7, 1974.

"Inflation, Credit Flows and Interest Rates," address before the Association of American Railroads' Treasury Division Convention, Phoenix, Ariz., October 23, 1973.

"Timing the Turn," address before the Second Annual Conference of the Securities Industry Association, New York, September 12, 1973.

"Federal Debt Management: An Economist's View from the Marketplace," address before the Federal Reserve Bank of Boston Conference, "Issues in Federal Debt Management," Melvin Village, N.H., June 27–29, 1973.

"The Challenges Confronting the American Money and Bond Markets," *Euromoney,* June 1973.

"Discipline and the Marketplace," address before the Annual Meeting of the New York Society of Security Analysts, New York, May 29, 1973.

"Supply and Demand for Credit in 1973," coauthored with James McKeon and Albert Gross, Salomon Brothers, February 21, 1973.

Statement before the Joint Economic Committee of the Congress of the United States, Washington, D.C., February 13, 1973.

"The Presidency: Post-Election Economic Challenges and Opportunities," address before the Fall Dinner Meeting of the Money Marketeers, New York, November 9, 1972.

"The Unfolding Drama in the Money Market," address before the 23rd Annual Investment Seminar, sponsored by the New York State Bankers Association in cooperation with the Graduate School of Business Administration of New York University, New York, September 22, 1972.

"The Coming Challenge to Freedom of Choice in Investment Decisions," address before the Financial Analysts Federation 25th Annual Conference, New York, May 23, 1972.

"The American Economic and Financial Scene," address at Banque Rothschild, Paris, March 13, 1972.

"The Bond Market in 1972," address before the American Bankers Association 53rd Midwinter Trust Conference, New York, February 7, 1972.

"Henry Kaufman, Portrait of the Economist as an Activist," *Institutional Investor,* January 1972.

"Supply and Demand for Credit in 1972," coauthored with James McKeon, Salomon Brothers, January 18, 1972.

"The Bond and Stock Markets in Phase II," address before the Municipal Finance Forum of Washington, Washington, D.C., November 24, 1971.

"The Significance of the President's New Economic Program for the Credit Markets," address before the 22nd Annual Investment Seminar, sponsored by the New York State Bankers Association in cooperation with the Graduate School of Business Administration of New York University, New York, September 24, 1971.

"Information Needs for the Financial Economist in the 1970's," address before the American Statistical Association at the 1971 Joint Statistical Meetings, Colorado State University, Fort Collins, August 26, 1971.

"Warnings from Interest Rates," address before the New York Society of Security Analysts, New York, May 24, 1971.

"Is the United States in a Two-Year Financial Cycle?" address before the Annual General Meeting of the Association of International Bond Dealers, Paris, April 16, 1971.

"Discipline and Stimulation in the 1971 Credit Markets," address before the Sixth Annual Financial Conference, sponsored by The Conference Board, New York, February 17, 1971.

"Supply and Demand for Credit in 1971," coauthored with Sidney Homer and James McKeon, Salomon Brothers, December 1970.

"The Prospects for Interest Rates and Liquidity," address before an Investment and Property Studies Conference, sponsored by the *Financial Times* and *Investors Chronicle*, London, October 28, 1970.

Remarks at the Federal Reserve Bank of Boston Conference, "Housing and Monetary Policy," Melvin Village, N.H., October 16, 1970.

"The Credit Crisis and Its Aftermath," address before the 21st Annual Investment Seminar, sponsored by the New York State Bankers Association in cooperation with the Graduate School of Business Administration of New York University, New York, September 18, 1970.

Statement before the Joint Economic Committee of the Congress of the United States, Washington, D.C., July 9, 1970.

"The Outlook for Interest Rates in an Unprecedented Setting," address before the 50th Annual Conference of the National Association of Mutual Savings Banks, New York, May 13, 1970.

"The New Supply and Demand Dimensions in the Stock Market," address before the New York Society of Security Analysts, New York, March 6, 1970.

"Living It Up in a 'Salomon-Sized' World," *Fortune*, April 1970.

"The Changing Bond Market and Implications for the Corporation in 1970," address before the *Business Week* Conference on Money and the Corporation, New York, December 9, 1969.

"Financing the U.S. Economy," address before the First Annual European Institutional Investor Conference, London, December 2, 1969.

"The Challenging Seventies," address before the 40th Anniversary Forum of the Security Analysts of San Francisco, San Francisco, Calif., October 28, 1969.

"Monetary Policy in 1970," address before the National Industrial Conference Board Business in 1970 Conference, New York, October 1, 1969.

"My Third Credit Crisis," address before the 20th Annual Investment Seminar, sponsored by the New York State Bankers Association in cooperation with the Graduate School of Business Administration of New York University, New York, September 19, 1969.

"The Forthcoming Rally in Bonds," address before the Annual Forecasting Conference, cosponsored by the American Statistical Association, University of Illinois, and Chicago Association of Commerce and Industry, Chicago, June 20, 1969.

"The Financial Outlook for Business Corporations," address before the 1969 Northeastern Area Conference of the Financial Executives Institute, Boston, May 9, 1969.

"The Changing Investment Climate," address before the New York Society of Security Analysts Portfolio Management Seminar, New York, April 17, 1969.

"The Money and Bond Market in 1969," address before the New School Conference, "Wall Street and the Economy '69," New York, March 8, 1969.

"The Money and Bond Market Outlook for 1969," address before the Investment Bankers Association of America 57th Annual Convention, Miami Beach, Fl., December 4, 1968.

"At the Crossroads: Economic Growth or Inflation?" address before a group of Philadelphia business and financial executives at the Provident National Bank, Philadelphia, October 31, 1968; and before the Hartford Society of Financial Analysts, Hartford, Conn., November 13, 1968.

"The Role of the Economist in the Money Market," address before the 10th Annual Meeting of the National Association of Business Economists, New York, September 27, 1968.

"Institutional Credit: Near-Term Outlook and Long-Term Challenge," address before the 19th Annual Investment Seminar, sponsored by the New York State Bankers Association in cooperation with the Graduate School of Business Administration of New York University, New York, September 13, 1968.

"The Financial Outlook," address before the Tenth Annual Forecasting Conference of the New York Chapter of the American Statistical Association, New York, April 26, 1968.

"The Financial Outlook and Savings Institutions," address before the 35th Annual Stockholders' Meeting of the Federal Home Loan Bank of New York, New York, April 10, 1968.

"The Market Implications of Poor Official Policy Timing," address before the Municipal Finance Forum, Washington, D.C., February 20, 1968.

"Interest Rates and the Defense of the Dollar," address before the Omaha-Lincoln Society of Financial Analysts Federation, Omaha, Neb., December 14, 1967; and before the Business Outlook Conference, sponsored by the University of Washington, Seattle, December 15, 1967.

"Financing the 1968 Boom," address before the Conference on Business in 1968, sponsored by the National Industrial Conference Board, New York, October 3, 1967.

"Capital Market Prospects in the United States," address before the First Annual Meeting of the Investment Section of the Canadian Life Insurance Association, Toronto, May 3, 1967.

"The Outlook for the bond and Money Market," address before the 14th Annual Alumni Business Conference, Graduate School of Business Administration, New York University, New York, March 18, 1967.

"The Financial Outlook for 1967," address before the 22nd Annual Conference for Senior Executives in Mortgage Banking, sponsored by the Graduate School of Business Administration, New York University, in cooperation with the Mortgage Bankers Association of America, New York, January 13, 1967.

"Monetary Policy and the Investment Outlook," address before the 52nd Annual Meeting of the Church Pensions Conference, New York, December 2, 1966.

"Financial Strains, War, and the Outlook for Interest Rates," address before the Municipal Bond Club of Baltimore, Baltimore, Md., October 19, 1966; and before a group of institutional investors, The Chaparral Club, Dallas, Tex., October 24, 1966; and before The Headliners Club, Austin, Tex., October 25, 1966.

"Supply and Demand for Credit through Mid-1967," address before the 17th Annual Investment Seminar, sponsored by the New York State Bankers Association in cooperation with the Graduate School of Business Administration of New York University, New York, September 9, 1966.

"The Economic Outlook for 1966 and Beyond," address before the 19th Annual Conference of the Financial Analysts Federation, New York, May 23, 1966.

"The Pressures in Our Financial Markets," address before the Annual Conference of the Municipal Finance Officers Association, San Diego, Calif., May 16, 1966.

"The Outlook for Interest Rates in 1966," address before the Municipal Forum of New York, New York, January 20, 1966.

"Another Look at Commercial Bank Investments," address before the National Convention of the National Association of Bank Auditors and Controllers, St. Louis, Mo., October 26, 1965.

"Viet Nam and the Outlook for Interest Rates," address before the American Mutual Insurance Alliance Investment Conference, New York, September 21, 1965.

"Commercial Bank Investments in the New Environment," address before the Investment Officers of the Clearing House Banks of the Twin Cities; the Twin Cities Society of Security Analysts; and a group of insurance investment officers, Minneapolis, Minn., May 14, 1965.

"The Forces Shaping Our Future Economic and Financial Environment," address before the Missouri Valley Conference of Robert Morris Associates, Lincoln, Neb., May 14, 1965; and before the Savings Bank Women of New York, New York, February 17, 1965.

"The Secular Trend of Long-Term Interest Rates," address before the New York Society of Security Analysts, April 14, 1965; and before the Boston Security Analysts Society, Boston, February 15, 1965.

"A Long Look at Future Fiscal and Monetary Policy," address before the New York Society of Security Analysts, New York, December 31, 1964.

"The Outlook for Interest Rates," address before St. John's University Annual Business Conference, Brooklyn, N.Y., November 17, 1964.

"Opportunities in the Money Market," address before the Consumer Credit Management Conference, Graduate School of Business, Columbia University, Harriman, N.Y., June 17, 1964.

"Opportunities in the Money Market," address before the Trust Investment School, Binghamton, N.Y., October 2, 1963.

"Federal Agency Obligations in Today's Bond Market," address before the Fraternal Investment Association, Bedford Springs, Penn., June 6, 1963.

"The Capital Markets in 1963," address before the New York Society of Security Analysts, New York, March 13, 1963.

"Perspectives on the Money Market," address before the Sixth Alumni Consumer Credit Management Conference, Graduate School of Business, Columbia University, Harriman, N.Y., February 13, 1963.

"Recent Money Market Developments and Their Significance to Consumer Credit Institutions," address before the Consumer Credit Management Program, Columbia University, New York, June 6, 1962.

INDEX